Modern Germany Reconsidered, 1870–1945

Modern Germany Reconsidered, 1870–1945

Edited by

Gordon Martel

London and New York

First published 1992
by Routledge
11 New Fetter Lane, London EC4P 4EE

Simultaneously published in the USA and Canada
by Routledge
a division of Routledge, Chapman and Hall, Inc.
29 West 35th Street, New York, NY 10001

© 1992 Gordon Martel

Typeset in 10 on 12 point Garamond ITC by
Columns Design and Production Services Ltd, Reading
Printed in Great Britain by
The University Press, Cambridge

British Library Cataloguing-in-Publication Data
Modern Germany reconsidered, 1870–1945
  I. Martel, Gordon
  943.08

Library of Congress Cataloging-in-Publication Data
Modern Germany reconsidered, 1870–1945 / edited by Gordon Martel.
  p. cm.
  Includes index.
  1. Germany – History – 1871– I. Martel, Gordon.
  DD220.M53 1991
  943.08–dc20 91–4047

ISBN 0–415–078180
ISBN 0–415–078199 pbk

for:

Warren Wolfe

respected colleague,

cherished friend

Contents

Preface

This is the second collection of 'Reconsiderations', the first of which dealt with A.J.P. Taylor's *Origins of the Second World War*. The aim of the present book, like the first one, is fairly simple: to serve undergraduate students taking courses in the history of modern Germany. The origins of the first book reveal how this ambition was conceived and realized: in an attempt to demonstrate R.G. Collingwood's concept of 'secondary history' to a class of first-year history students, I had them read A.J.P. Taylor's *Origins* and then look at a series of reviews, articles and books written on the subject since he wrote. This experiment proved to be a great success, as students were challenged by his provocative interpretation and eager to see how professionally trained historians reacted to it. Thus, both the nature and the value of historical debates were demonstrated to students who could also test Collingwood's hypothesis that it was the secondary history of a subject with which one should begin.

What I found to be difficult and frustrating was the process of putting together a coherent and accessible set of readings for my students to consider; the best that I could do was to collect a miscellany of materials that varied considerably in size, scope and style and were cumbersome to use. With this in mind I approached a number of leading experts to see if they would be interested in writing an essay on various aspects of Taylor's interpretation and to talk about the responses to it and the 'state of the art' of the debate today. Simultaneously, I found a receptive and enthusiastic editor in Jane Harris-Matthews, formerly of Allen & Unwin, who was convinced of the utility of such a book. Her assessment has proved accurate, and that first book is now used regularly in undergraduate history courses around the world.

The original formula has been expanded upon for this book, which is not tied to any one historian or interpretation. But the aim remains similar: to provide students with clear and accessible summaries of the most important controversies and developments in the interpretation of German history from 1870 to 1945, and thus to enable both instructors and students to overcome the limitations imposed by reliance upon a single-author survey of the period, a form which usually leaves little room for a discussion of debates.

The chapters in this book are not intended to be original in themselves, and I am indebted to the contributors who were willing to forego originality for the sake of producing a book that would be useful for students. They apparently share my conviction that we must do what we can to see that scholars speak to more than one another and that there are some crucial gaps in the literature between the textbook and the monograph. If this book proves to be a useful one it will be due to the commitment of these scholars to their craft. I thank each of them.

I am also indebted to a number of my colleagues here at Royal Roads Military College, where I found support and encouragement in some unusual places: in the departments of physics and mathematics. Early on in the process of putting these chapters together, I became convinced that it was time to learn to use something other than paper and pencil, that I ought to become 'literate' in the use of computers. I owe a word of thanks to Sherman Waddell and Jim Lacombe for their willingness to help me out on a number of occasions, and particularly to Joe Buckley, who, having the misfortune to occupy the office next door to mine, frequently came running when he heard my anguished cries of pain and frustration. I am also indebted to Manuela Fedorak who assisted me in the English rendering of Dieter Langewiesche's contribution.

But my greatest debt is to my friend and colleague, Warren Wolfe, who has come to personify for me the meaning of colleagiality. It was Warren who, becoming aware of the various projects in which I was engaged, convinced me that the new technology had a good deal to offer, and that I ought to take the plunge. He has since paid a high price for his persuasiveness. During the year in which I was editing, he devoted countless hours in teaching me how to acquire the skills which I needed and in designing special programs to meet my requirements. I often thought, as I called him on the telephone for the fifteenth or sixteenth time that day, that this would be the call that broke the camel's back – but that back never bent. Without the slightest glimmer of self-interest, Warren persisted, day after day, in assisting and encouraging someone whose greatest triumph in the use of technology had hitherto been mastering the use of a remote-control for a television set. And, what is most remarkable, he did so cheerfully and unwaveringly. If he were the model for all colleagues, universities would be wonderful places indeed. He has been an inspiration to me and I offer him my most sincere gratitude.

Gordon Martel
Royal Roads Military College,
Victoria, British Columbia

1 *Bismarckian Germany*

GEOFF ELEY

TRADITIONS AND REVISIONS

Constitutional crisis – Austro-Prussian War – North German Confederation – Franco-Prussian War – proclamation of the Reich – Congress of Berlin – Dual Alliance. This is one way, an older conservative way, of presenting the birth of the German empire. A sequence of political, military, and diplomatic events brought it into being. Germany was unified politically by 'blood and iron', the armed agency of Prussia. Geopolitically, it was a revolutionary creation. Disraeli, commenting on the Franco-Prussian War in the House of Commons, declared that

> This war represents the German Revolution, a greater political event than the French Revolution of the last century – I don't say a greater, or as great, a social event. What its social consequences may be are in the future. Not a single principle in the management of our foreign affairs, accepted by all statesmen for guidance up to six months ago, any longer exists. There is not a single diplomatic tradition which has not been swept away.[1]

For Anglo-American historians especially, German unification had a disturbing effect on the European balance of power. In one venerable tradition of German historiography, beginning with Ranke and continuing through the Borussian School of patriotic realists, this geopolitical meaning was not refused so much as given a positive construction: because of the *Primat der Aussenpolitik* (primacy of foreign policy), Germany's fate was decided by its central continental location and consequent embroilment in Europe's interstate power struggles. This certainly focused on diplomatic, military and political events as the primary stuff of history. But as a theory of German historical

1

development it also integrated political and socioeconomic aspects, seeing Prusso-German social and political structures as a function of Germany's Central European vulnerability.

In the 1960s a number of works challenged this assumption. They abandoned the traditional political–diplomatic perspective for one that assigned priority to social and economic developments.[2] The most direct reinterpretation in this sense was probably Helmut Böhme's *Deutschlands Weg zur Grossmacht*. Böhme sees the empire's foundation less as a formal act of political unification, of state making in a heroic nineteenth-century sense, than as the consequence of long-term developmental processes that set Prussia against Austria in an *economic* struggle for supremacy in Germany. Thus

> The quarrel over the *Zollverein* (Customs Union) became of central importance for the development of the German question, and it can be asserted that the '*kleindeutsch*' [small-German] national state arose chiefly from the Prussian defence against the economic order conceived by Austria for the great Central European region. For, in defending itself against the Schwarzenberg-Bruck conception, Prussia developed the basis for its own future hegemony.[3]

The struggle for control of the *Zollverein* and its smaller German character was decisive between 1853 and 1868 in destroying Austria's efforts at reducing Prussia to secondary status. Given this shift of focus from a political to an economic logic, therefore, 1858 and the opening of the 'New Era' in Prussian government becomes less crucial than 1857 and the economic depression, which widened the gap between the Austrian and Prussian-led German economies; 1862 is important less for Bismarck's appointment as Minister-President of Prussia than for the treaty of free trade with France; Austria's *military* defeat in 1866 is less decisive than its exclusion from the *Zollverein* two years before.

The implications of this approach are all the more radical when applied to the succeeding period, between the defeat of Austria and Bismarck's change of course in 1879. Böhme substitutes 1879 for 1871 as the terminal date of the German empire's foundation, and claims that effective, as opposed to formal, unification was not complete until the economic and political settlement of 1878–9. The government's parliamentary base of 1871–3, comprising National Liberals and Free Conservatives, and corresponding to the dominant free trading interest of east Elbian agriculture, merchant capital and light manufactures, was replaced during this settlement by a new protectionist front of Free Conservatives, Conservatives, National Liberals, and Catholic Center. Through the tariffs of 1879, Böhme argues, Bismarck forged a new combination of agrarian and industrial capital that formed the sociopolitical foundation of the empire until the collapse of 1918. The importance of this departure amounted to a 'refounding of the German Reich'.[4] Thus, 'the *Kulturkampf*, the formation of the first interest groups, the transition to protection, the rejection of the Liberal Party, and the transition to Anti-Socialist Law, Dual Alliance, and colonial policy are all to be counted within the foundation period of the Reich'.[5] In 1879–81, 'the first terminal point was reached in the 30-year creation of the German Reich'.[6]

This 'economizing' of the approach to German unification – a shift of emphasis from politics and statecraft towards economics, from Bismarck and Prussian militarism to the rise of a national market and the political economy of industrialization – was matched by a similar change of approach to the 1870s and 1880s. Bismarckian politics was reinterpreted through the lens of economic interest. Böhme was himself a pupil of Fritz Fischer, who played some part in urging Fischer to press ahead with his arguments about German aggression in the First World War, and Böhme's own work on the foundation of the Reich was meant to lend depth to Fischer's analysis. It was concerned with the origins of the interest-based politics whose primacy Fischer found crucial to the dynamics of Germany's foreign expansionism: that is, an anti-socialist and anti-democratic authoritarianism linked to the traditional privileges of pre-industrial elites (aristocracy, military, bureaucracy), but regrounded during industrialization in a new coalition of large-scale industry and big-estate agriculture. The continuity of this reactionary politics between the unification years and the First World War has come to be seen as the main obstacle to Germany's 'political modernization' (meaning the creation of a liberal political system) and, over the longer term, it is thought, led to structural instabilities that ultimately explain Germany's susceptibility to the rise of Nazism. Much ink has been spent in the unfolding and discussion of these ideas during the last three decades, and here I would like to highlight three main aspects, each of which reflects a strong belief in the power of socio-economic causality, and which are now crucial to how the Bismarckian era has come to be understood.

The first concerns the importance of the Great Depression of 1873–96 and the argument that the political history of the Bismarckian years was powerfully defined by economics. Just as the shaping of a national market and the long boom of the 1850s and 1860s provide the main context of unification, in Böhme's view, so does the Great Depression provide the context of the 'refoundation of the Reich' in 1878–9. The key text here has been Hans Rosenberg's *Grosse Depression und Bismarckzeit*, published in 1967 as the socioeconomic revisionism of the 1960s was moving into high gear, but originating in arguments first developed by Rosenberg in the 1940s.[7] For Rosenberg, the big political changes of

1878–9 were causally related to the economic problems produced by the crash of 1873, so that the Kondratiev downswing of 1873–96 is thought to have been reproduced in definite movements of social and political life. Most immediately, these included the turn by major industrial and agrarian interests to protectionist economic policies and away from free trade, culminating in the Bismarkian tariffs of 1879 (the theme of the later part of Böhme's book). But government policy in the 1880s also consisted of the search for successful 'anti-cyclical therapy' to handle the problems of overproduction and declining prices set off by the depression, and the turn to a forward policy of overseas imperialism through colonies and other means has also been read as a response to the structural pressures of the economic downturn.[8] More radically, Rosenberg's argument also sees a general atmosphere of uncertainty and crisis as the result of the post-unification economic situation: 'gloom and the feeling of tension, insecurity and anxiety' dominated the new German society, and the 'centre of gravity of political agitation shifted from issues of political policies...to a crude emphasis on economic objectives'. Apart from reorienting policy thinking in business and government, this also mobilized wide sections of the populace into activity, from workers to *Mittelstand* and farmers, and compelled a refashioning of outlooks in the political parties. Liberalism was the main loser in this process, because its free-trading and universalist ideals dramatically lost ground to the new politics based on sectional economic interest, and to an emerging 'anti-modern' ideological complex containing romantic, corporatist, and anti-semitic forms of belief. In the strongest versions, all manner of social, cultural, and intellectual developments were attributed to the originating impact of the depression in this way, including social Darwinism and psychoanalysis, as well as the various phenomena already mentioned.[9]

Second, anti-socialism was a vital aspect of the crisis mentality the depression created. For one thing, the German labour movement, organized into the united Social Democratic Party (SPD) in 1875 and already the strongest socialist movement in Europe, was historically a product of the depression years. But a large part of the anxieties described by Rosenberg became focused on the rise of socialism as a revolutionary and subversive threat to the interests and values of the Prusso-German ruling system and as such built up the momentum for some form of anti-socialist legislation. Thus, if the protectionist demands of industry and agriculture provided the positive materials for a new political settlement at the end of the 1870s, anti-socialism was the ideological cement that bound the somewhat disparate interests of the protectionist coalition together and simultaneously broadened its appeal in the electorate. As with the turn to protection, it was again the liberals who tended to suffer: not only did the anti-socialist rhetoric alienate their former working-class supporters and help drive them to the SPD standard, but the demands for exceptional legislation and restrictions of civil freedoms badly compromised liberal principles of constitutional liberty. Moreover, Bismarck manipulated this situation for all it was worth.

Bismarck genuinely shared the fear of revolution and consequently believed in the necessity of anti-socialist measures for their own sake. But at the same time, he hoped to use that fear to break the independent influence of the liberal parties and bring their middle-class supporters more directly to his own side – that is, behind the more right-wing parliamentary coalition being assembled around the demand for tariffs. The protectionism of the mid- to later 1870s was a movement from within the economy to which Bismarck was mainly in the position of responding; anti-socialism was an issue which he manipulated far more creatively in his own favour. In this sense, the Anti-Socialist Law of 1878 was the political complement to the tariffs of 1879.

The third feature of the post-1960s revisionism I wish to highlight is the idea of social imperialism, which illustrates a similar dualism of emphasis on socioeconomic causality and political manipulation. On the one hand, the problem of overproduction during the depression produced a remarkably broad consensus in business, journalistic, academic, political, and governmental circles behind the need for protected markets overseas, and during the late 1870s and early 1880s this translated into a powerfully orchestrated demand for colonies. Thus, so far from being an opportunistically motivated diplomatic maneuver (the commonest older explanation), Bismarck's grab for colonies in 1884–5 was a necessary response to pressures developing in the economy, just as the tariffs of 1879 had been. Colonial markets and investment opportunities would help counteract the irregularities of economic growth, stimulate renewed expansion, and in the process ease the pressures that were fuelling socioeconomic discontent. On the other hand, colonial acquisitions could become objects of popular enthusiasm and were skillfully manipulated by Bismarck for political purposes, most immediately in the 1884 elections, when he used the colonial issue to build support for the government parties and win votes away from the left-liberal opponents of an overseas empire. More generally, Bismarck's colonial policy amounted to 'social imperialism', or the deliberate attempt to use the economic and political arguments for empire to strengthen popular support for the governing system and its elites. Thus, the expansionist foreign policy of the 1880s and later is related by this explanation to the same combination of factors noted above: the economic context of depression, resulting social tensions and conservative political manipulation in the shape of Bismarck. As social imperialism, it involved 'the diversion outwards of internal tensions and forces of change in order to preserve the social and political status quo';

it was a 'defensive ideology' against the 'disruptive effects of industrialization'.[10]

Taken as a whole, this has been a persuasive and influential approach to the history of the Bismarckian period. It casts German state making in the light of social and economic history, but without turning Bismarck into the cipher of impersonal forces. For, while upholding the importance of economic factors in the unifying and consolidation of the new state, and while relating the political history of the 1870s and 1880s to the irregularities of economic growth and social tensions resulting from industrialization, such an approach also stresses the effects of a particular kind of manipulative politics. In fact, the turn to economic and social history has done very little to dislodge Bismarck from his role as the directive genius of German history between 1862 and 1890, and the works of Böhme and Wehler in particular leave him right at the centre of the historical narrative.[11]

The story such historians tell is one of a backward state and a modern economy – that is, an essentially unreformed Prusso-German state presiding over a massive process of economic modernization and seeking to preserve its traditional structures of authoritarian rule against the disruptive social and political effects of that process. The political history of the Bismarckian era, they argue, is contained in that contradiction, for the stability of the new state could be guaranteed over the long term only by building those 'modern' *political* institutions – Western parliamentary ones – adequate for dealing with the new forms of social conflict. Otherwise, a gap would open between the narrow base of the regime in the privileged interests of pre-industrial elites and the broader, more complicated range of interests in the emerging industrial society; and without structural reform that gap could be bridged only by artificial forms of 'secondary integration', of which social imperialism was the strongest and most dangerous example. Thus, beginning with Bismarck's colonial policy, it is argued, popular nationalism was consistently exploited as a 'long-term integrative factor' that was supposed to 'stabilize an anachronistic social and power structure'. Support for expansion abroad was used to 'block domestic progress' and the chances for 'social and political emancipation', an effective 'technique of rule' for defeating 'the advancing forces of parliamentarization and democratization'.[12]

What, more precisely, were the social interests and relations of domination such diversionary techniques of rule were meant to defend? At the institutional level of the state these are easy to see: the monarchy and its traditions of military and bureaucratic independence; the relative freedom of the executive from parliamentary controls; Prussia's special status in the empire; a restricted franchise in most of the individual states; the socially weighted tax system in Prussia and elsewhere; and so on. But within this framework of institutions, historians have also detected a more specific social interest, namely, 'the predominance of the feudal aristocracy'.[13] The social basis of Germany's constitutional authoritarianism, in this view, was the ability of a 'pre-industrial elite' of landowners to preserve the essentials of their power by subordinating the state machinery to their interests. The instruments of aristocratic power were control over the military and bureaucratic apparatuses of the state, a privileged position in the Prussian Landtag, fiscal immunities and a transmuted seigneurial authority over a dependent rural population east of the Elbe. To these factors may be added the preferential economic treatment that emerged from the tariff settlement of 1879. Thus, despite the capitalist transformation of German society and industry's growing predominance in the economy, it is argued, 'political power remained in the hands of the economically weakened pre-capitalist ruling strata (Junkers, bureaucracy, military)'.[14]

To maintain itself in this way the landed interest needed allies, not least because of its diminishing economic base. To deal with this aspect of the question another concept has been devised by recent historians, namely, that of *Sammlungspolitik*. A term of contemporary usage taken up historiographically at the end of the 1960s, *Sammlungspolitik* (literally, the 'politics of rallying-together') refers to a defensive alliance of industrialists and landowners, convergent protectionist interests united by a fear of foreign competition and democratic reform – 'the compromise-ideology of the ruling strata of industry and agriculture, with its basis in the common...anti-liberal and anti-socialist calculation', as one historian has called it.[15] The coalescence of this bloc in the later 1870s was facilitated by the pressures of the depression and the rise of the organized working class, realized in Böhme's 'refoundation of the Reich', the Bismarckian settlement of 1878–9, with its twin pillars of protective tariffs and Anti-Socialist Law. Moreover, this also inaugurated a lasting tradition of right-wing politics to which government strategy also consistently recurred. After a brief interruption in the early 1890s, when the short-lived chancellorship of Leo von Caprivi saw an opening of tension between agrarians and industrialists, *Sammlungspolitik* was successfully revived in the years 1897–1902 (culminating again in a new high tariff settlement). The years immediately before 1914 saw another concerted revival of the industrial–agrarian *Sammlung*, consummated in the *Kartell der schaffenden Stände* ('Cartel of the Productive Estates') of 1913; and the same bloc of interests dominated government politics in the First World War.[16]

Thus the politics laid down in the Bismarckian period are also thought to have cast a long shadow. They established powerful continuities that extended through the imperial period to that of Weimar and played the key part in rendering German society vulnerable to Nazism. The deep origins of the latter are thought to have lain in the persistent authoritarianism of the Bismarckian empire's political culture, the efforts of its ruling elites to fend off the potentially democratizing effects of industrialization and the political techniques and strategies they devised for neutralizing the challenge of the liberal and socialist opposition. Thus, in characterizing the continuity between the Second and Third Reichs, Wehler lists a 'long catalogue of historical handicaps' that burdened the Weimar Republic, including: the susceptibility to authoritarian politics; the hostility to democracy in education and party politics; the influence of pre-industrial leadership groups, norms and ideals; the tenacity of the German ideology of the state; the mystique of the bureaucracy; the manipulation of political anti-Semitism.[17] In other words, the revisionist interpretation of German history produced for the Bismarckian era in the wake of the Fischer controversy and other stimuli of the 1960s has also anchored a longer interpretation of the German past focused on the origins of Nazism. Although discussion of this continuity question would burst the bounds of this chapter, it is important, when considering the Bismarckian period, to be aware of these larger implications. Nor is it possible here to develop a full-scale critique of the approach described above. Instead, I would like to do two things: first, to show how these perspectives can structure a political narrative of the Bismarckian years; and, second, to propose an alternative reading of German unification, which suggests how the new picture might easily need to be redrawn. I will then close with some brief comments on how a new agenda of questions may be taking shape.[18]

THE POLITICS OF BISMARCKIAN GERMANY

We may begin our account of the political history with the moving element in Böhme's story, namely, the movement for protection. The first sign of such a movement in the aftermath of the 1873 crash came when the advocates of free trade in the Reichstag failed to secure the passage of the Tariff Suspension Bill, which instead was postponed until 1 January 1877. The fixing of a date then provided protectionists with a concrete focus for their efforts. Proceeding from the iron and steel industry in Rhineland-Westphalia, a series of organizational initiatives created a new pressure group structure designed to shift business opinion and the government in a protectionist direction: the Association of German Iron and Steel Industrialists (VDESI) launched in spring 1874; the Central League of German Industrialists (CVDI) formed in February 1876 around an active core of iron and steel, in coalition with textiles, leather, chemicals, paper and glass; and the agrarian Association of Tax and Economic Reformers (VSWR) a week later. These new organizations moved quickly to broaden their basis in the larger business community. Thus the South German governments of Württemberg and Bavaria swung round to protectionism, and by the end of 1874 the VDESI had already created an impressive front of chambers of commerce in the south, west and eastern regions of Germany, until by the end of 1876 the national umbrella of chambers of commerce (DHT) passed into protectionist hands. Nonetheless, the lobbyists were rebuffed by spokesmen in government; they failed to stop the renewal of the Austrian free trading treaty in September 1875; and VDESI petitions to the Reichstag, Bundesrat, and Prussian Ministry of War in October 1875 were all rejected. If the movement was to progress, it needed broader support in the Reichstag and a more sympathetic ear in the government.

If the agrarian alliance was to provide the first of these conditions, Bismarck offered the second. A foretaste occurred in 1875 when Kaiser Wilhelm I began to express concern over the growing protectionist pressure. In April he received simultaneous memoranda from the liberal head of the Imperial Chancellory, Rudolf von Delbrück, rejecting a petition from Westphalian steel producers, and from the Cologne banker, Abraham Oppenheim, calling for tariffs. The Kaiser minuted: 'Delbrück looks backward – Oppenheim and the steel producers look forward and refer to the facts of firms out of production, ruined finances, slumped share prices, and French export premiums'. On 6 August he wrote to Bismarck that he had been 'occupied since June...with the question of duties on steel products'. Bismarck took this as a 'warning sign' and immediately severed trade talks with Italy. Delbrück's departure from office in April 1876 should also be seen in the same terms, and Bismarck had actively connived at the parliamentary attacks on his own government that had maneuvered Delbrück into resigning. In fact, Bismarck was now working closely with a group of Free Conservative parliamentarians, including Wilhelm von Kardorff, Carl Friedrich Stumm and Lucius von Ballhausen, who were emerging as the main brokers of the putative protectionist turn. In March 1878 Bismarck told Kardorff: 'I want to have tariffs on tobacco, spirits, possibly even on coffee. I do not even shrink from imposing tariffs on corn...Germany has to establish her own tariffs according to her own needs.' Around the same time, the accession of a new pope provided an opening for negotiating an end to the confrontation with the Catholic church through the *Kulturkampf*, thereby allowing the Catholic Center Party's participation in the emerging protectionist front. In fact, in this period, the Center and the newly formed Conservative Party (in 1876) were natural allies, speaking for the heavily agrarian southern, western and eastern peripheries of the new empire. By this time the National Liberals, the majority grouping of German liberalism, had also become divided on the tariff issue. The tariff reform was passed by a cross-party coalition in July 1879, consisting of

Conservatives, Free Conservatives, Center, and a section of National Liberals.[19]

This new parliamentary majority – with 210 seats in the 397-seat Reichstag the two conservative parties and the Center could in theory replace the National Liberals as the main basis of government after the elections of 1878 – was certainly far more congenial for Bismarck and the Kaiser. The foundation of the Reich in 1867–71 had hinged on an uneasy compromise with the liberal constitutionalist movement of the 1860s. In the first half of the decade the latter had immobilized government in Prussia with its pressure for constitutional reform, while the liberal momentum in the south and central German states had helped convert this Prussian stand-off into a renewed demand for German unity. With breathtaking audacity Bismarck had then placed himself at the head of the national movement (to the extreme disquiet of Prussian Conservatives), unifying Germany through the three wars of 1864 (over Schleswig-Holstein), 1866 (against Austria) and 1870 (against France). Most German liberals appreciated the significance of the change. The North German Confederation of 1867 and the empire of 1871 may have fallen short of the full-scale parliamentary constitution the liberal consensus desired (and in other respects went beyond it, as in the provision for universal manhood suffrage). But they represented a fundamental transformation of the existing situation and provided a secure framework for further constitutional advance. As one senior National Liberal wrote at the time of the North German Confederation: 'If there is success . . . in organizing all north and central Germany with the help of parliament militarily and economically, and in these areas some emergency bridges are built to south Germany, a very firm basis for further development will have been achieved. The nation cannot ask for more at this time'.[20]

This prediction seemed to bear fruit in the events of 1870–1. The very fact of a single national state organized constitutionally was a profound advance from a liberal point of view. Moreover, aside from the Reichstag's ambiguous budgetary power, National Liberals secured the chancellor's potential accountability in the requirement that he countersign all acts of government and thereby accept responsibility: thus a new national official became the focus of the new regime, rather than the representative of the King of Prussia, and the principle of responsible government (that is, to the Reichstag) was entered onto the evolving political agenda. On this basis, the Prussian liberals had voted for the Indemnity Bill in September 1866, which retroactively legalized the Prussian government's collection of taxes during the constitutional stalemate with the liberals after 1862 (the bill passed by 230 votes to 75); and in the Reichstag of the North German Confederation the National Liberals provided the swing votes for approval of the new constitution (contributing 79 of the 230 votes that passed it, against the 53 of the opposition).[21] Moreover, from Bismarck's point of view, the situation had stabilized reasonably well: a united Germany was a liberal panacea, it is true, but the actual process of unification had remained under Prussian military control and brought a major accretion of international prestige, dramatically elevating Prussia-Germany to the status of an imposing great power. Constitutional government had been conceded, but on terms which Bismarck felt he controlled. Moreover, in the hey-day of international free trade, it was impossible not to base the conduct of government on a practical parliamentary majority of the elements of the propertied classes who were economically progressive: in political outlook this majority may have been liberal, but sociologically it comprised a solid coalition of industrial entrepreneurs, high finance, railway interests, the more liberal factions of the landed interest, and the urban Protestant *Bildungsbürgertum* (educated middle class) of Rhineland-Westphalia and the newly acquired north-central German provinces of Prussia – hardly a subversive threat to the social and political order.[22]

Bismarck's aim during the drama of unification was to steer a course between the specter of a fully constitutionalized Germany (a liberal-dominated nation–state equipped with a fully parliamentary constitution) and the last resort of a *coup d'état*, and thereby to preserve what he called the 'substance' of royal power, as opposed to the 'form in which the King exercises his rule', which was far more dispensable.[23] As against more traditionalist and dogmatic conservatives, Bismarck upheld less the principle of monarchical legitimacy and the mystique of throne and altar than the hard power relations binding the army to the Crown and its aristocracy. Otherwise, government had to be grounded in the 'productive classes of society', the 'producing people', the propertied pillars of the existing order; and in the 1860s and early 1870s it was clear that the majority inclinations of the latter were national, free-trading and moderately liberal. But negotiating a constitutional settlement that appeased such needs and aspirations without sacrificing the substance of Prussian traditions was a tricky business. The line between governing with the liberals and allowing the liberals to govern was extremely fine. By creating a parliamentary framework, Bismarck also gave parliamentary politics a chance to flourish, and after 1871 much of his political efforts were devoted to heading off a possible new constitutional challenge. His main goal was to 'avoid the supreme choice which threatened his work from beginning to end, the decision between the parliamentary monarchy or the conservative-dynastic *Staatsstreich* [*coup d'état*]', and the radical pragmatism of his politics in the 1860s had been precisely an attempt to break out of the polarizing logic the constitutional crisis had set off.[24]

In his memoirs Bismarck stated what Arthur Rosenberg called his 'basic sociological conception':

The greater caution of the more intelligent classes may quite likely arise from the materialistic basis of preservation of property...[and] for the security and advancement of the state, it is more useful to have a majority of those who represent property.... Every great community in which the careful and restraining influence of the propertied classes is lost on material or intellectual grounds will always develop a pace that will cause the ship of state to founder, as happened in the case of the French Revolution.[25]

This was the firm, principled basis of Bismarck's pragmatism: it led him to move radically to prevent the alienation of the liberally inclined *Bildungsbürgertum* in the 1860s; and it now led him to respond to the demands of the industrial bourgeoisie and the landed interest for protection in the 1870s. In that sense the tariffs of 1879 were a consistent reflection of this underlying political philosophy. Bismarck's practical dependence on National Liberal parliamentarians as he emerged from the unification settlement in 1867–71 threatened to recreate the constitutionalist deadlock he had originally broken open in the 1860s, except this time on an already liberalized constitutional terrain. The attractions of the protectionist movement of the 1870s were that it promised a new escape from the old dilemma:

> Bismarck's relationship to the pressure groups was not moulded by considerations of industrial or agrarian protective tariffs. His aim was far more political than economic. Bismarck's aims were first, to interweave the interests of the various producing classes of Prussia and to satisfy them in the economic field, and secondly, to bind these classes to the monarchical state which was led by him.[26]

An early intimation of the difficulties of cooperating with the liberals came in 1872, when the Conservative majority in the Prussian Herrenhaus (the non-elected upper chamber) rejected a government education bill for its secularist implications and followed this up with obstruction of the government's local government reform, both of which measures were also favored by the liberals. Bismarck responded by threatening to reform the Herrenhaus or to create sufficient new nobles to change its political complexion, together with a purge of those local and regional civil servants who had voted down the government's measures. Flooding the Herrenhaus with ennobled businessmen and bankers would in any case be consistent with his belief in the primacy of productive property: 'The Herrenhaus in my opinion must take into itself those elements of our national life that are more important than the ones presently on top.'[27] Simultaneously, though, the launching of the *Kulturkampf*, also strongly backed by the liberals in Prussia and elsewhere, promised to strengthen the incipient opposition of Prussian Conservatives, as well as counterproductively raising the Center Party to a key position of strength in the Reichstag (amounting to 91 seats in the elections of 1874). Such Conservative opposition was beginning to limit Bismarck's ability to keep up the reformist momentum necessary to ensure the National Liberal parliamentary group's acquiescence in his rule. The 1872 crisis was highly instructive in these ways: the original measures had been a low-cost substitute for genuine liberalization at the level of the Reich, which simultaneously achieved a streamlining of Prussian administration; yet Conservative obstructionism ended in strengthening the very liberal critique of Prussian particularism which Bismarck had originally hoped to appease. As Delbrück stated in the Crown council that discussed the affair, a failure of Prussia to set its own house in order would be followed inevitably by National Liberal demands for an increase in the powers of the Reichstag.[28]

Even greater cause for concern came with the 1874 elections and the startling success of the National Liberals. They now claimed 155 seats, or 38 per cent of the total (up from 125 in 1871), thereby reducing the Conservative representation from 57 to a pathetic 22. Constructing a majority was now impossible *without* the National Liberals, whereas they themselves could build one either to the right with the Free Conservatives (the 'Bismarckian party' *par excellence*, with 33 seats dropping slightly from 37) or to the left with the progressives (the left liberal rump from the 1860s, who held steady at 49, up slightly from 46 in 1871). The ceasefire between government and National Liberals over parliamentary control, workable in the empire's founding years, stood in danger of breaking down once a serious issue arose. The 1874 military budget, the likeliest early sticking-point, was ultimately approved on the basis of the so-called *Septennat* compromise formula, but Bismarck took careful note of the new parliamentary situation. The position of the Center was also a source of disquiet (91 seats, up from 63), for it could easily become a rallying-point for all dissatisfied elements – including Poles, Alsatians, Guelphs (i.e. Hanoverian particularists) and Danes (adding another 34 seats) – not least if the clergy became an effective organizational base. In the autumn of 1874, the National Liberals' abortive effort at participating in a censure motion (the so-called Majunke Affair) again dramatized the problem of the government's parliamentary support. Until an effective vote of confidence took shape, Bismarck had been ready to force matters to a crisis – by threatening to resign, dissolving the Reichstag and raising the electorate against the parties. In a Crown council of 18 December 1874, the Kaiser had said that 'it must be brought to the awareness of the Reichstag that it had become confused and that its power did not extend outside certain boundaries'; and the Ministry of State had to table a proposal by Bismarck to escalate matters by an attack on the Reichstag's existing powers.[29] In such circumstances the demand for protection – which gathered pace during 1875–6 – dovetailed neatly into Bismarck's growing anxieties about the political status quo.

In the second half of the 1870s Bismarck's politics were driven by the desire to extricate himself from dependence on the National Liberals and construct an alternative parliamentary base for his government. They proceeded through a succession of crises – from the Majunke Affair through the Press Bill of 1874 and amendments to the Penal Code in 1876 to the Anti-Socialist Law itself – in which he sought to maneuver the Reichstag into a position of responsibility for not taking measures against the threat of socialism. This tactic became clear during the preparation of the amendments to the Penal Code in 1875–6. Writing to Delbrück on 5 November 1875 Bismarck addressed himself with equanimity to the possibility of the bill's failure:

> If an evil is felt, then the public makes the government responsible for the fact that no measures have been taken for its relief; but if such an effort fails on the vote of the Reichstag, then the responsibility. . .passes onto the Reichstag and can become a corrective for the next elections.[30]

The tactical purpose of such a measure transcended its legislative content. More specifically, Bismarck played cynically on the fear of revolution and by exploiting the National Liberals' opposition to the anti-socialist legislation planned to split them from their constituency. This dualism was a constant of the anti-socialist initiatives of the 1870s: on the one hand, a genuine desire to stop the growth of social democracy; on the other hand, simultaneous exploitation of the fear of revolution to undermine the influence of the liberal parties and to bring either them or their supporters into a parliamentary bloc of order. Such initiatives were as much anti-liberal as anti-socialist.[31]

The 1877 elections were encouraging for Bismarck: they brought a National Liberal decline from 155 to 128 and a Conservative increase from 22 to 40, restoring the more manageable configuration of 1871–3, while the marginal growth of the SPD (from 9 to 12) could still be exploited in the manner described above. The pressure for tariffs and the anti-socialist calculation now conjoined in a tight political unity. In the Ministry of State on 10 March 1878 Bismarck articulated his thinking: if a comprehensive financial and tariff reform was rejected by the Reichstag, this should be carefully used to

> prepare the ground for the next regular elections, so that hopefully the stupid Jew-boy Lasker and his retinue, these theoretical orators, would

be replaced by moderate Conservatives, whom, for the realization of material benefits, the people will put in the place of those who are concerned only with formalistic guarantees.[32]

This statement was also made at the conclusion of the abortive Bennigsen candidacy, which was Bismarck's final effort at reworking the National Liberal alliance to his own advantage. Where Bismarck hoped to bring the National Liberals into greater conformity by an act of incorporation (by bringing their leader, Rudolf von Bennigsen, into the ministry), Bennigsen himself tried to use the negotiations for leverage on a gradual parliamentarization, and this must have entrenched Bismarck further in the desire to break with the existing party configuration. In their place he envisaged a system of economic groupings spanning the older political alignments. All being well, if economic fronts could be formed outside the present party lines, the government could 'enter the elections with some hope of seeing the predominance of doctrinaires in the parliamentary formations diminished'.[33]

In the immediate term, however, matters were almost deadlocked, and during late 1877 and early 1878 Bismarck made little progress with either the fiscal package of tariff reform or the other legislative measures high in his priorities; the parliamentary fragmentation still gave the National Liberals centrality as the largest single faction and allowed them to evade the traps Bismarck was laying for them. The assassination attempt on the Kaiser on 11 May 1878 (by a 21-year-old plumber named Hödel) supplied Bismarck with the opportunity he needed – that is, to exploit the fear of revolution in a situation of crisis in order to bring the National Liberals to heel or separate them from their constituency. As Bismarck telegraphed from his estate after the shooting: 'Ought not the assassination attempt be taken as grounds for an immediate Bill against the Socialists and their press?'[34] The prospective anti-socialist measures now became the main leverage on the liberals and their electorate. In effect Bismarck could now use the carrot and the stick – tariff reform to entice the electorate into the government camp, the specter of revolution to drive it. The importance Bismarck now attached to the Anti-Socialist Law and the sanctions he was willing to invoke to secure its passage made it the tactical key to the rapidly evolving situation.

This tactical significance mirrored exactly the maneuvering around the abortive legislation of 1875–6. As Christoph von Tiedemann, the head of the Reich chancellory, wrote in an internal memorandum of 19 May 1878, there were three factors at work in the new bill: (a) it was not essentially a product of the assassination crisis, but a longstanding government intention going back, for instance, to the attempted criminal law amendment in 1875–6; (b) it was meant to absolve the government from charges of inaction and transfer responsibility for future violence clearly to the Reichstag, if the bill were rejected; and (c) the issue should not be treated as a vote of confidence in the government, but simply as a means of forcing the Reichstag majority into an unequivocal statement.[35] Bennigsen put this more graphically: the bill had the 'intention of a war against the Reichstag and the preface to its dissolution'.[36] But while the National Liberals opposed the bill, as expected, they pledged themselves to a comprehensive law of association in the autumn and thereby took much of the wind from Bismarck's sails. It was the second assassination attempt on 2 June 1878, this time by a disturbed academic agronomist called Karl Nobeling, that pushed matters beyond doubt. Bismarck's immediate reaction was: 'Then we'll dissolve the Reichstag!'. A further exchange, possibly apocryphal, was also reported:

> 'Now I've got the scoundrels!'
> 'Your Highness means the Social Democrats?'
> 'No, the National Liberals.'[37]

The electorate could now be mobilized successfully against the 'doctrinaires'. It scarcely mattered that a majority of National Liberals would probably now support a second bill without a dissolution. Undermining National Liberal credibility with the voters was more important than forcing the measure through. In the Ministry of State on 5 June 1878 Bismarck overrode the views of his colleagues and pushed for immediate dissolution rather than presenting the bill in the same session. He was not to be diverted; working with the liberals was to be abandoned and a conservative orientation announced. Neither the Reichstag nor the Bundesrat could obstruct the process. On 13 June 1878 he commented to the Württemberg ambassador: 'If I don't threaten a coup, I get nothing through.'[38] In the relative calm after the elections, he reflected on the implications. He was prepared to push things much further: if the new Reichstag rejected the Anti-Socialist Law again, he would make a new dissolution the condition of his remaining in office; and 'if the dissolution is again unsuccessful, then a legal *Staatsstreich* would be necessary'. In that eventuality, he envisaged the dissolution, not only of the existing constitutional framework of the Reichstag, but of the Reich itself in its current form. Even Saxony would recognize the need for annexation by Prussia in such circumstances, and if Bavaria did not, it could be partitioned with Austria. The smaller states would be shown the examples of Nassau and Hesse (which had been subject to annexation in 1866). In conclusion Bismarck pointed out that the only alternative as chancellor was Ludwig Windhorst, the leader of the Center Party, and so no alternative at all.[39] As one National Liberal Reichstag deputy said to Bennigsen: 'If he doesn't get his way, he can dissolve yet again and then a third time; he doesn't want that, but we can come to it'.[40]

LIBERALISM AND REVISIONISM

On the face of it Bismarck's strategy of undermining the National Liberals' self-confidence and credibility worked. Between the elections of 1877 and 1878 the crisis atmosphere reduced National Liberal strength in the Reichstag from 126 seats to 99, and the left liberal Progressives from 35 to 26. In percentage of the popular vote, the declines were less (from 27.2 to 23.1, and from 7.7 to 6.7 per cent respectively), and the liberal parties lost more ground to effective coalition-building among their opponents than they did to the direct defection of their own voters. Moreover, by the next elections of 1881 the National Liberals had split: matching the 16 deputies who had voted with the tariff majority in 1879 (representing mainly regions with an interest in protection, such as Bavarian textiles or west German heavy industry), 28 deputies defected in summer 1880 to form the Liberal Union or Secessionists on a mainly free-trading platform. This halved the National Liberal representation for the next elections in 1881 (down to 47 seats, 14.7 per cent of the vote), but produced a combined left liberal strength of 115 seats (60 Progressives, 46 Secessionists, and 9 for the regionally based South German People's Party), or 23.1 per cent of the popular vote.

Thoughts of a lasting liberal revival, however, which caused Bismarck more than a momentary anxiety in the early-1880s, soon passed. Within the liberal camp as a whole there was still some fluidity between the National Liberal and left liberal sectors in the 1880s, but by 1893 the levels of support had stabilized at levels dramatically lower than the heroic days of unification and state-building in the 1870s: the National Liberals consistently returned some 45–55 deputies in the Reichstag elections of 1893–1912 (for some 12–13 per cent of the vote), while the combined left liberal strength hovered around 36–49 seats (or 9–14 per cent of the vote). This compared with a bloc of 208 liberal deputies in 1874, commanding 39.7 per cent of the popular vote.

Thus Bismarck's relationship with the National Liberals seems to have acted out the scenario described in the first section of this chapter – that of a conservative empire (the unreformed Bismarckian Prusso-German state) and its pre-industrial ruling elites defending authoritarian traditions against the liberal and democratic challenges thrown up by the process of industrialization and economic change by a mixture of crude power (the politics of 'blood and iron', repressive legislation like the Anti-Socialist Law, and Bismarck's threats of a *Staatsstreich*), political manipulation (Bismarck's personal skills and techniques of rule), and artfully mobilized nationalism (from the *Kulturkampf* to the economic nationalism of the tariffs and the 'enemy-within' rhetoric of anti-socialism). In fact, during the 1880s, the period not dealt with in detail here, the manipulated nationalism became all the more important with Bismarck's exploitation of the colonial idea and the campaign for the military budget, which successfully dominated the 1884 and 1887 elections respectively from the government's point of view. This history can easily be made to fit the model of liberal compromise and defeat in which the National Liberals in particular were continuously outmaneuvered into sacrificing the core principles of liberal democracy on the altar of Prussian-dominated national-state power. Given this framework, nationalism becomes the nemesis of the liberal democratic political modernization that German history failed to undergo during the *Kaiserreich*. This was true of nationalism both in its state-building dimensions (the process of German unification in the 1860s and the strengthening of the central state capacities in the following two decades) and in its manipulative ones (Bismarck's use of nationalist enthusiasms for cementing the status quo in the sense of 'secondary integration'). As Pflanze puts it in summary form: 'The essence of the Bismarckian Constitution was its conservation, through revolutionary means, of the Prussian aristocratic, monarchical order in a century of increasingly dynamic economic and social change'.[41]

However, there is another way of viewing the politics of the 1870s, which is not completely antithetical to the post-1960s revisionism, in the sense that it can preserve some of the latter's particular interpretations, but which does require a fundamental shift of perspective on the political complexion of the empire and the identity of its dominant social groups. In effect, I want to argue, the binary oppositions of reactionary/backward versus liberal/modern, and pre-industrial/aristocratic versus bourgeois, need to be deconstructed, because the real character of the Bismarckian empire confuses the clarity of these distinctions. In what follows I will present the argument under three heads: (a) the liberal, as opposed to the conservative or reactionary, qualities of the unification settlement; (b) the meanings of the *Kulturkampf*; and (c) the local contexts of liberal political life.

(a) German historians have strongly denied liberal credentials to the Prusso-German state created during 1867–71, pointing to the limited powers of the Reichstag under the constitution, the monarch's executive authority and the Prusso-German dualism that guaranteed the special privileges of the Junkers in Prussia (via the undemocratic three-class franchise, the aristocracy's relative immunity from taxation, its dominance within the army and parts of the civil bureaucracy and its special access to the kaiser-king). But if we look at what actually was accomplished during the unification settlement, this amounted to an impressive concentration of forward-looking economic legislation, an elaborate framework of capitalist enabling laws. During 1867–73 liberal demands for national economic integration formed the centerpiece of the emerging constitutional order, consummating the process begun by the launching of the *Zollverein* (customs union) several decades before. Such measures included: freedom of movement for goods, capital, and labor; freedom of enterprise from guild regulation; the 'emancipation of credit'; favorable legal conditions for company formation; the metric system of weights and measures, a single currency and unified laws of exchange; a federal consular service and standardized postal and telegraphic communications; patent laws; and the general codification of the commercial law. Central financial institutions then followed. As industrialization proceeded, the state did other things to reorganize the social environment for capitalist development – by regulating rail and water transportation, by managing external trading relations via commercial treaties and/or tariffs, by colonies and the protection of markets, by contracts for army and navy and by a host of social interventions (in welfare, education, labor legislation, and so forth). To all of this we might add the codification of criminal law, the standardizing of judicial procedure, and the eventual adoption of a new Code of Civil Law (this last not until 1896–1900). This legal and constitutional edifice presupposed the achievements of unification. The defeated left liberal opponents of Bismarck's settlement might speak dismissively of 'a customs parliament, a postal parliament, and a telegraph parliament'.[42] But these were precisely the areas in which the German social order was being reconstituted.[43]

Within limits, we can say that these are the functions common to all specifically capitalist states, in the sense that the accumulation and centralization of capital within nation–states structurally requires or presupposes a certain range of state interventions – that is, the basic guaranteeing of property rights, liberalizing the economy, standardization and codification of commercial practices, management of external relations to the benefit of trade, and so on. Alone, the creation of a single German state was a major progressive or modernizing achievement by the criteria of the time, given the previous territorial fragmentation of state jurisdictions in Europe's German-speaking region. Moreover, the overcoming of that region's myriad pre-national survivals – the petty monarchical, ecclesiastical, and aristocratic sovereignties only partially rationalized by Napoleon in the 1800s – was not the spontaneously embraced achievement of either the Prussian state or the pre-industrial aristocratic elites. The creation of a united Germany was placed on the political agenda by organized radical and liberal agitation between the 1830s and 1860s. The process of proposing the category of the German nation and of organizing public life into a new political community of citizens owed little to the initiative of the Prussian government. In fact, the real work of constituting the German nation had to be conducted in *opposition* to the existing sovereign authorities by civil initiative and voluntary association, and eventually by full-scale political action, first in the 1840s and then again in the 1860s. It was the liberal revival of the 1860s that compelled Bismarck's pragmatic response; and when he placed himself 'at the head of the revolutionary party' (as he is said to have put it), it was again the specifically liberal program which he proceeded to put into place.[44] The very creation of a centrally constituted national political arena on the ruins of the region's historic particularist jurisdictions (the new constitutional territory of the German empire) was a decisive liberal advance; and this simultaneously created the legal and institutional conditions for a process of capitalist industrialization throughout Germany, including the political consolidation of a national market and an impressive body of modernizing economic legislation. As Stürmer says: 'Bismarck produced the policies that liberal Germany desired'.[45]

(b) Thus, there may be good grounds for seeing German unification not as the capitulation and compromising of German liberalism, but as its highest achievement in this classical 1850s and 1860s phase. But unification was also a political act; which necessarily left much of the nation's social and cultural consolidation incomplete. Böhme, as we saw, proposed one way of understanding the process of completion, in the socioeconomic refoundation that hitched the imperial government to the stable alliance of 'iron and rye' in 1878–9. But this again emphasized the dynamics of liberal obsolescence, the growing inadequacy of the liberal political outlook when faced with the rise of protection and the new politics of interest. Similarly, one might stress the state-building aspects of Bismarck's politics in the 1870s – the strengthening of the Reich executive in an administrative and fiscal sense and the use of anti-socialist and nationalist appeals of various kinds to achieve 'secondary integration' in a German society that was badly fissured along religious, ethnic, social, and regional lines, with a narrow governing basis in the privileges of pre-industrial elites (this would be the view, for example, of Wehler). In that case, the *Kulturkampf* becomes another illustration of how the logic of official German-national politics worked to compromise liberal principles and entrap the National Liberal Party in a governmental alignment that militated against the possible liberalization of German society. The *Kulturkampf* was also contrary to liberal self-interest for it drove an unnecessary wedge between the liberals and German Catholics. From a liberal point of view, it was both unprincipled and short-sighted. As Margaret Anderson puts it:

Liberal democracy failed to develop strong roots in Germany not least because liberalism defined itself as anti-Catholic in a country where Catholics made up a third of the electorate and hence were necessary for the formation of any democratic majority with a hope of confronting the government for the purpose of exercising power.[46]

However, to imply that German liberals somehow had a choice whether to become anti-clerical or not is rather unhistorical. In Germany, no less than elsewhere in continental Europe, the critique of the Catholic church and its societal power was a strategic rather than an accidental commitment. For liberals the *Kulturkampf* (which in any case was well under way in many south German centers of liberal strength *before* Germany was unified) was simply the next stage of unification. It meant exactly what the term said – a struggle for progress, to unlock the potential for social development and free German society's dynamism from the dead hand of superstition and archaic institutions. The resources and apparatus of the Catholic church were thought to be obstructing this potential, so that any reordering of social priorities of the kind liberals desired necessarily entailed an attack on the church's traditional practices and privileges. Furthermore, it was no accident (liberals thought) that the Catholic regions were precisely the economically backward ones (a critique of Catholic backwardness that was later taken up by many bourgeois Catholic commentators themselves around the turn of the century). Thus, if the people were to be emancipated from their mental subjugation, a determined effort would be needed to capture the cultural initiative, dismantle Catholicism's obstructive strengths and redirect educational and cultural activity. This was clearest in the localities of south-west Germany and the Rhineland, where the *Kulturkampf* was most bitterly conducted. For the defenders of Catholic tradition, the church was the indispensable basis of community cohesion, both as an institutional resource and as a moral guardian. As far as liberals were concerned, however, clerical control of charities, poor-houses and schools simply tied up capital, kept the poor in dependent ignorance and shackled the chances of genuine social emancipation.[47]

Thus the *Kulturkampf* perfectly illustrates the two-sidedness of the liberal experience in the 1870s. On the one hand, it was a natural extension of the Bismarckian solution to the German question (that is, the Prussian, small-German one), because it emphasized the north German, Prussian and Protestant bias of the new state. It also had positive functions for state formation, by cutting back the independent public authority of the church and strengthening government control of education. In this sense, perhaps, it did work against the grain of liberal principle and did nothing to lay the groundwork for further liberalization of the political institutions, even damaging the latter by the restrictions on civil liberties that were entailed by limiting the practice of Catholicism. But on the other hand, the *Kulturkampf* strengthened the momentum of exactly those forces in civil society – the liberal movement for German unity – that in the 1860s Bismarck sought hardest to control. After liberalizing the economy, the *Kulturkampf* was the object of greatest liberal effort in the 1870s and also saw the greatest liberal penetration of the state apparatus (under Adalbert Falk's tenure at the Prussian Ministry of Culture and his counterparts in the other states). In this sense, it threatened to upset the uneasy compromise between Bismarck and the National Liberals on which the empire had been founded. Liberals were fighting a secular crusade against the very values, institutions and vested interests that Bismarck's constitution was meant to defend. After attacking social and cultural traditionalism in Catholic regions, what was to prevent liberals from turning their sights on the heartlands of Protestant conservatism too? The ideal of German-national citizenship that spoke through the liberal campaigning implied an attack on corporate particularism and a strengthening of local self-government, and neither was possible within the terms of Bismarck's constitution. This drive for progress in its sociocultural (as opposed to more directly economic or political) dimension was what the *Kulturkampf* was all about.

(c) We can view these processes most effectively in the local arena. One very good example is a collective study of the Konstanz region of south-west Germany in the period of unification, organized around the problem of the region's growing 'peripheralization' during industrialization.[48] In effect, Konstanz liberals saw themselves forced to embark on a visionary program of progressive regional development if this structural disadvantage was to be overcome. Faced with the preponderance of the industrial north in their state of Baden as a whole, with a resistant structure of local pre-capitalist interests, and with an indifferent central bureaucracy in Karlsruhe, liberals in Konstanz seized the initiative. They formed themselves as a political vanguard, proclaiming an ideal of progress whose material conditions they had yet to create. They then pursued the latter through the manufacture and management of public opinion, by dominating the town's cultural life, by creating new commercial institutions and by mounting a sustained attack on the institutional bulwarks of the existing social order (the Catholic Church, the clericalized charities, the lethargy of the surrounding countryside). Resting on the assured control of local institutions, this broadened into a wider offensive on the Karlsruhe government. The goal was to free the region's human and capital resources for a process of autonomous social development. Control of the charities, whose financial resources were considerable, assumed a central place in this conception. Not only did they trap the region's economic potential, but, to liberal minds, they stifled the chances for self-improvement by keeping the poor in a state of moral and spiritual dependence.

As in the rest of Germany, the height of liberal success came in the mid-1860s. Re-emerging from the post-1849 reaction, Konstanz liberals regrouped at the end of the 1850s and after 1860 began a new period of buoyancy. Conquering new positions of influence by the eve of the

Austro-Prussian War, they seemed on the brink of success. But the transformed circumstances of a partially unified Germany decisively changed the agenda. The formation of the North German Confederation forced Konstanz liberals to rethink their views on the national question, which so far had taken second place behind the campaign for internal reform. Moreover, a series of economic factors – the disruptions of the war, the burdens of the new pro-Prussian course (that is, the military reform, with its impact on taxation and the loss of rural labor), and the bad harvest of 1867–8 – opened a period of tension between liberals and the small property-owners whose support was essential to their cause. Aware of such disaffection, the liberals chose to press ahead and break with a political practice which had been fairly open and potentially democratic. They ceased to submit policy matters to public discussion, veiled the executive in secrecy and applied the local state apparatus in an impatiently authoritarian way. This alienated the wider petty-bourgeois coalition that had been so patiently assembled in the preceding decade and left the liberal leaders increasingly marooned on a rock of municipal office. The climax of this deteriorating situation came in January 1870, when an independent popular mobilization disputed liberal control of public opinion and defeated the key proposal for dissolving the *Allmende*, the common lands over the Swiss border.

The most interesting aspect of this process was the dynamics of political mobilization. At one level, Konstanz reproduced the familiar sociology of German liberalism in the nineteenth century, recruiting mainly from the local tradesmen and resident intelligentsia, such as it was. Of the 480 signatories of a petition supporting the liberal mayor Strohmeyer in 1869, some 17 per cent belonged to the *Bildungsbürgertum* of the free professions and some 30 per cent to the 'well-situated economic bourgeoisie (merchants, capital owners, manufacturers, inn-keepers)'.[49] But there were actually two different processes in the achievement of the local dominance by the liberals. One involved the gradual coalescence of a potential leadership in the early 1860s around the so-called Friday Circle, an informal discussion group. This reas-sembled the veterans of 1848 with some new recruits and a leavening of in-migrating intellectuals such as the journalist Edward Pickford.[50] But there was also a second process, which involved the wider stirring of public opinion, articulated from early 1865 through the new liberal institution of the *Bürgerabend*. Originating in a large public meeting to discuss the controversial charities issue, this was cleverly institutionalized into a regular forum for the airing of public affairs. Though the agenda was carefully stage-managed by the controlling group, such meetings became the main mechanism of public accountability and permitted a much larger degree of public participation. Some 37 per cent of those who signed the 1869 petition mentioned above were in handicrafts or agriculture, and at least 10 per cent belonged to the laboring poor ('those without a trade, day-laborers, servants'). Crucially, this involved the *Ortseinwohner*, those local residents who were disfranchised, in the political process and brought a new democratic potential into the town's public life.

This local example makes an important point about the social character of liberalism in the 1860s. It depended – in a dynamic and variable way – on the popular coalitions which specific political initiatives helped to create. For a brief time between early 1865 when they started the *Bürgerabend*, and 1867–8 when they stopped submitting themselves with any consistency to public debate, the Konstanz liberals successfully constituted themselves as the voice of a broadly based popular movement of reform. This emergent public opinion required a complex institutional fabric, the novelty of which cannot be overemphasized. The press was paramount. The *Konstanzer Zeitung* reported proceedings in the *Bürgerabend* in meticulous detail, praising their seriousness against the frivolity of the opposition – whose spokesmen were stigmatized as 'spineless lackeys', 'poorhouse parasites', and 'beggarwomen' (especially reserved for clerics). The public petition, orchestrated through the *Bürgerabend*, was another key medium. The role of the tavern as a center of information, discussion, and propaganda, and as a source of newspapers, was vital. Imaginative forms of public contestation, as in the practice of 'Radolfzellieren' (taking its name from the first event of this kind, in the nearby town of Radolfzell), in which liberals swamped Catholic meetings with their own supporters, were also important. Finally, the *Bürgerabend* was buttressed by an array of institutions stressing an ideal of progress and improvement: the choral society *Harmonie*, the workers' educational society, the fire brigade, the theater, and most of all the Commercial Society and the Credit Society, the spearhead of liberalism in the countryside.

It is here, within the cultural domain of political life – the extra-parliamentary sphere in the broadest sense – that the importance of the local arena can properly be seen. It was precisely through the minutiae of local politics, even though episodically and often intangibly, that the wider constituency of the liberals took shape. This was an informal politics of qualified participation, which stayed firmly in the managerial hands of the liberal leaders and was 'democratic' only in the most tendential of senses. In 1865–8, the *Bürgerabend* tended definitely towards a unified 'citizenry' by integrating wide sections of the people into a general reforming consensus. But once conditions deteriorated – especially when popular opposition developed to liberal designs on the *Allmende* and the charities – the new forms of participation could be dismantled as soon as they were built. To that extent, the new liberal public sphere had a decidedly instrumental character, with the liberals retreating into a more authoritarian practice of government once they held the reins of power and their popular support began to fragment. After 1868, the *Bürgerabend* lost its practical plebiscitary function. The politicization of rural Catholicism joined with the resentment at the costs of reform to push liberalism onto the defensive, and the more ambitious reforming plans were abandoned with resignation, from the general attempt to free capital resources to more particular projects like the idea of a theater reform.

GERMAN HISTORY AGAINST THE GRAIN

Thus if we read German history in the unification years against the grain – if we remember why unification had originally been forced onto the agenda of a political process that until 1867 was still 'pre-German', and what the meanings of the call for a united Germany actually were at this time (that is, liberal and radical rather than conservative); if we look at what was actually done in the unification settlement (in the shape of the constitution and the socioeconomic, administrative and cultural legislation of the early to middle 1870s) and at the social forces that were actually driving the policy-making process; and if we focus on how the politics of unification (which meant, for example, both the progressive economic legislation and the *Kulturkampf*) were made in the localities on the ground – then the character of the Bismarckian period begins to appear in a somewhat different light. While turning a critical spotlight on Bismarck and the authoritarian values and manipulative politics he locked into place, and while arguing for the harmful continuities he established with the authoritarian and demagogic politics of the future (from Wilhelmine imperialism to Nazism), there is a sense in which the post-1960s revisionist historians have still retained an excessively 'statist', Prusso-centric and 'Bismarckian' conception of how German history was made in the 1860s and 1870s. Moreover, in maintaining the traditional view that German liberals failed – capitulated and denied the essential principles of liberalism in fact – historians like Böhme and Wehler bring an unrealistically twentieth-century standard of successful liberalism to bear on the problem, in which advanced criteria of liberal democracy, welfare statism and civil rights are used to evaluate the consistency and effectiveness of a mid-nineteenth-century liberalism whose center of gravity and priorities were actually elsewhere.

If we locate German liberalism in the full European context of its own time, meaning the European-wide conjuncture of capitalist development and constitution-making in the 1860s, then the investment of liberal hopes in the Bismarckian settlement of 1867–71 appears not as a liberalism-denying compromise, but as a powerful, if unfinished, realization of liberal visions of the future. This was true *par excellence* of the very creation of the nation–state itself, of the laying of the institutional foundations for national economic development and of the cultural dimension of the drive for unification (that is, the *Kulturkampf*). 'Germany' was remade during the 1860s and 1870s, both territorially-constitutionally and socially-culturally, and it was re-made along the lines German liberals had broadly envisaged. In the event it was Bismarck who proved to be the manager of this process, but it was liberals who defined the agenda he carried out, not the pre-industrial and aristocratic elite on whom Böhme and Wehler want to focus, who were thrown by unification onto the defensive. The National Liberals were certainly outmaneuvered by Bismarck in the later 1870s, and his turn to the right in 1878–9 meant a serious weakening of their parliamentary and governmental position, but it is not clear that this negated the modernizing character of the unification settlement. To put this strongly, it may have been less the discrepancy between a modern industrializing economy and a backward social and political structure that produced both the imperialist nationalism and missing democratization of German history under Bismarck and his successors (that is, the view of the post-1960s revisionists), than the *very modernity* of the institutional framework created out of the unification settlement that made 'democratization' (or further liberalization) unnecessary. If this was so, we need to think again about how the history of German liberalism – and the character of the German empire under Bismarck – are best to be considered.[51]

In closing, I want to illustrate the possibilities of such a reassessment from two recent monographs of regional history. The first is a study by Heide Barmeyer of Prussia's annexation of Hanover in the Austro-Prussian War, which was negotiated during two ministerial conferences in March and the start of August 1867.[52] What she shows is less the simple 'Prussification' of Hanover than a more complex process of reform, in which the effort at protecting Hanover's distinctive administrative autonomies and traditions gave the leverage for the future overhaul of Prussia's own administrative system, based on 'decentralization and self-administration', and resuming the unfinished agenda of the Stein-Hardenberg reforms of the 1810s. In effect, the constitution of the Hanoverian provincial administration in 1867 provided the precedent for the general Prussian reforms of the next decade, including the district and provincial rationalizations of 1872 and 1875. The events of 1866–7 were an attempt 'to develop in and with Hanover a prefigurative reform-model for the general Prussian administration'.[53] The resulting settlement may not have been unambiguously liberal. But it was certainly *not* conservative in any given meaning of the term. In fact, the annexation of Hanover was irreconcilable with given conservative principles: 'the more modern, dynamic, and industrializing Prussia triumphed . . . over a

European order that was defined by monarchical legitimacy, solidarity of thrones and the received order of law'.[54] This may not have been the victory Bismarck wanted, but it was an irreducible effect of his actions. It was with liberals that he was now in alliance, and this was true above all in Hanover and the other annexed territories, where National Liberalism delivered the political language of national-cum-nationalist integration for the new state.

My second example is a study by Werner Blessing of secularization and schooling in nineteenth-century Bavaria.[55] Blessing shows how popular political identity was reshaped during the long transition between two contrasting structures of public legitimate authority – that of 'the feudal-corporative-confessional world of the old [Holy Roman] Empire', and that of the modern, secularized and associational world of the new nation–state. He explores this transition by analyzing a shifting picture of public institutional authority in Bavaria, composed of church, state and school, and its action on popular mentalities. Unification – and the incorporation of Bavaria into the Second Empire in 1871 – was the pivotal event in this process. It broadened the ideological and institutional context for the shaping of public consciousness, particularly for the bourgeois exponents of the emergent civil society, and eroded the basis for the older ritual apparatus of clerico-dynastic authority. At the same time, urbanization, industrialization and democratization (sum-marized by Blessing as 'the breakthrough of society') gradually undermined the parochialism that was hospitable to traditional forms of social and religious order. In the process one mode of popular religiosity gave way before another; organized Catholicism engineered a vital self-transformation; and the old monarchist cult of the Bavarian royal house subsided before a new bourgeois cult of the nation. After 1871, the expanding presence of the Kaiserreich gradually saturated Bavarian political culture. The real beneficiary was the elementary school, which emerges as the heroic protagonist of Blessing's tale. Thus, even where liberalism was less central as a directive political force in the 1870s, as in Bavaria, the social and institutional history of those years reveals processes of administrative reform, national integration and cultural change, which scarcely resemble the defence of a conservative social and political order historians such as Böhme and Wehler claim to detect.

There are certainly other major themes that might have structured this discussion of the Bismarckian years and the foundation period of German history in its modern, state-unified phase. The social history of the working class is one of these, for a major body of scholarship now exists which is distinct from the equally large literature on the labor movement and the SPD.[56] Similarly, a sudden rush of research in the 1980s has appeared on the German bourgeoisie, which takes seriously the question of bourgeois culture and the 'embourgeoisement' of the mores of the Kaiserreich.[57] Finally, the growth of German women's history has begun to have an impact on the late nineteenth century as well as the period during and since the First World War, where research is much thicker on the ground.[58] Here I have chosen to focus on the political history of the German nation–state's founding years in order to indicate how the main lines of interpretation and argument have developed.

NOTES

1 Benjamin Disraeli, speech in the House of Commons, 9 February 1871, in John C. G. Röhl, *From Bismarck to Hitler* (London, 1970), p. 23.

2 Hans Rosenberg, *Grosse Depression und Bismarckzeit. Wirtschaftsablauf, Gesellschaft und Politik in Mitteleuropa* (Berlin, 1967); Helmut Böhme, *Deutschlands Weg zur Grossmacht. Studien zum Verhältnis von Wirtschaft und Staat während der Reichsgründungszeit 1848–1881* (Cologne and Berlin, 1966); Hans-Ulrich Wehler, *Bismarck und der Imperialismus* (Cologne and Berlin, 1969).

3 Böhme, *Deutschlands Weg*, p. 15.

4 ibid., p. 411.

5 Helmut Böhme (ed.), *Probleme der Reichsgründungszeit 1848–1879* (Cologne and Berlin, 1968), p. 14.

6 Böhme, *Deutschlands Weg*, p. 9.

7 See Hans Rosenberg, 'Political and social consequences of the Great Depression of 1873–1896 in Central Europe', *Economic History Review*, vol. 13 (1943), pp. 58–73.

8 Here the argument has been developed at great length by Wehler, *Bismarck und der Imperialismus*. English summaries can be found in two essays: 'Bismarck's imperialism, 1862–1890', *Past and Present*, no. 48 (1970), pp. 119–55; 'Industrial growth and early German imperialism', in Roger Owen and Bob Sutcliffe (eds), *Studies in the Theory of Imperialism* (London, 1972), pp. 71–92.

9 E.g. this is tendentiously present in Hans-Ulrich Wehler, 'Der Aufstieg des Organisierten Kapitalismus und Interventionsstaates in Deutschland', in Heinrich August Winkler (ed.), *Organisierter Kapitalismus. Voraussetzungen und Anfänge* (Göttingen, 1974), p. 51. I have developed a full critique of Rosenberg's argument in Geoff Eley, 'Hans Rosenberg and the Great Depression of 1873–96: politics and economics in recent German historiography, 1960–1980', in *From Unification to Nazism. Reinterpreting the German Past* (London, 1986), pp. 23–41.

10 Wehler, *Bismarck und der Imperialismus*, p. 115. For a similar exploration of the domestic context of Bismarck's colonial policy, see Klaus J. Bade, *Friedrich Fabri und der Imperialismus in der Bismarckzeit: Revolution – Depression – Expansion* (Frieburg, 1975); and 'Imperial Germany and West Africa: colonial movement, business interests, and Bismarck's "colonial policies"', in Stig Förster, Wolfgang J. Mommsen and Ronald Robinson (eds), *Bismarck, Europe and Africa. The Berlin Africa Conference 1884–1885 and the Onset of Partition* (Oxford, 1988), pp. 121–47. For direct critiques of Wehler's stress on 'counter-cyclical therapy', see Hartmut Pogge von

Strandmann, 'Domestic origins of Germany's colonial expansion under Bismarck', *Past and Present*, no. 42 (1969), pp. 140–59; and 'Consequences of the foundation of the German Empire: colonial expansion and the process of political-economic rationalization', in Förster, Mommsen and Robinson, *Bismarck, Europe and Africa*, pp. 105–20. For my own critiques of the concept of social imperialism in Wehler, focusing more on the period after Bismarck: Geoff Eley, 'Defining social imperialism: use and abuse of an idea', *Social History*, vol. 1 (1976), pp. 269–90; and 'Social imperialism in Germany: reformist synthesis or reactionary sleight of hand?', in Joachim Radkau and Imanuel Geiss (eds), *Imperialismus im 20. Jahrhundert. Gedenkschrift für Georg W. F. Hallgarten* (Munich, 19?6), pp. 71–86, repr. in *From Unification to Nazism*, pp. 154–67.

11 In that sense, the recent major biography by Lothar Gall, which returns German history to a more explicit focus on Bismarck, is not at all incompatible with the earlier revisionism, whatever the particular differences of interpretation. See Lothar Gall, *Bismarck: the White Revolutionary*, 2 vols (London, 1986).

12 Wehler, 'Industrial growth and early German imperialism', pp. 89, 87, 88.

13 This phrase is taken from the chapter heading in Siegfried Mielke, *Der Hansa-Bund für Gewerbe, Handel und Industrie 1909–1914. Der gescheiterte Versuch einer antifeudale Sammlungspolitik* (Göttingen, 1976), p. 17: 'The political system: preservation of the predominance of the feudal aristocracy'.

14 ibid., p. 181.

15 Dirk Stegmann, *Die Erben Bismarcks. Parteien und Verbände in der Spätphase des Wilhelminischen Deutschlands. Sammlungspolitik 1897–1918* (Cologne, 1970), p. 13.

16 Stegmann, *Erbens Bismarcks*, provides an exhaustive treatment of the years 1909–13. For critical discussion: Geoff Eley, 'Sammlungspolitik, social imperialism and the Navy Law of 1898', in *From Unification to Nazism*, pp. 110–53.

17 Hans-Ulrich Wehler, *Das Deutsche Kaiserreich 1871–1918* (Göttingen, 1973), pp. 238 ff. (now translated as *The German Empire 1871–1918* (Leamington Spa, 1985)).

18 Critical discussions of the approach I have described can be found in: David Blackbourn and Geoff Eley, *The Peculiarities of German History. Bourgeois Society and Politics in Nineteenth-century Germany* (Oxford, 1984); Richard J. Evans, *Rethinking German History. Nineteenth-century Germany and the Origins of the Third Reich* (London, 1987); Robert G. Moeller, 'The Kaiserreich recast? Continuity and change in modern German history', *Journal of Social History*, vol. 17 (1984), pp. 655–83; James N. Retallack, 'Social history with a vengeance? Some reactions to H.-U. Wehler's "Das Deutsche Kaiserreich"', and Roger Fletcher, 'Recent developments in German historiography: the Bielefeld school and its critics', both in *German Studies Review*, vol. 7 (1984), pp. 423–50, 451–80. With the exception of Blackbourn and Eley, *Peculiarities*, these texts focus mainly on the post-Bismarckian era.

19 This account is taken from Helmut Böhme, 'Big business pressure groups and Bismarck's turn to protectionism, 1873–1879', *Historical Journal*, vol. 10 (1967), pp. 218–36, which usefully summarizes the author's detailed treatment in *Deutschlands Weg*. Böhme's use of sources and many detailed aspects of his work need to be treated with extreme care: see Hans-Ulrich

Wehler's extraordinary hatchet-job in *Neue Politische Literatur*, vol. 14 (1969), which, however leaves the basic principle of the argument intact. For another English-language account, see Ivo N. Lambi, *Free Trade and Protection in Germany* (Wiesbaden, 1963).

20 Rudolf. von Bennigsen, quoted by George G. Windell, 'The Bismarckian Reich as a federal state, 1866–80', *Central European History*, vol. 2 (1969), p. 295.

21 To clarify, the National Liberals were the majority tendency of German liberalism that made its peace with Bismarck's settlement of the German question, or at least, saw the latter as a good basis for future work. In effect, they split from the Progressive Party in 1867, leaving the original party as a left liberal rump.

22 An early analysis of the sociology of parliamentary liberalism in the unification era was Leonore O'Boyle, 'Liberal political leadership in Germany, 1867–1884', *Journal of Modern History*, vol. 28 (1956), pp. 338–52. The best synthetic accounts are now: James J. Sheehan, *German Liberalism in the Nineteenth Century* (Chicago, 1978); and Dieter Langewiesche, *Liberalismus in Deutschland* (Frankfürt, 1988).

23 Cited by Ernst Nolte, 'Germany', in Hans Rogger and Eugen Weber (eds), *The European Right* (London, 1965), p. 286.

24 Michael Stürmer (ed.), *Bismarck und die preussisch-deutsche Politik 1871–1890* (Munich, 1970), p. 34.

25 Otto von Bismarck, *Gedanken und Erinnerungen*, Vol. 2 (Stuttgart, 1898), p. 59; Arthur Rosenberg, *Imperial Germany. The Birth of the German Republic 1871–1918* (New York, 1970), p. 27.

26 Böhme, 'Big business pressure groups', p. 235.

27 Stürmer (ed.), *Bismarck*, p. 57.

28 ibid., p. 36.

29 Michael Stürmer, 'Staatsstreichgedanken im Bismarckreich', *Historische Zeitschrift*, vol. 209 (1969), pp. 584 ff. Editor of the Berlin *Germania*, Paul Majunke was a Center Reichstag deputy sentenced to a year in prison for press offenses, whose arrest in December 1874 triggered a parliamentary crisis, in which the passage of a parliamentary motion affirming parliamentary immunity was countered by Bismarck's threat of resignation.

30 Stürmer (ed.), *Bismarck*, pp. 77 ff.

31 See Werner Pöls, *Sozialistenfrage und Revolutionsfürcht in ihrem Zusammenhang mit den angeblichen Staatsstreichplänen Bismarcks* (Düsseldorf, 1960), pp. 32–40.

32 Stürmer (ed.), *Bismarck*, p. 118 f. Eduard Lasker was a leading left liberal parliamentarian.

33 ibid., pp. 117 ff.

34 Gall, *Bismarck*, Vol. 2, p. 93. In fact, Hödel had been expelled from the SPD.

35 Stürmer (ed.), *Bismarck*, p. 120 f.

36 Stürmer, 'Staatsstreichgedanken', p. 592.

37 ibid., p. 593; A. J. P. Taylor, *Bismarck. The Man and the Statesman* (London, 1955), pp. 172 ff.

38 Stürmer, 'Staatsstreichgedanken', p. 601.

39 Stürmer (ed.), *Bismarck*, pp. 131 ff.

40 ibid., p. 130.

41 Otto Pflanze, *Bismarck and the Development of Germany, 1815–1871* (Princeton, NJ, 1963), p. 168.

42 Benedikt Waldeck of the Progressive Party, cited by Theodor S. Hamerow,

The Social Foundations of German Unification 1858–1871, Vol. 2: *Struggles and Accomplishments* (Princeton, NJ, 1972), p. 330.

43 Paradoxically, this catalogue is also similar to the composite criteria used to describe the rise of the interventionist state in the era of organized capitalism by Hans-Ulrich Wehler, who is otherwise one of the strongest advocates of the 'pre-industrial' argument regarding the backwardness of the Prusso-German state. See Wehler, 'Aufstieg des Organisierten Kapitalismus'.

44 Pflanze, *Bismarck*, p. 301.

45 Stürmer 'Staatsstreichgedanken', p. 580.

46 Margaret Lavinia Anderson, *Windthorst. A Political Biography* (Oxford, 1981), pp. 195–7.

47 See David Blackbourn, *Class, Religion and Local Politics in Wilhelmine Germany. The Center Party in Württemberg before 1914* (London and New Haven, Conn., 1980), esp. pp. 233–5; and the three essays on 'Catholics and politics', in Blackbourn, *Populists and Patricians. Essays in Modern German History* (London, 1987), pp. 143–214. See also Jonathan Sperber, *Popular Catholicism in Nineteenth-century Germany* (Princeton, NJ, 1984); and Gert Zang, 'Die Bedeutung der Auseinandersetzung um die Stiftungsverwaltung in Konstanz (1830–1870) für die ökonomische und gesellschaftliche Entwicklung der lokalen Gesellschaft. Ein Beitrag zur Analyse der materiellen Hintergründe des *Kulturkampfes*', in Zang (ed.), *Provinzialisierung einer Region. Regionale Unterentwicklung und liberale Politik in der Stadt und im Kreis Konstanz im 19. Jahrhundert. Untersuchungen zur Entstehung der bürgerlichen Gesellschaft in der Provinz* (Frankfürt, 1978), pp. 307–73; Werner Trapp, 'Volksschulreform und liberales Bürgertum in Konstanz. Die Durchsetzung des Schulzwangs als Voraussetzung der Massendisziplinierung und qualifikation', ibid., pp. 375–434.

48 This account is distilled from Dieter Bellmann, 'Der Liberalismus im Seekreis (1860–1870). Durchsetzungsversuch und Scheitern eines regional eigenständigen Entwicklungskonzepts', ibid., pp. 183–263.

49 Zang, 'Bedeutung', p. 334.

50 The original center of 1840s liberalism in Konstanz was – characteristically, from what we know of such clubs elsewhere – the *Bürgermuseum*, the local elite social club. After 1850 liberal ranks were depleted by emigration and general depoliticization of the town's associational life, so that the *Bürgermuseum* drastically changed its character. When liberalism revived after 1860, it was natural for the re-emerging leaders to seek an alternative rallying-point: hence the so-called *Freitagskreis*.

51 A start in this direction may be found in Blackbourn and Eley, *Peculiarities*.

52 Heide Barmeyer, *Hannovers Engliederung in den preussischen Staat. Annexion und administrative Integration 1866–1868* (Hildesheim, 1983).

53 ibid., p. 6.

54 ibid., p. 1.

55 Werner K. Blessing, *Staat und Kirche in der Gesellschaft. Institutionelle Autorität und mentaler Wandel in Bayern während des 19. Jahrhunderts* (Göttingen, 1982). For an excellent companion study of Bavarian politics in the Bismarckian years, see Karl Möckl, *Die Prinzregentenzeit. Gesellschaft und Politik während der A ra des Prinzregenten Luitpold in Bayern* (Munich and Vienna, 1982).

56 There is some discussion of the literature on social democracy and the labor movement in James Retallack's chapter in this volume.

57 For the current research on the bourgeoisie, see the volumes edited by

Jürgen Kocka: *Arbeiter und Bürger im 19. Jahrhundert* (Munich, 1986); *Bürger und Bürgerlichkeit im 19. Jahrhundert* (Göttingen, 1987); and *Bürgertum in 19. Jahrhundert. Deutschland im europaischen Vergleich*, 3 vols (Munich, 1988). See also Werner Conze and Jürgen Kocka (eds), *Bildungsbürgertum* in 19. *Jahrhundert* Part I: *Bildungssystem und Professionalisierung im internationalen Vergleich* (Stuttgart, 1985); Lothar Gall, *Bürgertum in Deutschland* (Berlin, 1989). Hans-Ulrich Wehler's recent essays on the subject are conveniently collected in Wehler, *Aus der Geschichte lernen?* (Munich, 1988), pp. 161–255. For an English-language collection, see David Blackbourn and Richard J. Evans (eds), *The German Bourgeoisie* (London, 1989). For a major case study, see Michael John, *Politics and the Law in Late Nineteenth-century Germany. The Origins of the Civil Code* (Oxford, 1989). Again, this discussion was originally set in motion by Blackbourn and Eley, *Peculiarities*, which was first published in an earlier German edition in 1980.

58   For gender and women's history in general, see Eve Rosenhaft's chapter in this volume. Some access to the literature in English may be had through two collections: Ruth-Ellen B. Joeres and Mary Jo Maynes (eds), *German Women in the Eighteenth and Nineteenth Centuries* (Bloomington, Ind., 1986); and John Fout (ed.), *German Women in the Nineteenth Century* (New York, 1984).

2 *Wilhelmine Germany*

JAMES RETALLACK

For 30 of the 45 years since the collapse of Hitler's regime, questions about the structure and dynamic of the Wilhelmine empire have been crucial in explaining the origins of Nazism. It is difficult to imagine now the outlook of the late 1940s and 1950s when the most important historians in Germany insisted that Hitler had come out of nowhere to 'dupe' the German people into supporting his regime. This portrait of Hitler as an aberration, as something unique in German history, was advanced by conservatives in the profession who, for a variety of reasons, could not address the Nazi catastrophe directly.[1]

In order to lay a foundation for a closer examination of the major turning points in the historiography of the Second Reich, this chapter will begin with a discussion of the period immediately following the First World War. These turning points include the 'Fischer controversy' that emerged in the 1960s, the publication of *The German Empire* in 1973 – an important book by Hans-Ulrich Wehler – and subsequent critiques of the Wehler interpretation, which continue to dominate German historiography today. The second half of the chapter adopts a thematic approach in order to suggest how a unitary view of Wilhelmine Germany has disintegrated in the last fifteen years – and what might follow. Debates to be examined include the role of Wilhelm II, more positive aspects of German society and culture, the importance of regionalism, the (alleged) ascendancy of the bourgeoisie, and the predicament of 'under-privileged' groups in society. The chapter concludes with a prognosis for historical writing on Wilhelmine Germany in the 1990s, in effect posing the question: where next for the Kaiserreich? It is perhaps worth hinting at the outset that the reader will find few definitive answers here. New paradigms of historical analysis are emerging only slowly and a consensus about Wilhelmine Germany remains elusive. Therefore, even as we 'take our bearings' and consider how far this historiographical journey has brought us, we are unlikely to find an entirely satisfying synthesis waiting around the corner.

LEGACIES OF A CONSERVATIVE HISTORICAL TRADITION

During the Weimar Republic a majority of German historians rejected the premise of the 'war guilt' clause (Article 231) in the Treaty of Versailles, according to which Germany alone was responsible for the outbreak of war in August 1914. Most historians – led by Gerhard Ritter, Hans Rothfels, and Hans Herzfeld – believed instead that Europe as a whole had 'slid' into war and that Germany bore no special blame. From this followed their insistence that no connection existed between German aggressiveness and the structure of German society in the pre-1914 era.[2]

Even before the rise of Hitler a few dissenting voices struggled to be heard. Thorstein Veblen, for instance, suggested in 1915 that a fateful incongruence existed between Germany's modern industrial-military capacity and her retarded sociopolitical development.[3] Students of Friedrich Meinecke – including Eckart Kehr and Hans Rosenberg – used historical tools derived from social analysis in a more eclectic way, relying particularly on the work of Max Weber. Stressing the irresponsible nature of Wilhelmine decision making and foreign policy, Kehr and Rosenberg tended to reject the traditional 'narrative' approach in favor of a 'problem-based' analysis.

Because this new 'critical social history of politics' was unorthodox and provocative, the German historical establishment felt less invigorated than threatened. This promising new beginning began to disintegrate when the Weimar Republic collapsed and then disappeared altogether when the Nazis suppressed intellectual freedom in the 1930s. Many liberal historians were forced to emigrate, including Kehr, who died at the tragically young age of 30. But even those who stepped into academic posts in America tended to concentrate on the history of ideas rather than social and political history. Meanwhile, the majority of historians who remained in Germany had little difficulty in accommodating themselves to a regime whose main concerns lay outside the realm of academe.

After 1945, even those with some complicity in the crimes of Nazism were able to win back their posts and reintegrate themselves in the German historical tradition. In general, their writing revealed how little they understood the need for a decisive confrontation with Germany's past. This quite understandable difficulty inclined conservative historians to argue that German development in the late nineteenth and early twentieth centuries had differed little from that of other nations in western Europe. Indeed, as a spokesman for this generation, Gerhard

Ritter laid the foundations for all those who continued to deny any link between fascism and developments in Wilhelmine Germany. Instead, Ritter argued, the roots of Nazism stretched no further back than November 1918, after which an era of revolution, inflation and depression led to the Nazi seizure of power. Thus, it was not in 1890 but only after the First World War that German history began to go off the rails. Only the political innovations that followed the abdication of Wilhelm II were responsible for the Nazi dictatorship.

Although many in the historical profession did not fully appreciate it at the time, this explanation of the roots of Nazism did, in fact, suggest a particular interpretation of society and politics in imperial Germany. Because Ritter and others tended to see Christian values as an essential moral defence against 'materialism', their histories often blamed socialism and Marxism for later disasters. By ascribing Hitler's success to the rise of 'mass politics' after 1918, Ritter argued in effect that up to that point the old ruling class had helped preserve solid virtues against the vulgarity and self-interest of the masses. Germans had turned to Nazism not because liberal democracy failed but because Germany had become too democratic: it was not Frederick the Great and Bismarck who prepared the way for Hitler, but Robespierre and Lenin.[4] Older elites, 'men who were socially and financially independent, who knew something about politics', were overwhelmed by demagogues and party bureaucracies. Mature political judgment and a sense of individual responsibility were left behind.

THE FISCHER CONTROVERSY AND A NEW VIEW OF IMPERIAL GERMANY

Ritter's views were neither quite so categorical as this bald summary implies, nor were they universally shared. Yet in the 1950s most German historians still believed, as they had in the 1920s, that the most fateful 'crime' of 1918 was the war guilt clause. In light of this consensus, it came as a tremendous shock to both academic and public opinion when a distinguished historian, Fritz Fischer, produced the 'blockbuster' book of 1961 – a meticulously researched monograph that refuted the idea of Germany's innocence in the outbreak of war in 1914.[5] This book inaugurated the so-called 'Fischer controversy', which dominated German historiography through most of the 1960s.

There are many ironies to the Fischer controversy. Fritz Fischer, born in 1908, was anything but an outsider in the German historical profession. Moreover, his study of German war aims departed little from the conventional methods of narrative history and he relied mainly on the traditional sources of state documents and private papers. On neither count, therefore, did Fischer seem a likely candidate to upset the German historical guild. Most ironic of all, although Fischer set out to reconsider the aims of German foreign policy just before and during the war, in the long run his principal effect was to revolutionize thinking about German *domestic* politics for the *entire* period from 1871 to 1918 – and beyond.

Fischer presented three main theses. First, he argued that the German government in July 1914 accepted – indeed hoped – that a major European war would result from its enthusiastic backing of Austria against Serbia. Second, Fischer illustrated that the annexationist war aims of the Imperial government not only predated the outbreak of war, but also shared a remarkable similarity with the plans made by the Nazis for conquest after 1933. Both these theses have been revised and moderated by subsequent research. Nonetheless, thanks to Fischer's work, the 'continuity debate' has fundamentally changed the way we view the transitions from Kaiserreich to Weimar and from Weimar to the Third Reich.[6] Third, Fischer argued that the sources of German expansionism were to be found less in her international position than in her social, economic and political situation at home on the eve of war. It was this third conclusion, eagerly taken up first by Fischer's own students in Hamburg and then by a younger generation of German academics, which changed the tone and substance of writing about Wilhelmine Germany much more decisively than the war-aims debate itself. These changes were most recognizable in the flood of new works on imperial Germany that were published in the late 1960s and early 1970s.

According to Fischer and his like-minded colleagues, the seeds of German aggression in 1914 and 1939 could be found in the 1860s and 1870s. They were sown by Bismarck and the military-political 'revolution from above' that unified and industrialized modern Germany. Not popular revolution from below, but the imposition of authoritarian structures from above, shaped the imperial constitution and party system of the Kaiserreich. Those structures, and the people who profited in maintaining them, proved insufficiently flexible to adapt to the modern age. The hierarchies of status, power and wealth continued to be dominated by socioeconomic and functional elites closely allied with the imperial state.

Members of the German middle classes could never hope to overcome such entrenched interests, this argument continued, but they found many of their other ambitions fulfilled by a rapidly expanding industrial economy. Thus German burghers 'sold out' in accepting the defeat of the revolution in 1848, but they also 'bought in' to an imperial establishment that offered national unity, economic liberalism, patents of nobility and other symbols of prestige. Never having undergone a bourgeois revolution as occurred earlier in England and France, Germany subsequently diverged further from the western democracies under the rule of Wilhelm. This divergence, or 'special path' (*Sonderweg*), not only explained the persistence of 'feudal' elites in German society, but it also illustrated the dangers of late industrialization in a nation without the parliamentary traditions necessary to safeguard the diffusion of power. Social, economic and political tensions arising from rapid industrial change were incompletely deflected by ruling elites, resulting in an aggressive drive for world-wide influence (*Weltpolitik*) and territorial expansion. In short, Germany's unique misdevelopment at home in the nineteenth century explained her responsibility for twice unleashing war on Europe in the twentieth.

This brief synopsis may help to explain why, after the Second World War, explanations of the Hitler phenomenon underwent such critical scrutiny. By 1970 the broad socioeconomic development of central Europe, rather than any particular German susceptibility to fascist ideology, seemed to be the historical terrain whose reworking promised the greatest rewards. Though the aim was still to lay bare the roots of Nazism, new tools were already being forged to complete the task.

As it happened, a number of German historians beginning their careers in the late 1960s discovered that some of those tools had already been fashioned by early proponents of 'critical social history'. At the same time the unsettled political and intellectual climate of West Germany gave this historiographical revolt added piquancy. It was no accident that the work of a classic outsider, Eckart Kehr, was rediscovered, republished and translated into English as a symbolic statement of this rebellion.[7] For Kehr, before he died in New York, had already turned the Rankean maxim of 'the primacy of foreign policy' on its head; he preferred to write history based on the premise of the 'primacy of domestic policy'. The winds of change blew from other quarters as well, including Cologne and Heidelberg, where many students (including Wehler) passed through seminars in social history conducted by two members of the 'middle generation' of German historians, Theodor Schieder and Werner Conze. Hans Rosenberg, writing since the 1930s, was recognized as another key contributor. In his study of the Great Depression of 1873–96, Rosenberg never sought to narrate the events of 'high politics' by relying simply on documents that revealed the role of personalities and ideas in history.[8] Rather, by keeping alive traditions of sociological and economic analysis, Rosenberg explored more fundamental determinants of political conflict.

When a new generation of historians set out to follow these impressive leads, they produced a mountain of scholarship so imposing that it can be reviewed only in outline. The most noteworthy contributions included Helmut Böhme's account of Germany's path to nationhood; Hans-Ulrich Wehler's analysis of Bismarck's imperialism; Jürgen Kocka's work on white-collar workers; Dirk Stegmann's analysis of parties and nationalist pressure groups after Bismarck; and Peter-Christian Witt's examination of government financial policy.[9] At virtually every point it seemed that Fischer's concern with the domestic roots of German aggression found its perfect complements in methodological innovation and an active commitment to the ideals of liberal democracy. In resurrecting Marx and Weber; in importing methodological advances from other countries (for instance the Annales School in France or modernization theory in the United States); in trying to satisfy the demands of the student movement; even in establishing new historical journals to bolster their position within the profession, this new scholarship tried to ensure that academic conservatism would not again triumph.

HANS-ULRICH WEHLER'S SYNTHESIS

In 1973 the University of Bielefeld historian, Hans-Ulrich Wehler, believed that the time had come to pull together the strands of this research and attempt a synthesis. Wehler has won much credit – and probably more than his share of blame – for acting upon this insight. The synthesis he produced was more comprehensive than any previous contribution to the debate. Although derived from notes for lectures first delivered in Cologne, *The German Empire* only masqueraded as a textbook for students.[10] Far from seeking to present a 'balanced' narrative of events, its argument was intentionally critical. With the explicit aim of stimulating further debate, its tone was provocative and its conclusions 'preliminary'. All too often, however, the book was not received in this spirit.

And understandably so. Wehler pulled no punches in presenting a view of imperial Germany that ascribed the most manipulative intentions to elite groups and the government. He believed the Kaiserreich was immeasurably more anti-democratic, materialistic and brutish than it had appeared to Gerhard Ritter. Wehler was particularly uncompromising in condemning the willingness of the old ruling classes to protect their position by resorting to demagoguery and other modern weapons they found in the arsenal of mass politics. Grain-growing Junkers, heavy industrialists, courtly sycophants, Protestant clerics, Prussian generals and a whole range of less powerful 'in-groups' used these weapons ruthlessly and with fateful success. Modern propaganda, electoral chicanery, courtly ceremony, elementary education and other 'Bonapartist' techniques of rule channelled hatreds and prejudices into avenues designed to deflect revolution and perpetuate the enjoyment of privilege and power. In Wehler's account, there was no room for doubt about where these elites received their political education: demagogues and tricksters may have conveyed some of the lessons of mass politics, but the schoolhouse of authoritarian rule was designed and built by Bismarck. At root, German domestic politics owed its immaturity to Bismarck's 'dictatorial' determination to prevent the growth of democratic institutions. German foreign policy owed its restless dynamic to the influence of a militarist spirit and the moral neutrality of *Realpolitik* as practised by Bismarck during the wars of unification in the 1860s. German society owed its willingness to discriminate against minorities to Bismarck's campaigns against Poles, Guelphs, Catholics, socialists and left liberals (all designated at one time or another as 'enemies of the Reich'). And German capitalism, despite its rapid efflorescence, served only the interests of employers' associations, industrialists and agrarian interest groups. All those who stood to lose through an equitable distribution of income and wealth found a willing patron in Bismarck.

The unity of perspective between Wehler and Fischer is clear. Fischer wrote in his second major book, *War of Illusions*, that the aim of German policy between 1911 and 1914 was 'to consolidate the position of the ruling classes with a successful imperialist foreign policy', and 'it was hoped a war would resolve the growing social tensions'.[11] Both historians agreed that although manipulatory elites had had things pretty much their own way in deflecting the rise of liberal democracy, a dead-end was reached (or at least perceived) in 1914. But the implications of their revisionism did not stop there, because Fischer and Wehler also believed that when the social and economic tensions seething underneath the surface of Wilhelmine Germany finally broke through in the political realm, the effect was all the more devastating precisely because the delaying tactics employed by anti-democratic elites had been so successful. The real explosion at home came not in 1914, when the socialists agreed to support the war, but four years later, in the wake of economic collapse and total defeat on the battlefield. Because imperial elites had evaded political reform for so long, they paid the price many times over. Although they finally revenged themselves on liberalism in 1933 by holding the stirrups for Hitler, they mistakenly believed that they could oust 'the little corporal' from the saddle once the business of dismantling Weimar democracy was completed.

The stunt backfired, of course. It was Hitler who revenged himself on the old gang. But the continuities remain the same: they tie together modern German history just as tightly whether they are conceived as stretching 'from unification to Nazism' or 'from Hitler to Bismarck'.[12] Because Fischer and Wehler both compelled historians to address the period from 1860 to 1945 as a unity, the rethinking of German history they introduced unequivocally constituted a watershed. Their scholarship produced nothing less than a 'paradigm shift' in the way Germans sought to come to grips with their past.

It is a tribute to the scholarship produced between 1961 and 1973 that James Sheehan – though perhaps to his regret – used the term 'new orthodoxy' in 1976 to describe the influence of the Fischer–Wehler interpretation.[13] In fact a 'new revisionism' was already waiting in the wings and it is arguable that a new orthodoxy comparable to the consensus of the 1950s never did establish itself. This was in part because the institutional structure of the German university system ensured some diversity, in part because the intellectual and political climate changed in the early 1980s, and in part because new challenges from outside Germany were mounted so quickly. Nevertheless, Wehler's account served so well as an anvil of perceived orthodoxy, and the output of his Bielefeld workshop continued to be so prolific, that his 'school' became the obvious target for revisionists hammering to enter the field. If the rest of this chapter tends to give disproportionate emphasis to these revisionists, this is not to diminish the value of previous research that was conducted with different scholarly, political and pedagogical agendas in mind.

Many criticisms of Wehler's *Kaiserreich* are too singular and specific to be reviewed here. There are, nonetheless, some interpretive categories that allow us to organize their main themes. A number of early reviewers concentrated on Wehler's methodology in the broad sense: they disliked the Marxist overtones to his analysis and they objected to his apparent willingness to imprison chronology and personality within a straitjacket of economic determinism. Other critics were more interested in chronicling the selectivity with which Wehler chose his citations from the contemporary record: for every socialist or left liberal quoted by Wehler to underscore the plutocratic and illiberal nature of society, one could find ten Germans who felt completely at home in the empire. Some historians said Wehler looked backward exclusively from the political turning-point of 1933; others objected that his interpretation was based too much on economic developments in the 1860s and 1870s. Finally, many critics claimed that Wehler grossly overestimated the success of anti-democratic elites who used social imperialism, nationalism, militarism and other pre-fascist techniques to preserve the old order. Is it particularly helpful, they wondered, to speak so broadly of success or failure? Were these meaningful historical terms?

As Wehler's critics began to answer their own queries, some argued simply that Wehler's synthesis was attempted too early, before the necessary empirical groundwork had been laid to support such a weighty interpretive construct. Others suggested, with more merit, that historians could take up Wehler's interpretive challenge but at the same time press ahead with other theoretical and empirical inquiries designed to fill remaining gaps. Two such approaches have taken direct aim at Wehler's portrait of Bismarck as an evil godfather whose crimes rebounded on the German people after 1890.

KAISER WILHELM II AND 'ANOTHER' GERMANY

Wilhelm's dismissal of Bismarck from the Reich chancellory on 20 March 1890 was correctly seen at the time as a sea change in German politics. To many it was a presumptuous and premature act, undertaken by a young ruler who had been on the throne less than two years. How would the empire operate under anyone who lacked Bismarck's will of iron? This feeling of unease upon 'dropping the pilot' was understandable and, incidentally, one that Bismarck deliberately cultivated. But Wilhelm appeared determined to be a 'social Kaiser' who would alleviate the suffering of his most underprivileged subjects. And the new chancellor, Leo von Caprivi, seemed willing to challenge the power of the agrarian Junkers and to pursue a foreign policy that was less devious than Bismarck's. For these reasons we cannot dismiss lightly the remarkable feeling of relief that characterized the reactions of many Germans to the dramatic news from the chancellory on that spring day in 1890. The more articulate liberal spokesmen of the day were able for the first time to contemplate those breakthroughs in the economy, in the arts and even in politics, whose partial realization gave a distinctly Wilhelmine imprint to the age. The fact that many liberal reforms from those first years later faded from view, or that the right left its own mark as well, does not mean that Wilhelmine Germany was any more doomed to end in disaster than Bismarckian Germany had been.

It is not difficult to see why biographers of Wilhelm and students of court society objected when Wehler labelled their focus as 'personalistic'. In fact Wehler's *German Empire* relegated Wilhelm to the sidelines: '"Wilhelminism" [is] a term often used quite inappropriately to sum up this era. ... It was not Wilhelm II who imposed his will on government policy during this period, but the traditional oligarchies in conjunction with the anonymous forces of an authoritarian polycracy.'[14] The most comprehensive response to this view was published in 1982, in a volume of essays collected by the British historian, John Röhl.[15] It is worth emphasizing that both Röhl and Wehler are concerned with 'high politics' or what might be called 'politics from the top down'. In this context, however, Röhl argues that concentration on court society need not neglect theory or structures. The 'kingship mechanism', the 'palace perspective', and the 'role strain' inherent in Wilhelm's ceremonial duties are all analytical devices illustrating how personalities and structures complement one another in history. Therefore, contrary to Wehler, there is no reason why we must accept 'polycratic chaos' and the Kaiser's 'personal rule' as mutually exclusive. Wilhelm' s restless nature and his unpredictable influence on policy could well have caused the power vacuum that followed Bismarck's departure.

Many critics have noted, however, that biographers of the Kaiser often fail to practise what they preach, that they generally display a lack of interest in the structures of history, and that this undercuts their claim to offer a comprehensive analysis of Wilhelmine Germany 'with Wilhelm put back in'. We are treated to gruesome stories of Empress Victoria's amateur attempts to repair the damage to Prince Wilhelm's crippled arm. We learn much about Wilhelm's preference for generals and courtiers who were willing to dress up as ballerinas and poodles to amuse him. But all too often we are told nothing concrete about the policies that were actually implemented by Wilhelm's capriciously chosen men. Such studies continue to stimulate reflection and debate, and for that they are to be welcomed. One reviewer hit the mark, however, when he wrote that too often they have offered 'a baffling mixture of *aperçu* and cliché, insight and silliness'.[16]

A group of American historians has criticized Wehler's conclusions on very different grounds. They have suggested that Wilhelmine Germany was far less backward, authoritarian and outwardly aggressive than has been supposed. This view, too, offers food for thought. It is especially useful for students who may have begun their study of the Kaiserreich with Wehler's book, but who wonder whether everyday life in Wilhelm's reign could possibly have been as miserable as Wehler construes it. These American scholars have sought to overcome what Barbara Tuchman once called 'the trap built into all recorded history – the disproportionate survival of the negative'. Thus, they argue that by studying different historical clues than Wehler did, we can avoid describing the Wilhelmine era in the manner of a 'police blotter' and can discover another Germany that was 'more than the sum of its flaws'.[17] Within this 'other' Germany one finds cities that were vibrant and wholesome; universities and research institutions imbued with a progressive spirit; a free press able to check authoritarian excesses; a stabilizing and socially integrative army that provided a fruitful learning experience for its recruits; a progressive social ethos that combated religious and sexual discrimination; and a foreign policy that was modest and moderate in comparison with the strident and threatening postures assumed by French, British and Russian diplomats. Again, some contributions to this genre have been so one-sided that the charge of 'boosterism' is not unwarranted. The tendency has been to force the reader to choose between two Germanies – one virulent, the other benign.

Nonetheless, other contributions displaying a less dogmatic insistence on good and evil empires have prompted fruitful reflection about the potential for rational democratic reform in post-Bismarckian Germany. This line of inquiry, moreover, has helped to reintroduce a sense of 'contingency' into Wilhelmine history, necessarily reducing the emphasis on Bismarck's evil genius and – by extension – reducing the success we ascribe to his strategies for resisting democracy. This contribution is notable in work on a resurgent left-liberalism after 1900;[18] on why German citizens regarded voting in elections as a politically meaningful act;[19] and on partial successes in curtailing the Prussian militarist spirit at home.[20]

Even if these studies have so far yielded few definitive answers, they have made historians more skeptical about how well anti-democratic strategies actually worked in practice. Stuart Robson, a Canadian historian, expressed this feeling when he wondered aloud whether the established elites in Wilhelmine Germany could successfully have organized a cake-sale, let alone a ruthless, determined, coherent defense of the established order. Cavalier as Robson's remark may sound, it is consistent with the approach of scholars who are not satisfied with Wehler' s emphasis on the fateful success of political manipulation. This skepticism is arguably the closest thing to a consensus we are likely to find among those currently working on the Kaiserreich. In any case it is a perspective that seems more broadly based among active scholars than any inclination to focus on Wilhelm or to seek 'another' Germany.

SOCIETY AND POLITICS: FROM BELOW AND FROM THE PERIPHERY

Just as Wehler's synthesis gave a measure of coherence to the research conducted in the late 1960s, those who are skeptical about the value of Wehler's model owe much to a comprehensive statement of purpose that appeared at another critical stage of debate. What was needed by the late 1970s was another bold attempt to review the state of the art and to suggest agendas for future work. This time the call was answered by a British historian, Richard Evans, who in 1978 edited a volume of essays entitled *Society and Politics in Wilhelmine Germany*.[21] Collectively taking issue with Wehler's 'politics from the top down' approach, this volume brought together for the first time a group of younger British historians who wished to state the case – or cases – for a different perspective. These historians had no wish to examine point by point the devices by which Bismarck and the pre-industrial elites performed their wire-pulling act on the stage of Wilhelmine Germany. Instead they shifted their focus down to the level of ordinary people. Here they found not simply puppets and dupes of authoritarian stage managers. Nor did they find 'another' Germany. They found, rather, many Germanies. Led by, but extending well beyond, the trio of David Blackbourn, Geoff Eley and Richard Evans – who in any case disagree among themselves on many points – this revisionist assault kept British historians in the vanguard of English-language critics of Wehler for the next 10 years.

Space does not allow a discussion of each of the 'many Germanies' revealed by reappraisals of Wehler. They have proliferated rapidly and their contours have mutated constantly with the nourishment of new research and discussion.[22] Having said this, we can nevertheless note that recent studies have accorded special attention to those Germans in the empire who found themselves excluded from insider status in society. Such exclusion was made possible by barriers of geography, nationality, class, culture, religion and (perhaps most important of all) gender. This theme of underprivilege is worth examining in some detail in order to illustrate how new approaches to the history of society are deflecting and enriching our understanding of Wilhelm's empire on a broad front.

When we try to identify the 'out groups' in Wilhelmine society, we must consider not only those Germans at the bottom of the social, economic and political hierarchies, but other outsiders such as artists and criminals. This is not to imply that all of Wilhelm's subjects classified themselves in these specific terms or in mutually exclusive categories – as a worker, for instance, and nothing else. Rather, different categories of privilege and underprivilege crossed over and intersected with one another to produce a complicated matrix that objectively defined status and identity. Thinking in these terms helps bring to life the world of the underprivileged in a way that was formerly possible only for the study of great statesmen (who of course are more likely to leave a written record of their life). For example, it permits an unusual degree of empathy with one of the most striking figures of the Wilhelmine age, Rosa Luxemburg – a Pole, a socialist, a Jew and a woman.

Writing of 'out groups' implies that one can identify the 'in groups' in Wilhelmine Germany. But this is no easy matter either.

Geoff Eley and David Blackbourn believe that by the end of the nineteenth century the German bourgeoisie was possibly as influential as the aristocracy in the social and economic spheres – though still disadvantaged in the realm of politics.[23] Together they have argued that 'bourgeois revolutions' may bring to ascendancy bourgeois manners, laws, and economies even while helping mold a political system that falls far short of the liberal democratic ideal (as Wilhelmine Germany clearly did). They have also reminded us that bourgeois revolutions need not be sudden or violent. On the contrary, such revolutions may be most successful where they are least noticed: the process of establishing bourgeois hegemony may be a long, drawn-out affair. This suggests that further study of Wilhelmine Germany might hold the key to understanding all that changed, rather than all that remained static, during the empire. We are more conscious than ever that forms of negotiated consent between elites and subordinate groups had to be renegotiated again and again. Therefore we now tend to study Wilhelmine Germany in terms of the processes and changes that constantly reshaped it, rather than the structures and institutions inherited from Bismarck in 1890.

Undoubtedly, one of the most important such changes was the new impact of local and regional concerns on decision making in Berlin. When scholars in the 1960s wrote loosely about the Prusso-German empire and neglected developments in non-Prussian German states, they opened the door for those who wished to provide another perspective. Of course Prussian circumstances had a profound influence on the way Germany was unified in 1871 – and continued to do so long afterwards as well. Nonetheless, a number of contributors to Richard Evans' 1978 collection, and many historians since, have been intent to describe a Germany that was more than just an enlarged Prussia. Their Germany includes Prussia, to be sure – but a Prussia that was itself undergoing rapid modernization and 'in many ways a composite, artificial entity, containing a wide variety of social and political formations'.[24] The same could be said of other regions as well: the major states of Bavaria, Baden and Württemberg – to name only three of the most prominent members of the federal empire – were all fractured by confessional, occupational and cultural disparities.

Since Evans's volume appeared in 1978, local and regional studies have mushroomed, but a great deal of work remains to be done. In part this is because a new sophistication of analysis has arrived. Historians have successfully resisted the temptation to discard the central question – who ruled in Berlin? – which Wehler and Röhl answered so differently, with the narrower substitute – who ruled in Munich? Instead they have begun to address problems of political consciousness and the inter-relationship of local, regional and national identities.[25] These studies tend to show that Junkers, industrialists, state officials, Protestant pastors, and schoolmasters – all those to whom Wehler ascribed such potent manipulative influence – found that the power of political deference in Berlin did not necessarily prevail in the hinterland.[26] The particularities rather than the uniformity of circumstances in the different regions of Germany largely determined how the rise of mass politics was accommodated or incompletely deflected. These particularities, more-over, affected not only individuals and political parties, but also class relationships, nationality conflicts and religious controversies.[27]

SOCIAL DEMOCRACY, THE LABOR MOVEMENT AND WORKERS' CULTURE

None of Wilhelm's subjects suffered more discrimination than industrial workers in imperial Germany. Yet the major political representative of the working classes, the Social Democratic Party, was the pride of the Second International. On the face of it, the SPD fully deserved this honor. It won more votes than any other German party from 1890 onwards. After the 'red elections' of January 1912 it fielded the largest parliamentary caucus in the Reichstag. However, European socialism encountered its blackest day on 4 August 1914, when German socialists voted the government of Chancellor Bethmann Hollweg the necessary funds to pursue a European war. The SPD is considered to have missed a second, even more momentous, opportunity in the winter of 1918–19, when it allegedly 'failed' to follow the Bolshevik example, for reasons that still defy easy explanation.

Early studies sought to explore these triumphs and shortcomings of German socialism by focusing on theoretical debates within the party and on prominent party leaders. The scholarship of the 1960s and 1970s extended this work, looking particularly at the susceptibility of workers to the lures of nationalism, at the legacy of Bismarck's anti-socialist laws (1878–90), and at the way the Wilhelmine state and big business reacted to the (apparently) increasing threat of revolution. This wave of research has been sustained and once again redirected by those who have taken issue with Wehler. Quite naturally, their focus on the experiences of 'plain people' has highlighted the plight of those at the base of the socioeconomic pyramid.[28] Although much of the scholarship on the SPD has appeared only in German, even the English-language reader may be quite overwhelmed by the mass of material available. Fortunately, one can turn to a number of highly readable surveys of the SPD's history.[29] To these can be added other studies on more specific themes. Two of the most important highlight the place of women within the industrial workforce and – not at all the same question – the role of feminism within the labor movement.[30] As well, the complex struggle within German socialism between orthodox Marxists, revisionists, and reformists is more accessible than ever before.[31]

Most historians now agree that it is incorrect to conceive of the German working class as ascribing to positions that were either uniformly reformist or uniformly revolutionary. Yet they still disagree on how to address a crucial question dominating the debate: how did workers perceive their own interests and respond to their under-privileged status? One set of answers is provided by historians who study the labor movement. While these scholars previously tended to consider the role of the SPD in isolation and overestimated the common worker's understanding of theoretical debates, newer research stresses the diversity of German labor and the reception of ideology in a more sophisticated way. The history of the labor movement now addresses strikes, lock-outs and many individual forms of protest – including alcoholism and absenteeism. Useful distinctions are being drawn between the tendency of trade unions to concentrate on long-term achievements and that of individual workers to concentrate on short-term concerns within life and labor cycles. Early views of a sharp disjunction between a revolutionary SPD leadership and a reformist rank and file are also being reconsidered.[32] Whereas the role of ideology was not highlighted in much of the social history written in the 1970s, historians are once again trying to understand how ideologies were transmitted, how they were received and how they changed over time.

On the other side of the argument are historians who prefer to study workers' culture. They do so in part because institutional studies of the SPD told us so little about the concrete experiences of individual workers in the workplace, in school, within the family and neighborhood and at leisure. It must nevertheless be noted immediately that the best contributions to this genre overlap substantially with more conventional political perspectives. This overlap is crucial to understand how radical and militant positions on narrow political questions emerged from a broader cultural environment.[33] There still exists a danger that if social history and political history diverge too far, if the politics of everyday life is not related to events of national significance, we may find ourselves trying to write the history of Germany's working classes 'with the SPD left out'.[34]

In light of this difficulty, many historians have taken issue with earlier approaches that focused narrowly on the institutions of the Social Democratic Party, ignoring the vast everyday world of those who never affiliated themselves formally with the SPD.[35] Such critics charge that older interpretations conceived of German workers as 'passive receptacles waiting to be filled with ideas poured down from above',[36] not as free actors making rational decisions about their best interests. This reaction has fueled a tremendous growth in the social history of the Kaiserreich generally and, since the late 1970s, in the 'history of everyday life' (*Alltagsgeschichte*). Neither inquiry need focus exclusively on workers, of course. As well, although *Alltagsgeschichte* has recently been hailed as the 'most important new departure in West German historiography during the last decade',[37] it may be argued that it has had more of an impact on the study of the Third Reich than on that of Wilhelmine Germany. Nonetheless, this new perspective has cast working-class experience in pre-1914 Germany in a new light, because it allows historians to conceive of workers' culture in a remarkably new way.

For proponents of *Alltagsgeschichte*, the word culture does not mean merely the arts, or literature, or entertainment. Rather, its usefulness lies in its ability to suggest a broader dimension of history that transcends the social, economic, intellectual and political spheres. It allows analysis of class and power relationships, to be sure, but it also considers consciousness, mentalities, inner experiences and ways of life. Paul Willis helped explain the breadth of this conception of culture when he wrote: 'Culture is not artifice and manners, the preserve of Sunday best, rainy afternoons and concert halls. It is the very material of our daily lives, the bricks and mortar of our most commonplace understandings, feelings and responses.'[38] With this broad conception of culture, current research is moving away from a concentration on the leisure activities of workers and devoting more attention to everyday workplace experiences, social mobility, communal environment, housing, health, family life, religion, education, reading habits and those elements of mass culture that were just beginning to have an impact at the end of the Wilhelmine age, such as cinema and spectator sports.

Lastly, there is growing interest in the rough side of working-class culture. To explain how workers deviated from bourgeois Germans in their social values and norms, historians are turning to working-class crime, prostitution, heavy drinking, fairs and carnivals, workplace sabotage and pilferage, and what Alf Lüdtke has called 'horse-play'.[39] Again, methodological innovation provides new insights. Reading police reports 'against the grain,' as it were, yields some startling conclusions about those being repressed, but also about those allegedly wielding the authority supplied by the dominant culture. Far from constituting a casual or trivial side of workers' culture, law-breaking and other patterns of nonconformity can help us assess how workers were or were not integrated into society.[40] In this way conventional distinctions between the public and the private are being fundamentally rethought. Never before have historians had open to them more avenues to discover the 'inner experiences' of life in the Wilhelmine empire.

CONCLUSION

The reader was warned at the outset to expect no grand synthesis, no unitary paradigm, no happy ending to the tortured tale of Wilhelmine historiography since 1945. Anyone still looking for the Holy Grail of German history may be comforted to know that experts in the field are equally reluctant to abandon their quest. This was revealed by a recent conference devoted to charting a course for studying the Kaiserreich in the 1990s. Despite the impressive new work that was presented, the assembled scholars could only agree to disagree – on the very first day – about what directions and agendas would prevail for the next decade.[41] This serves as a comment on the course of Wilhelmine historiography for the previous 30 years as well. Since Fritz Fischer demanded a new confrontation with Germany's past in 1961, the 'medium' of German historical scholarship has been inextricably linked with its 'message'.

When new forms of political pluralism and student protest renewed the assault on traditionalism in the late 1960s, the substance and tone of writing on Wilhelmine Germany began to change even more rapidly.

Because the political discourse has not ceased, the rethinking and rewriting of Wilhelmine history has not ceased either. This chapter has tried to take account of these parallel developments. As it has moved thematically from concentration on elites and emperors to consideration of 'plain people', it has introduced schools of thought that may be characterized – however simplistically – as history from above and history from below. The fact that holders of coveted professorial chairs have criticized the history of everyday life for idealizing and romanticizing the masses further emphasizes the importance of understanding the political and intellectual contexts in which reassessments of imperial Germany have taken place. Precisely because the status quo in both West German politics and the historical profession will be challenged repeatedly during the 1990s, historians will continue to conceive of an empire that was extraordinarily diverse and dynamic. We now know that Wilhelm ruled over not just Protestant Prussians, but also over Catholics, Jews, Poles and Bavarians. The empire was not entirely bad. It was neither completely urban nor completely rural. It was not populated only by men. Aristocrats did not exclusively set the tone of everyday life – but neither did the Social Democrats. Manipulative strategies to deflect change did not always work as planned; often they went disastrously wrong. The empire that Bismarck constructed in January 1871 was transformed by social, economic and political developments of such magnitude that it was almost unrecognizable when it passed into the history books in November 1918.

Does this mean we should throw up our hands and despair of ever understanding this disparate thing called Wilhelmine Germany? Does it mean we have to choose only one of the many Germanies presented by recent scholarship? Of course not. Nor do we have to start rebuilding Wilhelmine Germany from the ground up whenever a new interpretation is introduced. An emphasis on historical deconstruction and new directions does not mean that we throw out older research because it was undertaken previous to the most recent shift of paradigm. A much more useful approach is to take what is valuable from past analyses, combine it with what we find convincing from newer work, identify remaining gaps and then set out to fill them.

My point is this: any attempt to sum up the essential features of life in Wilhelmine Germany is determined by our overall conceptual and methodological approach. We can find in Wilhelmine Germany – as elsewhere in the past – more or less what we go looking for. If we expect individuals to be longing for, say, *liberté, égalité* and *fraternité* on the one hand, or authority, community and a charismatic leader on the other, we are very likely to find Germans who espoused these ideals. But that does not mean we may apply a uniform label of liberal or fascist sympathies to the whole of Wilhelmine society. Do we really believe that every German in the empire was equally moved when a new colony in east Africa was founded, when a wildcat strike was suppressed, when a local zoo was established, when a Polish estate was confiscated, when a law of assembly was liberalized, when the price of bread fell by 5 Pfennigs, when the first woman entered a German university, or when Sergei Diaghilev's *Ballets russes* introduced avant-garde dance to the German stage? The different yardsticks by which we measure the most immediate events, trends and thoughts of an age yield many different interpretations. We know that Diaghilev's company left a trail of 'excitement, incredulity, and rapture' when it toured Berlin shortly before the First World War.[42] But could not exactly the same emotions of excitement, incredulity and rapture – or similarly intense ones – have been generated by the other historical events just catalogued, depending on the perspective of the individual? Are the events of everyday life not just as worthy of the historian's attention as the frivolous excesses of court society or the deadly calculations of the Prussian General Staff? This chapter, though it has also provided a survey of research on Wilhelmine Germany, has sought to prompt reflection on exactly these questions.

NOTES

1 In the notes below I refer whenever possible to English translations of German works; other selections from the literature have also been weighted heavily toward the English reader.
2 This analysis relies heavily on Richard J. Evans, 'Wilhelm II's Germany and the Historians', in R. J. Evans, *Rethinking German History* (London, 1987), pp. 24–32; and Georg Iggers (ed.), 'Introduction' in *The Social History of Politics* (Leamington Spa, 1985), esp. pp. 12–31.
3 See further, Ralf Dahrendorf, *Society and Democracy in Germany* (Garden City, NY, 1965); Arthur Rosenberg, *Imperial Germany* (Boston, Mass., 1964).
4 See Iggers, *Social History*, p. 20.
5 For references see the chapter in this volume by Holger Herwig.
6 See further, Robert Moeller, 'The *Kaiserreich* recast? Continuity and change in modern German historiography', *Journal of Social History*, vol. 17, (1984), pp. 655–83.
7 See Gordon Craig (ed.), *Economic Interest, Militarism, and Foreign Policy* (Berkeley, Calif., 1977); E. Kehr, *Battleship Building and Party Politics in Germany, 1894–1901* (Chicago, 1983).
8 Rosenberg, *Grosse Depression und Bismarckzeit* (Berlin, 1967); further references in Geoff Eley, 'Hans Rosenberg and the Great Depression of 1873–96', in G. Eley, *From Unification to Nazism* (Boston, Mass., 1986), pp. 23–41; Moeller, '*Kaiserreich* recast?', pp. 656–7.

9   For detailed references see the chapters in this volume by Geoff Eley and Holger Herwig.

10 *The German Empire 1871–1918* (Leamington Spa, 1985). Initial reactions to it and guides to the literature are provided in J. Retallack, 'Social history with a vengeance? Some reactions to H.-U. Wehler's *Das Deutsche Kaiserreich*', *German Studies Review*, vol. 7 (1974), pp. 423–50; and Moeller, '*Kaiserreich* recast?'

11 *War of Illusions* (London, 1975), p. viii.

12 Eley, *From Unification to Nazism*; R. J. Evans, 'From Hitler to Bismarck: Third Reich and *Kaiserreich* in recent historiography', in Evans, *Rethinking German History*, pp. 23–54.

13 *Journal of Modern History*, vol. 48 (1976), p. 567.

14 Wehler, *The German Empire*, p. 64.

15 J. C. G. Röhl and Nicolaus Sombart (eds), *Kaiser Wilhelm II: New Interpretations* (Cambridge, 1982); see also Isabel Hull, *The Entourage of Kaiser Wilhelm II, 1888–1918* (Cambridge, 1982); Lamar Cecil, *Wilhelm II* (Chapel Hill, NC, 1988); compare G. Eley, 'The view from the throne: the personal rule of Kaiser Wilhelm II', *Historical Journal*, vol. 28 (1985), pp. 469–85; Evans, 'From Hitler to Bismarck', pp. 58–63; and David Blackbourn, 'The kaiser and his entourage', in D. Blackbourn, *Populists and Patricians* (London, 1987), pp. 45–54.

16 Blackbourn, 'Kaiser and entourage', p. 48.

17 Joachim Remak and Jack Dukes (eds), *Another Germany* (Boulder, Colo., 1988), p. 207; see further criticisms in R. J. Evans, *In Hitler's Shadow* (New York, 1989), p. 176, and my review in *Canadian Journal of History*, vol. 24 (1989), pp. 271–3.

18 See, for example, Beverly Heckart, *From Bassermann to Bebel* (New Haven, Conn., 1974); a large gap will be filled by the publication of Stuart Robson's study, 'Left liberalism in Germany, 1900–1919', D.Phil. thesis, University of Oxford, 1966.

19 Stanley Suval, *Electoral Politics in Wilhelmine Germany* (Chapel Hill, NC, 1985); Brett Fairbairn, 'The German Reichstag elections of 1898 and 1903', D.Phil. thesis, University of Oxford, 1987.

20 David Schoenbaum, *Zabern 1913* (London, 1986).

21 London, 1978.

22 One might also note research in areas not addressed directly in this chapter, including Konrad Jarausch, *Students, Society, and Politics in Imperial Germany* (Princeton, NJ, 1982); Peter Jelavich, *Munich and Theatrical Modernism* (Cambridge, Mass., 1985); Geoff Eley, *Reshaping the German Right* (New Haven, Conn., 1980); and Roger Chickering, *We Men Who Feel Most German* (Boston, Mass., 1984). On East German historiography see Andreas Dorpalen, *German History in Marxist Perspective* (Detroit, Mich., 1988), esp. ch. 6.

23 D. Blackbourn and G. Eley, *The Peculiarities of German History* (Oxford, 1985); see also R. J. Evans, 'The myth of Germany's missing revolution', reprinted in Evans, *Rethinking German History*, pp. 93–122.

24 Evans, 'Introduction', *Society and Politics in Wilhelmine Germany*, p. 25.

25 An early exemplar of this genre was D. Blackbourn, *Class, Religion, and Local Politics in Wilhelmine Germany* (New Haven, Conn., 1980); cf. Dan White, *The Splintered Party* (Cambridge, Mass., 1976); William W. Hagen, *Germans, Poles, and Jews* (Chicago, 1980); David Crew, *Town in the Ruhr*

(New York, 1979); Rudy Koshar, *Social Life, Local Politics, and Nazism* (Chapel Hill, NC, 1986); and R. J. Evans, *Death in Hamburg* (Oxford, 1987).

26   cf. J. Retallack, 'Anti-Semitism, conservative propaganda, and regional politics in late nineteenth-century Germany', *German Studies Review*, vol. 11 (1988), esp. p. 395; J. Retallack, *Notables of the Right* (London, 1988), Part II.

27   Attention to distinctions between 'out-groups' and 'in- groups', both at the center and on the periphery of national politics is currently paying dividends in research on the German *Mittelstand*, comprising artisans, small shopkeepers, white-collar workers and peasants. For introductions to the literature see David Blackbourn, 'Between resignation and volatility: the German petty bourgeoisie in the nineteenth century'; 'Peasants and politics in Germany, 1871–1914'; and 'The Politics of Demagogy in Imperial Germany'; all three essays are reprinted in Blackbourn, *Populists and Patricians*; cf. Richard J. Evans and W. R. Lee (eds), *The German Peasantry* (New York, 1986); Robert Moeller (ed.), *Lords and Peasants in Modern Germany* (Boston, Mass., 1986), pp. 1–23; and David Crew, '"Why can't a peasant be more like a worker?": social historians and German peasants', *Journal of Social History*, vol. 22 (1989), pp. 531–9.

28   This perspective was especially evident in studies emanating from the former German Democratic Republic; see Dorpalen, *German History in Marxist Perspective*, esp. pp. 244–5.

29   Including Helga Grebing, *The History of the German Labour Movement* (Leamington Spa, 1985); Willi Guttsman, *The German Social Democratic Party, 1875–1933* (London, 1981); see also the short essays in Roger Fletcher (ed.), *Bernstein to Brandt* (London, 1987).

30   See the essays by Ute Frevert, Alfred Meyer, and Ute Daniel in ibid.; Ute Frevert, *Women in German History* (Oxford, 1989), esp. chs 9, 12 and 13; August Bebel, *Women under Socialism* (New York, 1971); R. P. Neumann, 'The sexual question and social democracy in imperial Germany', *Journal of Social History*, vol. 7 (1976), pp. 271–86; Jean Quataert, *Reluctant Feminists in German Social Democracy* (Princeton, NJ, 1979).

31   Begin with Carl Schorske, *German Social Democracy, 1905–1917* (Cambridge, Mass., 1955).

32   cf. Stephen Hickey, *Workers in Imperial Germany* (Oxford, 1985); and Mary Nolan, *Social Democracy and Society* (Cambridge, 1981).

33   See Dick Geary, 'Identifying militancy: the assessment of working-class attitudes towards state and society', in R. J. Evans (ed.), *The German Working Class 1888–1933* (London, 1982), p. 230.

34   See G. Eley, 'Combining two histories: the SPD and the German working class before 1914', *Radical History Review*, vols 28–30 (1984), pp. 13–44.

35   For example, Guenther Roth, *The Social Democrats in Imperial Germany* (Totowa, NJ, 1963); see the critique in R. J. Evans, 'Introduction: the sociological interpretation of German labour history', in Evans, *The German Working Class*, p. 19.

36   ibid., p. 25.

37   G. Eley, 'Labor history, social history, *Alltagsgeschichte*: experience, culture, and the politics of the everyday – a new direction for German social history?', *Journal of Modern History*, vol. 61 (1989), p. 297; cf. Iggers, *Social History*, pp. 36–43; and Lynn Abrams, *Workers' Culture in Imperial Germany* (London, forthcoming [1991]).

38   Cited in David Crew, 'Interpretations of working-class culture', in M. Ferro and S. Fitzpatrick (eds), *Culture et révolution, Éd. de l'École des Hautes*

Études en Sciences sociales (Paris, 1989), p. 34; cf. Dieter Langewiesche, 'The impact of the German labour movement on workers' culture', *Journal of Modern History*, vol. 59, (1987), pp. 506-23; Richard J. Evans, 'Social democracy and the working class in imperial Germany', *European History Quarterly*, vol. 18 (1988), pp. 77–90; and Eve Rosenhaft, 'History, anthropology, and the study of everyday life', *Comparative Studies in Society and History*, vol. 29, (1987), pp. 99–105; cf. Kathleen Canning, 'Gender and the culture of work: ideology and identity in the world behind the millgate, 1890–1914', in Larry Eugene Jones and James Retallack (eds), *Elections, Mass Politics, and Social Change in Modern Germany* (New York, forthcoming [1992]).

39 Alf Lüdtke, 'Cash, coffee-breaks, horseplay: *Eigensinn* and politics among factory workers in Germany circa 1900', in M. Hanagan and Charles Stephenson (eds), *Confrontation, Class Consciousness and the Labor Process* (New York, 1986), pp. 65–95.

40 A useful documentary account is Alfred Kelly (ed.), *The German Worker* (Berkeley, Calif., 1987).

41 'The *Kaiserreich* in the 1990s: New research, new directions, new agendas', held at the University of Pennsylvania, 23–25 February 1990.

42 Modris Eksteins, *Rites of Spring* (Toronto, 1989), p. 26.

3 Industry, Empire and the First World War

HOLGER H. HERWIG

The historical debate in the Federal Republic over the 'German question' as it pertains to the early part of the twentieth century is most intimately associated with two scholars: Fritz Fischer of Hamburg University and Hans-Ulrich Wehler of Bielefeld University. The former dominated discussion in the 1960s with his provocative assertion that imperial Germany in 1914 had undertaken a planned 'grab for world power' (*Griff nach der Weltmacht*) by unleashing a world war designed to secure German political, economic and military domination of the continent and its periphery; the latter in the 1970s aroused a storm of protest with his attempts to define the history of the Second Reich primarily in terms of impersonal structural processes (*Strukturgeschichte*) and to found a school of critical 'historical science' (*Geschichtswissenschaft*).

To be sure, there were other avenues of approach suggested in order to rethink the peculiar nature of German history (*Sonderweg*) since Otto von Bismarck, but space does not permit – nor would it be reasonable to attempt – a sweeping *tour d'horizon* of all paths leading to Clio's altar.[1] Thus, I will offer some observations on and evaluations of where the great historiographical revolutions associated with Fischer and Wehler stand today, as well as where future investigations might be heading. A third major section will provide an overview of the most recent work in the field of 'industry and war' for the period of the First World War, specifically with regard to armaments policy and the attempted mobilization of the nation for 'total war'.

Finally, the reader should be forewarned that Germany's 'empire' – that disparate and far-flung collection of largely undesirable real estate in Africa and Asia – is omitted in this chapter. It played a role neither in the origins nor in the outcome of the First World War. When war came in 1914, it fell – with the notable exception of German East Africa – almost without serious resistance to the Allies. At no time did it constitute the cherished El Dorado of colonial enthusiasts: Berlin's colonial trade in 1914 represented only 0.5 per cent of its total trade; the colonies, for their part, attracted but 3.8 per cent of Germany's total overseas investment.[2] For the most part, the 'empire' had been collected at random, and largely for reasons of national prestige and pride. Germany's future was, and remained, in Europe.

THE FISCHER CONTROVERSY

In 1961 Fritz Fischer launched what can only be described as a historiographical revolution with his massive tome, *Griff nach der Weltmacht*.[3] The Hamburg historian leveled three critical charges at previous interpretations of the origins of the First World War: that continuity in German aims and policies could be found from Wilhelm II to Adolf Hitler; that Germany did, in fact, bear the main responsibility for the outbreak of war in 1914; and that the Second Reich's vast annexationist schemes and downright racism in the First World War presaged the darker chapters of the Third Reich. The book, largely researched and compiled by a host of postgraduate assistants, was firmly based upon fresh and extensive documentary materials culled especially from archives in Austria and in the German Democratic Republic.

The reaction of Fischer's conservative colleagues was both immediate and personal.[4] Gerhard Ritter of Freiburg deemed the work a 'self-deprecation of the German historical consciousness', and in 1964 he joined forces with Karl Dietrich Erdmann at Kiel to persuade the West German Foreign Office of Gerhard Schröder to deny Fischer funds already granted by the Goethe Institute for a lecture tour of the United States – a tour which Ritter equated with a 'national tragedy'.[5] For a decade, Ritter, Erdmann, Egmont Zechlin, Erwin Hölzle and others engaged in a vituperative press war with Fischer and his students in which no provincial newspaper was considered too remote or too insignificant to trumpet charges and countercharges.

In the first book, offered in an abridged English-language version under the much more modest (and misleading) title of *Germany's Aims in the First World War*,[6] Fischer argued that Germany in 1914 deliberately chose not only to abandon Bismarck's moderate policy of semi-hegemony in Europe in favor of a Napoleonic policy of hegemony, but also to seek world-power status at the expense of Great Britain and Russia. The vaunted 'grab for world power' implied in the book's German title caused Fischer to abandon a number of well-established positions: the distinction between the radical war aims of the military and the moderate ones of the civilians was erased; Chancellor Theobald von Bethmann Hollweg was depicted not merely as the vacillating 'philosopher of Hohenfinow', but rather as the prime agent of expansionism;

and the appointment of Generals Paul von Hindenburg and Erich Ludendorff to head the General Staff in the fall of 1916 was characterized by Fischer as no longer a major turning point to a more aggressive form of imperialism, but simply as a change in the tempo of expansionism. Therewith, Fischer struck at the heart of the accepted defense of 'moderate' civilians such as Bethmann Hollweg by Ritter and his supporters. Above all, Fischer's suggestion that continuity in war aims could be traced from Wilhelm II to Adolf Hitler infuriated his critics.

Fischer rested his case upon a detailed exposition of the chancellor's annexationist program of 9 September 1914 – an incredibly comprehensive shopping list of German war aims drafted even before the battle of the Marne. Therein, Bethmann Hollweg had called for German security in Europe 'for all imaginable time': France was to be destroyed as a great power, Russia reduced to the dimensions reached under Peter the Great, Belgium turned into a German 'vassal state', Luxemburg annexed outright, French and Belgian coastal areas and ore-mining districts likewise annexed, Russia and Britain replaced by Germany as the dominant power in the Middle East and Persia, the Scandinavian states and Holland brought into the German orbit, a 'Central African Colonial Empire' created as a reservoir of raw materials, and the states of central and eastern Europe from the North Sea to the Black Sea – friend, foe and neutral alike – gathered under the umbrella of an economic alliance dominated by Germany (the early-nineteenth-century concept of *Mitteleuropa*). Ottoman Turkey as well as Habsburg Austria-Hungary, in effect, were to become German satellites. Finally, Fischer argued that this September program remained valid in its basic contours throughout the war – as evidenced not only in the Draconian settlements with Russia and Rumania in the spring of 1918, but also in Foreign Secretary Paul von Hintze's annexationist demands as late as August 1918. Bethmann Hollweg's grand design entailed nothing less than 'a complete revolution in European political and economic power relationships'.

Three key points emerged for Fischer: the September program was not the brain child simply of Bethmann Hollweg but rather 'it represented the ideas of leading economic, political, and also military circles'; it remained the keystone of German war aims throughout the war; and it was 'conceived as a program of moderation'. Fischer further suggested that the well-publicized differences during the war between civilian and military leaders were ones of form rather than of substance. The source of expansionism, he argued, was not Germany's international situation but rather its economic, social and political structure. Moreover, Fischer suggested that vast annexations were seen, especially in right-wing circles, as a means of maintaining their domestic dominance. He also detected a 'continuity of error' in so far as German leaders constantly underestimated the strength of others while concurrently overestimating their own. Finally, Fischer pointed to the emergence of racism in the various proposals to 'resettle' Poles and Jews from the Polish 'border strip' in the eastern 'space' – as well as in the proposals to 'resettle' the Baltic states and to transform the Crimea into a 'German Mediterranean'.[7]

Fischer's adversaries, both at home and abroad, first reacted by accusing him of 'fouling his own nest', and then by resuscitating David Lloyd George's hackneyed comment that in 1914 'the nations slithered over the brink into the boiling cauldron of war'.[8] In other words, they suggested yet again that the war had been brought on by dark, devious, impersonal forces that lay beyond the control of mere mortals. In the Federal Republic, Erdmann and Zechlin championed this line of argument; in the United States, Paul Schroeder used the analogy of a 'Galloping Gertie' to explain the events of July 1914.[9] The alliance system, military mobilization, railway timetables, and the 'tragic fate' of the German nation had all combined to deprive Berlin's statesmen and soldiers of room to maneuver. Ritter accused Fischer of being unable to understand the 'mood of 1914', of being unable to place the decision makers of 1914 within the mentality of the era. The Hamburg historian, Ritter asserted, had failed to approach his documents either with empathy or with historical understanding. Indeed, it was only after Ritter immersed himself in the Viennese military archives that he confided privately that he was 'shaken' by what they revealed about July 1914.[10]

Fischer reacted to the storm created by his first book by producing a second: *Krieg der Illusionen*, quickly published again in an abridged English-language version as *War of Illusions*.[11] Examining the period from 1911 to 1914, Fischer stressed the interaction between domestic social, economic and political problems and the Reich's external position. The book combined a little of Leopold von Ranke's *Primat der Aussenpolitik* and Eckart Kehr's *Primat der Innenpolitik*.[12] Three thematic insights emerged: industrialists and financiers had resisted all attempts by the workers and their organized representatives to aspire to political power; the Prussianization of Germany after Bismarck's victorious wars had created an anti-democratic, authoritarian state that decried both the Enlightenment and the ideals of 1848; and cultural pessimism led Germany's leaders to view a military solution as the only way of breaking the 'encirclement' of Germany by her enemies. Werner Sombart's stark contrast between British traders and German heroes (*Händler und Helden*) in 1915 served as the epitome of this *mentalité*.

Above all, Fischer's second book emphasized that Germany had been a latecomer to imperialism, that its chronic capital shortage and export problems had hampered its overseas efforts, and that its dominant Junker elite had sought to plaster over cracks in the domestic domain by 'exporting the social question', that is, by a policy of 'social imperialism'. Right-wing mobilization of support for a 'great overseas policy' was to serve as a bulwark against social reform (if not revolution) at home. While Fischer admitted that Wilhelm II was inclined to avoid making decisions and that Bethmann Hollweg did *not* share the view of the Pan-Germans that war would enhance domestic stability, he nevertheless continued to insist that war in 1914 constituted a *Flucht nach vorn*, a bold leap forward designed to establish German hegemony in Europe by war – especially before Russia became too powerful.

New and dramatic was Fischer's contention that the path to war had been chosen at a special 'war council' convened by Wilhelm II on 8 December 1912 upon receiving news that 'perfidious Albion' would not stand idly by, as she had in 1870, and permit German domination of the continent. Fischer suggested that war was postponed in 1912 only because Bethmann Hollweg insisted that Germany must first prepare herself diplomatically, economically and psychologically, and because Admiral Alfred von Tirpitz argued that the Kiel Canal must first be completed – which it was in June 1914.[13]

Fischer received staunch support for his position from both German and foreign scholars, who zealously searched the archives of Europe for pieces of the puzzle that was created after 1919 when 'patriotic self-censors' in the German Foreign Office had 'sanitized' the historical record in a concerted attempt to erase evidence of German responsibility for the war.[14] Imanuel Geiss of Bremen University published 1,168 documents to establish that Germany and Austria-Hungary had taken the first fateful steps toward war in July 1914, and then escalated a local Austro-Serb war into a continental conflagration that pitted Triple Alliance against Triple Entente, and finally into a world war.[15]

Faced with such staggering evidence, Fischer's critics changed tactics. No longer denying the validity of his research or his methodology, they instead fell back upon the theory of the 'calculated risk' first enunciated in 1913 by Kurt Riezler, the chancellor's Foreign Office counsellor.[16] According to this theory, while Bethmann Hollweg appeared willing to risk war in 1914 over the Austro-Serbian conflict, in reality he was merely playing a game of diplomatic bluff designed to push the Entente powers to the wall and to break that alliance once it faced the prospect of a general European war – something that Germany had previously tried unsuccessfully during the first Moroccan crisis in 1905. Only when Russia refused to be bluffed, the argument went, did war become inevitable. Thus, a major share of responsibility for the war rested with St Petersburg.

Andreas Hillgruber was the first to resurrect Riezler's rationale. Concessions, Hillgruber argued, could be wrung from Germany's opponents only through a high-stakes diplomatic bluff. Only if the Central Powers held firm could the 'Russian danger' be mastered. Such quick and decisive action alone would halt the 'moral' decline of Berlin and Vienna. And since Russian and Austrian interests in the Balkans did not immediately touch the vital interests of the other great powers, the risk was a calculated one. Rather than seeking to isolate Britain through neutrality, Hillgruber suggested, Bethmann Hollweg and Riezler merely sought to keep London as a distant partner in international crises – a step which would have loosened the Anglo-Russian entente of 1907.[17]

Hillgruber's interpretation of Riezler was embraced with alacrity in the United States by Konrad Jarausch. Ingeniously, Jarausch suggested that while the German effort to split the Entente was *offensive*, overall German policy in July 1914 'was, indeed, *defensive*'.[18] Later, in his biography of Bethmann Hollweg, Jarausch reiterated this theme. Bethmann Hollweg emerges from these pages as an 'enigma'; Germany as beset by 'hubris'. The same impersonal, tragic, fateful forces discovered by the apologists of the 1920s appear again. Bethmann Hollweg is accorded 'human greatness', depicted as a dedicated statesman who stayed in office during the war 'out of duty and responsibility' in order to head off worse alternatives. Eventually, the 'weight of fate' caught up with him.[19] The centerpiece of evidence for all this is the Riezler diary,[20] the critical passages for July 1914[21] Erdmann apparently carefully 'editing'. One begins to wonder who was in charge in Berlin, Riezler or Bethmann Hollweg?

What is the student to conclude from all this? By and large, most of the works on the July crisis written before 1961 are now out of date; the tremendous outpouring of new materials that resulted from Fischer's first book has rendered inadequate these earlier treatments. Second, I would agree with Annelise Thimme that the current proponents of the theory of the 'calculated risk' offer little but 'new wine in old wine skins'.[22] Research seems to lie with Fischer. Indeed, if one takes away Fischer's dogged obsession with the 'war council' of 8 December 1912 and his equally rigid assertion that July 1914 constituted a 'grab for world power' rather than an attempt to enhance Germany's *continental* position, then one has the story of July 1914 pretty much in place. I concur with Hans-Ulrich Wehler's conclusion that three-fourths of Fischer's assertions are today accepted as valid.[23]

Above all, it is time once and for all to discard Lloyd George's worn-out phrase that Europe 'slithered' into war in 1914. Great powers throughout history have rarely, if ever, 'slithered' into major wars; rather, they undertake this most difficult of all human endeavors only after carefully weighing the advantages and disadvantages. In this sense, and only in this sense, can one speak of a 'calculated risk' in July 1914.

And where does the future lie in terms of scholarly investigation? It would appear that only the Serbian documents remain to be unearthed, and conservative estimates indicate that it will be well into the next century before Yugoslavian scholars progress to 1914 with their publication of diplomatic documents. At best, these materials will shed light only upon whether Serbia did, in fact, seek (and receive) a Russian 'blank check' after being handed the Austro-Hungarian ultimatum on 23 July 1914.

More promising, on the other hand, seems to be recent work undertaken on what James Joll has termed the 'mood of 1914'. While the view that Europe went to war with great enthusiasm, indeed euphoria, has been widely accepted by historians, fresh work on regional responses to the war in France and Germany has suggested that this conclusion may be too simplistic; but major revision of accepted perceptions of the popular mood in Europe's cities in the summer of 1914 awaits further study.[24]

THE WEHLER THESIS

A second historiographical (and methodological) revolution swept the Federal Republic in the 1970s and is most intimately associated with Hans-Ulrich Wehler of Bielefeld University. Armed with indefatigable energy, buoyed by generous research leaves every other semester, supported by a host of postgraduate assistants and in possession of what almost amounts to a personal publishing house at Göttingen, Wehler has flooded the market with essays, anthologies and books critically re-evaluating the social, economic and political history of the Second Reich. Of immediate concern here are his two major analyses of the German state from Bismarck to the Weimar Republic: *Krisenherde des Kaiserreichs, 1871–1918* and *Das Deutsche Kaiserreich, 1871–1918*, which appeared in an English-language edition as *The German Empire, 1871–1918*.[25]

It should be stated from the outset that Wehler does not seek to offer a balanced account of the Second Reich; rather, he presents a highly critical, provocative re-examination of the major social, economic and political problems that confronted the state of Bismarck and Wilhelm II. There is no room for subtlety or complexity. Wehler paints his pictures in black and white. Moreover, Wehler's ideal model is the liberal, democratic Anglo-Saxon constitutional state, especially its American variant. Finally, Wehler closely follows Kehr in maintaining the 'primacy of domestic politics'. Foreign affairs are seen only as a manipulative means of controlling domestic unrest; they are accorded barely ten pages in *The German Empire*, less than ten per cent of the book.

Wehler's overarching thesis, paralleling not only the work of Fritz Fischer but also that of the political scientist Karl Dietrich Bracher, is that there exists continuity from the Second to the Third Reich – in fact,

Wehler argues that the traditional ruling elite merely served as 'stirrup holders for Hitler'. 'Continuity' for Wehler means that there existed a straight line from the 'dictatorial Bonapartist regime' of Bismarck to the 'pseudo-constitutional, semi-absolute' Wilhelmian state, and finally to the totalitarian order of National Socialism. The glue that held together each of the three states was social imperialism: 'Social imperialism served to defend the traditional social and power structures of the Prusso-German state, and to shield them from the turbulent effects of industrialization.'[26] Education, family, church, the military and the courts also acted as agents of social control and class preservation.

Wehler explains the internal dysfunction of the German state as a dialectical process, as a conflict between the largely Prussian conservative, agrarian ruling elite and the forces of social and political change in a rapidly industrializing German state; he treats the history of the Second Reich as 'the defence of inherited power positions by pre-industrial elites against the onslaught of new forces'. Throughout this dialectical conflict theory, he interweaves the impotence of political parties, the extra-parliamentary role of special interest groups and the mobilization (*Sammlung*) of the traditional classes threatened by economic modernization. The only escape for many was anti-Semitism, imperialism, integral nationalism and, finally, war. The German *Rechtsstaat* under Wilhelm II is depicted as a thinly veiled absolutism in which the state acted as a 'princely insurance firm against democracy'.[27]

In this rigid schematism, there is no room for the generally acknowledged growth of parliamentarism in the Reichstag. Germany was doomed from birth due to the fact that it only 'partially modernized' after 1870 – and thus remained, as Marx once put it, an 'anachronism'. In other words, Wehler argues that the system possessed built-in tensions between the forces of change and industrialization, on the one hand, and those of the status quo among the pre-industrial agrarian elite, on the other. Only the artificial 'magical triangle' of social imperialism, social protectionism and social militarism could preserve elite politics. This functionalist approach in the end owes much to the works not only of Marx, Engels and Kehr, but also to those of Max Weber and Thorstein Veblen.

The First World War, according to Wehler, changed none of this. The *Burgfrieden* (domestic truce) of 1914 and its intended creation of a German *Volksgemeinschaft* is dismissed as 'a yarn spun with grandiose words', as a 'mask' constructed to preserve the ruling elite. War aims after 1914 served only to 'legitimize' the 'noble-monarchical' elite. Prewar conflicts of interest remained irreconcilable. And the attempt to defuse demands for domestic reform by way of successes on Europe's battlefields 'ran like a red thread' through all war-aims proposals between September 1914 and August 1918.[28] Total mobilization of the nation for war ('social romanticism'), as demanded by General Ludendorff and Colonel Max Bauer, was merely a final, desperate attempt to plaster over domestic class differences. The 'Fatherland Party' of Wolfgang Kapp and Alfred von Tirpitz with its 1.25 million members in July 1918 only presaged the advent of fascism. Social Darwinism, racism and anti-Semitism were the legacy that the Second Reich bequeathed to the Third.

It is not difficult to criticize Wehler's approach. Obviously, nations other than Germany were beset by social Darwinism and anti-Semitism and enamored of social imperialism; what state in 1914 did not have its lunatic fringe? And what state in 1914 did not view war as a legitimate means of conducting politics? The concept of continuity is far too rigid: Bismarck was no Hitler, and his policies were at least based squarely upon reality. The state *was* on the way to greater parliamentarization; the working classes and their representatives had conquered almost every major city hall. Moreover, for all his emphasis on social and economic history, Wehler ignores the role of women despite the fact that by 1914 Germany had some 500,000 females organized in various clubs, and would add more than 700,000 women to its labor force during the First World War.

There is in all of Wehler's work a deplorable lack of appreciation for and understanding of foreign policy, an exaggerated stress upon social imperialism and an omission of the human factor in decision making, characteristics that reduce the drama of the historical process to something akin to a marionette theater. Above all, one takes umbrage at the constant polarization of historical verdicts, at the lack of shades of grey between the poles of white and black.[29] For, as David Schoenbaum has argued, imperial Germany was 'neither significantly more nor less repressive than other Western societies' and 'was endowed, like others, with a fragile and complicated social and political equilibrium'.[30] Finally, as Thomas Nipperdey has suggested, history cannot be presented totally without the human factor if professional historians wish to escape their self-imposed isolation from modern society.[31]

And yet, one cannot ignore Wehler. Like Fischer before him, he has changed the parameters of the historical debate. Above all, he has challenged the basically conservative West German historical guild (*Zunft*) to confront the issue of the reaction of German society to modernization and industrialization. He has stimulated debate, stirred investigation into the long-range origins of the Third Reich and has firmly added a social and economic component to traditional political and diplomatic history. In the process, Wehler has taken delight in becoming the gadfly of the profession, a role previously perfected in England by A.J.P. Taylor.

Wehler's critical and functionalist approach to the history of the Wilhelmian empire was taken to its most radical form by his erstwhile colleague at Bielefeld, Jürgen Kocka, in *Klassengesellschaft im Krieg*, or *Facing Total War: German Society, 1914–1918*.[32] Using an overtly Marxist model, Kocka suggests that the intensity of class conflicts increased throughout the war until, by 1918, they became dominant. He too eschews the study of human beings and chooses to focus on impersonal forces: the interaction between the interests of the capitalist class and those of the working class. Given this rigid and dominant class structure, it is not surprising to find that the state is accorded only a semi-independent role in the historical process. Socioeconomic processes, either speeded up or created by the war, alone dominate Kocka's landscape. It is *Strukturgeschichte* in its most stringent form.

Kocka marshals massive statistical data to make the case that the war impoverished the working class, especially after 1916, as a result both of a decline in real wages and of a shortage (hence greater cost) of foodstuffs. With regard to industry, the picture was more complex: while war industries enjoyed sharp rises in profits, consumer-oriented industries suffered declines. Especially after the Hindenburg program of enhanced industrial output for armaments industries and the accompanying Auxiliary Service Law designed to mobilize the nation's labor pool in 1916, many small-scale businesses were forced out of the market place. Kocka identifies a group of 120,000 entrepreneurs and managers as the winners in the war, the 6.2 million laborers as the losers. The position of the upper middle class deteriorated significantly as a result of protracted war: while the new *Mittelstand* of white-collar employees was proletarianized, the old bourgeoisie of high-ranking civil servants was likewise on the losing side with regard to both income and inherited property. In other words, while the numerically small industrial elite did very well during the war, both the middle class and the working class drew closer together in terms of loss of income and property. Hence, Kocka explains, it is hardly surprising that the workers remained loyal throughout most of the period 1914–18 and rejected revolution in favor of gradualism.

Both Kocka's model and his conclusions ought to be challenged for their rigidity. Wolfgang Mommsen[33] has suggested that profits at the top were not nearly as impressive as Kocka would have it, and that Kocka's attempt to identify 120,000 entrepreneurs and managers as a distinct social class is too imprecise. Above all, the workers' loss of income and prestige *vis-à-vis* the middle class does not by itself suffice to explain their lack of protest throughout much of the war. For, if the Wilhelmian state were beset by the sort of severe class dichotomy depicted by Kocka, one can only wonder why this did not readily translate into political activity and class confrontation. The answer would seem to be that neither trade unions nor workers suffered as much as Kocka would have us believe. Reality, it would appear, refuses to correspond to his model.

The most radical socioeconomic interpretation of the First World War comes, not surprisingly, from Marxist historians in East Germany, especially from a collective group of scholars such as Alfred Müller, Alfred Schröter, and Hermann Weber,[34] who are associated with Fritz Klein's Institut für Geschichte at the Akademie der Wissenschaften. In 1968 this group published a three-volume history of Germany in the First World War[35] that set the tone for much of the East German historiography on the war.

For Klein and his associates, the First World War constituted a 'quarrel among the imperialists for a new division of the world'. Monopoly capitalists and Junker agrarians, assisted by the military, unleashed the war, which was inevitable owing to the 'conflicts inherent to the capitalist social order'. Europe's 'Great Folly' ushered in the 'final crisis phase of capitalism' – just as before 1914, imperialism had emerged as the 'last phase of capitalism'. Predictably, the winners were 'armaments monopolists, large landowners, profiteers, and speculators'; armaments manufacturers alone reaped profits of 5,000 million Mark. Only the right-wing opportunism of the Social Democratic Party kept the monopoly capitalists and Junker agrarians in power and prevented the German people from being 'liberated from the bonds of the imperialist system' by forging 'a solid alliance with the Soviet Union'.[36]

Although the three volumes offer invaluable and oft-overlooked social as well as economic data, they are nevertheless too narrowly conceived owing to the need of the editors to prove the underlying Marxist thesis and are, thus, disappointingly predictable. The state emerges as nothing more than 'an instrument of power in the hands of the ruling classes'. The Auxiliary Service Law of 1916, designed to mobilize the nation's manpower reserves, is dismissed by Klein as a vehicle to 'create a *military prison* for the workers (and partly also for the farmers) and a *paradise* for bankers and capitalists'.[37] The fact that the private sector frequently objected to state interference in the economic domain is blithely ignored; conversely, industrialists such as Walther Rathenau who sought to coordinate the efforts of the government and the private sector are denounced as constituting the 'liberal wing' of the German monopoly bourgeoisie.[38] Evidence to support these radical assertions is not presented as it probably does not exist. In the end, the Marxist theory that monopoly capitalism and the state were 'fused' into one – naturally under the dominance of the former – simply does not correspond to reality. Again, monocausal explanations brazenly ignore the complexity of a German society engaged in modern industrial warfare for the first time.

Much more useful is the pioneering study of *Army, Industry, and*

Labor in Germany 1914–1918 by Gerald Feldman.[39] Feldman posits the thesis that the army – almost by default, given the incompetence of the imperial bureaucracy and the narrow interest of the Reichstag – was forced to plan and direct the nation's wartime economic mobilization. Thus projected into a field for which they were utterly unprepared, military leaders for the first time were brought face to face with the social and economic factors which, long before the war, had destabilized the Wilhelmian state and which, even as the war raged on, would continue to transform it. Unable to refuse the demands made by the organized labor movement and unwilling to curb either the profits or the power of heavy industry, the military helped to legitimize collective bargaining and to lay the foundations of postwar inflation. According to Feldman, neither soldiers nor statesmen were motivated by the national interest; rather, they became entangled in the web of intrigues spun by the bureaucratic-military elite that governed Germany.

Feldman's book is at its best on 1916, with its treatment of the Hindenburg program for increased armaments production and the Auxiliary Service Law for mobilizing labor. Driven by the battlefield urgency to mobilize the nation's material and manpower reserves for war, Ludendorff and Bauer in particular agreed to major concessions to both labor and industry; conversely, they forced heavy industry to accept this 'onerous' arrangement. For nearly eighteen months the agreements held. Excessive war profits and waste as well as occasional labor unrest were overlooked as production did, in fact, increase. By June 1918, however, the pact unravelled. Unable to control labor and unwilling to curb industry, Ludendorff and Bauer had to admit defeat: the nation was not prepared to undergo the sacrifices necessary to conduct 'total war'. Feldman thus stresses the limits of Ludendorff's alleged dictatorial powers. Much like Fischer and Wehler, he depicts Germany's wartime program of vast annexations both in Europe and overseas mainly as a new form of 'social imperialism', as a bulwark against revolution at home. In terms of the subsequent history of Germany, he argues that Ludendorff's failure to mobilize the nation set the stage not only for the postwar 'stab-in-the-back' legend, but also the eventual 'revolution from above'. In Feldman's pages, the *Dolchstoss* legend becomes plausible, if not actual.

If Feldman offered a necessary and welcome corrective to the 'critical' school of Wehler and Kocka as well as to the dogmatic East German Marxists, then Karl Erich Born's recent study of the 'Economic and social history of imperial Germany 1867/71–1914' seeks to revise their interpretations completely.[40] Born argues vociferously that Germany experienced more continuity at the social and economic levels than on the political plane. His interpretation is moderate and sympathetic: while he concedes that the Second Reich was beset by the problems arising from a premodern and pre-industrial social structure and mentality, Born nevertheless suggests that on the whole it was liberal, constitutional and respectable, and certainly as advanced as many of the more progressive nations of the West. Therewith, Born, like Schoenbaum before him, seeks to restore the debate to its pre-Wehler state.

What does the future portend for the socioeconomic history of the Second Reich? The immediate future would seem to belong to a group of young historians loosely associated with the Max Planck Institute for History at Göttingen who seek to combine narrative and analysis in their history. Taking the British historian E.P. Thompson as well as the French *Annales* School as their models, scholars such as Clifford Geertz, Hans Medick and Carlo Ginzburg have sought to shift the focus to the everyday life of those men, women and children who come from the traditionally neglected (*ausgegrenzt*) strata of society. Their approach centers squarely upon the narrative history of how human beings have been affected by the great social and economic developments of late nineteenth-century Germany, and thus offers an alternative (or correction?) to the stark, analytical school of historical social science championed by Wehler and Kocka. Whether this latest development will end in mere romantic nostalgia, as Wehler has suggested, or whether it truly will shed light upon those who paid the price for modernization and industrialization remains to be seen.[41]

GERMANY IN THE AGE OF TOTAL WAR

The vaunted 'German Question', of course, partly revolves around the peculiarly militaristic nature of that state and society. A growing number of scholars both in Germany and abroad have analyzed what now is commonly called the military-industrial complex in order to compare and to contrast the German way of war against especially the Anglo-Saxon way of war. In other words, how well did Germany conduct 'total war' between 1914 and 1918? To what degree was it willing and able to mobilize both manpower and material reserves toward victory? To date, this third and final field of historical inquiry has remained relatively free of the personal and methodological bitterness associated with Fischer and Wehler.

A first attempt to analyze the role of labor and armaments production during the war was undertaken by Robert B. Armeson in *Total Warfare and Compulsory Labor: A Study of the Military-Industrial Complex in Germany during World War I*.[42] Armeson stressed Germany's economic unpreparedness for war in 1914, and suggested that it was only in the wake of the serious manpower shortage of 1915, occasioned by the forced induction of skilled workers into the armed forces, that the government proved willing to address economic problems. Even so, it was not until the appointment of Generals Hindenburg and Ludendorff in late 1916 that the opposition of the trade unions and the General Staff was overcome and the Auxiliary Service Law instituted in December 1916.

The law was not a success. In the short run, too many loopholes and special exemptions undermined its effectiveness. Armeson saw its real value in its long-range implications: it accorded Parliament an unprecedented voice in administering the law, it effectively ended the *Burgfrieden* of 1914, it laid the groundwork for the future Weimar political coalition, and it provided the Third Reich with a precedent for its drastic system of manpower controls two decades later.

In West Germany, Lothar Burchardt took up themes first broached in the 1920s by Hans Herzfeld in his pioneering work on German industry and the military.[43] Burchardt, like Armeson, argued that, despite Fritz Fischer's charge that Germany had begun to plan by December 1912, there had been no systematic preparation for conflict before war broke out, that nothing had been done to assure adequate supplies of food for the people, raw materials for industry, or manpower and material resources for the military. With a few notable exceptions such as Generals August Keim and Colmar von der Goltz as well as Heinrich Class, both the public and the private sectors had been indifferent to economic planning for war. General Alfred von Schlieffen's magical recipe for a quick, victorious operational campaign against France and Russia emphasized mobilization rather than protracted war. Only under Schlieffen's successor, General Helmuth von Moltke, the Younger, was some attention paid at last to economic mobilization. Especially after the conclusion of the Anglo-Russian entente in 1907, Germany began to include 'perfidious Albion' among the Reich's probable adversaries, and to contemplate the difficulties of facing a naval blockade. Such disparate theorists as Friedrich Engels and Field Marshal Helmuth von Moltke, the Elder, had predicted that future wars were bound to be of long duration; and since the Reich imported nearly half of its foodstuffs and raw materials, it readily became apparent that it was in no position to fight a lengthy war.

Little was done to remedy these obvious problems, Burchardt asserts, due to the inertia of the bureaucracy as well as to the prejudices of the Reich and Prussian agencies most directly affected. While Admiral von Tirpitz was not interested in the economic aspects of preparing for war, Clemens von Delbrück, the Minister of the Interior, was opposed in principle to government involvement in industrial and economic planning. In addition, the Imperial Treasury was concerned that any economic preparations for war would seriously jeopardize an already severely strained budget. Most Prussian agencies, on the other hand, resisted even the suggestion of federal offices cutting into the fiscal 'fat' of the individual states. Again, while the Reich Treasury felt that providing foodstuffs was a matter for the states to resolve among themselves, the *Länder* believed it to be a purely military question, and hence to fall into the federal domain. Finally, Burchardt shows that there existed virtually no contacts in this matter either between the various agencies of government, or between the public and private sectors. The end result, unsurprisingly, was that almost nothing had been done to provide systematic planning for war.

Study of the German home front and the military during the First World War received great impetus in 1970 with Wilhelm Deist's publication of 511 documents pertaining to 'Military and Domestic Politics in the World War 1914–1918'.[44] Deist analyzes the dual function of the German army as both guarantor of domestic stability and executor of national policy. Above all, he emphasizes the complexity of the military's role; far from being the monolithic, authoritarian institution depicted by many Anglo-Saxon scholars, the German military was a multifaceted and diffuse organization. Its major offices ranged from the General Staff, War Ministry, War Office, Navy Office and Admiralty Staff down to the roughly two dozen commanding generals of military districts. The latters' function as official censors reveals the impossibility of neatly dividing military and political spheres of influence and control. Overlap was the norm. On the other hand, the military *was* sufficiently united to resist successfully all attempts at reform.

Deist also disagrees with the generally held notion that the Third Supreme Command under Hindenburg and Ludendorff constituted a military dictatorship; Ludendorff, he argues, could never quite bring himself to assume political responsibility for the fate of the nation.[45] Deist concurs with Feldman that the military was divided on the question of organized labor. While the War Office was willing to make concessions to labor, the General Staff tended to side with heavy industry and, under Colonel Bauer, sought to create a repressive right-wing dictatorship with proto-fascist trappings.[46] Bauer failed, mainly because no one could be found who was willing to assume the burden of leadership. Yet, the military became so heavily involved in national politics during the war that the revolution of 1918–19 ought to be regarded as a revolt against militarism rather than as a political movement. Perhaps most importantly, Deist's documentary collection is designed to spur further research into military–civilian relations during the First World War.

The same can be said of a new collection of 135 documents edited by Deist and Volker Berghahn that shed light upon German military and naval armaments policies up to 1914. The editors argue that the European armaments race prior to 1914 was the prototype of modern arms races among industrial nations, and thus suggest that it can shed light upon present American-Soviet armaments relations. The edition is especially welcome since most German military records were destroyed by Allied air raids in 1942 and 1945, and since the only published collection containing some of these materials is out of print.[47]

Finally, Michael Geyer of Chicago has sought to rekindle critical examination of the German military with a highly provocative analysis of 'German Armaments Politics 1860–1980'.[48] Basically, Geyer asks his colleagues to rethink the role of the German military in the 'age of machine warfare'.[49] He rejects the widespread notion that armaments develop a life of their own, that they become automatic and irreversible; rather, they are made 'by human beings for human beings' and serve primarily to preserve the existing order. Like Deist, Geyer argues that the notion that the German military coopted heavy industry into its domain during the war is too simplistic as their interests were far from identical. Change and adaptability were the hallmarks of German armaments policies.

The period from 1871 to 1916, Geyer suggests, was one of 'personnel-intensive armament' in which the Prussian War Ministry concentrated on men rather than machines. The Third Supreme Command of Ludendorff and Bauer in 1916–18, however, brought about an 'explosive fusion', a 'symbiosis between the military and industry', in which machines replaced men as the primary agents of state-organized violence. Trench warfare levelled classes. Military status was defined more by technical expertise than by rank as machines 'synthesized' class and rank differences. Frontline soldiers, in the words of Ernst Jünger, became 'workers' of war. The First World War catapulted the German military under Erich Ludendorff into twentieth-century industrialized society by 'fusing' the new 'frontline mentality' with an equally novel 'machine culture', and, in the process, produced a military system based on 'freedom and equality'.[50]

The works of Berghahn, Deist and Geyer, among others, augur well for the future of military history. Gone, it would seem, are the days not only of 'drums-and-trumpets' operational histories, but perhaps also of Anglo-Saxon 'war-and-society' studies. The 'new' military history promises to be a composite of diplomatic, economic, operational, political, psychological and social analyses.

THE FUTURE

The historiography of the 'German question' remains alive and well on both sides of the Atlantic. While the Fischer controversy has largely been relegated to anthologies designed for use by undergraduates,[51] the critical history of Wehler and Kocka currently finds itself under attack by the advocates both of 'neutral' narrative history (Nipperdey) and of 'history from below' (Medick). The coming years thus are likely to witness continued heated debate between the proponents of *Strukturgeschichte* and those of *Alltagsgeschichte*.

Unfortunately, the West German *Zunft* remains intent on insisting that only one approach – whichever it may be – is viable. If there is a lesson to be learned from the academic donnybrooks of the 1960s and 1970s, surely it must be that the study of history is sufficiently abundant and elastic to allow for more than one methodological approach. Domestic and foreign policies are *not* mutually exclusive; rather, they interact constantly to produce the national polity, in which one, and then the other, may dominate. Neither are narrative and critical history mutually exclusive. A judicious mix of narrative case studies and functional analysis is dictated, it would seem, by common sense alone. The current trend toward *Alltagsgeschichte* can only serve to enrich our understanding of the past – without necessarily negating other approaches.

The charm of historical investigation, as R.G. Collingwood pointed out almost half a century ago, is that history does not consist exclusively of 'events causally determined and scientifically comprehensible', but rather that it also entails 'the discerning of the thought which is the inner side of the event'.[52] When German historians accept this postulate they will be able to jettison the sterile 'either-or' debates of the past and to produce a richer, more mature and multifaceted historiography.

NOTES

1 See the Introduction to Georg Iggers (ed.), *The Social History of Politics: Critical Perspective in West German Historical Writing since 1945* (New York, 1985), pp. 1–48.

2 Holger H. Herwig, *'Luxury' Fleet: The Imperial German Navy 1888–1918* (London and Atlantic Highlands, NJ, 1980), pp. 95–110. The 'prestige' component in German empire-building has recently been examined by Holger H. Herwig, *Germany's Vision of Empire in Venezuela 1871–1914* (Princeton, NJ, 1986).

3 Fritz Fischer, *Griff nach der Weltmacht. Die Kriegszielpolitik des kaiserlichen Deutschland 1914/18* (Düsseldorf, 1961).

4 See John A. Moses, *The Politics of Illusion: The Fischer Controversy in German Historiography* (New York, 1975), for a brief overview.

5 Ritter to Schröder, 17 January 1964, in Klaus Schwabe and Rolf Reichardt (eds), *Gerhard Ritter. Ein politischer Historiker in seinen Briefen* (Boppard, 1984), p. 587.

6 *Germany's Aims in the First World War* (New York, 1967).

7 ibid., pp. 105–6, 211, 573, 636. See also Fischer's most recent English-language publication: *From Kaiserreich to Third Reich: Elements of Continuity in German History, 1871–1945* (London, 1986).

8 David Lloyd George, *War Memoirs* (London, 1924), Vol. 1, p. 32.

9 Paul W. Schroeder, 'World War I as Galloping Gertie: a reply to Joachim Remak', *Journal of Modern History*, vol. 44 (1972), pp. 319–45. 'Galloping Gertie' refers to the Tacoma Narrows Bridge, which collapsed in 1940 under pressure from high winds.

10 In a letter to Fritz Hartung on 11 March 1960, Ritter confessed that he had been 'morally somewhat shaken' by studies in the Viennese Military Archive. Schwabe and Reichardt, *Gerhard Ritter*, p. 538. See also Gerhard Ritter, 'Eine neue Kriegsschuldthese? Zu Fritz Fischers Buch "Griff nach der Weltmacht"', *Historische Zeitschrift*, vol. 194 (1962), pp. 646–68. Also, the various responses to Fischer by Egmont Zechlin, *Krieg und Kriegsrisiko. Zur deutschen Politik im Ersten Weltkrieg* (Düsseldorf, 1979).

11 *Krieg der Illusionen. Die deutsche Politik von 1911 bis 1914* (Düsseldorf, 1969); *War of Illusions: German Politics from 1911 to 1914* (New York, 1975).

12 Eckart Kehr, *Der Primat der Innenpolitik. Gesammelte Aufsätze zur preussich-deutschen Sozialgeschichte im 19. und 20. Jahrhundert*, ed. Hans-Ulrich Wehler, (Berlin, 1965). Gordon A. Craig edited an English-language edition: *Economic Interest, Militarism, and Foreign Policy* (Berkeley, Calif., 1977).

13 Fischer, *Krieg der Illusionen*, pp. 231–41. Fischer was most vigorously supported in this claim by John Röhl, *1914: Delusion or Design? The Testimony of Two German Diplomats* (London, 1973), pp. 28–32; and *Kaiser, Hof und Staat. Wilhelm II. und die deutsche Politik* (Munich, 1987), pp. 175–202.

14 See especially Adolf Gasser, 'Deutschlands Entschluss zum Präventivkrieg 1913/14', in M. Sieber (ed.), *Discordia Concors. Festgabe für Edgar Bonjour zu seinem 70. Geburtstag am 21. August 1968* (Basel, 1968), Vol. 1, pp. 171–224; and Gasser, *Preussischer Militärgeist und Kriegsentfesselung 1914. Drei Studien zum Ausbruch des Ersten Weltkrieges* (Basel and Frankfurt, 1985). Also, Volker R. Berghahn, *Germany and the Approach of War in 1914* (New York, 1973); and Imanuel Geiss, 'The outbreak of the First World War and German war aims', *Journal of Contemporary History*, vol. 1 (1966), pp. 75–91. For a recent evaluation of the 'patriotic self-censors', see Holger H. Herwig, 'Clio deceived: patriotic self-censorship in Germany after the Great War', *International Security*, vol. 12 (1987), pp. 5–44.

15 Imanuel Geiss (ed.), *Julikrise und Kriegsausbruch 1914. Eine Dokumentensammlung*, 2 vols (Hanover, 1963–4); *Juli 1914. Die europäische Krise und der Ausbruch des Ersten Weltkriegs* (Munich, 1965); *July 1914: The Outbreak of the First World War. Selected Documents* (New York, 1968).

16 Kurt Riezler, *Die Erförderlichkeiten des Unmöglichen. Prolegomena zu einer Theorie der Politik und zu anderen Theorien* (Munich, 1913); and J.J. Ruedorffer [Kurt Riezler], *Grundzüge der Weltpolitik in der Gegenwart* (Stuttgart and Berlin, 1914).

17 Andreas Hillgruber, 'Riezlers Theorie des kalkulierten Risikos und Bethmann Hollwegs politische Konzeption in der Julikrise 1914', *Historische Zeitschrift*, vol. 202 (1966), pp. 331–51.

18 Konrad H. Jarausch, 'The illusion of limited war: Chancellor Bethmann Hollweg's calculated risk, July 1914', *Central European History*, vol. 2 (1969), p. 75.

19 Konrad H. Jarausch, *The Enigmatic Chancellor: Bethmann Hollweg and the Hubris of Imperial Germany* (New Haven, Conn., 1973), especially p. 405.

20   Karl Dietrich Erdmann (ed.), *Kurt Riezler. Tagebücher. Aufsätze. Dokumente* (Göttingen, 1972).

21   Charges of 'editing' the Riezler diary were first made by Bernd Sösemann, 'Die Tagebücher Kurt Riezlers: Untersuchungen zu ihrer Echtheit und Edition', *Historische Zeitschrift*, vol. 236 (1983), pp. 327–69; Erdmann defended himself in the same issue; 'Zur Echtheit der Tagebücher Kurt Riezlers. Eine Antikritik', ibid., pp. 371–402. An interim evaluation now exists by Bernd F. Schulte, *Die Verfälschung der Riezler Tagebücher. Ein Beitrag zur Wissenschaftsgeschichte der 50er und 60er Jahre* (Frankfurt, 1985). A recent biography of Riezler by Wayne C. Thompson, *In the Eye of the Storm: Kurt Riezler and the Crises of Modern Germany* (Iowa City, Iowa, 1980), basically accepts Riezler's notion of the 'calculated risk' in July 1914.

22   See Thimme's review of Jarausch's *Enigmatic Chancellor* in *Journal of Modern History*, vol. 48 (1976), p. 734.

23   Hans-Ulrich Wehler, *Entsorgung der deutschen Vergangenheit? Ein polemischer Essay zum 'Historikerstreit'* (Munich, 1988), p. 125.

24   'The Mood of 1914' in James Joll, *The Origins of the First World War* (London, 1984), pp. 171–200; Jean-Jacques Becker, *The Great War and the French People* (New York, 1986); and Volker Ullrich, *Kriegsalltag: Hamburg im Ersten Weltkrieg* (Cologne, 1982).

25   Hans-Ulrich Wehler, *Krisenherde des Kaiserreichs, 1871–1918. Studien zur deutschen Sozial- und Verfassungsgeschichte* (Göttingen, 1970 and 1979); and *Das Deutsche Kaiserreich, 1871–1918* (Göttingen, 1973 and 1979), which appeared with the Berg Press in England as *The German Empire, 1871–1918* (Leamington Spa, 1985). Vandenhoeck & Ruprecht has published much of the work being done by Wehler and his associates.

26   See also Hans-Ulrich Wehler, 'Bismarck's imperialism 1861–1890', *Past and Present*, vol. 48 (1970), p. 153.

27   Wehler, *Kaiserreich*, pp. 177, 96.

28   ibid., p. 208.

29   For incisive critiques of Wehler's works, see the various reviews in the *Historische Zeitschrift* by Andreas Hillgruber (vol. 216 (1973), pp. 529–52); Hans-Günter Zmarzlik (vol. 222 (1976), pp. 105–126); and Klaus Hildebrand (vol. 223 (1976), pp. 328–57).

30   David Schoenbaum, *Zabern 1913: Consensus Politics in Imperial Germany* (London, 1982), p. 184. After all, industrial unrest such as Haymarket, Homestead and Pullman was hardly a German occurrence; and the 'continuation of politics by bloody means' can be seen best perhaps not in Berlin but in Paris *(mur des fédérés)* and St Petersburg ('bloody Sunday').

31   Thomas Nipperdey, 'Wehlers "Kaiserreich". Eine kritische Auseinandersetzung', *Gesellschaft und Geschichte*, vol. 1 (1975), pp. 539–60.

32   Jürgen Kocka, *Klassengesellschaft im Krieg. Deutsche Sozialgeschichte 1914–1918* (Göttingen, 1973); in English, *Facing Total War: German Society, 1914–1918* (Cambridge, Mass., 1984).

33   See Wolfgang J. Mommsen, 'Society and war: two new analyses of the First World War', *Journal of Modern History*, vol. 47 (1975), pp. 529–38.

34   Alfred Müller, *Die Kriegsrohstoffbewirtschaftung 1914–1918* (East Berlin, 1955); Alfred Schröter, *Krieg–Staat–Monopol 1914–1918* (East Berlin, 1965); and Hermann Weber, *Ludendorff und die Monopole. Deutsche Kriegspolitik 1914–1918* (East Berlin, 1966).

35   Fritz Klein *et al.* (eds), *Deutschland im ersten Weltkrieg*, 3 vols (East Berlin, 1968). Largely neglected is Ruth Andexel, *Imperialismus – Staatsfinanzen,*

Rüstung, Krieg; Probleme der Rüstungsfinanzierung des deutschen Imperialismus (East Berlin, 1968).

36 Klein, *Deutschland im ersten Weltkrieg*, Vol. 3, pp. 565–9.

37 ibid., Vol. 2, pp. 140, 488. The emphasis is Klein's.

38 ibid., Vol. 1, pp. 363 ff.; Vol. 2, pp. 131, 138 ff.

39 Gerald D. Feldman, *Army, Industry, and Labor in Germany 1914–1918* (Princeton, NJ, 1966).

40 Karl Erich Born, *Wirtschafts- und Sozialgeschichte des Deutschen Kaiserreichs 1867/71–1914* (Wiesbaden, 1985).

41 A recent collective volume by Robert Berdahl (ed.), *Klassen und Kultur. Sozialanthropologische Perspektiven in der Geschichtsschreibung* (Frankfurt, 1982), offers an overview of the new 'history from below'.

42 Robert B. Armeson, *Total Warfare and Compulsory Labor: A Study of the Military-Industrial Complex in Germany during World War I* (The Hague, 1964).

43 Lothar Burchardt, *Friedenswirtschaft und Kriegsvorsorge: Deutschlands wirtschaftliche Rüstungsbestrebungen vor 1914* (Boppard, 1968); Hans Herzfeld, *Die deutsche Rüstungspolitik vor dem Weltkrieg* (Leipzig, 1923).

44 Wilhelm Deist (ed.), *Militär und Innenpolitik im Weltkrieg 1914–1918*, 2 vols (Düsseldorf, 1970).

45 See Martin Kitchen, *The Silent Dictatorship: The Politics of the German High Command under Hindenburg and Ludendorff, 1916–1918* (New York, 1976). The thesis of the book is embodied in its title.

46 See Martin Kitchen, 'Militarism and the development of fascist ideology: the political ideas of Colonel Max Bauer, 1916–1918', *Central European History*, vol. 8 (1975), pp. 199–220.

47 Volker R. Berghahn and Wilhelm Deist (eds), *Rüstung im Zeichen der wilhelminischen Weltpolitik. Grundlegende Dokumente 1890–1914* (Düsseldorf, 1988).

48 Michael Geyer, *Deutsche Rüstungspolitik 1860–1980* (Frankfurt, 1984).

49 See also Michael Geyer, 'German strategy in the age of machine warfare, 1914–1945', in Peter Paret (ed.), *Makers of Modern Strategy from Machiavelli to the Nuclear Age* (Princeton, NJ, 1986), pp. 527–97.

50 Geyer, *Deutsche Rüstungspolitik*, especially pp. 90–105.

51 For example, D.C. Heath is presently reissuing its time-honored anthology on *The Outbreak of World War I* in order to update the historiography of the Fischer controversy.

52 R.G. Collingwood, *The Idea of History* (Oxford, 1946), pp. 150, 222.

4 Culture and Politics in the Weimar Republic

LARRY EUGENE JONES

From beginning to end, Weimar culture was intensely political. Not only did the greatest cultural achievements of the Weimar era mirror the political struggles that after 1918 were to become such a familiar trademark of German life, but culture itself was enlisted in the struggle over the political future of the German people. No matter how much Weimar intellectuals may have prided themselves upon the superiority of *Geist*, or spirit, to the amoral world of power politics, the culture they created was part of a much larger struggle for cultural and intellectual hegemony. It was a struggle waged not so much between different social classes as within the German bourgeoisie between those who believed in cooperation across class lines on the basis of parliamentary democracy and those who categorically rejected the social and political compromises upon which the Weimar Republic had been founded. That this struggle was eventually decided in favor of the latter of these two groups contributed in no small measure to the delegitimation of the Weimar Republic and helped to narrow the range of options that was available to Germany's political leadership once the failure of Weimar democracy had become an established fact of life. Any study of Weimar culture, therefore, must devote careful attention to the burning political issues that infiltrated virtually every corner of German life from 1919 to 1933. Conversely, any study of Weimar politics must also seek to understand the way in which Weimar culture not only replicated the struggle for social and political hegemony, but entered into that struggle with a sense of engagement that has few parallels in modern history.[1]

The purpose of this chapter is to sketch the outlines of the relationship between culture and politics in the Weimar Republic and to suggest how the rise of cultural modernism and the reaction against it helped to define the broader context in which the struggle for the survival of German democracy was ultimately decided. This approach follows the lead of a new generation of French historians who have shifted the focus of their attention from the socioeconomic to the cultural determinants of historical change.[2] In this respect, however, one must be careful not to assign cultural determinants the sort of causal primacy they enjoyed in the works of pre-eminent intellectual historians such as Fritz Stern and George Mosse. Although Stern's *The Politics of Cultural Despair* (1961) and Mosse's *The Crisis of German Ideology* (1964) played an important role in identifying the irrational, racist and anti-modern currents that were at work in Germany's political culture, their approach to German history was both too fatalistic and one-dimensional. Not only did their work on the intellectual origins of the Third Reich make it appear that there was no alternative to the Nazi seizure of power in January 1933, but their commitment to exposing the cultural and intellectual roots of Nazism made it difficult for them to appreciate the diversity and heterogeneity of German culture. More importantly, their cultural determinism made it unnecessary for them to explain the specific historical conditions under which these and not other aspects of Germany's cultural tradition became manifest.

In *The Politics of Cultural Despair* Stern concentrated his attention on three self-styled 'conservative revolutionaries' – Paul de Lagarde, Julius Langbehn and Arthur Moeller van den Bruck – whose critique of Germany's cultural and historical development since 1871 helped to till the soil in which the seeds of Nazism took root.[3] Although Stern did not explain how these ideas were disseminated throughout German society, his general conclusion, both here and in a collection of essays subsequently published as *The Failure of Illiberalism*, was that by 1918 illiberalism had become so pervasive at all levels of German society – and particularly within Germany's conservative elites – that the Weimar Republic stood little, if any, chance of survival.[4] For Mosse, on the other hand, the most surprising feature of Germany's recent historical development was not that Hitler came to power in January 1933 but that he – or someone like him – had not done so earlier. To support his argument, Mosse traced the development of what he called the *völkisch* tradition from its intellectual origins at the beginning of the nineteenth century through its institutionalization in a plethora of middle-class parties, interest organizations and patriotic associations between 1871 and 1918 to its eventual triumph in 1933. By the end of the 1920s Germany's political culture had, in Mosse's mind, become so thoroughly saturated with racist, anti-Semitic and anti-liberal ideas that Hitler would have come to power even without the runaway inflation of the early 1920s or the onset of the Great Depression a decade later.[5]

Both Stern and Mosse subscribed to a monocausal, if not deterministic, interpretation of modern German history that reduced the Weimar Republic to little more than a dress rehearsal for the triumph of Nazism.

It took the publication of Peter Gay's *Weimar Culture: The Outsider as Insider* in 1968 to recapture the sense of diversity, innovation and experimentation that characterized Germany's cultural and intellectual development between 1918 and 1933. Although Gay's attempt to analyze the relationship between culture and politics in Freudian categories such as the 'revolt of the son' and the 'revenge of the father' may be more tantalizing than persuasive, his portrait of Weimar culture serves as a constant reminder of its creativity and diversity. For Gay, Weimar culture was 'a precarious glory, a dance on the edge of a volcano', that consisted of many different and often contradictory strands existing in a state of unresolved tension with each other.[6] From Gay's perspective, therefore, it would be a serious mistake to suggest that the establishment of the Third Reich represented the inevitable culmination of Germany's cultural development. The more relevant problem, as Geoff Eley suggested in a somewhat different context, is 'that of establishing how certain "traditions" become selected for survival rather than others – how certain beliefs and practices came to reproduce themselves under radically changed circumstances, and how they become subtly transformed in the very process of renewal'.[7] This chapter will show how specific social, economic and political factors converged during the Weimar Republic to favor one particular aspect of Germany's cultural tradition at the expense of others.

It is impossible to understand the specific configurations of Weimar culture without first examining Germany's cultural and intellectual development during the last decades of the Wilhelmine empire. From the middle of the nineteenth century to the outbreak of the First World War, Germany's cultural and intellectual life was dominated by a relatively thin, but immensely influential social stratum known as the *Bildungsbürgertum*.[8] Drawing its inspiration from the revival of neo-classical humanism at the end of the eighteenth century, the *Bildungsbürgertum* espoused a moral vision that emphasized the emancipation of the individual from anything that might interfere with the free development of his – or, under extraordinary circumstances, her – personality. Regarding the formation of character and the development of the human reason as the highest goals of cultural activity, this ideal presupposed the sublimation of instinctual energy, including sexuality, into work or cultural achievement. Culture, therefore, served as a vehicle for the refinement of passion and for the elevation of the instinctual to the level of the spiritual. This avowedly elitist, unabashedly male and inherently repressive moral ethos offered emancipation on narrowly defined terms that denied the instinctual bases of human activity. Not only was this ethos internalized in the behavior structure of the individual through the agency of the patriarchal family, but it also came to play a crucial role in the formation of Germany's bourgeois elite by virtue of its incorporation into an educational philosophy known as *Bildungsliberalismus*.[9]

In the second half of the nineteenth century, the cultural and intellectual hegemony of the German *Bildungsbürgertum* was undermined by a combination of factors. The onset of the Great Depression in the mid-1870s and the development of a new, more highly concentrated form of industrial capitalism severely weakened the more traditional, individualistic foundations of Germany's economic system. At the same time, the rise of the masses to social and political consciousness and the emergence of mass political parties on both the left and the right constituted a direct challenge to the elitist character of those institutions through which the German bourgeoisie had traditionally exercised its social and political hegemony.[10] The increasing anxiety which the German *Bildungsbürgertum* began to feel as a result of these developments could be seen in its gradual retreat from the liberal ideas of progress and reason and in the emergence of philosophical irrationalism as an increasingly powerful force in German culture. The rapture with which a sleepless Thomas Buddenbrooks picked up the second volume of Arthur Schopenhauer's *The World as Will and Idea* and read of how death was nothing but redemption from the pain of individual existence bore subtle, yet persuasive testimony to the way in which the tenets of philosophical irrationalism had begun to penetrate the awareness of Germany's educated elite.[11] By the same token, the operas of Richard Wagner became an enormously influential vehicle for the dissemination of an inherently irrational view of the world – and in this case one that was imbued with a particularly virulent dose of nationalism and cultural anti-Semitism – throughout the German bourgeoisie.[12]

No thinker exercised as powerful, yet as diffuse, an influence on German cultural and intellectual life in the last years of the Wilhelmine empire as Friedrich Nietzsche. As the self-proclaimed apostle of cultural rebirth, Nietzsche took special pains to expose the inherently repressive and moribund character of nineteenth-century, bourgeois-Christian Europe.[13] Nietzsche's enormous popularity stemmed ultimately from the fact that his philosophical legacy was so ambiguous that it could be interpreted in any number of ways. At the very least, Nietzsche's disdain for the political aspirations of 'the herd' and his idealization of war as the testing ground of human greatness reinforced the anti-democratic prejudices of Germany's ruling classes and encouraged them to think of war as a panacea for their nation's domestic problems.[14] At the same time, Nietzsche's exhortation to 'live dangerously' and his crusade to liberate human instinct from the crippling weight of Christian morality helped to articulate the frustration that German youth had come to feel at the repressive moral conventions of bourgeois society.[15] Nietzsche's influence was most profoundly felt, however, among those young artists and aesthetes who rejoiced in his devastating critique of the nineteenth century's misplaced faith in science, progress and reason and who responded to his call for cultural rebirth with a passionate intensity that echoed Nietzsche's own messianic zeal. In the final analysis, it was not the reactionary but the apocalyptic and revolutionary Nietzsche who had the greatest impact upon the cultural life of Wilhelmine Germany.[16]

Nietzsche's ruthless dissection of European cultural decadence and his apocalyptic vision of cultural rebirth through the agency of the artist turned *Ubermensch* found resonance in the rise of cultural modernism. Although its origins were not German but Viennese and Parisian, the modernist revolt had a profound impact upon Wilhelmine culture and did much to disturb the intellectual equilibrium of Germany's *Bildungsbürgertum*. The receptivity of Wilhelmine Germany to modernist culture stemmed not so much from the crisis and dissolution of liberal hegemony, as it did in *fin de siècle* Vienna,[17] as from the effects of the extraordinarily rapid pace of social and economic modernization that Germany experienced between 1871 and 1914. The dramatic transformation of the German economy in the last decades of the Second Empire produced two discernible, yet antithetical cultural responses. The first was a sense of increasing pessimism and a nostalgia for the past on the part of those elements of Germany's educated elite that felt most directly threatened by the changes that were taking place in the social and economic structure of German life.[18] This was, after all, the mood that pervaded Thomas Mann's *Death in Venice* and informed the image of the 'iron cage' which Max Weber used at the end of *The Protestant Ethic and the Spirit of Capitalism* to describe the conditions of modern life. But the cultural pessimism of Germany's educated elite was complemented by a second impulse that looked beyond the decadence of contemporary culture to its revitalization and rebirth at the hands of a new generation of artists who had freed themselves from the dead weight of convention and tradition. Fascinated by the sudden and dramatic changes that seemed to be taking place at all levels of German life, this cadre of disaffected artists and intellectuals provided fertile soil in which the seeds of modernist culture could take root and flourish.[19]

The principal manifestation of cultural modernism in prewar Germany was an artistic and literary movement known as expressionism.[20] The various strains of German expressionism were united by a disdain for the materialistic trappings of bourgeois life and an apocalyptic longing for a spiritual breakthrough to what its partisans called the 'new man'.[21] Beyond this, however, there were important differences between the two major schools of prewar German expressionism. Founded in Dresden in 1905, *Die Brücke* was deeply influenced by Nordic and African art and sought to project an image of man uncorrupted by the hypocrisy of modern life and in touch with the instinctual or mythic dimension of human existence. The bold use of color and line in paintings such as Ernst Ludwig Kirchner's *Portrait of a Woman* (1911) or Karl Schmidt-Rottluff's *Rising Moon* (1912) constituted an affront to bourgeois taste, while the thematic content of Max Pechstein's *Nudes by the Sea* (1913) represented a stinging indictment of the ossification and artificiality of life during the last years of the Second Empire. Yet whereas *Die Brücke* sought to escape the evils of modern civilization by returning to a more primitive mode of human existence in which the instincts were celebrated as the source of artistic inspiration, *Der Blaue Reiter*, established some five years later in Munich, sought to achieve this by means of a breakthrough into what Wassily Kandinsky portrayed as the realm of pure spirit.[22] The impulse that animated Kandinsky's abstract compositions and Franz Marc's *Fate of the Animals* (1913) was profoundly apocalyptic and sought nothing less than the total redemption of man and society through art.[23]

Although expressionism was avowedly apolitical and eschewed a political solution to the crisis of modern man, it represented a frontal challenge to the cultural and intellectual hegemony of Germany's *Bildungsbürgertum*. Whatever uneasiness Germany's educated elite may already have felt about the momentous changes that were taking place in the objective conditions of German life could only have been exacerbated by the rise of cultural modernism. The shock of non-representational art and atonal music, the discovery of the unconscious, the development of new literary techniques such as the stream of consciousness mode of narration and, perhaps most important, the challenge of Einstein and the new physics to the Newtonian view of the world all had a disorienting effect upon the *Bildungsbürgertum* and severely compromised its ability to function in its traditional capacity as the mediator of cultural values between the ruling classes and society as a whole.[24] A further symptom of the cultural crisis that existed in Germany on the eve of the First World War was the increasingly powerful longing, particularly within the younger generation, for some sort of redemptive act that would usher in a new age of humanity and brotherhood. The deracination, or bankruptcy, of traditional bourgeois culture thus combined with the millenarian fervor of the modernist revolt to create a cultural environment in which war was no longer abhorred, but welcomed as the moment of apocalyptic resolution.[25]

The outbreak of the First World War provided an intellectually beleaguered *Bildungsbürgertum* with a much-needed respite from its own ennui and gave it an opportunity to reaffirm its utility to the nation by defending German *Kultur* against the artificiality and superficiality of French *Zivilisation*. Thomas Mann's *Reflections of the Non-Political Man* was only the most celebrated example of the way in which Germany's cultured elite rallied to the cause of the German war effort.[26] For the disciples of the new modernist culture, on the other hand, the war afforded a rare opportunity to participate in the mystical process by which a new world was being reborn out of the ashes of the old. But neither the rationalizations of Germany's cultural elite nor the promise of apocalyptic rebirth could sustain the nation through the four years of hard and relentless fighting that were to follow. As the war dragged on, the euphoria and unity of purpose that had captivated the nation in August 1914 gave way to a mood of increasing exhaustion and disgruntlement.[27] When the war finally ended with a defeat for which the German public was largely unprepared, the people took its revenge and overthrew the imperial monarchy. With the collapse of the Second Empire, Germany had entered a new age, an age whose dominant spirit was that of cultural modernism. Germany had, in the words of historian Detlev Peukert, entered the age of the 'classical modern'.[28]

From the moment of its birth, the Weimar Republic was the scene of a pitched battle for cultural and intellectual hegemony between two competing sectors of the German bourgeoisie, one of which was committed to cooperation across class lines on the basis of parliamentary democracy and the other to the destabilization of Germany's fledgling democratic order and the restoration of prewar power relationships. Indeed, the very choice of Weimar as the site of the constitutional convention had been dictated as much by cultural as by political considerations. In choosing the seat of Germany's late eighteenth-century neo-classical revival as the birthplace of the new republic, the leaders of German democracy hoped not only to invoke the spirit of Weimar against that of Potsdam but also to provide the new political order with an aura of legitimacy by identifying it with the humanistic legacy of Goethe and Schiller. Moreover, the principal architects of the Weimar Constitution – Hugo Preuß , Max Weber and Conrad Haußmann – were all bourgeois liberals who remained deeply committed to the social and cultural values of the German *Bildungsbürgertum*. As a result of their efforts, the new constitutional order carried a distinctly liberal imprimatur even though the party to which they belonged was the weakest member of the governmental coalition.[29] Yet not even the pride that German liberals could take in having established the constitutional foundations of the new republican system could fully assuage the apprehension that made itself felt, for example, in the closing passages of Weber's 'Politics as a vocation' or in his lament over the 'demystification of the world'. It was, as Weber reminded a student audience at the University of Munich in February 1919, not 'summer's bloom . . . but rather a polar night of icy darkness and hardness' that awaited the German nation.[30] For those who subscribed to the social and cultural values of the German *Bildungsbürgertum*, the new age that had dawned with the collapse of the Second Empire and the founding of the Weimar Republic was one fraught with anxiety and doubt.

Efforts to legitimize the Weimar Republic by appropriating the cultural legacy of the German *Bildungsbürgertum* were hampered from the outset by the lack of any sort of clear political consensus on the part of Germany's educated elite. While many prominent representatives of the German *Bildungsbürgertum* rallied to the support of the pro-republican German Democratic Party (Deutsche Demokratische Partei, or DDP) in the January 1919 elections to the National Assembly, a far more significant portion of Germany's educated elite seems to have voted for the decidedly more conservative German People's Party (Deutsche Volkspartei) or, in some cases, for the militantly anti-republican German National People's Party (Deutschnationale Volkspartei). Bourgeois loyalties to the new republican order were severely strained not only by the compromises which the leaders of the DDP had to make to the Social Democrats in the area of fiscal and economic policy, but also by the deep-seated bitterness which the imposition of the Versailles peace treaty produced within virtually every sector of the German bourgeoisie. By far the most damaging blow to these loyalties, however, came in the form of the runaway inflation of the early 1920s. The inflation had a devastating effect upon the German academic community and reduced the various forms of private investment with which the *Bildungsbürgertum* had traditionally supplemented its income to a fraction of their original worth.[31] The inflation thus destroyed the economic substance of a significant portion of Germany's educated elite and left it permanently estranged from a system of government that had originally sought to portray itself as the heir to the humanist legacy of Goethe and Schiller. Not even Thomas Mann's impassioned defense of the German republic following Walther Rathenau's assassination in the summer of 1922 could halt the progressive disaffection of Germany's cultured and elite from the new political order.[32]

The plight of the German *Bildungsbürgertum* was one aspect of the enormous social price that Germany had to pay for the rapid modernization of her economy in the first third of the twentieth century. Modernization, however, had many different faces. In the economic sphere, modernization manifested itself primarily in the rationalization of German industry and in the increasing concentration of economic power in the hands of large capitalist enterprises that, to all outward appearances, were more powerful than the state itself.[33] In the political realm, modernization was associated with the introduction of parliamentary democracy and the displacement of traditional bourgeois *Honoratiorenparteien*, or parties of notables, by mass political parties that relied upon a high degree of organization and the most sophisticated techniques of popular mobilization in their bid for public favor.[34] In the social sphere, modernization not only encompassed the process of urbanization and increased mobility across class lines but also entailed a radical redefinition of gender relations and the 'emancipation of the modern woman' from the traditional straitjacket of *Kirche, Küche* and *Kinder*.[35] And, in the cultural sphere, modernization involved the emergence of a new type of intellectual who, in the spirit of Nietzsche's call for the 'transvaluation of all values', rejoiced in the destructive power of his own reason as traditional values, beliefs and standards of aesthetic taste came under its relentless onslaught. In the final analysis, therefore, it was not so much the social and cultural values of the German *Bildungsbürgertum* as the modernist revolt of the early twentieth century that left its imprint most indelibly impressed upon the cultural profile of Weimar Germany. To Germans and non-Germans alike, Weimar became synonymous with the spirit of modernity.[36]

The First World War and the revolution that followed Germany's military defeat had a dramatic impact on the development of cultural modernism in the postwar period. Whereas before the war the modernist revolt had been essentially apolitical and had defined human emancipation more in aesthetic and psychological than in political terms, the postwar period witnessed the emergence of a radically new strand of cultural modernism that sought to forge an alliance between cultural and political revolution. The marriage of art and revolution was most apparent in Munich, where Ernst Toller, Erich Mühsam and several other literati of the left placed their talents at the service of the ill-fated Soviet Republic from February to May 1919.[37] At the same time, a split developed within the ranks of the modernist movement between those who continued to define culture in exclusively elitist terms and those who sought to bridge the gap between elite and popular culture by addressing themselves directly to the masses. Although the fact that this split existed had already become apparent before 1914 in Munich and other centers of urban culture,[38] after the war the desire to make art more accessible to the masses merged with the revolutionary impulses on the German Left to produce a new concept of art that sought to exploit its potential as an instrument of popular enlightenment and agitation. Erwin Piscator's *agitprop* and Bertholt Brecht's 'Epic Theater' were only two of the better known examples of the way in which the notion of art for art's sake gave way to a more politicized concept of art that was allied to the social and political emancipation of the German worker.[39]

Just as the expressionist quest for the 'new man' was fuelled by recurrent eruptions of revolutionary unrest between 1918 and 1923, so the runaway inflation of the early 1920s lent credence to Marxist claims that the old bourgeois order was in its death throes and that the birth of a new age was at hand. Driven by the need to explain the collapse of socialist unity in August 1914 and the failure of the revolutionary movement after the end of the First World War, Marxist theory in the immediate postwar period demonstrated remarkable vitality. Among the most important developments was the attempt by Georg Lukacs and Karl Korsch to return Marxism to its Hegelian origins and to infuse it with the basic values of bourgeois humanism. Lukacs's *History and Class Consciousness* (1923) represented an intellectual *tour de force* that sought to reconstruct Marx's early thought through a critical reinterpretation of Hegel, the left Hegelians and the little that Marx himself had published in the 1840s. Lukacs's central thesis was that at the heart of Marx's critique of the capitalist system lay a concept of man rooted in the highest principles of bourgeois humanism. Marx's revolutionary passion, therefore, stemmed from his realization that the humanist concept of man was incompatible with the forms of social and economic organization that had developed in industrial capitalism and that only the overthrow of capitalism would enable man to reappropriate his alienated human essence. By portraying Marxism both as the heir to the humanist tradition of Goethe and Schiller and as the philosophy of action by which that tradition would be translated into practice, Lukacs sought to legitimize Marxist claims to social and political hegemony by appropriating the neo-classical heritage of the German *Bildungsbürgertum*.[40]

The emergence of Marxist humanism represented an important response to the question that had come to occupy more and more of Thomas Mann's attention during the course of the 1920s: could humanism survive the dissolution of the social order to which its emergence and pre-eminence had been so closely tied? For the champions of the modernist revolt, this question could only have been answered in the negative. To them, the collapse of the bourgeois social order was both part and parcel of a more fundamental transvaluation of values that would culminate in the emergence of the 'new man' and in the liberation of human instinct from the dead hand of morality and tradition. Yet, while the widespread prostitution and sexual libertinism of the early 1920s might have suggested that such a transvaluation was in fact under way, the millenarian impulse that had played such an important role in the expressionist vision of the 'new man' was unable to sustain itself in the face of the repeated blows that Germany suffered between 1919 and 1923. The defeat of the revolutionary left in 1919–20 and again in 1923, the murder first of Matthias Erzberger in 1921 and then of Rathenau a year later and the complete collapse of the German currency in 1922–3 all combined to exhaust the expressionists' faith in the redemptive power of their own art. Expressionism, as John Willett has suggested in his recent study of theater in the Weimar Republic, had 'run out of steam'.[41]

The stabilization of the mark in the winter of 1923/24 marked the beginning of an apparent return to normality that was to last for five years. In many essential respects, however, the stabilization of the mark was to prove every bit as damaging to the future of Weimar democracy as the inflation. The various measures taken to stabilize the mark inflicted additional and in some cases severe economic hardship upon those social strata that had already been forced to bear the brunt of the inflation. Moreover, the authoritarian manner in which the mark had been stabilized did much to aggravate the incipient legitimacy crisis that had plagued the Weimar Republic ever since its founding in 1919. More important still, the uneven economic recovery that Germany experienced between 1924 and 1929 bypassed economically and politically significant elements of the German middle class, with the result that they became increasingly disaffected from the existing system of government.[42] Not even the election of war hero Paul von Hindenburg as president of the Weimar Republic in 1925 or the Nobel Peace Prize that Foreign Minister Gustav Stresemann won two years later could erase the trauma of inflation or ease the frustration of stabilization.

Ephemeral though it was, Germany's economic and political stabilization in the second half of the 1920s was nevertheless accompanied by a marked change in aesthetic sensibilities. In the visual arts this could be seen most dramatically in the eclipse of the messianic idealism of *Die Brücke* and *Der blaue Reiter* in favor of a new school of expressionism known as the *Neue Sachlichkeit*, a term alternately rendered as the 'new objectivity' or the 'new sobriety'.[43] The *Neue Sachlichkeit* was closely allied to the political left, and its chief exponents, Georg Grosz and Rudolf Dix, were relentless in exposing the moral and spiritual depravity of Germany's ruling classes. Despite its hostility towards the German bourgeoisie, however, the art of Grosz and his associates after 1923 was devoid of any genuine revolutionary conviction. The defeat of the German left between 1919 and 1923 had a profound effect upon Grosz, and he was never able to recover the passion of his early commitment to the cause of revolutionary socialism.[44] Nowhere was the gulf that separated Grosz from the messianic idealism of the first generation of German expressionists more apparent than in a watercolor from 1928 entitled *A Man of Opinion*. Here the true nature of the 'new man' was finally revealed as a Nazi in a brownshirt with a swastika on his arm.

The combination of resignation and biting satire that characterized the art of the *Neue Sachlichkeit* could also be seen in the development of German theater in the second half of the 1920s. In drama, as in the visual arts, the messianic idealism of early German expressionism gave way to a new conception of theater that was politically committed, yet devoid of revolutionary conviction. The most innovative force in Weimar theater was Bertholt Brecht, who in the mid-1920s had been converted to a highly idiosyncratic and non-doctrinaire form of Marxism by Walther Benjamin and Karl Korsch. Deeply distrustful of both the excessive emotionalism and the stylized subjectivism of the expressionist movement, Brecht began to formulate the outlines of a new dramatic idiom that would enable him to use the stage as a forum for the discussion and propagation of ideas. According to Brecht's theory of 'Epic Theater', the purpose of drama was not to effect an emotional catharsis on the part of the audience through its identification with the tragic fate of a great hero but to raise the consciousness of the masses and to instil in them a clearer awareness of the universal class conflict that constituted bourgeois capitalist society.[45] In *Man Is Man* (1924–5) Brecht parodied the expressionist notion of the 'new man' by portraying the transformation of Galy Guy, a simple and carefree porter from the barracks in Kilkoa, into the intrepid Jeriah Jip, who singlehandedly captured the fortress guarding the Tibetan frontier. The inspiration behind the play came from Brecht's conviction that human nature was infinitely malleable and that expressionist dreams of the 'new man' were problematic, if not patently absurd. Brecht followed this in 1928 with his greatest success, *The Three Penny Opera*, a play expressly designed for society's flotsam and jetsam. Here Brecht not only exposed the moral hypocrisy of bourgeois society – hence his famous trope 'Erst kommt das Fressen, dann kommt die Moral' (first comes the meal, then comes the moral) – but used animal imagery to dramatize the dehumanization of man and the impoverishment of his social relationships under capitalism. That Brecht's characters were ultimately incapable of meaningful political action was in itself a function of the self-alienation and reification that permeated their social universe.[46]

Trends similar to what was happening in art and drama could also be seen in the development of the German cinema. Early Weimar cinema was profoundly influenced by the expressionist rebellion in art and literature. Not only did *The Cabinet of Dr Caligari* (1919) and other film classics of the early 1920s employ sets that had been designed by painters schooled in the expressionist idiom, but the jerky and exaggerated gestures of actors in films like Fritz Murnau's *Nosferatu* (1922) paralleled the distortion of object and feature that had become such a familiar trademark of expressionist art. Moreover, the thematic content of early Weimar cinema, with its fascination for characters of monstrous proportions who stood outside the pale of conventional morality, was fully consistent with the way in which the first generation of German expressionists had openly flaunted their disdain for the basic values of traditional bourgeois culture.[47] With Germany's economic and political stabilization in the second half of the 1920s, however, the character of German cinema underwent a dramatic change that closely paralleled what was happening in art and drama. No film better epitomized the eclipse of the expressionist impulse in Weimar cinema than G. W. Pabst's *The Joyless Street* (1925). With stark and unrelenting realism, Pabst used the fate of a typical Viennese family to depict the moral and economic decay of the Austrian and – by way of extension – German middle class under the impact of the postwar inflation. At no point in his film did Pabst offer a political solution to the moral and social crisis of the great inflation. Life on the joyless street was a life without hope, a life of unremitting despair.[48]

For those whose sympathies were on the left, the second half of the 1920s offered a particularly dismal picture of Germany's political future. As short-lived as it might have been, the stabilization of the Weimar Republic also meant the stabilization of Germany's bourgeois capitalist order and the emergence of a new cultural style that had little in common with the millenarian zeal of early Weimar expressionism. To those who still identified themselves with the basic values of the bourgeois humanist tradition, on the other hand, it seemed as if their very culture was collapsing around them. The popularity of jazz, the public infatuation with Josephine Baker, the sexual licence of the 'Golden Twenties', the rebellion of the younger generation – all of this betrayed a culture in crisis, a culture divided against itself, a culture torn between the claims of the past and the hopes of the future. As Harry Haller, the anti-hero of Hermann Hesse's *Steppenwolf* (1927), lamented in a commentary on the Middle Ages that was pregnant with meaning for his own times:

> Human life is reduced to real suffering, to hell, only when two ages, two cultures and religions overlap.... Now there are times when a whole generation is caught in this way between two ages, two modes of life, with the consequence that it loses all power to understand itself and has no standard, no security, no simple acquiescence.... A nature such as Nietzsche's had to suffer our present ills more than a generation in advance. What he had to go through alone and misunderstood, thousands suffer today.[49]

Or, as Karl Jaspers wrote in his essay on *Man in the Modern Age* (1931):

> Beyond question there is a widespread conviction that human activities are unavailing; everything has become questionable; nothing in human life holds good; that existence is no more than an unceasing maelstrom of reciprocal deception and self-deception by ideologies. Thus the epochal consciousness becomes detached from being, and is concerned only with itself. One who holds such a view cannot but be inspired with a consciousness of his own nullity. His awareness of the end as annihilation is simultaneously the awareness that his own

existence is null. The epochal consciousness has turned a somersault in the void.[50]

These were but two of the voices that bemoaned the spiritual crisis that had descended upon Germany in the second half of the 1920s. To theirs one might also add those of Oswald Spengler, Thomas Mann, Martin Heidigger, Carl Gustav Jung and Sigmund Freud, to mention only a few of those who tried to come to terms with the demise of their cultural heritage. Their despair, however, was to find a powerful complement in a longing for regeneration that had far from exhausted itself in expressionism's quest for the 'new man' and that now manifested itself in the call for a 'conservative revolution'. A term first coined by the Austrian poet and playwright Hugo von Hofmannstahl in a famous speech he delivered at the University of Munich in January 1927, the 'conservative revolution' sought to overcome the estrangement of spirit (*Geist*) from life and to create a 'new German reality in which the entire nation could take part'.[51] Against the fragmentation of German social and political life Hofmannstahl sought to invoke the healing power of German culture. To be sure, it is unlikely that Hofmannstahl ever appreciated the political implications of what he was saying. Still, his lament over the estrangement of spirit from life struck a responsive chord among those who sought to enlist German culture in the struggle against the hated Weimar system. In its more blatant political manifestations, the doctrine of the conservative revolution was directed not merely against the individualistic and materialistic trappings of modern mass democracy but also against the reactionary social vision of oldline conservatives such as the newly elected chairman of the German National People's Party, Alfred Hugenberg. In a broader sense, the conservative revolution defined itself in essentially moral and spiritual terms and sought nothing less than the rebirth of the human spirit.[52]

The doctrine of the conservative revolution was only the tip of the seismic shift that began to take place in Germany's political culture in the second half of the 1920s. If, as Charles Maier has suggested in his *Recasting Bourgeois Europe*, the first decade after the end of the Second World War was characterized by 'the new primacy of interest politics and the eclipse of ideology',[53] then the last years of the Weimar Republic witnessed a sharp and powerful reaction against the increasingly prominent role that organized economic interests had come to play in the German political process. This reaction, which drew its impetus from the idealism of the German youth movement and the nationalism of patriotic organizations like the Stahlhelm and Young German Order (Jungdeutscher Orden), sought to reassert the primacy of the ideological and national moment in German political life over the purely economic and was directed specifically against the role that conservative economic interests like the National Federation of German Industry (Reichsverband der Deutschen Industrie) and the National Rural League (Reichs-Landbund) had played in Weimar's political and economic stabilization after 1924. In trying to give this sentiment a political content and a political direction, self-proclaimed conservative revolutionaries such as Edgar Jung and Ernst Jünger lay claim to the millenarian legacy of modernist culture and harnessed it to the hegemonic aspirations of Germany's anti-republican right.[54] The impulse that lay behind the notion of the conservative revolution, however, was anything but revolutionary. Not only were Jung and Jünger outspoken elitists who resolutely opposed every emancipatory impulse of the nineteenth and twentieth centuries, but they regarded the various manifestations of modernist culture as symptoms of the spiritual malaise that had descended upon their beloved Germany. The 'new nationalism' of Jung, Jünger and their associates on the radical right precluded any sort of compromise with the pluralistic character of Weimar culture.[55]

The conservative critique of modernist culture anticipated Nazi diatribes against the cultural decadence of the postwar age. To the Nazis, expressionist painting, jazz and the 'modern woman' were but specific symptoms of a overly cerebral and alien culture that had lost its contact with the *Volk*. To be sure, Nazism manifested that same disdain for the traditional bourgeois order that had found expression in the modernist revolt. By the same token, Nazism portrayed itself as a millenarian movement with rhetoric and imagery that had been either consciously or unconsciously appropriated from the modernist movement.[56] And the Nazis – like Jünger, Oswald Spengler and other champions of the conservative revolution – were fascinated with the extremely rapid pace of technological change that seemed to be taking place all around them and clearly sought to incorporate technological revolution into their vision of the German future.[57] Yet for all of its anti-bourgeois and millenarian rhetoric and for all of its fascination with the technological trappings of the modern age, there remained something inherently *spießbürgerlich*, or philistine, about the Nazi movement that emerged most clearly in its crusades against degenerate art, jazz and the emancipated woman of the 'Golden Twenties'. Nazism was not so much the political analogue to the modernist revolt as the liquidator of that revolt's cultural legacy.[58]

Although Weimar may have been synonymous with the spirit of modernity, cultural modernism contributed little to the political legitimation of Weimar democracy. The deracination of Germany's traditional bourgeois culture had created a sense of uprootedness on the part of the German *Bildungsbürgertum* that effectively militated against its acceptance, except perhaps on the most tenuous of terms, of the new republican order. By the same token, the modernist revolt, with its apocalyptic imagery and longing for the 'new man', placed the most important cultural movement of the early 1920s in fundamental opposition to the existing social and political order. As a result, neither those bourgeois humanists in whose name the republic had supposedly been founded nor those cultural modernists with whose cause the republic had become so closely identified were prepared to come to Weimar's defense in its hour of need. In the meantime, Weimar's close identification with cultural modernism provided its detractors with much of the negative symbolism they needed to mobilize popular sentiment against the new republican order.

Bedevilled by the twin legacy of defeat and revolution and beset by economic problems that were to prove insurmountable, the Weimar Republic never succeeded in developing the record of positive accomplishment that would have been necessary for it to legitimize itself in the eyes of Germany's disaffected middle classes.[59] At the same time, the forces of cultural reaction enjoyed a preponderant advantage in terms of the economic resources that were necessary to imprint their vision of Germany's national destiny upon society at large. The struggle for cultural hegemony, therefore, was never a struggle between equals but one in which the anti-republican right enjoyed a decisive material advantage in the form of the publishing houses they controlled and the financial support they received from conservative economic elites.[60] Moreover, this struggle took place on linguistic terrain that had been derived in large part from the corporatist vocabulary of nineteenth-century German conservatism, a factor that not only inhibited the republic's political legitimation but obliged its supporters to formulate their arguments on its behalf in a language that was inimical to their own basic principles.[61] To be sure, none of these factors, either by itself or taken together, provides a sufficient explanation of how and why Hitler came to power. Still, their net effect was to narrow the range of options that was available to Germany's political leaders in the last years of the Weimar Republic and to help create a moral and intellectual environment in which the rise of Nazism and Hitler's appointment as chancellor could take place.

NOTES

Dedicated with appreciation and affection to my colleagues in the John M. Olin Seminar on Political History at the National Humanities Center, 1988–9, but most of all to Franklin Ford, Sarah Maza and Patricia O'Brien.

1 On the analytical and explanatory potential of the concept of hegemony, see T. J. Jackson Lears, 'The concept of cultural hegemony: problems and

possibilities', *American Historical Review*, vol. 90 (1985), pp. 567–93. For all of its empirical shortcomings, David Abraham's work has made an important contribution by introducing the concept of hegemony into the theoretical discussion of how Weimar democracy failed and the Nazis came to power. Abraham, however, has used the concept almost exclusively as a category of political analysis and never addressed the broader cultural dimensions of the term. For varying statements of the Abraham thesis, see D. Abraham, 'State and classes in Weimar Germany', *Politics and Society*, vol. 7 (1977), pp. 229–66, and 'Constituting hegemony: the bourgeois crisis of Weimar Germany', *Journal of Modern History*, vol. 51 (1979), pp. 417–33, as well as the revised version of his controversial book, *The Collapse of the Weimar Republic*, 2nd edn (New York, 1986), esp. pp. 1–41. On the political dimensions of Weimar culture, see the work of two East German scholars B. Schraeder and J. Schebera, *The 'Golden' Twenties: Art and Literature in the Weimar Republic*, tr. K. Vanovich (New Haven, Conn., 1988).

2   In this respect, see the collection of essays published by M. Baker (ed.), *The Political Culture of the Old Regime* (Oxford, 1987), as well as the review essay by S. Maza, 'Politics, culture, and the origins of the French Revolution: notes on the Tocquevillian revival', *Journal of Modern History*, vol. 61 (1989), pp. 704–23. See also L. Hunt (ed.), *The New Cultural History* (Berkeley, Calif., 1989).

3   F. Stern, *The Politics of Cultural Despair: A Study in the Rise of the Germanic Ideology* (Berkeley, Calif., 1961), esp. pp. 326–61.

4   In this respect, see F. Stern, *The Failure of Illiberalism: Essays on the Political Culture of Modern Germany* (New York, 1971), esp. pp. ix–xxix. For a critique of the explanatory claims that Stern and others – most notably Ralf Dahrendorf in his classic study on *Society and Democracy in Germany* (Garden City, NY, 1967) – have made on behalf of the concept of illiberalism, see K. H. Jarausch, 'Illiberalism and beyond: German history in search of a paradigm', *Journal of Modern History*, vol. 55 (1983), pp. 268–84.

5   In his analysis of the rise of Nazism, Mosse completely discounts the role of economic developments. Neither the runaway inflation of the early 1920s nor the Great Depression of the early 1930s receive mention in Mosse's treatment of this problem. See G. L. Mosse, *The Crisis of German Ideology: Intellectual Origins of the Third Reich* (New York, 1964), pp. 237–93.

6   P. Gay, *Weimar Culture: The Outsider as Insider* (New York, 1968), esp. pp. xiii–xv.

7   G. Eley, 'What produces fascism: preindustrial traditions or a crisis of the capitalist state?', *Politics and Society*, vol. 12 (1983), p. 63.

8   One of the most important developments in recent German historiography is the amount of attention that has been devoted to the social and intellectual history of the German *Bildungsbürgertum*. For example, see K. Vondung, *Das wilhelminische Bürgertum. Zur Sozialgeschichte seiner Ideen* (Göttingen, 1976); W. Conze and J. Kocka (eds), *Bildungsbürgertum im 19. Jahrhundert*, Vols 1 and 4 (Stuttgart, 1985 and 1989).

9   In this respect, see the classic study by W. H. Buford, *The German Tradition of Self-Cultivation: 'Bildung' from Humboldt to Thomas Mann* (New York, 1975), as well as the more recent contribution by C. McClelland, 'The wise man's burden: the role of academicians in imperial German culture', in G. Stark and B. K. Lackner (eds), *Essays on Culture and Society in Modern Germany* (Arlington, Va, 1982), pp. 45–69. See also the exemplary study of higher education in the Second Empire by K. H. Jarausch, *Students, Society*

and Politics in Imperial Germany: The Rise of Academic Illiberalism (Princeton, NJ, 1982).

10 In this connection, see H. Mommsen, 'Die Auflösung des Bürgertums seit dem späten 19. Jahrhundert', in J. Kocka (ed.), *Bürger und Bürgerlichkeit im 19. Jahrhundert* (Göttingen, 1987), pp. 288–315, and more recently K. H. Jarausch, 'Die Krise des deutschen Bildungsbürgertums im ersten Drittel des 20. Jahrhunderts', in Kocka, *Bildungsbürgertum*, Vol. 4, pp. 180–205.

11 T. Mann, *Buddenbrooks*, tr. H. T. Lowe-Porter (New York, 1926), pp. 512–14. My reading of Mann is indebted to the seminal essay by G. Lukacs, 'In search of bourgeois man', in Lukacs, *Essays on Thomas Mann*, tr. S. Mitchell (London, 1964), pp. 13–46. A more recent and more successful attempt to relate the thematic content of Mann's works to the times in which he lived can be found in T. J. Reed, *Thomas Mann: The Use of Tradition* (Oxford, 1974).

12 On the extent of Wagner's influence on European culture, see the collection of essays published by D. C. Large and W. Weber (eds), *Wagnerism in European Culture and Politics* (Ithaca, NY, 1984). On the philosophical content of Wagner's operas, see L. J. Rather, *The Dream of Self-Destruction: Wagner's Ring and the Modern World* (Baton Rouge, La, 1979).

13 K. Löwith, *From Hegel to Nietzsche: The Revolution in Nineteenth-Century Thought*, tr. D. Green (New York, 1964), pp. 260–2, 303–5, 368–72.

14 The extent of Nietzsche's influence upon the thinking of Germany's political elites before the First World War remains a matter of some disagreement. See the conflicting interpretations in A. J. Mayer, *The Persistence of the Old Regime* (New York, 1981), pp. 275–324, and R. H. Thomas, *Nietzsche in German Politics and Society, 1890–1918* (Manchester, 1983), pp. 112–24.

15 Thomas, *Nietzsche*, pp. 96–111.

16 Nietzsche's influence on the cultural and intellectual life of late imperial Germany has yet to be systematically analyzed. For the best discussion of the apocalyptic implications of Nietzsche's thought, see T. Strong, *Friedrich Nietzsche and the Politics of Transfiguration* (Berkeley, Calif., 1975), esp. pp. 108–34, 218–93.

17 On the origins of Viennese modernism, see C. Schorske, *Fin-de-Siècle Vienna: Politics and Culture* (New York, 1981), esp. pp. xxvi–xxvii, 5–10, 116–20.

18 F. Ringer, *The Decline of the German Mandarins: The German Academic Community, 1890–1933* (Cambridge, Mass., 1969), esp. pp. 42–61, 253–304.

19 The indigenous roots of German modernism have received increasing attention in the last decade. In this connection, see J. McFarlane, 'Berlin and the rise of modernism, 1886–96', in M. Bradbury and J. McFarlane (eds), *Modernism 1890–1930* (Middlesex, 1974), pp. 105–19, as well as the excellent monographs on specific aspects of the modernist revolt in Germany by P. Paret, *The Berlin Secession: Modernism and its Enemies in Imperial Germany* (Cambridge, Mass., 1980); P. Jelavich, *Munich and Theatrical Modernism: Politics, Playwriting, and Performance 1896–1914* (Cambridge, Mass., 1985); and most recently M. Eksteins, *The Rites of Spring: The Great War and the Birth of the Modern Age* (Boston, Mass., 1989), esp. pp. 85–94.

20 For an introduction to the various strains of German expressionism, see the excellent collection of essays published by S. E. Bronner and D. Kellner (eds), *Passion and Rebellion: The Expressionist Heritage* (New York, 1988). Of particular interest is Kellner's own essay, 'Expressionism and rebellion',

pp. 3–39. See also the classic study by B. Myers, *The German Expressionists: A Generation in Revolt* (New York, n.d. [1957]). On the expressionist movement in drama and poetry, see W. Sokel, *The Writer in Extremis* (Stanford, Calif., 1959), and M. Patterson, *The Revolution in German Theatre 1900–1933* (London and Boston, Mass., 1981). On expressionist painting, see P. Selz, *German Expressionist Painting* (Berkeley, Calif., 1974).

21 D. Kellner, 'Expressionist literature and the dream of the "New Man"', in Bronner and Kellner, *Passion and Rebellion*, pp. 166–200.

22 For Kandinsky's artistic theories, see W. Kandinsky, *Concerning the Spiritual in Art*, tr. M. T. H. Sabler (New York, 1947). The apocalyptic dimension of Kandinsky's art has been explored by R.-C. Washton Long, *Kandinsky: The Development of an Abstract Style* (Oxford, 1980), esp. pp. 13–41, 75–87, 108–22. For further information, see M. Kester, 'Kandinsky: the owl of Minerva', in Bronner and Kellner, *Passion and Rebellion*, pp. 250–75, as well as the excellent monographs by P. Weiss, *Kandinsky in Munich: The Formative Jugendstil Years* (Princeton, NJ, 1979).

23 For an intriguing analysis of Marc's *Fate of the Animals*, see F. Levine, *The Apocalyptic Vision: The Art of Franz Marc as German Expressionism* (New York, 1979), pp. 76–103.

24 In this respect, see the perceptive essay by D. Langewiesche, 'Bildungsbürgertum und Liberalismus im 19. Jahrhundert', in Kocka, *Bildungsbürgertum*, Vol. 4, pp. 95–121, esp. pp. 109–13.

25 This point has been argued most persuasively by Eksteins, *Rites of Spring*.

26 On the German intellectual community and the First World War see Ringer, *Decline of the German Mandarins*, pp. 180–99. On Mann's response to the war, see Reed, *Mann*, pp. 179–225.

27 Eksteins, *Rites of Spring*, pp. 139–238.

28 D. Peukert, *Die Weimarer Republik: Krisenjahre der Klassischen Modern* (Frankfurt, 1987). For a summary of Peukert's argument, see his article, 'The Weimar Republic – old and new perspectives', *German History*, vol. 6 (1988), pp. 133–44.

29 For further information, see E. Portner, *Die Verfassungspolitik der Liberalen – 1919. Ein Beitrag zur Deutung der Weimarer Reichsverfassung* (Bonn, 1973). On Weber's role in drafting the Weimar constitution, see W. J. Mommsen, *Max Weber and German Politics, 1890–1920*, tr. M. S. Steinberg (Chicago, 1984), pp. 332–89.

30 M. Weber, 'Politics as a vocation', in H. Gerth and C. W. Mills (eds), *From Max Weber: Essays in Sociology* (London, 1948), p. 128. Weber's pessimism is a well-established feature of his intellectual profile. For differing explanations of this aspect of Weber's thought, see A. Mitzman, *The Iron Cage: An Historical Interpretation of Max Weber* (New York, 1970), and W. J. Mommsen, *The Age of Bureaucracy: Perspectives on the Political Sociology of Max Weber* (Oxford, 1974), pp. 95–115, as well as the recent study by L. Schaff, *Fleeing the Iron Cage: Culture, Politics, and Modernity in the Thought of Max Weber* (Berkeley, Calif., 1989).

31 For further information, see Ringer, *Decline of the German Mandarins*, pp. 62–66.

32 For differing interpretations of Mann's political views and their relation to his art, see K. Sontheimer, 'Thomas Mann als politischer Schriftsteller', *Vierteljahrshefte für Zeitgeschichte*, vol. 6 (1958), pp. 1–44, and H. Pross 'On Thomas Mann's political career', *Journal of Contemporary History*, vol. 2 (1967), pp. 64–79, as well as the more critical assessment of Mann's politics

by K. Bullivant, 'Thomas Mann and politics in the Weimar Republic', in K. Bullivant (ed.), *Culture and Society in the Weimar Republic* (Manchester, 1977), pp. 24–38.

33 See Gerald D. Feldman, 'The Weimar Republic: A problem of modernization?', *Archiv für Sozialgeschichte*, vol. 26 (1986), pp. 1–26.

34 See the classic study by S. Neumann, *Die deutschen Parteien. Wesen und Wandel nach dem Kriege* (Berlin, 1932), pp. 98–114.

35 Peukert, *Die Weimarer Republik*, pp. 87–111. On the limits of women's emancipation in the Weimar Republic, see U. Frevert, *Women in German History: From Bourgeois Emancipation to Sexual Liberation*, tr. S. M. Evans (Oxford, 1989), pp. 168–204.

36 For the best general surveys of Weimar culture, see W. Z. Laqueur, *Weimar: A Cultural History, 1918–1933* (New York, 1974), and J. Hermand and F. Trommler, *Die Kultur der Weimarer Republik* (Munich, 1978). See also the collections of essays published by L. Reinisch (ed.), *Die Zeit ohne Eigenschaften. Eine Bilanz der zwanziger Jahre* (Stuttgart, 1961); K. Bullivant (ed.), *Culture and Society in the Weimar Republic* (Manchester, 1977); and A. Phelan (ed.), *The Weimar Dilemma: Intellectuals in the Weimar Republic* (Manchester, 1985), as well as H. Pachter, *Weimar Etudes* (New York, 1982). For a useful survey of literature in the Weimar Republic, see R. Taylor, *Literature and Society in Germany, 1918–1945* (Sussex, 1980), pp. 1–177.

37 For further details, see S. Lamb, 'Intellectuals and the challenge of power: the case of the Munich "Räterrepublik"', in Phelan, *The Weimar Dilemma*, pp. 132–61, as well as the study by Joan Weinstein, *The End of Expressionism: Art and the November Revolution in Germany, 1918–19* (Chicago, 1990).

38 For example, see P. Jelavich, 'Popular dimensions of modernist elite culture: the case of theater in fin-de-siècle Munich', in D. La Capra and S. L. Kaplan (eds), *Modern European Intellectual History: Reappraisals and New Perspectives* (Ithaca, NY, and London, 1982), pp. 220–50.

39 On Piscator, see C. Innes, *Erwin Piscator's Political Theatre* (Cambridge, 1972), and J. Willett, *The Theatre of Erwin Piscator* (New York, 1979). On Brecht, see below in this chapter.

40 Above all else, see the classic chapter on reification and the consciousness of the proletariat in G. Lukacs, *History and Class Consciousness: Studies in Marxist Dialectics*, tr. R. Livingstone (Cambridge, Mass., 1968), pp. 83–222. For a short, though extremely useful elucidation of this work, see G. H. R. Parkinson, *Georg Lukacs* (London, 1977), pp. 34–57. On the place of this text in the development of Marxist humanism, see the seminal study by A. Arato and P. Breines, *The Young Lukacs and the Origins of Western Marxism* (New York, 1979), pp. 113–41, 190–209. See also L. Congdon, *The Young Lukacs* (Chapel Hill, NC, 1983), and M. Cluck, *Georg Lukacs and His Generation 1900–1918* (Cambridge, Mass., 1985).

41 Willett, *Theatre of the Weimar Republic*, pp. 73–92. See also Sokel, *Writer in Extremis*, pp. 192–226.

42 For further details, see L. E. Jones, *German Liberalism and the Dissolution of the Weimar Party System, 1918–1933* (Chapel Hill, NC, 1988), pp. 208–11, 225–6, 251–65.

43 That such a shift in sensibilities took place has been persuasively argued by J. Willett, most notably in *Art and Politics in the Weimar Period: The New Sobriety, 1917–1933* (New York, 1979), pp. 67–94.

44   On Grosz's political and artistic development from 1923 to 1933, see B. Lewis, *George Grosz: Art and Politics in the Weimar Republic* (Madison, Wis., 1971), pp. 175–210, and M. K. Flavell, *George Grosz: A Biography* (New Haven, Conn., 1988), pp. 36–71.

45   For the most explicit statement of Brecht's dramatic theories, see his essay 'The modern theatre in epic theatre', in J. Willett (ed.), *Brecht on Theatre: The Development of an Aesthetic* (New York, 1964), pp. 33–43. For a fuller discussion of Brecht's aesthetic, see J. Willett, *The Theatre of Bertholt Brecht: A Study from Eight Aspects* (New York, 1960).

46   The best introduction to Brecht's thought and intellectual development is still M. Esslin, *Brecht: The Man and His Work* (Garden City, NY, 1960). On the character of Brecht's Marxism, see E. Lunn, *Marxism and Modernism: An Historical Study of Lukacs, Brecht, Benjamin and Adorno* (Berkeley, Calif., 1982), pp. 119–27.

47   By far the most comprehensive analysis of the expressionist influence on Weimar cinema is L. Eisner, *The Haunted Screen: Expressionism in the German Cinema and the Influence of Max Reinhardt* (Berkeley, Calif., 1969).

48   In this respect, see the classic study by S. Kracauer, *From Caligari to Hitler: A Psychological History of the German Film* (Princeton, NJ, 1947), pp. 131–99. For a critique of Kracauer's assumptions and methodology, see T. Elsaesser, 'Film history and visual pleasure: Weimar cinema', in P. Mellencamp and P. Rosen (eds), *Cinema History – Cinema Practices* (Los Angeles, Calif., 1984), pp. 47–84. See also P. Petro, *Joyless Streets: Women and Melodramatic Representation in Weimar Cinema* (Princeton, NJ, 1989).

49   H. Hesse, *Steppenwolf*, tr. B. Creighton and updated by J. Mileck (New York, 1973), pp. 24–25.

50   K. Jaspers, *Man in the Modern Age*, tr. E. and C. Paul (London, 1951), p. 21.

51   H. von Hofmannstahl, *Das Schrifttum als geistiger Raum der Nation* ([Munich], [1927]), p. 31.

52   The classic study of the conservative revolution is A. Mohler, *Die konservative Revolution in Deutschland 1918–1932* (Stuttgart, 1950). On the limits of its utility as an analytical category, see K. von Klemperer, *Germany's New Conservatism: Its History and Dilemma in the Twentieth Century* (Princeton, NJ, 1968), pp. 227–31. See also the recent contributions by K. Bullivant, 'The conservative revolution', in Phelan, *Weimar Dilemma*, pp. 47–70, and the relevant chapter in J. Herf, *Reactionary Modernism: Technology, Culture, and Politics in Weimar and the Third Reich* (Cambridge, 1984), pp. 18–48.

53   C. S. Maier, *Recasting Bourgeois Europe. Stabilization in France, Germany, and Italy in the Decade after World War I* (Princeton, NJ, 1975), p. 484.

54   The relationship between German industry and the conservative intelligentsia has been well documented in J. Petzold, *Wegbereiter des deutschen Faschismus. Die Jungkonservativen in der Weimarer Republik* (Cologne, 1978). On the ideas of Jung and Jünger, see W. Struve, *Elites against Democracy: Leadership Ideals in Bourgeois Political Thought in Germany, 1890–1933* (Princeton, NJ, 1973), pp. 317–52, 377–414, as well as L. E. Jones, 'Edgar Julius Jung: the conservative revolution in theory and practice', *Central European History*, vol. 21 (1988), pp. 142–74.

55   For a perceptive analysis of the neo-conservative critique of cultural modernity, see G. Stark, *Entrepreneurs of Ideology: Neo-conservative Publishers in Germany, 1890–1933* (Chapel Hill, NC, 1981), pp. 172–211. A

somewhat more problematic analysis of this problem is to be found in D. Barnouw, *Weimar Intellectuals and the Threat of Modernity* (Bloomington, Ind., 1988). For further information, see Laqueur, *Weimar*, pp. 78–109.

56 Eksteins, *Rites of Spring*, p. 311.

57 Herf, *Reactionary Modernism*, pp. 189–216.

58 The extent to which Nazism is to be regarded as a modern or an anti-modern movement remains a matter of considerable debate. For example, see H. A. Turner, Jr, 'Fascism and modernization', in H. A. Turner, Jr (ed.), *Reappraisals of Fascism* (New York, 1975), pp. 117–39. In point of fact, Nazi cultural policy was so fragmented that historians have had a difficult time reducing it to any sort of common denominator. For specific indications of Nazi hostility toward the various manifestations of modernist culture, see M. Kater, 'Forbidden fruit? Jazz experience in the Third Reich', *American Historical Review*, vol. 94 (1989), pp. 11–43, and Frevert, *Women in German History*, pp. 207–16.

59 For further details, see H. Mommsen, *Die gespielte Freiheit. Der Weg der Republik von Weimar in den Untergang 1918 bis 1933* (Berlin, 1989).

60 For further details, see Stark, *Entrepreneurs of Ideology* pp. 15–57, and H. Holbach, *Das 'System Hugenberg'. Die Organisation bürgerlicher Sammlungspolitik vor dem Aufstieg der NSDAP* (Stuttgart, 1981).

61 In this respect, see two recent studies by T. Childers, 'Languages of liberalism: liberal political discourse in the Weimar Republic', in K. H. Jarausch and L. E. Jones (eds), *In Search of a Liberal Germany: Studies in the History of German Liberalism from 1789 to the Present* (Oxford, 1990), pp. 323–59, and 'The Social language of politics in Germany: the sociology of political discourse in the Weimar Republic', *American Historical Review*, vol. 95 (1990), pp. 331–58.

5 The Nature of German Liberalism

DIETER LANGEWIESCHE

The history of German liberalism is commonly portrayed as a history of decline. The stages of this decline seem to be obvious.

First of all, the attempt to create a national constitutional state failed in the revolution of 1848–9. The nation–state, which the liberals had longed for, actually emerged in 1871, but they were unsuccessful in giving it a parliamentary system of government based on the British model. In the revolution of 1918–19 Germany finally became a parliamentary democracy, where liberals worked out the constitution and where they had some influence in politics. But only 14 years later the fall into a barbarian dictatorship began, a regime that destroyed every vestige of liberality, and one to which the liberals were unable to provide an alternative.

It is therefore understandable that shortly after the end of the Nazi dictatorship the historian Friedrich C. Sell described the history of German liberalism, so closely interwoven as it was with the history of Germany as a whole, as a 'tragedy'. His important book, published in 1953,[1] was hardly noticed by German historians at the time, although it was, until recently, the only comprehensive treatment of the development of German liberalism since the eighteenth century. And yet his interpretation prevailed, and those who concerned themselves with the history of German liberalism usually assumed that there was a chain of capitulations that led up to the catastrophe that began in 1933.

Sell's interpretation of German history was closely bound up with the vicissitudes of his own life. He was descended from a respectable liberal family of scholars and he maintained this tradition until the National Socialists took away his chair of history in Kassel in 1937 and forced him to emigrate a year later. In 1948–9, one hundred years after the failure of the first attempt to create a liberal German state, Sell came back to live in West Germany. The book that he wrote after his return consisted of an appeal to the Germans to learn from their history and thereby secure the future of the young democracy, which, at that time, was far from being consolidated.

Although four decades of political experience and intensive research on German history have gone by since Sell wrote, his book is not yet obsolete. It has maintained its status as one of the first historical works to classify National Socialism by placing it within a broader historical perspective, thereby demonstrating that this German past, although giving rise to the Nazi dictatorship, has also displayed moral standards that may provide guidance in the present and for the future. But modern research has not followed the path marked out by Sell. Above all, the development of liberalism can no longer be seen as a one-way street that led inevitably to the catastrophe of 1933. German liberalism, we now know, was much more varied than anyone was able to see so soon after the national socialist dictatorship. Being aware of this variety has, however, made it more difficult to define precisely the nature of German liberalism over a period of two hundred years. What liberalism actually meant to people has to be determined for each epoch anew, because liberalism changed as society changed.[2] What liberals did and what they aspired to at the beginning of the nineteenth century is quite distinct from liberal aspirations in the highly industrialized society of the late twentieth century. So the nature of German liberalism can be appreciated only if we do not equate every change with deviation from its original goals.

Any history of German liberalism must also consider seriously the fact that 'Germany' was an invented word which may have served to conceal the extent of the territorial divisions within the new state.[3] The Holy Roman Empire was an assembly of an inestimable variety of independent territories, whose traditions were still alive when this empire collapsed between 1803 and 1806 under the pressure of Napoleonic rule. The so-called 'Deutscher Bund' (German Alliance), founded in 1815, did not go back to this territorial division. But there still existed 38 states which were uncompromisingly concerned about maintaining their sovereignty and gaining the loyalty of their people. Germany was no political reality. There did not even exist a political center where decisions for the whole nation were made. No German equivalent of Paris or London existed and those who wished to play an active role in politics had to do so within the state in which they lived. This situation influenced liberalism very deeply. Liberalism in Baden was different from liberalism in Prussia, in Mecklenburg, or in Austria.[4] Even in the German nation–state, which was created in 1870, the federal traditions remained very strong, although the dynamic new nation–state did lessen these tendencies. Only the national socialist dictatorship destroyed German federalism. But even that could not extinguish completely the old traditions. Federalism came back to life in 1945, when the Federal Republic of Germany was created; and it emerged again in the midst of the democratic movement in the German Democratic Republic in 1989, when plans were made to restore the old historical *Länder*. Not even four decades of a communist central state could delete the memory of a federal past. The historical traditions of states and regions have always played an important part in the history of Germany, and this is still true today. Historians of German liberalism should not overlook it.

It is not my intention here to survey the development of German liberalism in its different regions and epochs. Instead, I wish to describe some of the most predominant aspects and problems in their long-term development in order to determine how the nature of German liberalism has changed in the two hundred years of its history.

BELIEF IN THE FUTURE AND FEAR OF REVOLUTION

The ideals of German liberalism came into being in the eighteenth century, during the Enlightenment, whose optimistic view of the future became one of the leading characteristics of liberalism.[5] To be a liberal meant, until late in the nineteenth century, to believe in progress. No liberal doubted that the future would be better than the present and the past had been. This faith in the inevitability of progress made the liberals sure of the future and tolerant towards the shortcomings of the present. What could not be achieved immediately would surely be gained later. Revolutions seemed unnecessary therefore and, as experience proved, dangerous.

The reign of terror during the French Revolution was never forgotten by the liberals and each of the following revolutions, so numerous in European history between 1789 and 1848, brought back this bloody memory.[6]

Timely reform which would make revolutions unnecessary was the liberal therapy to immunize society against the danger of revolution. Only if all other methods of achieving changes proved to be ineffective would German liberals be prepared to accept a revolution. In fact, revolutionary reform was the worst thing that they could imagine. When a revolution did break out – without their participation and against their will – liberals always tried, as quickly as they could, to have it legalized and to bring it under parliamentary control. In place of revolutionary upheavals they proposed to achieve change through parliamentary resolutions. It was according to this guideline that liberals acted during the political disturbances which struck some German states in 1830, following the July Revolution in France; the guideline was again adhered to during the wave of revolution that swept through Europe in 1848–9, and again in the revolution of 1918–19.[7] By fighting for immediate election to a constitutional Parliament they tried to end the revolution and to make reforms possible at the same time. The refusal to continue the revolution did not mean that liberals were prepared to abandon reform; rejecting both revolution and stagnation, they adopted evolution as their guiding principle.

The belief that violent revolutionary upheavals could be avoided through a program of progressive political and social change was not confined to liberalism alone. Social democracy also developed an understanding of revolution, in which both peaceful and bloody changes in state and society were envisioned as possible alternatives.[8] But in practice Social Democrats aimed to achieve reforms without violence – which was shown most clearly in the revolution of 1918–19, when they played much the same role as liberals had 70 years before, in the revolution of 1848–9. Both were pushed to the front of a revolution that they had neither created nor wanted, and both tried as quickly as they could to lead the revolution into parliamentary reforms by election to a constitutional assembly. The Social Democrats refused to lead a revolutionary dictatorship in 1918–19 just as the liberals had refused before them.[9]

German liberalism and German socialism shared more than a willingness to work for progressive reform even at moments when revolutionary opportunities beckoned; the movements also agreed on some fundamental ideological beliefs, and the way that these were to be put into practice. Social Democrats inherited the liberal belief in a progressive future although, ironically, this belief was weakening among liberals when the problems of industrial society became more apparent towards the end of the nineteenth century. Liberalism had no convincing answers to the questions posed by industrialization because its ideology was rooted in pre-industrial times. The liberal belief in the inevitability of progress broke down completely when Germany was defeated in the First World War and the imperial regime collapsed – a breakdown that was compounded by the great inflation of the 1920s, which deprived the middle class of the material basis that had enabled them to live a 'middle-class' life.[10]

In spite of disappointments in the Second Empire, and in the face of criticism of it, liberals regarded it as the high point of German history and considered it to be their own creation; when it unexpectedly collapsed in 1918, they had nothing left to hope for. After the collapse, liberalism became so discredited that the new organizations that took up the work of the old liberal parties no longer dared to call themselves liberal. The names by which they now chose to identify themselves were the Deutsche Demokratische Partei (German Democratic Party) and the Deutsche Volkspartei (German Peoples Party). The new names did not stand for new visions of the future, however, and fewer and fewer people believed that the liberal parties could lead Germany into a better future. The last free elections to the Parliament of the Weimar Republic, which were held in November 1932, brought both parties a combined total of only 2.9 per cent of the vote. The history of liberalism and the liberal parties as the main proponents of progress was over.

LIBERALISM AND BOURGEOIS SOCIETY: THE *BÜRGERLICHE GESELLSCHAFT*

The individual stood at the center of the liberal belief in progress and the attainment of individual rights was the primary goal of liberal organizations. But the question of *how* to secure individual rights was a controversial subject that was hotly debated even amongst liberals, and the solutions that were conceived of changed throughout the nineteenth and twentieth centuries along with the changing nature of the problems. The main goal of liberalism was to preserve the individual's freedom of decision making. The group must come second to the individual. This conviction distinguished liberalism from nationalism and socialism, the other dominant ideologies to emerge in the nineteenth century. It is true that liberals in Germany, as in other European states, cooperated closely with national movements and ideologies, but their insistence on the primacy of individual rights always separated their ideals from those who placed collective groups such as the people, or the nation, or class at the center. Liberalism gave up its basic convictions and changed its character when this dividing line was crossed. This happened in Germany (and not only there) in the last decades before the First World War, when many liberals adopted the ideology of the imperial regime. Here the needs of the nation were placed before the rights of the individual.[11]

In the nineteenth century liberalism conceived of a society as 'civil' if it guaranteed the same rights to all people and accepted the liberty of the individual as its supreme aim. It aimed to create not the *bourgeois* but the *citoyen*. The German language hides a distinction of fundamental importance here because the word *Bürger* can mean either 'bourgeois' or 'citizen'. In fact, *Bürger* can actually mean three different things. First, until sometime after the mid-nineteenth century, it could refer to the inhabitant of a town who enjoyed several rights in that town (and only in that specific town). These rights could determine his whole life. Only those who enjoyed the civic rights offered by a town could, for example, marry, or run a workshop on their own, or participate in elections of municipal institutions and – last, but not least – could claim support in cases of emergency.[12] Second, since the eighteenth century, *Bürger* could refer to the 'citizen' (*citoyen*) of a state in which the equality of rights for all those deemed to be citizens is recognized. And, third, the words *Bürger* and *Bürgertum* took on the meaning of the class terms *bourgeois* and *bourgeoisie* sometime in the course of the nineteenth century.[13] So the *Bürger* in nineteenth-century Germany could appear as a person in three ways: as the inhabitant of a town he enjoyed a variety of privileges; these were defended against egalitarian visions of the 'society of citizens' but, as *citoyen*, he tried to turn these visions into reality; and as a *bourgeois* he could finally come out against the egalitarian demand of the *citoyen* and the corporative thinking of the townspeople.

Liberalism became, in the first half of the nineteenth century, the political synonym for the ideal society of citizens that the *citoyen* sought to achieve. This ideal was directed against everything that limited the liberty of the individual. It was directed not only against absolutism and the privileges of the aristocracy, but also against the corporative privileges of manual workers' or merchants' guilds and, finally, against the preferential treatment of any particular religious denomination. To call oneself liberal meant, therefore, that one wished to create a society in which each citizen would enjoy equality before the law and in the practice of politics.

Theoretically, this liberal program was a revolutionary one because it demanded that society be radically changed. But practically, it developed into a long-term educational program that permitted inequality to continue for the present. Although such liberals believed that equality before the law should become reality at once, they also insisted that political equality could be granted only when certain conditions had been met.

The economically independent, educated man was the liberal ideal of the *citoyen*. In the liberal imagination, women did not belong to that section of the population which could become, either now or in the future, emancipated members of bourgeois society, and their thinking on this subject did not begin to change until late in the nineteenth century.[14] Liberals also preferred to establish a graduated scale of political rights for men in order to ensure the security of the state and society against sudden or irrational change. This explains why liberals attempted to circumscribe the political influence of those who were lacking either property or education by creating different grades of voters. This was not specifically German. During the revolutions of 1848, liberals throughout Europe tried to prevent universal, equal and direct elections of representatives. But in the end they had to submit to the bourgeois and proletarian democrats who claimed the unlimited right to vote for all men.[15] When, after the failure of the revolution, the German states eliminated the democratic right to vote, liberals welcomed the step. Even when the democratic right to vote was restored, first in 1867 in the Norddeutscher Bund, and later in 1871 when the Second Empire was created, the liberals were not responsible. Here the Prussian secretary, Bismarck, was the moving force: he used this initiative as one of his political weapons in his campaign against Austria, pulling the national movement onto the side of Prussia.[16] But in most of the German states and towns the right to vote was not made democratic until 1918. Liberals did nothing to bring about reform. On the contrary, they defended the existing system wherever they could, and it was only when the democratic suffrage could no longer be avoided that liberals would bring themselves to accept it.

Liberals did not see any contradiction between the egalitarian ideals of the bourgeois society of which they dreamed and their insistence on restricting the right to vote. They saw no contradiction because their belief in progress led them to envision rights as an evolutionary concept; theirs was a program of gradual improvement through education. Their message was: become bourgeois and you will become a member of bourgeois society with full political rights. Although the *citoyen* was to be found at the heart of the liberal conception, he was required to have property and education in order to qualify for the title.

This model of the state emerged in the first half of the nineteenth century and was therefore conceived on the basis of experience in pre-industrial society. Early liberals did not envision a bourgeois society characterized by class distinctions, but rather a 'classless' bourgeois society.[17] They wanted to destroy the old corporative society, but they did not wish to replace it with one they regarded as dissipated and *laissez-faire*. The mission of German liberalism was not to produce the conditions in which it would be possible for industrial capitalism to see the light, nor did German liberals propose to act as the mouthpiece of the industrialists. Instead, they reflected deeply on how Germany could avoid an English-style process of industrialization. The liberalism of the Manchester School found no support among the early German liberals. Their ideal economic unit was the small, middle-class business. They wished to create the conditions in which as many men as possible would be in a position to become the 'bourgeois' breadwinner of their family ('bourgeois' in this context meaning secure but moderate). The liberals, in fact, always refused to apply their claim for equal rights to the distribution of property, for they preferred to see property allocated in such a way that there would not be vast differences between the possessions of individuals. Carl von Rotteck, one of the best-known early German liberals opposed, like others, an 'accumulation of enormous industrial and financial capital in individual hands'. That, he said, would create an 'ugly aristocracy of money', consigning 'the mass of the nation to be dependent for their livelihood' and therefore doom 'the individual person to be completely at the goodwill or mercy or egoistic calculation of a big owner'.[18]

But even liberals did not know how to create a society in which the extremes of riches and poverty could be avoided. They simply hoped that if the old corporative barriers were removed, people would somehow become more reasonable. At the same time they were not afraid to have the state interfere in regulating the economy in order to prevent the distortions of wealth that were produced by competition, they put their trust in the ability of free men to build up a society in which progress would ultimately work for the benefit of all.

One should not regard this liberal vision as mere window-dressing, as an ideology that was cleverly designed to disguise the real aim of creating a society based on class distinctions. The model was developed during a time when large companies were rare and when many Germans wished to avoid the 'English way' of industrialization. The early liberal Utopian dream of a classless bourgeois society was born under pre-industrial circumstances and, ironically for those who held on to it, the model did not turn into an ideology until further economic developments had rendered it obsolete. In the middle of the nineteenth century the dynamic process of industrialization was initiated that would make Germany one of the leading industrial powers in the world by the century's end. This unexpected development meant that liberalism would have to accommodate its political and social visions of the future to the realities of the industrial society that was actually emerging in Germany. Liberals now began the painful process of abandoning their Utopian dream of a classless bourgeois society. They were not able, however, to develop a new model that held out the prospect of an adequate substitute for the socially integrative promises of the Utopian vision. This became one of the main weaknesses of the liberal model, and one which they never succeeded in overcoming.[19]

Until the 1860s many liberals looked to the possibility of cooperatives as instruments that might yet enable them to realize their old ideal of economic independence. The idea was that the cooperatives would place the earlier liberal Utopian dream of a society of owners on a new collective foundation.[20] This new plan envisioned that a group of people, not an individual, might be able to realize the dream of an independent 'bourgeois' livelihood. The young socialist labor movement was also attracted to the idea of cooperatives, seeing in them a real alternative to capitalism. But the great hopes that some liberals and socialists had for the cooperatives never materialized. They did not turn into anti-capitalistic bastions – neither for the socialists nor for small and middle-class businesses.

The last 30 years of the nineteenth century witnessed the emergence of new political and social models that were based on recent experience of the realities of a class-dominated society. Within the socialist labor movement in Germany the Marxist model of class struggle became more predominant than in other European countries.[21] The liberal movement, on the other hand, became more 'bourgeois' than it had been before, and it gradually lost the broad social basis that it had formerly enjoyed: workers began to withdraw from liberal parties in the 1870s.[22]

But the social visions of the movement were changing as well. Blinded by the bright future that seemed to be promised by the great economic boom of the 1860s, many liberals simply chose to ignore the poverty that surrounded them. Economic prosperity, they believed, would eventually resolve all social problems. Anyone who failed to overcome his difficulties by adapting to industrialization came to be regarded as a moral failure. This strict individualism connected the older liberalism of the pre-industrial period with the newer liberalism of the initial phase of industrialization. Participation in 'bourgeois society' was still seen as an individual achievement and as part of a process of education. But more and more people came to regard this interpretation as a bourgeois excuse for failing to address their problems, as the decline in liberal fortunes in elections to the Reichstag and to the Landtag demonstrates.

Although the German liberal parties became more and more bourgeois, they did not adopt the philosophy of the Manchester School, even in the late nineteenth century. The political atmosphere of Germany was too full of social questions for any party to avoid them, and liberals played their part in formulating those sociopolitical reforms by which Germany became the pioneer of active social intervention by the state.[23] German liberalism, though, did not have a unified sociopolitical policy. A number of famous liberals influenced the public with a variety of speeches and writings. Heinrich von Treitschke is a good example of how some members of the liberal educated classes tried to bring the old liberal model of society into line with the new reality of industrial capitalism. Such liberals divested themselves of the older liberal vision of an egalitarian bourgeois society and promoted the idea of state intervention to improve the condition of the working class. But they knew that such intervention would not eliminate inequality. Treitschke was not afraid of calling the society of imperial Germany a class society, and he was able to do so in good conscience because he believed that inequality is not only inevitable but necessary in order to produce the achievements of an elite culture: 'Millions must till the soil and forge and plane, that a few thousand can research, paint and rule. Socialism tries in vain to eliminate this cruel recognition by empty cries of rage.'[24]

Treitschke became the mouthpiece of those among the educated classes who saw the liberal vision of a bourgeois society coming into being in the capitalist class society of the present. Social inequality now came to be regarded as an integral component of this society, which represented a radical revision of the early liberal model of society. Those who shared Trietschke's view continued to claim precedence for the educated classes, however, because they were to perform the superior task of making culture possible in this new, industrialized, capitalist society. Through this ideology, those for whom Trietschke spoke were prepared to conform with the changing conditions of an industrial society. But at the same time, they abstained from making liberalism more attractive to all sections of the population, choosing instead to hold out the prospect of a bright future to those who had the academic qualifications to realize it. Only those who became the chosen few could expect to reap the fruit of their labors within the 'bourgeois society' envisioned by these liberals.

This elitist program was not the only one sketched by liberals during the period of industrialization in Germany. They offered various answers to the challenges posed by the emergence of a new mass society.[25] Some of them, especially professors and high officials, engaged in intensive debates through which they attempted to create parties, mobilize the bureaucracy, or create public support for social reforms. This process helped to lower the barriers that divided liberalism and socialism, which made it easier for the liberal parties and the social democrats to cooperate as they began to do during the First World War, and as they continued to do during the Weimar Republic. Liberal social reformers began to reconsider their individualistic model and to propose collectivist social policies. The difficulties which the liberal parties confronted in attempting to adapt themselves to the new political and social conditions of the Second Empire became apparent during the 1880s when they were faced with the anti-socialist laws and with social welfare legislation. It is true that left-wing liberals voted against these anti-socialist laws, which were designed by Bismarck to destroy the socialist labor movement. But at the same time they rejected the social welfare legislation that marked the beginning of modern social insurance, health insurance, accident insurance and retirement and disability insurance. On the other hand, right-wing liberals were partly responsible for making possible these landmarks in the history of social reform. Yet it was liberalism's right wing that ensured the non-liberal anti-socialist laws of a majority in the Reichstag.

Political progress and social reform did not necessarily coincide with German liberalism, therefore, during the Second Empire. Those liberals who were close to the conservative power elites, such as the National Liberal Party, supported the social insurance policy initiatives of the state. But those who wished to reform the state itself, as did the left-wing liberals and the Social Democrats, refused to entrust it with such measures out of a fear of strengthening the conservative foundations of the state by providing it with modern socio-political equipment.

Until the First World War, liberals did not regard either the Reich or the individual states as the most important test cases in the cause of social progress. The towns were their primary concern, but, in spite of this, the great achievements of municipal liberalism have scarcely been considered in modern research.[26]

Municipal liberalism was deeply involved in resolving the large social problems that arose from the enormous increase in population during the latter half of the nineteenth century. Towns began to take on many new tasks. The construction of new waterworks and a conductive sewage system formed an important part of this expansion, as did the organization of street cleaning and refuse collection, the establishment of gasworks and power stations as well as the building of a tram system. Towns also provided educational institutions and cultural amenities such as new schools, museums, theaters, public swimming baths and parks. Contemporaries referred to this program as 'municipal socialism' in order to characterize the new dimensions of municipal politics.

Liberals played their part in this program and encouraged these policies. Liberalism had always found its strongest support in the towns, and in the second half of the nineteenth century it became deeply engaged in the political and social processes – an engagement that has scarcely been noticed in studies of German liberalism. In Germany the roots of what might be referred to as social liberalism are to be discovered in the towns and not in the politics of the Reich or the Land. And in the towns liberalism tried to bring its model of a bourgeois society into harmony with the conditions of a modern industrial society. In the course of this undertaking liberals again showed that they always had the *bourgeois* in view when they referred to the *citoyen*. Therefore they defended vigorously the undemocratic regulations that governed the right to vote in the towns. Nowhere was this right as limited as it was in the towns: sometimes only one-tenth of those who had the right to vote in elections to the Reichstag had the same right in local elections.

German towns were, in effect, walled in by the absence of democratic suffrage and within these walls liberals were better able to maintain their control of the political process than they could have done through elections to either the Reichstag or the Landtag. Only this very restrictive political system, by which liberals delayed the growth of stronger representation by Social Democrats in the municipal Parliaments, made it possible for municipal liberalism to promote the cause of sociopolitical reform. The towns seemed to offer a last refuge, where liberals could defend equally their ideal of a bourgeois society against both the superior strength of the state and the advance of social democracy. The development of social insurance by the state during the Second Empire had begun to undermine the local foundation upon which liberalism had come to depend; then, during the Weimar Republic, the tendency to centralize social policy continued and, with democratic suffrage now established in the towns, the old foundation was further weakened. When social policy provisions became even more extensive following the Second World War, liberal parties completely lost their stronghold in the towns. In the cities of the Federal Republic, the Freie Demokratische Partei (Free Democratic Party) has played only a minor role as a political force. The loss of its stronghold in local politics severely weakened its traditional base of support and altered the nature of German liberalism.

Before this decline became precipitous, a new form of social liberalism began to emerge that was less directly dependent upon control of the towns. In the early twentieth century some liberals on the left tried to create a new social basis for the old liberal ideal of a free individual. They supported equal rights for both the employer and the employee and they approved of a further extension of social welfare legislation. This made it easier for Social Democrats and liberals to cooperate and it was, in fact, upon this form of cooperation that the Weimar Republic was founded and upon which its ability to survive later depended. These attempts at more social openness died, however, with the decline of the liberal parties following 1920, and after the Second World War the FDP did not take them up. The sociopolitical basis of the Federal Republic was not only created without the help, but usually against the opposition of the Liberal Party. In the 1960s, the FDP at last took up the cause of sociopolitical modernization.[27] But even then the party failed to become the driving force behind political reforms, as it insisted on warning against the creation of an oversized welfare state. Demanding as little regulation as possible by the state in order to give the individual the greatest possible liberty places the FDP clearly in a line of continuity that stretches back to early liberalism. But what was at that time a liberal vision of the future promising greater liberty for all people, is now simply a policy of restriction. Few people today are attracted to this vision, with the result that the FDP must constantly be concerned that it will fail to receive the necessary 5 per cent of the popular vote at the elections to the Bundestag or the Parliaments of Länder.

WOMEN, CATHOLICS, WORKERS: PROBLEM GROUPS OF LIBERALISM

The liberal vision of the future in the nineteenth century was directed to all men, but not to women. Very few men, and not many women, claimed political equality of gender in the first few decades of that century.[28] Even the gymnastics clubs and choral societies, which were at that time the largest groups of organized opposition, did not admit women as members. So it is not really surprising that early liberals proposed to exclude women from their program of political emancipation. All men were similarly exclusionist, no matter what political organization they supported. But for liberals, the exclusion of women raised some fundamental philosophical questions. At the heart of the liberal model of state and society was the premise that all human beings have the same rights. But at that time they were convinced that women in married life must be legally subordinated to men. For liberal theorists, marriage and family formed the foundation of the state, and they believed that the state itself consisted of a mass of family units, in which the male head of the unit played the part of *citoyen*. But how can a state be legally egalitarian when it rests on a foundation of basic inequality of gender? This problem disturbed liberal theorists, and they attempted to resolve it through their definition of marriage: marriage should be a contract between two people, in which each party has certain rights. The 'law of nature', which determines that the man should be at the head of the family, ought to take precedence over the legal principle of equality. Therefore, liberal theory postulated a patriarchal marriage and family and yet retained its ideal of a legally egalitarian society. The National Liberal Party continued to adhere to this position at the end of the nineteenth century, and they consequently experienced no discomfort when the *Bürgerliche Gesetzbuch* (civil law) in 1900 awarded decision making in marriage to the man.

The liberals also defended male power regarding the right to vote. When, in 1908, women were allowed by law to join political parties, some leading feminists became committed to left-wing liberal organizations. But only a few liberals, such as Friedrich Naumann, claimed that women should be given the right to vote. But these few proponents failed to succeed even among left-wing liberals, where the women's movement encountered less disapproval than from other bourgeois parties. Liberals finally accepted the political equality of women only in the revolution of 1918–19, when they could no longer find a way to avoid it.

German liberalism came into being as a movement of Protestant males. Catholics sometimes voted for one of the liberal parties, but they remained a small minority. By the middle of the nineteenth century, if not earlier, 'liberal' and 'Catholic' had come to suggest conflicting political philosophies.[29] At that time, Catholicism started an intellectual and organizational renovation, with the result that the Catholic church became a tough ideological competitor for the liberals. In Germany liberalism was not only a political program, but also a laical ideology that would not tolerate the claim of a church to absolute truth. This explains why liberalism and Catholicism became bitter rivals when the Second Empire became a denominationally neutral state. Catholics considered the so-called *Kulturkampf* between state and church a liberal attempt to use the sanctions of the state to achieve a secular modern age. Liberals were regarded as the leading political representatives of the modernity which was so vehemently opposed by the Catholic church, as well as some other elements of German society. When Germany emerged as a dynamic industrial country in the second half of the nineteenth century, the dramatic social changes that this involved were too much for many people to bear. A large section of society could therefore be found to support those who opposed this modernity.[30] Catholicism profited from this. They created a broad network of organizations that strongly supported the *Zentrum*, a Catholic party formed when the German empire was constituted. Liberal parties could never find their way into this Catholic milieu. While in the eyes of the Catholics these parties remained political advocates of the Protestant nation-state of 1871, in the eyes of the liberals the Catholics were not sufficiently committed to the cause of the nation to be regarded as trustworthy. Liberals regarded the *Zentrum* as the political weapon of a supranational Catholic church. During the First World War these antagonisms were kept under restraint, and during the Weimar Republic the liberal parties and the *Zentrum* often worked together in government. But the organizational and ideological separation between liberalism and Catholicism remained and this division formed one of the historical continuities in Germany's political culture. Liberal parties were Protestant, but fewer and fewer Protestants actually voted for liberal parties. In attempting to attract the Protestant vote, liberals had to compete with social democracy, conservative parties and, later, with the National Socialists. The meaning of this denominational dividing line diminished in importance only in the secularized society of the Federal Republic. And even now the line is still visible.

The liberal dream envisioned a society of the *Mittelstand*, but this was not a vision of social exclusiveness: in time, liberals believed, everyone might be incorporated into the *Mittelstand*, thus producing a classless society. Throughout the first half of the nineteenth century, and well into the 1870s, this vision of a new bourgeois society had widespread appeal. In fact, men from all social strata supported liberal-inspired organizations. [31] And this included working men: around 1870, liberal unions still had about as many members as both socialist associations. In the first two elections to the Reichstag, the two labor parties combined were not able to win more than two seats. At that time it was far from clear that liberalism would lose the competition for the support of the working-class voter. The decline in working-class support for liberalism occurred in imperial Germany, and the process described above, in which the liberals became 'more bourgeois' and through which they attempted to utilize the new anti-socialist legislation to turn the socialists into outlaws goes far to explain this phenomenon. The 'class struggle from above' helped to inspire the formation of working-class organizations. All later liberal attempts to win back the support of the workers failed. Workers voted socialist, Catholic, or conservative; a great many even voted

National Socialist – but they rarely voted liberal. Liberal parties were never able to overcome the loss of their working-class support, which declined rapidly in the final decades of the nineteenth century and failed to revive even after 1945.

LIBERALISM AND 'NATION'

Until the first decade of the Second Empire, liberalism was more than merely a political party: it represented a national movement which was made up of numerous organizations.[32] The liberals were the spokesmen of nationalism, which offered such great opportunities to integrate the fragmented political and social forces of society that no other grand ideology of the nineteenth century could compete with it. The goals of a nation–state and progress were regarded as two sides of the same coin. Until a German nation–state was brought into existence the term was suggestive of a broad, progressive vision of the future: an end to borders that prevented the free movement of people, goods and ideas; improvement of living conditions for all; equal political rights for all men; and a strong Parliament, where representatives of the people would determine the politics of the state. Which territories the nation–state should contain and which political institutions it should incorporate were hotly debated subjects; but everyone shared the belief that this new state would become an instrument of progress. This is why liberals, democrats and socialists found the concept of the nation–state to be so attractive, in contrast to the conservatives – who finally brought themselves to accept it only after it had become a reality.

Liberalism did not demand the creation of a nation–state when the movement began; originally located in the towns, and fixing their attention on their own state, liberals attempted to institute civic and state reforms, and it was only when the various German states failed to respond favorably to these calls that liberals began to turn to the idea of the nation–state. Before long, the slogan of the 'nation–state' was trumpeted by liberals and democrats as an alternative to bureaucratic absolutism. Just how powerful a force nationalism could be was shown for the first time in the revolution of 1848–9, and the demonstration was repeated in the 1860s. Even Bismarck discovered that military force was insufficient to accomplish his Norddeutscher Bund in 1867, and then the Second Empire in 1871, against the wishes of Austria, other German governments, conservatives and all *Großdeutsche*.[33] He had to rely on the support of the broad national movement, of which the liberals formed the spearhead and were its most important advocates, inside and outside of the Parliaments. Together with them, Bismarck carried through the constitution first of the Norddeutscher Bund and then of the Second

Empire. Both sides had to make considerable compromises, which resulted in a splitting of liberalism into two parties. The right wing amalgamated with the National Liberals and supported Bismarck. The left wing formed itself into the Deutsche Fortschrittspartei (German Progress Party) and went into opposition. Both liberal parties, even the left-wing liberals, had positive attitudes towards the nation–state. They differed only in their willingness to compromise in the debates concerning the new constitution.

The National Liberals were not satisfied with the constitution because they had hoped to establish a true parliamentary system. They did not succeed. However, eventually they gave their consent to the constitution, leading some to argue that this capitulation was due to the weakness of the young labor movement. But this is not true. The National Liberals were simply convinced that the economic strength of the bourgeoisie would inevitably change the political structure of the nation–state in favor of liberalism: those who dominated society would eventually dominate the state. This was the firm conviction of the National Liberals, whose thinking was materialistic, not idealistic.

Developments in the first decade after the foundation of the Norddeutscher Bund seemed to confirm the validity of the National Liberal viewpoint. One of the great phases of reform in German history now began. Under the direction of the Reichstag, the legal and economic system of the German states was reformed and unified in only a few years. Standardized weights and measures were a part of this, as was the liberalization of the law. For the first time in Germany individuals were given the freedom to marry whom they wished, when they wished, or to open a commercial enterprise without asking for permission to do so. Contemporaries admired the period, referring to it as the 'liberal era': the liberals had called for and pushed through these reforms; the National Liberals had developed into a kind of ruling party without becoming formally involved in government.[34]

This turbulent phase of reform ended abruptly in 1878 when Bismarck abandoned his connection with the National Liberals and initiated the 'Second *Reichsgründung*' by securing the support of the Conservatives and the Catholic *Zentrum* instead. The liberals were shocked by this radical change. They had accepted political compromises because they were convinced that progress was on their side and that in the long run they would be able to carry out their program. The economic stagnation that began to be felt in 1873 had shattered liberal faith in the nation–state as the instrument that would guarantee permanent economic progress; now, in 1878, Bismarck's change of strategy shattered their faith in political progress. The liberal parties lost the most as a result of these developments: the public had learned to identify them with hopes that had now been dashed. The first great crisis that confronted the new nation–state had discredited German liberalism, and it never succeeded in regaining lost ground. Liberalism and progress ceased to be synonymous in the minds of most Germans.[35]

The political meaning of nationalism also began to be transformed, as what had been an ideology of the Left came to be captured by the Right.[36] This process was already becoming apparent during the period of unification, but after the 1870s it became obvious. Nationalism slipped away from the liberal leadership and became a political tool of the non-liberal parties and associations. Yet it remained an extremely effective ideology and a new, popular nationalism emerged which enabled conservatism to modernize in the age of imperialism.[37]

No other party, movement, or ideology was as devastated by the change in the meaning of nationalism as were the liberals. When the early liberal ideal of a bourgeois society lost its persuasive power during the emergence of the new industrial capitalism, liberals substituted the nationalist ideal for it – and their existence had come to depend upon it. In their use of nation and nation–state as the only integrative ideological terms the liberals tried to bind together their political clientèle and to revive the struggle for reform. But they cherished false hopes. The liberals could not compete with the new nationalist associations, neither in Wilhelminian times nor during the Weimar Republic.[38] Nevertheless, even in the first decade of the Federal Republic's existence, the liberals remained attached to the nation–state of 1871.[39] This is not really surprising when one considers that liberals regarded their predecessors as having been responsible for the creation of this state, which they regarded as the high point of German history. The FDP finally divested themselves of this tradition in the 1960s with the creation of the *neue Ostpolitik* (New Eastern Policy).

WHERE ARE THE LIBERAL TRADITIONS TODAY?

As already suggested, the Freie Demokratische Partei clearly fits within many of the dominant historical traditions of German liberalism. But these traditions are not embodied in the FDP alone. Some of the central ideas contained within the historical development of German liberalism have become constitutional standards in the Federal Republic. This is certainly true of those fundamental liberal objectives – that the constitution should guarantee individual liberty and give all citizens the chance to participate in the process of decision making. Liberalism never developed a similarly coherent strategy for the forming of economic and social structures, or for laying the foundations of everyday behavior. Generally, it can be said that liberalism has had an extraordinary influence on the formation of modern German society, in as much as it created a network of political, social, economic and cultural principles. In this respect one can speak of a renaissance of liberalism after the Second World War – but a renaissance that was not, and is not, tied to individual parties. This is a reason for optimism.

NOTES

1 F. C. Sell, *Die Tragödie des deutschen Liberalismus* (Stuttgart, 1953; 2nd edn, Baden-Baden, 1981).
2 cf. esp. J. J. Sheehan, *German Liberalism in the Nineteenth Century* (Chicago and London, 1978); D. Langewiesche, *Liberalismus in Deutschland* (Frankfurt, 1988).
3 See the impressive essay by J. J. Sheehan, 'What is German history? Reflections of the role of the nation in German history and historiography', *Journal of Modern History*, vol. 53 (1981), pp. 1–23.
4 cf. the essays in D. Langewiesche (ed.), *Liberalismus im 19. Jahrhundert: Deutschland im europäischen Vergleich* (Göttingen, 1988), ch. I.
5 cf. F. Valjavec, *Die Entstehung der politischen Strömungen in Deutschland* (Munich, 1951; reprint Düsseldorf, 1978); more recently D. Langewiesche, 'Spätaufklärung und Frühsozialismus in Deutschland', in E. Müller (ed.), '... *aus der anmuthigen Gelehrsamkeit'. Tübinger Studien zum 18. Jahrhundert* (Tübingen, 1988), pp. 67–80; J. J. Sheehan, 'Wie bürgerlich war der deutsche liberalismus?' in D. Langewiesche (ed.), *Liberalismus im 19. Jahrhundert*, pp. 28–44.
6 M. Neumüller, *Liberalismus und Revolution: Das Problem der Revolution in der deutschen Geschichtsschreibung des 19. Jahrhunderts* (Düsseldorf, 1973).
7 C. H. Church, *Europe in 1830: Revolution and Political Change* (London, 1983), pp. 95–106, 143–90; Langewiesche, *Liberalismus in Deutschland*, pp. 39–64, 251–60; L. E. Jones, *German Liberalism and the Dissolution of the Weimar Party System, 1918–1933* (Chapel Hill, NC, and London, 1988), pp. 15–29.
8 S. Miller, *Das Problem der Freiheit in Sozialismus: Freiheit, Staat und Revolution in der Programmatik der Sozialdemokratie von Lassalle bis zum Revisionismusstreit* (Frankfurt, 1964).
9 cf. the essays of Chapter 2 in R. Fletcher (ed.), *Bernstein to Brandt: A Short History of German Social Democracy* (London, 1987); Jones, *German Liberalism*, pp. 15–29; Langewiesche, *Liberalismus in Deutschland*, pp. 251–3.
10 cf. ibid., pp. 227–72; Jones, *German Liberalism*, pp. 162–222, 251–65.
11 W. J. Mommsen, 'Wandlungen der liberalen Idee im Zeitalter des Imperialismus', in K. Holl and G. List (eds), *Liberalismus und imperialistischer Staat: Der Imperialismus als Problem liberaler Parteien in Deutschland 1890–1914* (Göttingen, 1975), pp. 109–47; L. Gall, 'Südenfall des liberalen Gedankens oder Krise der bürgerlich-liberalen Bewegung? Zum Verhältnis von liberalismus und Imperialismus in Deutschland', in ibid., pp. 148–58; Langewiesche, *Liberalismus in Deutschland*, pp. 221–7.
12 The lifestyle and the civic community of the old German town is brilliantly described by M. Walker, *German Home Towns: Community, State, and General Estate, 1648–1871* (Ithaca, NY, 1971).

13 The results of recent research are to be found in J. Kocka (ed.), *Bürgertum im 19. Jahrhundert: Deutschland im europäischen Vergleich*, 3 vols (Munich, 1988) esp. Kocka's summary 'Bürgertum und bürgerliche Gesellschaft im 19. Jahrhundert: Europäische Entwicklungen und deutsche Eigenarten', ibid., pp. 11–76.

14 See below, pp. 77–79.

15 D. Langewiesche, 'Gesellschafts- und verfassungspolitische Handlungsbedingungen und Zielvorstellungen europäischer liberaler in der Revolution von 1848', in W. Schieder (ed.), *Liberalismus in der Gesellschaft des deutschen Vormärz* (Göttingen, 1983). This was also published in *Geschichte und Gesellschaft*, Sonderheft 9, pp. 341–62.

16 L. Gall, *Bismarck: Der Weiße Revolutionär* (Frankfurt, 1980), pp. 373–93.

17 L. Gall, 'Liberalismus und "bürgerliche Gesellschaft"', in L. Gall (ed.), *Liberalismus* (Cologne, 1976), pp. 162–86; Langewiesche, *Liberalismus in Deutschland*, pp. 27–34; H. Sedatis, *Liberalismus und Handwerker in Süddeutschland* (Stuttgart, 1979); R. Koch, '"Industriesystem" oder "bürgerliche" Gesellschaft: Der frühe deutsche Liberalismus und das Laisser-faire-Prinzip', *Geschichte in Wissenschaft und Unterricht*, 29 (1978), pp. 605–28.

18 C. V. Rotteck, 'Eigentum', in *Staats-Lexikon oder Encyklopädie der Staatswissenschaften*, vol. 4 (Altona, 1836/37), quoted in the valuable collection of sources in H. Brand (ed.), *Restauration und Frühliberalismus 1814–1840* (Darmstadt, 1979), p. 388.

19 cf. Th. Schieder, 'Die Krise des bürgerlichen Liberalismus', in T. Schieder, *Staat und Gesellschaft im Wandel unserer Zeit* (Darmstadt, 1970), pp. 58–88; Langewiesche, *Liberalismus in Deutschland*, pp. 111–27, 187–200; L. Gall describes this development in his book on the history of the Bassermann family from Mannheim, *Bürgertum in Deutschland* (Berlin, 1989); for the European perspective see D. Langewiesche, 'Liberalismus und Bürgertum in Europa', in J. Kocka (ed.), *Bürgertum*, vol. 3, pp. 360–94.

20 R. Aldenhoff, *Schulze-Delitzsch. Ein Beitrag zur Geschichte des Liberalismus zwischen Revolution und Reichsgründung* (Baden-Baden, 1984); H.-G. Haupt and F. Lenger, 'Liberalismus und Handwerk in Frankreich und Deutschland um die Mitte des 19. Jahrhunderts', in Langewiesche, *Liberalismus im 19. Jahrhundert*, pp. 305–31.

21 J. Kocka (ed.), *Europäische Arbeiterbewegungen im 19. Jahrhundert: Deutschland, Österreich, England und Frankreich im Vergleich* (Göttingen, 1983); D. Geary (ed.), *Labour and Socialist Movements in Europe before 1914* (Oxford, 1989); P. Weber, *Sozialismus als Kulturbewegung: Frühsozialistische Arbeiterbewegung und das Entstehen zweier feindlicher Brüder Marxismus und Anarchismus* (Düsseldorf, 1989).

22 See Langewiesche, *Liberalismus in Deutschland*, pp. 138–64, and esp. the tables, pp. 295–331. In the 1960s the defeat of liberalism in the battle for workers' votes was not yet decided, see J. Breuilly, 'Liberalismus oder Sozialdemokratie? Ein Vergleich der britischen und deutschen politischen Arbeiterbewegung zwischen 1850 and 1875', in Kocka, *Arbeiterbewegungen*, pp. 129–66.

23 R. vom Bruch (ed.), *'Weder Kommunismus noch Kapitalismus': Bürgerliche Sozialreform in Deutschland bis zur Ära Adenauer* (Munich, 1985); G. A. Ritter, *Sozialversicherung in Deutschland und England: Entstehung und Grundzüge im Vergleich* (Munich, 1983).

24 Quoted in Langewiesche, *Liberalismus in Deutschland*, p. 189.

25 The following summary is based on Sheehan, *German Liberalism*, chs 5 and

6; G. Hübinger, 'Hochindustrialisierung und die Kulturwerte des deutschen Liberalismus', in Langewiesche, *Liberalismus im 19. Jahrhundert*, pp. 193–208; Langewiesche, *Liberalismus in Deutschland*, ch. 4; Langewiesche, 'Bildungsbürgertum und Liberalismus im 19. Jahrhundert', vol. 4 (Stuttgart, 1989), pp. 95–121; R. V. Bruch, 'Gesellschaftliche Funktionen und politische Rollen Bildungsbürgertums im Wilhelminischen Reich', in ibid., pp. 146–79; D. Langewiesche, 'German Liberalism in the Second Empire 1971–1918', in K. Jarausch and L. E. Jones, *In Search of Liberal Germany* (Oxford, 1990).

26   A first outline is given by J. J. Sheehan, 'Liberalism and the city in 19th century Germany', *Past and Present*, 51 (1971), pp. 116–37; Langewiesche, *Liberalismus in Deutschland*, pp. 200–11. For the urban development and the social policy of the towns, see J. Reulecke, *Geschichte der Urbanisierung in Deutschland* (Frankfurt, 1985); Langewiesche, '"Staat" und "Kommune": Zum Wandel der Staatsaufgaben in Deutschland im 19. Jahrhundert', *Historische Zeitschrift*, 248 (1989), pp. 621–35.

27   See K. Holl, G. Trautmann and H. Vorländer (eds), *Sozialer Liberalismus* (Göttingen, 1986); H. Vorländer (ed.), *Verfall oder Renaissance des Liberalismus? Beiträge zum deutschen und internationalen Liberalismus* (Munich, 1987); H. G. Hockerts, *Sozialpolitische Entscheidungen im Nachkriegs-deutschland* (Stuttgart, 1980). The Weimar Republic is the most thoroughly researched period in the history of German liberalism; see esp. Jones, *German Liberalism*; a short outline is given in Langewiesche, *Liberalismus in Deutschland*, pp. 233–88; for the development after the Second World War see ibid., pp. 287–300; L. Albertin (ed.), *Politischer Liberalismus in der Bundesrepublik* (Göttingen, 1980).

28   The best summary gives U. Frevert, *Frauen-Geschichte. Zwischen Bürgerlicher Verbesserung und Neuer Weiblichkeit* (Frankfurt, 1986); cf. U. Frevert (ed.), *Bürgerinnen und Bürger. Geschlechterverhältnisse im 19. Jahrhundert* (Göttingen, 1988). There is no study of gender and liberalism. The following hints are based on Langewiesche, *Liberalismus in Deutschland*, pp. 33–4, 155, 208, 225.

29   The conflict between Catholicism and liberalism is not well researched. See ibid., pp. 180–87; D. Blackbourn, *Volksfrömmigkeit und Fortschrittsglaube im Kulturkampf* (Stuttgart, 1988); J. Sperber, *Popular Catholicism in 19th-Century Germany* (Princeton, NJ, 1984). On the relationship between religion and society in Germany see T. Nipperdey, *Religion im 22bruch: Deutschland 1870–1918* (Munich, 1988).

30   The most impressive work on these problems is H. Rosenberg, *Grosse Depression und Bismarckzeit: Wirtschaftsablauf, Gesellschaft und Politik in Mitteleuropa* (Berlin, 1967).

31   See Sheehan, *German Liberalism*, pp. 19–34; Sheehan, 'Liberalism and society in Germany, 1816–1846', *Journal of Modern History*, 45 (1973), pp. 583–604; Langewiesche, *Liberalismus in Deutschland*, pp. 34–8, 111–27, 133–64.

32   For the process of nation building in Germany, see esp. P. J. Katzenstein, *Disjoined Partners. Austria and Germany since 1815* (Berkeley, Calif., 1976); H. Schulze (ed.), *Nation-Building in Central Europe* (Leamington Spa, 1987); O. Dann (ed.), *Nationalismus und sozialer Wandel* (Hamburg, 1978); Langewiesche, '"Nation" und "Nationalstaat": Zum Funktionswandel politisch-gesellschaftlicher Leitideen in Deutschland seit dem 19. Jahrhunderts', in F. W. Busch (ed.), *Perspektiven gesellschaftlicher Entwicklung in beiden deutschen Staaten* (Oldenburg, 1988), pp. 173–82.

33   For further details see the chapter on 'Die "Revolution von oben"', in Gall, *Bismarck*, pp. 373–455; the same term is used by the Marxian author E. Engelberg, *Bismarck: Urpreusse und Reichsgründer* (Berlin, 1985); cf. D. Langewiesche, 'Revolution von oben? Krieg und Nationalstaatsgründung', in D. Langewiesche (ed.), *Revolution und Krieg: Zur Dynamik historischen Wandels seit dem 18. Jahrhundert* (Paderborn, 1989), pp. 117–33.

34   See Sheehan, *German Liberalism*, pp. 123–77; Langewiesche, *Liberalismus in Deutschland*, pp. 164–80; Langewiesche, *German Liberalism*, pp. 217–27.

35   In addition to the studies quoted in note 34 see H. Rosenberg, *Grosse Depression*, chs 2–4.

36   H. A. Winkler, 'Vom linken zum rechten Nationalismus: Der deutsche Liberalismus in der Krise von 1878/79', *Geschichte und Gesellschaft*, 4 (1978), pp. 5–28.

37   J. N. Retallack, *Notables of Right: The Conservative Party and Political Mobilisation in Germany, 1876–1918* (Boston, Mass., 1988); R. Chickering, *We Men Who Feel Most German: A Cultural Study of the Pan-German League, 1886–1914* (Boston, Mass., 1984); G. Eley, *Reshaping the German Right: Radical Nationalism and Political Change after Bismarck* (New Haven, Conn., 1980).

38   See Holl and List, *Liberalismus*; W. J. Mommsen, *Max Weber und die deutsche Politik 1890–1920* (2nd edn, Tübingen, 1974); P. Theiner, *Sozialer Liberalismus und Weltpolitik: Friedrich Naumann im Wilhelminischen Deutschland, 1860–1919* (Baden-Baden, 1983); Langewiesche, *Liberalismus in Deutschland*, pp. 211–86 for the most important studies concerning the Weimar Republic.

39   D. Hein, *Zwischen liberaler Milieupartei und nationaler Sammlungsbewegung: Gründung, Entwicklung und Struktur der Freien Demokratischen Partei 1945–1949* (Düsseldorf, 1985); T. Rütten, *Der deutsche Liberalismus 1945–1955* (Baden-Baden, 1984).

6 *The Rise of National Socialism 1919–1933*

JANE CAPLAN

THE INTERPRETIVE CONTEXT

Although the foundation of the Nationalsozialistiche Deutsche Arbeiter-partei (NSDAP) as a political movement was a symptom of the crisis of Germany in the revolutionary aftermath of the First World War, the sources of its ideology, its appeal and its social composition lay in the nineteenth century, perhaps even further back in German history.[1] Historians have disagreed, however, on the relative weight they would give to the long-term and short-term sources of the Nazi movement. Few would deny altogether that the origins of National Socialism as both an ideology and a social movement lay in some measure in the period before 1914. Similarly, few would contest the immediate contribution of the war itself – that deep scar in European cultural and political consciousness – and of the postwar conjuncture of defeat and revolution in Germany. No history of the radical right in interwar Europe could entirely ignore either of these influences, but at present historians tend to emphasize the conjunctural rather than the structural conditions for the emergence of National Socialism. This is not only a matter of stressing the two successive periods of systemic crisis in Germany – the first, between 1917 and 1923, that fostered the rise of a radical right including the NSDAP, and the second, between 1930 and 1933, that brought Hitler to power. In addition, the conjunctural explanation now relies heavily on the argument that the supporters who made the NSDAP the largest membership and electoral party in Germany by mid-1932 were animated less by the extreme histrionics of the party's leadership than by calculations of political rationality similar to those that prompted the choices of other voters or political activists.[2] In other words, the victory of National Socialism does not need to be ascribed to some deep-laid political or psychological deficiency in German culture and history, but

117

can be adequately explained by reference to the precise and temporary conditions of German history in the 1920s and early 1930s.

By contrast, older accounts, especially those written by Western or German emigré historians, tended to emphasize the extreme irrationalism of National Socialism as well as its deep-laid roots in Germany's earlier history. They located its ideological and social origins in the upheavals of German industrialization and Germany's failure to develop a rational liberal order capable of integrating its citizens. Creating a synthetic lineage for National Socialism in the history of ideas, some historians linked thinkers as varied as Hegel, Fichte, H. C. Chamberlain and Lagarde as representatives of a specifically German resistance to the age of European liberalism; they emphasized the neo-romantic, social Darwinist and *völkisch* currents that were prominent in the 'cultural pessimism' of *fin-de-siècle* German thought.[3] Although this crisis of modernity, which was also a crisis of classical liberalism in the face of mass society,[4] was a generic European phenomenon by the close of the nineteenth century, the very weakness of the liberal tradition in Germany encouraged a particular skepticism there about liberalism's political and ideological claims. This created a space for an anti-liberalism that also professed an especially profound contempt for the rationality and predictability of bourgeois culture. A more extreme, and now largely discredited, variant of this approach forged an even longer ideological heritage that linked Luther and other pre-modern German figures to Hitler as equivalent emanations of a peculiarly German, peculiarly vicious, and transhistorical anti-humanism.[5]

A more recent and subtle version of this view of National Socialism as a symptom of deep-seated structural weaknesses or failures in German history has relied less upon purely ideological explanations, but has concentrated rather on the effects of the survival of pre-capitalist, pre-industrial social and political institutions and relationships, which distorted the development of nineteenth-century Germany and bore bitter fruit after the war. According to this interpretation, Germany was peculiar among Western societies in its failure to develop the multifarious and resilient sociopolitical structure that has normally accompanied the rise of industrial capitalism. It lacked both a strong and self-confident bourgeoisie and the liberal political ideology that has been the intellectual and political tool of bourgeois leadership *vis-à-vis* other social classes. Successive failures by the German bourgeoisie to enter into its appropriate political inheritance – in 1848, in the 1860s and the 1890s – left Germany exposed to the reactionary obscurantism of the old agrarian and military ruling elites, and to the unsatisfied claims of the popular classes, both proletarian and petty bourgeois. The collapse of this rigid and antagonistic structure in 1918 merely created the conditions in which previously repressed or manipulated classes and ideologies began to confront one another more blatantly and with less restraint.[6]

A third influential interpretation of National Socialism is offered by Marxist theory, or theories, which combine structural and conjunctural elements in a single analysis.[7] Marxist theories have always emphasized the generic character of fascism, whether in interwar Italy and Germany or elsewhere in time and place, and the first explanations of this mass counter-revolutionary movement were contemporary with its Italian origins. The primary quest of Marxist interpretations in the 1920s and 1930s, when European communist parties directly confronted fascist movements and regimes, was to identify the social location and logic of fascist movements, within the twin contexts of an overarching theory of capitalism and class struggle on the one hand, and a conjunctural politics of revolutionary stalemate on the other. Structurally, Leninist theory held that capitalism had entered its final period of crisis by 1914, as the economic and political conditions for revolutionary transformation gathered strength. Conjuncturally, capital faced an increasing crisis of political representation after the war, yet the revolutionary momentum was blocked by the collapse of working-class unity in 1919, and by the left's failure to gain the support of the middle strata of society. Fascism entered here as a mass counter-revolutionary movement of the socially disorganized classes, mobilized by capital in a bid to recover its political hegemony.

A crucial element in these contemporary Marxist analyses of fascism was the distinction drawn between the class *composition* of the movement, and the class *interests* it served.[8] Thus National Socialism was seen as a largely petty-bourgeois party that nevertheless served the interests of monopoly capital in the latter's twin fight against small capital and the proletariat. And although both theoretical and polemical critiques of National Socialism by Marxists employed a vocabulary that emphasized its barbaric and counter-revolutionary character, the classic Marxist theory of fascism saw it primarily as a phenomenon not of backwardness but of hyper-development, at least sectorally – a conclusion they were logically compelled to reach, since the appearance of fascism was supposed to provide evidence of the final contradictions of capitalism.

Despite many differences of context, the concept of German peculiarity has thus played a striking role in recent explanations of Germany's modern history, as other chapters in this collection show. The temptation to employ some version of this to explain National Socialism is all the greater since the experience and consequences of Nazi rule seem to be literally without parallel in modern history – hence the appeal of interpretations that see National Socialism as a form of collective atavism or residual barbarism peculiar to the malformed process of

German history. Yet current reconsiderations of the question of Germany's 'special development' suggest that the issue is not so much whether German history has been peculiar by comparison with somewhere else, but in what ways, and for what reasons, the path of German history has been what it was, irrespective of any hypostatized model of normality against which it could be measured and found wanting. [9]

Debates about German history will surely benefit by being liberated from the constraining dualism that pitches Germany as the 'other' against a norm which is itself a construct,[10] and by being launched instead onto the open seas of multiple comparisons and shifting vantage points. The Anglo-American model of liberal capitalism will continue to do service here, to be sure; but what must also join the interpretive schema are the very different examples of, for example, petty capitalist France, Italy under unification and fascism, or Tsarist and Soviet Russia, not to mention the transnational vectors of normalization and rupture propounded by theorists such as Foucault.

This chapter will try to offer a path through the most significant interpretations and controversies that surround the rise and success of National Socialism between 1919 and 1933, but without losing sight of the thread of historical narrative. An explanation of the National Socialist rise to power in 1933 must seek to answer two related questions: how did the NSDAP grow from its insignificant beginnings as an obscure grouplet on the fringe right in 1919 to become one of the largest parties in Germany by 1930? And how did its leader, Adolf Hitler, then come to be appointed chancellor of Germany on 30 January 1933? These questions will be addressed in turn below.

THE NSDAP FROM FOUNDATION TO TAKEOFF, 1919–30

The origins and early history of the National Socialist movement have attracted less controversy than its later development and activities. Until the mid-1920s the NSDAP was a small and not particularly distinctive element in the multifarious and fragmented German *völkisch* movement, typical in its ideology and following, and unremarkable until the combination of Hitler's leadership and the politico-economic crisis of the late 1920s thrust it into a more prominent national role. A certain amount of historical effort has gone into exploring the early years of the party and clarifying Hitler's role in it before 1923, but this has been more a project of reconstruction than of reinterpretation. [11]

Nevertheless, this early history was marked by two features, each of which was to become more debated as the Nazi movement developed.

First, there was the extent to which the NSDAP enjoyed from its earliest days not only access to but also the active support of individuals and institutions more powerful than itself. Among these were the influential Pan-German establishment, which had provided a 'respectable' focus for ultra-nationalist, *völkisch* and anti-Semitic tendencies since prewar days; the Bavarian military; and the conservative-monarchist Bavarian government. At the same time, the NSDAP addressed its message not to these elite groups, but to ordinary Germans, including the working classes whom it hoped to wean from Marxism. From its inception, therefore, there was more than a whiff of indeterminacy about the NSDAP's social location and logic: it seemed to be sponsored by interests different from and more powerful than its socially inferior membership. Second, Hitler's early association with the NSDAP was crucial to the party's future.[12] Had Hitler not joined this group, it is virtually certain that the course of its history – and with it, perhaps, the course of German history – would have been very different in the 1920s and 1930s. To an extent unparalleled in other modern political movements, the success of the Nazi Party was intimately connected with the peculiar organizational and propaganda skills of one man. There is little disagreement among historians about the extraordinary importance of Hitler to National Socialism as far as the pre-1933 period is concerned. Far more debatable, on the other hand, is the extent to which the history of national socialist Germany after 1933 can be adequately explained by reference to Hitler's leadership alone.[13]

The party that Hitler joined in September 1919, the Deutsche Arbeiterpartei (DAP), was one of a number of anti-Semitic, extremist groups on the radical right that flourished in the highly politicized and tense environment of postwar Munich. Typically, these sectarian groups represented those who were most outraged by Germany's defeat and by the establishment of the republic by the socialist and democratic 'November criminals' – events for which they blamed the old elites almost as much as the 'Jewish-Bolshevik' conspiracy whose hand they saw everywhere. The party's Twenty-Five-Point Program, adopted in February 1920 (when the DAP also renamed itself the Nationalsozialistische Deutsche Arbeiterpartei, or NSDAP), drew on an amalgam of communal and petty bourgeois themes that had been typical of anti-capitalist and anti-socialist ideologies since the 1890s and were now embodied into most of the postwar fascist programs. These included a strongly racist and anti-Semitic nationalism, calls for strong political leadership, centralized government, and interventionist social and educational policies, and an economic anti-capitalism which included demands for land reform, profit sharing, nationalization, the abolition of 'interest bondage' and unearned incomes, and the creation of 'a healthy middle class' (*Mittelstand*).

As the NSDAP's membership grew (it reached about 55,000 by 1923) and disputes over strategy mounted, one of Hitler's chief rallying calls was his insistence that the NSDAP was to be a new kind of political movement, marked by both activism and populism. Like many of his contemporaries in the postwar racist and nationalist movement, he had nothing but contempt for the elitism and bourgeois hesitancy of the more traditional *völkisch* movement and the established political parties of the right. At the same time, it is clear that he saw the NSDAP as drummer rather than general in the battle for Germany's future: as a party whose job was to mobilize a mass movement on behalf of the more powerful forces that would then be in a position to topple the Weimar Republic, rather than to undertake this task itself. But the NSDAP's attempted putsch of 8–9 November 1923 revealed that Hitler had miscalculated the relationship between the old and the new politics. Kahr, Lossow and their associates in Bavarian government and military circles had their own political agenda, in which the primary objectives were separatism, monarchism and authoritarian rule, rather than the national populist revolution espoused by Hitler. It was their unwillingness to risk civil war with the German army that led to Hitler's downfall in November 1923.

During his imprisonment in 1924 Hitler revised his strategy in two crucial respects. First, he recognized the folly of aiming at power without the support of the army, and his political decisions through to 1934 were always co-determined by this new consideration. As a corollary, he rejected the use of direct force against the state in favor of a strategy of electoral persuasion by means of which the NSDAP would acquire a mass base large enough to become the deciding factor in German politics. In a well-known statement in 1924, Hitler explained that

> When I resume active work it will be necessary to pursue a new policy. Instead of working to achieve power by armed conspiracy, we shall have to hold our noses and enter the Reichstag against the Catholic and Marxist deputies. If outvoting them takes longer than outshooting them, at least the results will be guaranteed by their own constitution.[14]

These decisions presupposed a party capable of mobilizing popular support and commitment on a national scale. The sources and motives of this support have been the subject of continuous scrutiny and debate since the 1920s and this largely sociological project has gone hand in hand with the more general question of how to characterize National Socialism as a political movement. Contemporary political and academic observers who sought to explain the appeal of the Nazis were struck by the extent to which, like other European fascist parties, they represented a novel form of politics and ideology: the NSDAP's very self-description as a movement (*Bewegung*) rather than a party served to emphasize this.[15] Young, agitationist, counter-revolutionary, paramilitary in organization and violent in action, the Nazi Party seemed to flout the conventions of nationalist conservatism, liberalism and social democracy alike, while also usurping and recombining many of their ideological claims. The SA (Sturmabteilung), largely coterminous with the party's male membership, was heavily involved in propaganda work and in representing the physical power of the movement at meetings and on the streets.[16] Yet although the party cultivated this public image of novelty, youth and dynamism, it also developed a local organizational structure that was not in fact so different from the accepted traditions of German associational life, which linked sociability and political debate in a pub-based culture of male *Gemütlichkeit*.[17]

The social and temperamental gap between the volatile young activists of the SA, and the petty-bourgeois and professional sympathizers who ballasted the local party organization, was to bedevil the party up to and beyond the seizure of power. The Nazi movement contained on the one hand violently putschist and revolutionary tendencies in its paramilitary wing that constantly threatened to run out of control, especially as the political temperature heated up after 1930. These also stamped much of the party's propaganda activity – it was not accidental that the SA was assigned the task of propaganda vanguard, and that propaganda shaded almost imperceptibly into the political violence of confrontation and street brawling.[18] On the other hand, the movement also embraced a regular, complex and quasi-bureaucratic party organization that stabilized Nazi support on the middle ground and reflected the normalized pattern of associational life and political mobilization that had developed in Germany since the late nineteenth century.[19]

Until the late 1920s, the NSDAP addressed itself chiefly to an urban working-class audience which showed little interest in its message. As a result, the party did very poorly in local and provincial elections in the mid-1920s, never gaining more than 3.7 per cent of the vote, and remaining on the fringes of German party politics.[20] The Nazi breakthrough to the center of the German political stage came only after 1928, when reaction against the rationalizing and socializing trends of the late 1920s coincided with the beginnings of economic depression and political crisis to create a huge reservoir of potential support for the Nazis. The corporatist politics of the 1920s had tended to squeeze the middle and lower middle classes – farmers, artisans, shopkeepers, petty traders, salespeople, pensioners, small rentiers, and the like – between the more organized forces of big business and labor. These groups also felt especially burdened by high taxation and interest rates that seemed to serve the alien powers of government and high finance: indeed, it was rural tax revolts in Schleswig-Holstein and Oldenburg in 1927–8 that gave the NSDAP the first signals that the party's efforts might be better directed at the rural *Mittelstand* than at the urban areas on which the party had hitherto concentrated.[21] It was these groups that then deserted the moderate parties of the democratic middle, notably the Deutsche Demokratische Partei (DDP) and Deutsche Volkspartei (DVP), and the conservative and nationalist DNVP, often gravitating first to the splinter parties or withdrawing temporarily from the electorate altogether, and then flocking after 1929 into the ranks of Nazi voters. The shrinkage and fragmentation of support for the middle parties were also evidence of a crisis of voter confidence in these moderate representatives of liberal democracy, and it was the Nazis who were able to capitalize on this desertion – even if the loyalty it brought them was potentially fickle.[22]

Both the NSDAP's early membership profile and its successful appeal to the rural *Mittelstand* after 1928 led many contemporaries to conclude that it remained a primarily petty-bourgeois party through to 1933, even if leavened by the more volatile admixture of ex-combatants, *deraciné* intellectuals and social malcontents that had been seen as its core membership.[23] The classic Marxist argument too was that the postwar fascist parties drew their support largely from the petty bourgeoisie, a class that was simultaneously threatened by the organized proletariat and betrayed by big capital.[24] This lower middle-class thesis remained an orthodoxy until quite recently. But renewed empirical research since the 1970s, some of it drawing on sophisticated statistical techniques, has substantially revised this conventional account of the NSDAP's political identity.[25] The new consensus is that by 1932 the party was drawing on an unprecedentedly broad social spectrum of support among Protestant (but not Catholic) voters, including some workers and members of the professional and commercial elites, as well as members of the middle and lower-middle classes.

One reason for this success is that the Nazis appear to have been peculiarly adept at tailoring specific (though not necessarily compatible) messages to particular groups, while at the same time managing to present themselves as a party of universal appeal. Their astute propaganda enabled the party to capitalize on the prior breakdown of politics into narrower interest-group representation: in a sense, the political scene was already fragmented by 1928, and it was the NSDAP that swept the pieces into a single new movement.[26] But the reasons *why* any particular set of voters chose the Nazi party are not as easy to elicit as the actual electoral data. Strictly speaking, voter motivations cannot be inferred either from party propaganda or from aggregate voting statistics, yet, in the absence of public opinion surveys or other 'objective' evidence, historians have little choice but to fill the gap with educated guesses about motives. Inevitably, these will vary from case to case, but there has been a broadly developing consensus that German voters were drawn into the ambit of the NSDAP by frustration with the breakdown of politics and government on the middle ground, and by the NSDAP's promises of material relief in times of economic desperation – tax and interest relief for farmers and small businessmen, security of tenure for civil servants, revalorization of savings for pensioners, adequate support for the family. These promises were combined with relentless attacks on the corruption, mismanagement and foreign manipulation which, according to the Nazis, had held postwar Germany in a stranglehold. Perhaps most important, the party was able, for a time at any rate, to present itself *both* as a respectable *and* as an unprecedentedly dynamic political organization. All this enabled the Nazis to hollow out support from the liberal and conservative parties, and to present themselves as a national party of integration, rather than a class-bound or confessional interest group. They acquired, in other words, 'the coveted mantle of a *Volkspartei*'[27] that had eluded their rivals in German political history.

The question of working-class support for Nazism has proved particularly contentious, and the deep divisions in the historiography reflect those in past politics, where working-class immunity from fascism was the mirror image of petty-bourgeois susceptibility. Both the theoretical and the empirical dimensions of contemporary arguments have been extensively reviewed since the 1960s.[28] In general, it is clear that workers remained underrepresented in the membership of the NSDAP. A left-wing had, it is true, lodged itself within the Nazi movement in northern and western Germany by the early 1920s, when Gregor Strasser and associates such as Goebbels, Kaufmann and Terboven focused their efforts on winning proletarian support in heavily urban and industrial areas. Ideologically this group was closely related to the national Bolshevik, pro-Russian ideas that were then circulating on both the right and the left, and stood in stark contrast to Hitler's own rigid anti-communism. However, the party's attempt to recruit workers as members and voters in the 1920s was undoubtedly a failure, and this was partly the cause of the party's shift of electoral interest to a more middle-class electorate in 1928. Even after the economic disarray of the early 1930s, not more than a third of the NSDAP membership was working-class by 1933, while the class itself formed about half of the electorate.

The picture is, however, muddied by disagreements over the definition of 'worker': if the term includes artisans, shop assistants and clerks, then its representation will look more impressive than if it is restricted to manual workers alone.[29] After a good deal of debate, the best conclusion seems to be that the NSDAP was more successful than previously supposed in attracting workers from the handicrafts and small manufacturing sectors, and from rural areas and small towns. In general, however, the *organized* working class – those with links to the trade unions, the SPD, or the KPD – did remain largely impervious to Nazism, and this set limits to the party's ability to extend its support further.[30] At the same time, as Tim Mason has pointed out, the working-class parties had never succeeded in organizing more than about half of the German working class, at a crude estimate.[31] Those who were not in the working-class movement were, if Catholic, likely to have been Center Party voters, or might have been part of the large popular base of the Protestant DNVP, which by 1930 was losing heavily to the NSDAP.[32] By 1930, then, it was becoming more difficult to draw up a profile of the typical Nazi voter, or even party member. The core may have been Protestant, old petty-bourgeois, and small-town, but this was now the center of much more socially diverse congeries of supporters.

A related question that needs mention here is the representation of women in the Nazi movement. Until recently, discussion of the sources of support for National Socialism tended to ignore gender as an analytical category, or otherwise to operate with crude and empirically dubious assumptions about its role. Within the past 15 years, however, the new interest in women's history, feminism and sexual politics has transformed the context of debate.[33] After some disagreement about the extent and sources of women's support for National Socialism, the most recent research suggests that before 1930 the NSDAP was less attractive to female than to male voters, but that thereafter the party made disproportionate gains among women. By the final Reichstag elections of March 1933, more women than men were voting Nazi. The question why women supported the Nazis is more open. The older view was that this was an index of women's own anti-feminism, their rejection of the emancipation conferred by Weimar. More recently, it has been pointed out that the fruits of emancipation were dubious at most, especially in the context of the economic depression.[34] Moreover, just as Nazi propaganda did not make anti-Semitism a primary issue in its final, opportunistic drive for electoral power, so also the party's profound anti-feminism was not so prominent between 1930 and 1933. Women were not, it is true, visible within the leadership of the Nazi party, nor did they constitute much of its membership. At the same time, the party leadership before 1933 largely left its women supporters to organize themselves, and this contributed to expectations that women would play an appropriately prominent role in a Nazi regime.[35]

The final question to be discussed here is the degree of elite support for National Socialism. At one level, this is a straightforward issue which can be addressed by the same empirical techniques used for determining the social range of support in general (even if the definition of 'elite' is somewhat cloudy). Thus Kater's analysis of NSDAP membership records suggests that Germany's upper strata – for example businessmen, Protestant pastors, senior civil servants and the professions in general – were overrepresented before 1933, and that this was even more the case for the party's official cadres.[36] Hamilton's research into electoral results in some of Germany's largest cities also shows a clear pattern of support for the NSDAP in the wealthier districts.[37] This kind of evidence tends to undermine the argument that Nazism was predominantly a movement of the masses, and that it was disdained by more educated and socially superior Germans. However, the relationship between National Socialism and the German elites is also implicated in much more contentious arguments about the class character of the movement – not in terms of its class *composition*, but as a question of its class *identity*, in the sense of what interests it served. As already suggested, many contemporaries (including the democratic Weimar parties) saw fascism as a movement that served interests different from, and more powerful than, those professed by its members and overt supporters. This did not rule out the fact that some members of Germany's elites were openly active in the NSDAP, nor did it necessarily imply a belief in conspiracy theories and the power of behind-the-scenes manipulation. But it did suggest that the mass character of the movement was in some sense put to work for other agendas; that the policies of a future Nazi regime could not be discerned from the expressed interests of its mass membership; and that the Nazi seizure of power was assisted by Germany's economic and political elites.

That the backstairs machinations of influential political figures were partly responsible for the final crisis of Weimar in 1930–3 is scarcely in doubt, but the greatest historical controversy has concerned the question of industrialists' support for the NSDAP. Once again, this is a major political and historiographical debate that can only be described briefly here. One thread of argument, originating with the left in Weimar Germany and widely held since then in both liberal and Marxist historiography, maintains that National Socialism, despite the populist anti-capitalism of its program, ultimately served the interests of big capital. It aimed to eviscerate the working-class movement and discipline the proletariat, and then to embark on nationalist and militarist policies which would redound principally to the benefit of industry.[38] The Nazi leadership courted industrialists, and they responded by offering financial support to the party and by otherwise indicating their preference for a Nazi-led solution to the political and economic crisis after 1930. Whether or not it was the *intention* of the Nazi leaders, or their followers, to serve the interests of capital, objectively the movement was doomed by the balance of economic relationships within German capitalism to perform this labor. The party's anti-Semitism performed a valuable function here in identifying a specific group of capitalists (*Jewish* bankers, *Jewish* department-store owners) who could be lambasted without this appearing to be an attack on capitalism specifically.

The basic division here lies between those who subscribe to some version of objective or structural analysis of capital's relationship with fascism, and those who argue that there is insufficient empirical evidence of capitalists 'support for the party to warrant any claims about their interest in or responsibility for the Nazi seizure of power.'[39] Since these two arguments derive from different theories of historical causation and explanation, it is hard to adjudicate between them in their starkest form. It is true that, despite Hitler's attention to industrialist circles after 1927, there is only scant evidence that they gave *direct* financial support to the NSDAP, or that the party was dependent on these subventions before 1933. A few industrialists – the radical pan-German mineowner Emil Kirdorf, for example, and the steel magnate Fritz Thyssen – gave considerable sums to the NSDAP before 1933. Others, also mainly from heavy industry, were involved intermittently in discussions and other contacts with prominent Nazis, and these certainly became broader and more cordial as the power of the party waxed in 1932. At the same time, industrialist circles as a whole maintained a more cautious attitude towards the Nazis, and often spread their political donations across a wider range of parties. Financially, the NSDAP was certainly more dependent on the contributions of its mass membership than on handouts from a few magnates (though this was no longer true for the elections of March 1933, when the party's coffers, exhausted by the 1932 election campaigns, were replenished only by handsome large-scale donations).

However, to regard these facts as an adequate answer to the much more complex questions raised by the relationship between fascism and capitalism, both before and after the seizure of power, is to equate causation with determinable individual intentions alone, and to ignore the demonstrable though often indirect influences of corporate structures in politics, the economy and ideology. Big business, especially the highly cartelized heavy industrial sector, had no love lost for the Weimar Republic, whose social and labor-relations policies were, from their point of view, costly and interventionist. Even before the world depression hit Germany in 1929, Ruhr industrialists had mounted an offensive against both labor and the new social democratic coalition that came to power in 1928. And when the slump came, its destructive impact shattered not only Germany's economy, but also the fragile structure of interest-group politics on which heavy industry depended for its political clout. The electoral shrinkage of the DVP and even DNVP, together with the fragmentation of industrial interests by the depression, left industry without a clear or powerful political spokesman. In these circumstances, industrial interests were bound to consider, even with reservations, the advantages of collaboration with Germany's major anti-Marxist party. Certainly, they evinced little interest in supporting the mass parties of the left as the major alternative to the NSDAP.[40]

The accumulated modifications of older assumptions about the social origins of Nazi support have, finally, fed criticisms of the premise that class or social status in an objective sense is a meaningful index of political allegiance.[41] For example, Thomas Childers argues that Weimar political propaganda drew heavily on the language of occupational rather than class identity, addressing voters as craftsmen, farmers, pensioners, and so on, yet that this vocabulary of *Stand* belonged in a relatively autonomous sphere of political discourse and was not simply the reflection of an objective social reality.[42] This new debate about language and the limitations of the 'social interpretation' of Nazism remains somewhat preliminary and has not yet dislodged the latter as the dominant paradigm, even in its modified form. An echo of the older disputes also remains audible even in these latest debates. However, they are also in part evidence of the slow intrusion into the field of Nazi studies of interpretive paradigms drawn from the arena of linguistics, literary theory and the new intellectual and cultural histories. This process registers the break up of both the social-science premises and the Marxist-influenced theories that have been powerful in historiography for the past 20 or 30 years. It has been a good deal slower to affect the field of modern German history than, for example, French or British history, for a number of reasons. The resistance reflects not only the tenacity with which the earlier political and historiographical battles over class were fought in the German field, but also the sense that the new intellectual history might be inappropriate for the interpretation of a period so scarred by the material consequences of human action. This may be particularly true of the poststructuralist variants of current literary and historical theory, which appear to many critics to discount claims of rationality and truth that are peculiarly essential to the study of a politics as apparently irrational and mendacious as Nazism.[43] Against this, however, it is arguable that poststructuralist techniques may offer some new insights into the operations of ideology and may contribute to a non-trivializing historicization of National Socialism. Current critiques of class as an organizer of identity and social action, as well as the deconstruction of the rigidity of fragile dualisms such as fascist/communist, myth/science, reactionary/progressive, may open a field for reconsidering the relationships between mutually hostile ideologies and practices without discounting their historical power, yet also without accepting the terms of historical confrontation uncritically. As yet, however, these various approaches are in their infancy and it is unclear how far they will succeed in defining new paradigms for the history of National Socialism.[44]

FROM MASS MOVEMENT TO NATIONAL GOVERNMENT, 1930–3

It now remains to examine how the NSDAP became the beneficiary of the systemic crisis that engulfed the German polity after 1929. By the time of the Nazi electoral breakthrough in September 1930, the political situation in Germany had been transformed by the impact of the economic depression. The republic's legitimacy had never been secure since its inception in the troubled circumstances of defeat and revolution in 1918–19, and the stabilization of the mid-1920s had not been accompanied by any effective strengthening of Weimar's base in German political culture – rather the opposite, as the character of government became more technocratic in style and less politically rooted. The outcome of the 1928 elections had also sent mixed messages at best, with its fresh evidence of disaffection among middle-class voters and the anxieties that were provoked on the right by the recovery of the SPD. With the disastrous impact of the US stock market crash in October 1929, the German economy began to grind to a halt; industrial production plummeted, unemployment rocketed and standards of living declined.[45] From then on, the huge fiscal and social problems of collapsing profitability and mass unemployment dominated the political scene in Germany, and finally overwhelmed the republic.

The first signs of crisis came with the fall of the SPD-led coalition cabinet in March 1930, over the issue of financing the overstretched unemployment insurance program. Given the deep divisions within the Weimar coalition, Heinrich Brüning's appointment as chancellor, with access to the emergency powers wielded by Hindenburg under Article 48 of the Weimar constitution, clearly marked a turn towards the authoritarian reconstruction of Weimar government. Historical opinion has differed widely on how to interpret the collapse of the Weimar Republic – whether it was destroyed from within by its structural weaknesses and by failures on the part of its own supporters, or from without by hostile assaults; whether there was a logic in the processes that led to its collapse, or whether the final events were more in the nature of avoidable accidents.[46] However, these should not necessarily be regarded as mutually exclusive explanations; rather, they have served to indicate different research emphases – on the republic's origins, its structural history, both economic and political, its final phase and so on. Most historians would agree that a complex model of causation is required in order to explain the brevity of the Weimar Republic, and that it is also helpful to distinguish between the several questions of why Weimar democracy was so fragile, why it was narrowed after 1930 and why a National Socialist regime came to replace it from January 1933.

According to this periodization, Brüning's chancellorship inaugurated a period of profound transformation for the republic, one that paved the way for the governmental crisis that finally engulfed Germany in 1932–3. The specific question of his objectives – was he committed to the salvation of a recognizable if modified democratic system, or did his policies put this at deliberate risk? – remains controversial. Brüning operated under the major constraint of the economic crisis, whose effects on Germany continued to be catastrophic. Yet it is also clear that he was determined to use the economic emergency to force solutions to two major problems that were extraneous to the depression itself: reparations, and the constitutional dependence of the Weimar state on a democratic political process that had proved unable to deliver strong government. It is true that Brüning did achieve some fiscal and foreign policy successes in 1930–1.[47] But his policy priorities played into the hands of the more dedicated reactionaries within Germany's political and military elites, while his inability to overcome the depression ensured that economic leaders in industry and agriculture would also become increasingly amenable to more radical solutions.

Brüning's decision to force a parliamentary crisis in the summer of 1930 was mandated by these policy priorities and was in retrospect a major error. Instead of enhancing the power of the moderate right, the September 1930 elections saw a spectacular increase in support for the NSDAP: their representation shot up from 12 to 107 seats, while the DVP and DNVP lost massively, and the KPD improved its position substantially. Brüning was left dependent on the passive tolerance of the SPD on the one hand, and on Hindenburg and his reactionary circle on the other – a fragile balance of incompatible parliamentary and extra-parliamentary forces that was unlikely to prove durable. At the same time, Hitler and the Nazis were unable to benefit directly from their new political prominence. The party's Reichstag victory stimulated a rallying of anti-Nazi forces among the political parties and Land governments, some of which issued measures against extremist political activities. The political violence and anti-capitalist radicalism associated with the Nazi movement also unnerved many on the more conservative right, and Hitler himself had great difficulty in steering between the shoals of compromise and confrontation that were equally antagonizing to different constituencies in his divided party.

From 1930 Hitler established more direct contacts than before with representatives of the existing power structure: he talked with Brüning in October and with Hindenburg a year later; he attempted to revive collaboration with the DNVP in 1931; and he renewed openings towards the Ruhr industrialists in 1932. In September 1930, as a witness in the trial of three Reichswehr officers accused of illegal work for the NSDAP, Hitler made his famously ambivalent distinction (reminiscent of his private remarks in 1924) between procedural and substantive loyalty to the constitution.[48] This statement, prevaricating as it was, certainly bolstered the NSDAP's image as a legal party rather than a revolutionary movement. But the radical SA, now over 100,000 strong, was deeply suspicious of anything that smacked of negotiation or compromise with the existing order and maintained its revolutionary and combative stance. Despite Hitler's attempts at damage control, the risk of an SA defection from the Nazi movement loomed large both in Hitler's anxieties and in the hopes of his political opponents. And the frustration of the SA was but one manifestation of a basic and destructive imbalance in German politics after 1930, between the narrowing circle of decision making at the top and the expanding compass of mass mobilization at the grassroots.[49] This became particularly glaring in 1931 and 1932, when the prolonged series of regional and national campaigns threw the NSDAP and the other political parties into frenzied electioneering, the results of which seemed, however, unable to determine public policy.

Papen's appointment as chancellor in June 1932 intensified this gap between popular and high-level politics. Papen had no popular legitimacy; the Reichstag was paralyzed between opponents of the republic on the extreme right and left, and rebuilding effective support for it would have been a daunting task – even supposing that Papen and Hindenburg had been seriously interested in reconstructing Weimar democracy. By now, Hitler was refusing to support any cabinet in which he did not hold the chancellorship – an appointment resolutely resisted by Hindenburg, who disliked Hitler personally and distrusted him politically. But the period between these failed negotiations in August 1932 and Hitler's appointment as chancellor in January 1933 was one of great stress and uncertainty for the Nazis. Internally the movement was strained by Hitler's inability to achieve the chancellorship; advocates of force on the one hand, and of political compromise on the other, threatened the unity of the party. The elections of November, called by Papen in hopes of capitalizing on the NSDAP's problems, were a major setback: the radical tone given to the campaign on Goebbels's instructions offended many, and the party lost votes for the first time since 1930. It emerged from the campaign demoralized and virtually bankrupt, with the electoral evidence indicating that the NSDAP had reached the limits of its appeal as a party of protest and that its support might be as fragile as it was broad.[50]

In the circumstances, it was only the development of a further governmental crisis in December and January that finally brought Hitler to power, and it is here that the story of the NSDAP since 1923 comes full circle. Papen's successor, Schleicher, hoped to extend the base of his government to both the right and the left by splitting the radicals from the NSDAP and establishing a populist–labor alliance with the socialist and Catholic unions. This almost succeeded, but against Schleicher were arrayed not only Papen and Hindenburg, but other members of Germany's economic elites who were shaken at the prospect of such an alliance. The breakthrough came in the last week of January, when Hindenburg, moved both by his son and by an appeal from his fellow Junkers, finally agreed, though with reluctance, to offer Hitler the chancellorship. The critical change of circumstances here was something that returns us to Hitler's decision after the Munich putsch to take power with, not against, the state and the army: this was General von Blomberg's agreement to serve as defense minister in Hitler's cabinet, and thus to remove Hindenburg's fear of a Reichswehr revolt. On 30 January 1933 Hitler was sworn in by Hindenburg as chancellor of a rightist coalition cabinet; the Reichstag was dissolved, and Germany was to be ruled by presidential decree until new elections in March.

The full history of the Nazi seizure of power is not, of course, told at this point. How the Nazis outmaneuvered their coalition partners and informal allies to establish a terrorist dictatorship continues some of the significant themes already present in the story – most notably, the themes of political violence within the NSDAP, and political compromise and miscalculation among the old elites. Similarly, the character and policies of the Nazi regime after 1933 were in crucial ways stamped by the experience of the movement before it came to power.[51] We have, however, seen how the NSDAP rose to its position of pre-eminence in German political life, and how and why it became the chief beneficiary of the economic and political crisis that dominated Germany after 1930. The final months of maneuvering and negotiation underline the extent to which the NSDAP's ultimate achievement of power was the result not only of its own platform or electoral successes, but also of the internal crisis of the Weimar state between 1930 and 1933. To be sure, its capacity to attract a mass following was quite spectacular, and this can be ascribed to the party's ability to project itself as a *national* as well as *nationalist* party, to dissociate itself from the failed 'Weimar system' and to convey an image of political energy and imagination. Yet the movement's ruthlessness and brutality were also crucial to its political success, and it was Hitler's peculiar genius that he was able to maneuver the party's image in such a way that his supporters could largely repress whatever each of them found less attractive in the movement (a capacity that was to be mobilized to even more disastrous purpose after 1933). Furthermore, it was clearly the extreme circumstances of the depression that lifted the NSDAP from margin to center – a position that it might not have been able to occupy for much longer. And the significance of the depression was not simply that Germany was thrown into economic and social confusion, but also that it became the context in which conservative groups tried to force a solution to what they saw as the structural problems of the Weimar Republic – notably, its democratic constitution and its continued entanglement in the aftermath of military defeat and social revolution. The gap between the hyperactive politics of the grassroots and the anaemic and alienated gyrations of the political elite offered an ideal opening to the NSDAP, with its strident and repeated message of strong leadership, national unity and salvation. It was as if the party offered itself after 1930 as the only safe conduit through which the frustrated energy of the German people could be channeled once again into the work of national recovery. Yet the party's image as a *Volkspartei* had depended on repressing the internal differences that threatened to shatter its volatile unity.

It is for this reason that historians have labeled the NSDAP as a protest party more capable of mobilizing than sustaining or directing its supporters. And the implication that National Socialism was more adept at negative than positive achievements seems amply borne out by the subsequent history of the 'Third Reich'.

NOTES

1 The literature on the rise of National Socialism is, needless to say, vast and never-ceasing, and defeats recapitulation here. A good introduction is Martin Broszat, *Hitler and the Collapse of Weimar Germany* (Leamington Spa, Hamburg and New York, 1987). A useful summary of the recent historiography is Peter D. Stachura (ed.), *The Nazi Machtergreifung* (London, 1983); other useful collections include Thomas Childers (ed.), *The Formation of the Nazi Constituency 1919–1933* (London, 1986), and two editions by Isidor Dobkowski and Michael Walliman: *Towards the Holocaust: The Social and Economic Collapse of the Weimar Republic* (Westport, Conn., 1983), and *Radical Perspectives on the Rise of National Socialism in Germany, 1919–1945* (New York, 1989). There is an invaluable edition of documents by Jeremy Noakes and Geoffrey Pridham, *Nazism 1919–1945*, Vol. 1: *The Rise to Power 1919–1934* (Exeter, 1983). For a guide to interpretations of National Socialism, see Pierre Ayçoberry, *The Nazi Question. An Essay on the Interpretations of National Socialism 1922–1975* (New York, 1981). For a good general history of the Weimar Republic, see Eberhard Kolb, *The Weimar Republic* (London, 1988), which also contains a section summarizing the main historiographical debates. Ian Kershaw, *The Nazi Dictatorship. Problems and Perspectives of Interpretation* 2nd edn (London, 1989) and John Hiden and John Farquharson, *Explaining Hitler's Germany. Historians and the Third Reich* 2nd edn (London, 1989) mainly cover the post-1933 period. The most recent and valuable English-language publications on specific topics will be referred to below.

2 The evidence is discussed most exhaustively in Thomas Childers, *The Nazi Voter. The Social Foundations of Fascism in Germany,1918–1933* (Chapel Hill, NC, and London, 1983), and Richard Hamilton, *Who Voted for Hitler?* (Princeton, NJ, 1982).

3 See for example Fritz Stern, *The Politics of Cultural Despair* (Berkeley, Calif., 1961); George Mosse, *The Crisis of German Ideology. The Intellectual*

Origins of the Third Reich (London, 1964); Hermann Glaser, *The Cultural Roots of National Socialism* (Austin, Tex., 1978). Some important strands of late nineteenth- and early twentieth-century German thought are discussed in Geoffrey Field, *Evangelist of Race. The Germanic Vision of Houston Stewart Chamberlain* (New York, 1981); Daniel Gasman, *The Scientific Origins of National Socialism. Social Darwinism in Ernst Haeckel and the German Monist League* (New York, 1971); Walter Struve, *Elites against Democracy. Leadership Ideals in Bourgeois Political Thought in Germany, 1890–1933* (Princeton, 1973); and Jeffrey Herf, *Reactionary Modernism. Technology, Culture and Politics in Weimar and the Third Reich* (Cambridge, 1984).

4 For the mass society thesis, which saw fascism as an expression of the social and political anomie of modern society, see originally Reinhard Bendix, 'Social stratification and political power', *American Political Science Review*, vol. 46 (1952), pp. 357–75; Hannah Arendt, *The Origins of Totalitarianism* (New York, 1951); William Kornhauser, *The Politics of Mass Society* (Glencoe, Ill., 1959), and see also Bernd Hagtvet, 'The theory of mass society and the collapse of the Weimar Republic: A re-examination', in S.U. Larsen *et al.* (eds), *Who Were the Fascists? Social Roots of European Fascism* (Bergen and Oslo, 1980), pp. 66–115.

5 For example, Peter Viereck, *Metapolitics. From the Romantics to Hitler* (New York, 1941); Edmond Vermeil, *Germany's Three Reichs* (London, 1945).

6 For early interpretations, see Talcott Parsons, 'Some sociological aspects of the fascist movements', *Social Forces*, vol. 21 (1942/3), pp. 138–47 and 'Democracy and social structure in pre-Nazi Germany', *Journal of Legal and Political Science*, vol. 1 (1942/3), pp. 96–114. Ralf Dahrendorf, *Society and Democracy in Germany* (New York, 1967) extends this analysis. Among historical accounts, see, for example, Hans-Ulrich Wehler, *The German Empire 1871–1918* (Leamington Spa and Dover, NH, 1985). For other references and a critical discussion of the issues in this debate, see Geoff Eley and David Blackbourn, *The Peculiarities of German History. Bourgeois Society and Politics in Nineteenth-Century Germany* (Oxford, 1984), and Geoff Eley, 'What produces fascism? Preindustrial traditions or the rise of a capitalist state?', in Dobkowski and Walliman, *Radical Perspectives*, pp. 69–99.

7 The literature here is extensive. Important contemporary interpretations include Leon Trotsky, *The Struggle Against Fascism in Germany* [1930–40] (New York, 1971); R. Palme Dutt, *Fascism and Social Revolution* [1934] (Chicago, 1974); Georgi Dimitrov, *Report to the 7th Congress Communist International 1935* [1935] (London, n.d.); Daniel Guérin, *Fascism and Big Business* [1945] (New York, 1973). Translations of contemporary Marxist writing can be found in David Beetham (ed.), *Marxists in Face of Fascism. Writings by Marxists on Fascism in the Inter-War Years* (Totowa, NJ, 1984) and Tom Bottomore and Patrick Goode (eds), *Austro-Marxism* (Oxford, 1978). The most comprehensive recent analysis is Nicos Poulantzas, *Fascism and Dictatorship* (London, 1974); also interesting is Mihaly Vajda, *Fascism as a Mass Movement* (London, 1976). Alfred Sohn-Rethel, *The Economy and Class Structure of German Fascism* (London, 1987) contains both contemporary and later essays. For other discussions and references, see Ayçoberry, *Nazi Question*; Dobkowski and Walliman, *Radical Perspectives*; Martin Kitchen, *Fascism* (London, 1976); John Cammett, 'Communist theories of fascism', *Science and Society*, vol. 3 (1967), pp. 149–63; Anson Rabinbach, 'Towards a Marxist theory of fascism and national socialism: A report on

developments in West Germany', *New German Critique*, vol. 1 (1974), pp. 127–53. On the KPD, see Ben Fowkes, *Communism in Germany under the Weimar Republic* (London, 1984); on SPD attitudes to fascism, see Richard Breitman, 'Nazism in the eyes of German social democracy', in Dobkowski and Walliman, *Towards the Holocaust*, pp. 197–212. For the East German literature, see Andreas Dorpalen, *German History in Marxist Perspective: The East German Approach* (Detroit, Mich., 1985). There are also, of course, extensive contemporary and current literatures in German.

8   This sense of the ambiguity of fascism has not, of course, been confined to Marxist analyses. Thus Ortega y Gasset wrote in 1927 that 'whichever way we approach fascism we find that it is simultaneously one thing and the contrary, it is A and not A'; quoted in Ernesto Laclau, 'Fascism and ideology', in his *Politics and Ideology in Marxist Theory* (London, 1977), p. 81. This question will also be explored further below.

9   See Eley and Blackbourn, *Peculiarities of German History*; also Richard Evans, 'The myth of Germany's missing revolution', *New Left Review*, no. 149 (1985), pp. 67–94; and the more recent literature on the *Historikerstreit*, for example, Geoff Eley, 'Nazism, politics and public memory: thoughts on the West German Historikerstreit', *Past and Present*, no. 121 (1988), pp. 171–208. The advantages of a more molecular historiography are suggested by the valuable study by Rudy Koshar, *Social Life, Local Politics, and Nazism. Marburg 1880–1935* (Chapel Hill, NC, and London, 1986), which examines the membership and views of Marburg's local voluntary associations, their tensions with regard to national politics and their eventual affiliations with National Socialism.

10   And which is also constructed, as norms tend to be, by excluding or repressing what is shared in common with the 'other', so that the abjected 'other' functions in an important sense to confirm the otherwise fragile unity and authority of the norm.

11   On the founding of the DAP, see Reginald Phelps, 'Hitler and the *Deutsche Arbeiterpartei*', in Henry Turner (ed.), *Nazism and the Third Reich* (New York, 1972), pp. 5–19; on the organizational history of the party in general, see Dietrich Orlow, *The History of the Nazi Party: 1919–1933* (Pittsburgh, Pa, 1969).

12   Hitler's early role as leader is discussed in Joseph Nyomarkay, *Charisma and Factionalism in the Nazi Party* (Minneapolis, Minn., 1967) and Ian Kershaw, *The 'Hitler Myth'. Image and Reality in the Third Reich* (Oxford, 1987), ch. 1.

13   It is beyond the scope of this chapter to discuss this question, but see the chapters by David Kaiser and Richard Breitman below.

14   Quoted in Noakes and Pridham, *Nazism*, p. 37.

15   See Hans Mommsen, 'National Socialism: continuity and change', in Walter Laqueur (ed.), *Fascism. A Reader's Guide* (Harmondsworth, 1979), pp. 151–92; Martin Broszat, *German National Socialism 1919–1945* (Santa Barbara, Calif., 1966).

16   For the SA, see principally Richard Bessel, *Political Violence and the Rise of Nazism. The Storm Troopers in Eastern Germany 1925–1934* (New Haven, Conn., 1984); Conan Fischer, *Stormtroopers. A Social, Economic and Ideological Analysis* (London, 1983); Eric G. Reiche, *The Development of the SA in Nürnberg 1922–1934* (Cambridge, 1986), and Peter H. Merkl, *Political Violence Under the Swastika* (Princeton, NJ, 1975).

17   See Koshar, *Social Life, Local Politics, and Nazism*, p. 81. Classic accounts of the tactics and appeal of Nazism are William Sheridan Allen, *The Nazi*

Seizure of Power. The Experience of a Single German Town 1930–1935 (London, 1966), and Theodore Abel, *Why Hitler Came Into Power* [1938] (Cambridge, 1986). A recent account of the texture of local politics in Weimar is Peter Fritzsche, *Rehearsals for Fascism. Populism and Political Mobilization in Weimar Germany* (New York, 1990).

18 For the SA, see references in n. 16 above, also Richard Bessel, 'Violence as propaganda: the role of the storm troopers in the rise of National Socialism', in Childers, *Formation of the Nazi Constituency*, pp. 131–46. For the other side of political violence, see Eve Rosenhaft, *Beating the Fascists? The German Communists and Political Violence 1929–1933* (Cambridge, 1983).

19 For a discussion of this division, see Bessel, *Political Violence and the Rise of Nazism*, ch. 6; a further aspect is discussed in Rudy Koshar, 'Two 'Nazisms': the social context of Nazi mobilization in Marburg and Tübingen', *Social History*, vol. 7 (1982), pp. 27–42.

20 See Broszat, *Hitler and the Collapse of Weimar Germany*, pp. 64–5.

21 See Jeremy Noakes, *The Nazi Party in Lower Saxony 1921–1933*, Part 2 (Oxford, 1971). For Schleswig-Holstein, see Rudolf Heberle, *From Democracy to Nazism* (New York, 1970; [1st edn, 1945]).

22 The crisis of the liberal parties in Weimar has been exhaustively examined by Larry E. Jones, *German Liberalism and the Dissolution of the Weimar Republic 1918–1933* (Chapel Hill, NC, and London, 1988).

23 See especially Harold Lasswell, 'The psychology of Hitlerism', *Political Quarterly*, vol. 4 (1933), pp. 373–84, and the classic statement by Seymour Martin Lipset, *Political Man. The Social Bases of Politics* (New York, 1960), ch. 5. A less clear but nonetheless related sociological profile was drawn by proponents of the mass society thesis; see references in n. 4 above. Further references and discussion in Hamilton, *Who Voted for Hitler?*, chs 1 and 2.

24 See references in n. 7 above.

25 The most important contributions here have been Childers, *Nazi Voter*; Hamilton, *Who Voted for Hitler?*; the essays in Childers, *Formation of the Nazi Constituency*; Michael Kater, *The Nazi Party. A Social Profile of Members and Leaders, 1919–1945* (Cambridge, 1983); and a number of essays by Jürgen Falter, including (in English) 'Radicalization of the middle classes or mobilization of the unpolitical?' *Social Science Information* vol. 20, (1981), pp. 389–430, and (with Reinhard Zintl), 'The economic crisis of the 1930s and the Nazi vote', *Journal of Interdisciplinary History*, vol. 19 (1988), pp. 55–85.

26 For propaganda, see Childers, *Nazi Voter*; Lothar Kettenacker, 'Hitler's impact on the lower middle class', in David Welch (ed.), *Nazi Propaganda* (Beckenham, 1983), pp. 10–28; Richard Bessel, 'The rise of the NSDAP and the myth of Nazi propaganda', *Wiener Library Bulletin*, vol. 33 (1980), pp. 20–9; Ian Kershaw, 'Ideology, Propaganda, and the Rise of the Nazi Party', in Stachura, *Nazi Machtergreifung*, pp. 162–81.

27 Childers, *Nazi Voter*, p. 265.

28 For theoretical work, see the works cited in n. 7 above. Empirical studies include Tim Mason, 'National Socialism and the working class, 1925–May, 1933', *New German Critique* (1977), pp. 49–93; Detlev Mühlberger, 'The sociology of the NSDAP: the question of working-class membership', *Journal of Contemporary History*, vol. 15 (1980), pp. 493–511; Max Kele, *Nazis and Workers* (Chapel Hill, NC, 1972).

29 This point was first made by Tim Mason in a critical review of Kele, *Nazis and Workers*: 'The Coming of the Nazis', *Times Literary Supplement*, 1

February 1974. It has since been debated in connection with the SA in particular; see the works cited in n. 16 above, and also the debate between Richard Bessel and Mathilde Jamin on the one hand, and Conan Fischer and Carolyn Hicks on the other, in *Social History*, vol. 4 (1979), pp. 111–16, and vol. 5 (1980), pp. 131–40.

30   Mason, 'National socialism and working class'; see also James Wickham, 'Working-class movement and working-class life: Frankfurt am Main during the Weimar Republic', *Social History*, vol. 8 (1983), pp. 315–43. The practice of *Alltagsgeschichte*, or reconstructing the history of everyday life, could throw new light on the nature of class consciousness in Weimar, but has so far had more impact on the historiography of working-class experience in the late nineteenth century and under Nazism; see Geoff Eley, 'Labor history, social history, *Alltagsgeschichte*: experience, culture, and the politics of the everyday', *Journal of Modern History*, vol. 61 (1989), pp. 297–343.

31   Mason, 'National Socialism and the German working class', p. 60.

32   For the DNVP as mass party, see Hamilton, *Who Voted for Hitler?*, ch. 10.

33   See principally Helen L. Boak, '"Our last hope": women's votes for Hitler – A reappraisal', *German Studies Review*, vol. 12 (1989), pp. 289–310; also Jill Stephenson, 'National Socialism and women before 1933', in Stachura, *Nazi Machtergreifung*, pp. 33–48; Tim Mason, 'Women in Nazi Germany', *History Workshop Journal*, vol. 1 (1976), pp. 74–113; and Claudia Koonz, *Mothers in the Fatherland* (New York, 1986), chs 3 and 4.

34   Mason, 'Women in Nazi Germany, Part I'; Renate Bridenthal and Claudia Koonz, 'Beyond *Kinder, Küche, Kirche*: Weimar women in politics and work', in Renate Bridenthal *et al.* (eds), *When Biology Became Destiny. Women in Weimar and Nazi Germany* (New York, 1984), pp. 33–65.

35   This evidence is discussed especially by Koonz, *Mothers in the Fatherland*, ch. 3.

36   Kater, *Nazi Party*, chs 2, 3 and 7; see also Brian Peterson, 'Regional elites and the rise of National Socialism, 1920–33', in Dobkowksi and Walliman, *Radical Perspectives*, pp. 172–93; Koshar, *Social Life, Local Politics, and Nazism*, Part 2; Geoffrey J. Giles, 'National Socialism and the educated elite in the Weimar Republic', in Stachura, *Nazi Machtergreifung*, pp. 49–67; and Konrad Jarausch, 'The crisis of the German professions, 1918–33', *Journal of Contemporary History*, vol. 20 (1985), pp. 379–98.

37   Hamilton, *Who Voted for Hitler?*, chs 4–8.

38   See Dobkowksi and Walliman, *Radical Perspectives*; Breitman, 'Nazism in the Eyes of German social democracy'; also other works cited in n. 7 above.

39   The difference is best observed by comparing David Abraham, *The Collapse of the Weimar Republic. Political Economy and Crisis* 2nd. edn (New York, 1986) and Henry A. Turner, *German Big Business and the Rise of Hitler* (New York, 1987). The argument over Abraham's book reached beyond the usual scholarly proportions; see particularly the exchange between Abraham and Gerald Feldman in *Central European History*, vol. 17 (1984), pp. 159–290.

40   Dick Geary, 'The industrial elite and the Nazis in the Weimar Republic', in Stachura, *Nazi Machtergreifung*, pp. 85–100, offers a useful overview; see also the sources in n. 39 above, and Gerald Feldman, 'The social and economic policies of German big business 1918–1929', *American Historical Review*, vol. 57 (1969), pp. 47–55; also Bernd Weisbrod, 'Economic power and political stability reconsidered: heavy industry in Weimar Germany',

Social History, vol. 4 (1979), pp. 241–63. Once again, the bulk of this literature is in German.

41   Hamilton, *Who Voted for Hitler?* is the most sustained argument for this; see also the debate between Hamilton and Childers, and the comment by William Sheridan Allen, in *Central European History*, vol. 17 (1984). The issue has since been taken a step further in a critical essay by Peter Baldwin, 'Social interpretations of Nazism: renewing a tradition', *Journal of Contemporary History*, vol. 25 (1990), pp. 5–37.

42   Thomas Childers, 'The social language of politics in Germany: the sociology of political discourse in the Weimar Republic', *American Historical Review*, vol. 95 (1990), pp. 331–58. The party's appeal to a variety of social groups is discussed in the essays in Childers, *Formation of the Nazi Constituency*.

43   Charles Maier has questioned the value of poststructuralist interpretation in *The Unmasterable Past* (Cambridge, 1988); the recent controversies (not mainly conducted by historians, however) over the attitudes to fascism of Martin Heidegger and Paul de Man, seen as apostles of poststructuralist theory, have heightened the sense that its opening of texts to multiple interpretation is inimical to the premises of historiography; on Heidegger see *Critical Inquiry*, vol. 15 (1989), and on de Man see ibid., and Werner Hamacher *et al.* (eds), *Responses. On Paul de Man's Wartime Journalism* (Lincoln, Nebr., 1989).

44   A review of the issues is attempted in Jane Caplan, 'Postmodernism, poststructuralism, and deconstruction', *Central European History*, vol. 22 (1989), pp. 260–78.

45   Harold James, *The German Slump: Politics and Economics* (Oxford, 1986); see also Richard Evans (ed.), *The German Unemployed. Experiences and Consequences of Mass Unemployment from the Weimar Republic to the Third Reich* (New York, 1987), and Peter D. Stachura (ed.), *Unemployment and the Great Depression in Weimar Germany* (New York, 1986).

46   Kolb, *Weimar Republic*, ch. 6, offers a useful overview of the mainly German literature on this question. The classic text on the collapse, Karl Dietrich Bracher's *Die Auflösung der Weimarer Republik* (Villingen, 1955), has never been translated; but see Abraham, *Collapse of the Weimar Republic*; and most recently Ian Kershaw (ed.), *Weimar: Why Did German Democracy Fail?* (London, 1990), which was not available to me in time to consult for this chapter.

47   For an assessment of Brüning's financial policies, see James, *German Slump*.

48   Quoted in Noakes and Pridham, *Nazism*, p. 90.

49   Thus in 1930 the Reichstag held 94 sessions, while five emergency decrees were adopted; by 1932 the figures were 13 and 57 respectively (Childers, *Nazi Voter*, p. 192); concomitantly, the electoral participation rate, 74.6 per cent in 1928, reached 83.4 per cent in July 1932; between 1928 and 1930, NSDAP membership increased from 108,717 to 293,000, and probably reached well over a million by the end of 1932.

50   Childers, 'Limits of National Socialist mobilisation'.

51   See Mommsen, 'National Socialism'.

7 Women in Modern Germany

EVE ROSENHAFT

The historiography of modern Germany, as of all countries and periods, now includes a considerable body of work on the history of women and, increasingly, of gender relations. Although it is still possible for mainstream social and political histories to ignore the 'woman question', the study of women and gender is well established as a branch of German history. The particularities of women's situation in Germany since the nineteenth century have generated their own objects of interest and controversy. These, though often arising out of the special concerns of international feminist scholarship, tend to echo more general historiographical debates about the characteristic features and failings of German society. Indeed, the historical moments and movements that are most characteristic of German society involved an explicit sexual politics or were accompanied by anxieties about the stability of gender identities and the balance of power between the sexes.

At the end of the nineteenth century Germany had a large female workforce and the largest women's movement in the world. At the same time, German women were among the most severely restricted in Western Europe, in terms not only of civil rights but also of rights within marriage. Until 1908 Prussian women (about two-thirds of the female population of the Reich) were barred from joining political organizations. Granted the franchise in 1918 and formal equality under the Weimar constitution of 1919, they remained subject to discriminatory employment legislation during the 1920s in spite of the continued growth in the numbers of working and professional women and the popularization of the image of a 'new', independent and emancipated woman. National Socialism came to power in 1933 with the explicit policy of recovering the distinctions between masculine and feminine roles that had become blurred, restoring men to the position of social leadership and healthy, 'Aryan' women to their primary function as bearers of racially pure

140

children. Both the social and the racial policies of the Nazi regime thus had distinct and quite deliberate implications for women, as workers and as mothers. In self-conscious reaction against the experience of National Socialism, the identities of the new German states after 1949 were expressed in distinct public attitudes to women's role. Where the German Democratic Republic set full formal equality and integration into the workforce against the Nazi insistence on separate spheres, the social policy of the Federal Republic aimed to reassert the sanctity of the patriarchal family against the imagined consequences of *Gleichschaltung*. West German civil law continued to prescribe housekeeping and child-raising as the primary duties of married women until 1975.[1]

In these developments, and particularly in the period before the Second World War, the women's movement played an ambivalent role. In the late nineteenth and early twentieth centuries, in spite of the relatively backward position of German women in terms of legal status, Germany witnessed no equivalent of Britain's militant suffragism. The demand for full legal and civil equality was raised by the Social Democratic women's movement, but among Social Democrats women's demands were understood as part of a broad socialist program whose achievement required the subordination of women's special needs to working for the victory of the labor movement. The work of organizing and mobilizing women around issues specific to women fell to the bourgeois women's movement, most of whose leading representatives subscribed to a vision in which emancipation meant freeing women to make a full contribution to society in terms of their characteristically feminine qualities and talents. This approach to feminist politics had a contradictory flowering in the 1920s and 1930s. On the one hand the expansion of public health and welfare services during the First World War and during the Weimar Republic placed the 'feminine' concern for children, family and service to others at the center of state policy. However, in so far as the Nazis promised to prosecute in more effective form the welfare state policies of the Weimar Republic and at the same time to give practical support to the principle of separate spheres and the protection of family life, the ideological heritage of the bourgeois women's movement predisposed many women's organizations to look favorably on the Nazi take over and cooperate in Nazi programs.

In this sense, the question of the origins and consequences of National Socialism has structured research and debate in the history of women and gender. This appears paradoxical: in speaking of National Socialism one invokes a *political history* of radical discontinuity, or at least of shifting balances of class power within a continuity of capitalist production relations, while women's history appears to confirm a continuity in the balance of power between the sexes that even the abolition of capitalism in the German Democratic Republic (GDR) did not succeed in suspending. Since the 1970s, however, trends in research have led to a fruitful convergence of the two themes. On the one hand, historians and social scientists have increasingly been interested in situating National Socialism within a continuous development of modern Western society, in considering it as a characteristic product of that development and looking for the features of the Nazi system that permitted it to be experienced as 'normal' by the people who operated within it. On the other, the emphasis in women's history has shifted from demonstrating the continuity of women's subordination and elaborating its functionality to the attempt to historicize it, that is to identify the relationship between the particular gender identities accepted as normal in modern Western society and other characteristic features and values of that society. The result of this convergence has been to open up new dimensions in the historical account of both National Socialism and the situation of women, even if the opportunities it provides for a general reinterpretation have not yet been taken up.

WOMEN, WORK AND FAMILY IN NATIONAL SOCIALISM

Perhaps the most important insight of recent research into the situation of women under National Socialism has been to underline its ambivalence and to emphasize the extent to which this ambivalence reflected a dual thrust in Nazi policy. In particular, it is no longer possible to assert simply that National Socialism pursued a conservative (or reactionary) policy of returning women to the home.[2] On the contrary, within the context of a general determination to subordinate women to institutionalized male power, the Nazi system identified a place for women at work as well as in the family. What was peculiar to National Socialism was its intention to rationalize the process of deciding which women should perform which functions.

National Socialism first attacked women's employment on political grounds; active discrimination was directed at removing women from positions of power and authority, or preventing them from reaching such positions.[3] A woman remained conspicuously at the top of the Nazi Women's Organization, and women leaders were prominent in other mass organizations which claimed extensive competence to organize the education of women and girls for their social role and contribution to the national effort. But women were immediately and systematically excluded from political appointments and decision-making posts. They retained the right to vote (in a political order in which the franchise had become meaningless), but could no longer stand for office and were excluded from sitting on juries. The system of marriage loans introduced in 1933 was designed to tempt women out of the workforce, rather than force them out. It also manifestly served wider purposes in which women were implicated but were not the principal targets of policy: making jobs available for unemployed men, raising the birth rate and (perhaps most important, in terms of the characteristic preoccupations of the regime) providing a mechanism for the expansion of eugenic screening and regulation. Similarly, the only measure aimed at directing women into acceptably 'feminine' occupations was the introduction of an incentive to the employment of domestic servants (backed up by the use of the Labor Service system after 1935 to introduce girls to menial agricultural and domestic work). The only women who were denied the right to work were women in managerial positions in the public sector, beginning with married women civil servants. Here, Nazi policy followed previous practice, both in the specific attack on *Doppelverdienertum* ('double-earning' households) and in limiting the full deployment of executive power to the area in which the state was the employer. Lower salaries were introduced for women civil servants, quotas on promotions severely disadvantaged women in the education service and women teachers and public servants were forced into lower-status posts. From 1936 on women were barred from acting as judges or lawyers. Women doctors were prohibited from practising independently and women's access to medical training and practical experience was severely restricted. Nazi policy also aimed at cutting off the supply of female professionals by progressively denying girls the kinds of secondary education that would qualify them for university places and replacing academic subjects with domestic science. Even before the introduction of full-blown sex discrimination, the racial and political purging of the lower ranks of the public service and the professions, carried out by a combination of legislation and voluntary 'Aryanization' of professional associations, along with the transformation of the functions of such public agencies as health and marriage counselling centers, had a disproportionate impact on women, because their presence in these posts often reflected a moral and political commitment to public service.[4]

Official measures to enforce the conservative familialist ideology conventionally associated with National Socialism were thus limited in their scope, and the consequence was that even in peacetime the participation of women in the labor force increased twice as sharply as that of men. By 1939 a higher proportion even of married women were in work than in 1933.[5] In the last two years before the outbreak of war, moreover, the demand of the armaments industry for scientifically and technically trained personnel led to a new policy of encouraging girls to go into higher education. With the onset of war, the shortage of qualified men led to large numbers of women in education, training and paid work at all levels, and also offered women already employed in some areas (such as white-collar work) undreamt-of opportunities for upward mobility.[6] This occurred in spite of the fact that the official propaganda of home and family, the legal fixing of women's industrial wages at lower rates than men's and the practice of paying generous allowances to the dependents of soldiers in order to secure public support for the war effort provided married women with both a rationale and a good reason to avoid war work. (Compulsory labor registration was introduced for women only in 1943 and the regulations were full of loopholes and inconsistently applied.) This pattern has led some historians to identify a fundamental contradiction in national socialist policy: on the one hand, the ideology that denied women the right to work was so powerful that it hindered the mobilization of female labor even in the wartime emergency.[7] On the other, in spite of its conservative ideology, National Socialism was an essentially modernizing force in gender relations (as reflected in patterns of women's work), contributing in the long term to the emancipation of women from traditional roles.[8]

In so far as these two assertions are based on statistical evidence, the contradiction that they propose is open to question. The view that the Nazis were 'unsuccessful' in any objective terms in mobilizing female labor in wartime, although widely held, has been challenged on the grounds that the potential pool of female labor was already effectively exhausted at the outbreak of war. Before the war, it has been argued, Germany had already achieved the degree of mobilization of women that the other combatant powers still had to aim for, so that the relatively low increase in the female labor force after 1939 is not remarkable. By 1943, women made up 36.4 per cent of the British workforce, but 48.8 per cent of the German; over half of German women of working age were already at work or engaged in some form of labor service in 1939.[9] Those who remained to be mobilized in wartime were primarily women who had never worked before, members of the middle and upper classes, and their resistance to making such a major contribution to the national effort could be surprising only to Nazi ideologues.

Moreover, it was more the concern with general civilian morale than an attachment to familialist ideology that produced the policies that made staying at home more attractive than working. (These authors do not deny the real strains put on the economy and on those women who did work by the continuing labor shortage, or the social strains implicit in the manifest fact that it was working-class women who were most often forced to work.) The use of rising rates of female employment to support an argument about long-term emancipatory processes is problematic considering that the participation of women in the West German labor force in 1950 (30 per cent) was lower than it had been at any time since the First World War and still had not achieved the level of 1939 by the 1980s.[10] Qualitative evidence suggests that the principal element of modernization in the gendered labor market between 1939 and 1945 was the opening up to women of certain jobs, particularly clerical work – a process that by no means implied emancipation or equality for women.[11]

What an earlier empirical historiography had identified as contradictions in Nazi policy have found a kind of resolution since the late 1970s in new attempts at a feminist synthetic account of Nazism. These efforts challenge both the idea that the national socialist vision of gender and family was essentially conservative and the related view that the Nazis held and aimed to enforce a traditional, undifferentiated view of female character. They see it as characteristic of National Socialism that its policy makers (whatever the vision presented in mass propaganda) harbored different ideals of womanhood for different groups of women. The process of enforcing these ideals implied at once the radical subordination of all women and the abandonment of the idea of a single feminine character shared by all women as a socially relevant category. And it was more than compatible with a vision of a future social order which was outspokenly anti-traditional and progressive in terms of contemporary technologies and programs of labor discipline. Annemarie Tröger has shown a continuity of official and managerial policies directed at training girls for a career that would combine raising a family with employment in semi-skilled industrial work; after 1933 these policies became part of the program of the Deutsche Arbeitsfront for the women of the working class. The argument that women were psychologically and physiologically well adapted to assembly-line work was elaborated in the course of the rationalization of German industry in the 1920s. Nazi ideology added the qualification that physically and mentally undemanding work of this kind was best suited to allow women workers the time and energy to reflect on and carry out their maternal duties more effectively.

This idea of women's work as non-work was characteristically supplemented by the conviction that other women, those suited to be full-time mothers, should be discouraged from working, and still others, namely those unfit for motherhood, should be compelled to work until the state found other ways of disposing of them.[12] In Nazi theory, the distinctions between these three groups were biological; in practice, the criteria applied were social and behavioral, as a growing body of research on medical and eugenic screening in the Third Reich has made clear. In her work on compulsory sterilization, which was carried out on some 400,000 Germans (approximately half of them women) under Nazi eugenic legislation, Gisela Bock insists that the Nazi ideal of motherhood was reserved for the eugenically select and illustrates the brutal machinery and invidious terms of the selection process. Bock, in a radical formulation of the combined process of subordination and differentiation outlined above, describes the logic of Nazi policies as the 'intended elimination of the female sex'.[13] (It ought to be noted that both Bock and

Tröger, among others, have identified a significant amount of resistance on the part of women, particularly young women, to being pressed into the roles and occupations assigned to them by Nazi policy.)

DESTABILIZING AND RESTORING GENDER ROLES

The idea of an 'intended elimination of the female sex' implies a desire on the part of National Socialists to do away with women in the sense of reducing them absolutely to the minimum necessary function of vessels for biological reproduction. It may equally be read as referring to the relationship between National Socialist gender ideology and the cultural definitions of masculinity and femininity that are characteristic of Western culture, but which were being increasingly challenged in the early twentieth century. Extensive research in the history of literature, political and social theory and psychology has identified the emergence in the course of the eighteenth century of a systematic vision of the polarization of 'sexual characters'. In this view, men and women had distinct but complementary qualities, which were seen as suiting them for the spheres or aspects of human activity that were coming to be seen in similarly polarized terms. Men embodied intellect, activity, creative production, and were fitted by nature to act in the public sphere of political and economic life, while the characteristic gifts of women were instinct and affection, patience and effortless reproduction, their sphere the private sphere of home and family. This world-view has been interpreted as a direct reflection of the division of labor in the households of the service bourgeoisie of the eighteenth century, in which home and workplace were separate and the household lost its economic functions and took on those of providing education for children and recreation for the economically active father.[14]

National Socialism radically challenged the polarities of bourgeois ideology in two respects: first, in its brutal disregard for the distinction between public and private, its determination to subject every relevant aspect of individual life to the control of the state; and, second, in its repudiation of the myth of a unitary femininity that would make all women mothers. The study of women's history in the light of the National Socialist experience has therefore given considerable attention to illustrating the ambivalence in the bourgeois idea of femininity and the feminine sphere itself.

For one thing, it is clear that by the end of the nineteenth century ever fewer people were prepared to accept that the denial of basic rights to women was compatible with the needs and expectations of a modern society. In 1896 a new Civil Code was passed, to go into effect in 1900, which included the first codification of family law for the whole of the

German Reich. The debates around the provisions of the draft code provided a focus for public discussions about the rights of women within the family, while the Bund Deutscher Frauenvereine (BDF, the umbrella association of non-socialist women's organizations) twice organized campaigns of petitions and public meetings to demand that wives at last be given an equal say in domestic decisions and control over their own property and that the law governing the rights of illegitimate mothers and children be reformed.[15] They were largely ignored, the code's principal reform being the introduction of the right of working wives to keep control of their own earnings. This was a concession to the reality of expanding women's work; in 1895 12 per cent of married women were earning, an increase of three percentage points over 1882 (between 1882 and 1907 the female proportion of the manual labor force increased from 13.3 to 18.2 per cent).[16] The new provision also implied the recognition and sanction of a range of roles for women – although middle-class women remained firmly bound to their role in the patriarchal family.

In 1908 the ban on the participation of women in political meetings and associations was lifted. By then, the BDF had adopted the demand for women's suffrage, although the demand was actively pursued only by a relatively small section on the association's left wing. A more eye-catching form of activity of the women's movement in these years was the campaign against the legal regulation and policing of prostitution. Like similar campaigns in the United States and Great Britain, this campaign raised under the banner of 'morality' a direct challenge to the sexual double standard and the demand that all women be treated with respect as persons whose physical integrity was inviolable. (The central protest was against the powers of the police arbitrarily to detain individual women and subject them to medical examination.)[17] Since it presented the spectacle of 'respectable' middle-class women speaking in public about 'indecent' things (even if only to denounce them as an affront to feminine 'honor'), the morality campaign represented a further challenge to conventional gender stereotypes and to the security of male dominance.[18] The turn of the century witnessed a burst of scientific, pseudo-scientific and polemically anti-feminist literature designed to reassert the essential differences between men and women, now couched increasingly in terms of women's inferiority.[19] At the same time, the idea of companionate marriage was beginning to be canvassed among progressive intellectuals, while the new youth movements, which cultivated a range of attitudes from androgyny through desexualized homophilia to sexual partnership, put generation before the gender as an object of allegiance and concern.

If the 'traditional' relationship between the sexes was already being challenged before 1914, the experience of the First World War brought a very severe shock indeed, as women demonstrated their capacity to function effectively in administration and the economy in the absence of men. At the outbreak of the war the middle-class women's associations came together to form the Nationaler Frauendienst (National Women's Service), which took over extensive functions as the war went on, not only in maintaining morale through propaganda but also in administering the social services that proliferated in wartime to aid the families of soldiers and war-workers. Working-class women took on a more immediate burden of responsibility, as the sole providers of income and representatives of parental authority in households where the fathers had been conscripted. The anxiety engendered by the absence of male authority figures on the home front was reflected in the anticipation of a rise in juvenile delinquency, in fears about the disruption of domestic and social order that often accompanied complaints about the increasing insolence of the working class. The image of women's work also began to change. Called upon to replace conscripted male workers, women were spectacularly visible in public transport, and were drafted into munitions work on a large scale; the Krupp arms factories, which before the war had employed between 2,000 and 3,000 women, had 28,000 women workers at the beginning of 1918; the proportion of women in the Krupp workforce had risen from 3.2 per cent to 37.6 per cent.[20]

Since the 1920s, most of the literature on women's work in the First World War has assumed that the war gave a significant boost to the participation of women in the labor force, with large numbers entering the workforce for the first time between 1914 and 1918 and an atmosphere significantly more encouraging to women's paid employment after 1918.[21] The implicit vision of the war and the Weimar Republic as a period of emancipation for women has been challenged from two directions. Ute Daniel has recently argued that it was not so much the scale of women's labor-force participation that changed as the kind of work they did; the war effort shifted women who were already working out of 'women's industries' such as clothing and food processing and into heavy industry, and the typical working woman was still more likely to be single than married.[22] In the light of recent research that has emphasized the official perception of women's work as a temporary measure, and the relative ease with which women were persuaded to give up their jobs to returning soldiers in 1918–19,[23] Daniel makes the radical argument (on the basis of local studies) that the war had no long-term effect on women's work. For the Weimar Republic, Renate Bridenthal has argued persuasively that the spectacle of women going out to work was to some extent a function of a real shift from home-working, and especially domestic service, to industrial work, which made women's work more visible. Far from being liberating, however, the kinds of women's work that were characteristic of the 1920s both in industry and in domestic and agricultural work were more demanding of time and effort and brought less status and income than ever before.[24] The more radical proposition that a cataclysmic event such as the First World War had no concrete consequences for the lives of women will continue to be challenged. But the overall effect of critiques of this kind has been to shift the attention of historians to the interplay between perceptions of women's situation and policies. Women's high visibility in previously male industrial preserves during the war had consequences both for perceptions of gender roles and for state and employer policies towards workplace organization.

In the realm of gender roles, as in society and the economy generally, the slogan of the years following the First World War was rationalization.[25] Within the realm of industrial work, the drive towards rationalization, already under way before 1914, was accelerated by the demands of wartime production and intensified in the 1920s in response to the threat to profitability posed by the terms of currency stabilization after 1923. The concentration of firms and, in particular, the transformation of the labor process through managerial and technological means (the assembly line) that rationalization involved had dual implications for women. On the one hand, rationalization was designed to cut labor costs by easing the employment of untrained operatives with low expectations, of whom young women represented the most obvious supply. At the same time, the experience of efforts to attract and hold married women workers during the war had taught many large industrial employers the value of providing services for workers' families. In wartime, these services had been provided by the state. In the wake of industrial rationalization, 'progressive' employers such as Siemens, the electrical giant, introduced a new variation on employer paternalism designed to 'rationalize' the relationship between work and family in the sense of preventing any perception of a conflict of interest between the two. This might mean maintaining measures to make it possible for women to combine low-paid industrial work with looking after their families; it might, as in the case of Siemens, mean treating the whole family of the (male) worker as the unit of production, and taking steps to influence the workers' home life in such a way as to guarantee that it fulfilled the function of keeping the worker happy and healthy and providing a new generation of reliable workers.

The slogan of rationalization came to be applied during the 1920s to a number of areas of everyday life, and in each case its implication was that the idea of a polar difference, or even a relationship of complementarity, between the masculine and feminine spheres was no longer tenable. The movement for the rationalization of housework, drawing on both managerial (time-keeping) and technological (electrical household appliances) models, insisted that the household was a workplace subject to the same principles as the shop floor. The movement for the rationalization of sexuality was based on the conviction that even the most intimate sphere of human relations was subject to demystification through scientific analysis, which if properly applied could improve performance; it insisted that women were as capable of sexual response and had as much right to sexual satisfaction as men.[26]

In its relationship to women, rationalization has thus been interpreted as both confirming the breakdown of traditional gender polarities and attempting to restore women to their family and reproductive functions by reinscribing them in a new, less polarized scheme of social and sexual relations. On the one hand, rationalization in industry contributed to the general postwar phenomenon of the increased visibility of women at work, in politics and in new forms of popular leisure such as the cinema. Even if life did not change very much for most women, the controversial type of 'new woman' – economically independent, unemotional and calculating, sexually self-aware, oriented towards entertainment and consumption and positively androgynous in her hairstyle and dress – was significant both as a symbol of perceived change and as a model to which young women in particular aspired.[27] She was a product of the rationalized labor market and the forms of consumption it encouraged, as well as of more diffuse challenges to traditional femininity. Outside the rationalization movement, the reaction against this figure, and against the fear of decline of the family and loss of male authority associated with it, has been identified in a range of preoccupations of Weimar culture, including the movement for the introduction of Mother's Day as a national holiday and the treatment of the theme of motherhood in war memorials.[28] Analysis of the writings of extreme conservative and proto-fascist authors of the 1920s has revealed a characteristic misogyny which was expressed as an association between powerful women and the threatening revolutionary mass.[29]

WOMEN, THEIR POLITICS AND THE PATHOLOGY OF BOURGEOIS SOCIETY

Both the verbal preoccupation of the Nazi movement with reversing women's emancipation and the prosecution under the Nazi regime of schemes to subordinate the definition of women's role entirely to the combined demands of production and reproduction may thus be read back into the 1920s' efforts to redefine the relationship between masculinity and femininity in ways that would stabilize the attachment of women to the family. In this light, Nazism accommodated both a 'modern' and a 'conservative' answer to the perceived breakdown of traditional gender roles. Much was made in the past of National

Socialism's attraction for women, which was perceived as being considerable and also as paradoxical in the light of the commitment of the Nazis to reversing what emancipation women had experienced. Close attention to the voting figures has shown that while women, who tended on the whole to vote more conservatively than men of the same class, showed relatively little enthusiasm for National Socialism before the depression, they contributed (though still at a slower rate than men) to the Nazis' electoral upswing in 1930 and, by 1932, were outnumbering male voters in their support for the NSDAP in some areas. (Their support, however, continued to vary with class and, especially, religion.)[30] Historians have shown more interest in National Socialism's success after 1933 in winning the assent of many active and self-conscious women organized within the women's movement, a phenomenon that reflects the continued vitality of a 'separate spheres' model of the role of women. Not least because of this, the 'failure' of the largest section of the non-socialist women's movement in Germany to establish and defend a strictly egalitarian position on women's rights has been the subject of considerable historical research and argument.

The shift of frames of reference within the English-language literature is well illustrated by the approaches of Richard Evans, in his 1976 study of the bourgeois feminist movement in Germany, and Claudia Koonz, in her 1986 work on women and national socialism. Evans's concern was to challenge both the classical structuralist view that the Wilhelmine period witnessed the failure of modern political forms to develop alongside a rapidly modernizing industry and a revisionist view that cited the rise of the women's movement as a sign of social progress. His work characterizes the position of the prewar BDF as having nothing to do with feminism or with the interests of women as identifiable from a contemporary perspective, and explains the successive freezing out of egalitarians, militant suffragists and advocates of sexual and reproductive rights for women as a paradoxical consequence of the expansion of BDF membership following the (unquestionably progressive) lifting of the ban on women's political activity. He thus treats the fate of liberal feminism as an aspect of the contradictory fate of German liberalism itself, and as evidence for the wider argument that liberal individualism is not to be regarded as the quintessence of political modernity.[31] Claudia Koonz describes the acceptability of National Socialism to organized women as the longer-term consequence of the abandonment of liberal individualism by the women's movement in favor of familialist, collectivist, *völkisch* and nationalist positions, and its popularisation of the idea that the most effective contribution of women to society would be in fields that represented an extension of their maternal role. She sees the position of the women's movement not as a denial of feminism, however, but as a manifestation of a particular kind of feminism, namely, the separatist feminism that has become increasingly influential in the United States since the 1970s. Her work has to be seen as a polemic against a politics based on the assertion that women have special qualities that make them different from men in socially and politically significant ways.[32]

Within the last 10 years, then, there has developed a tendency to attempt to situate the peculiarities of the nineteenth-century women's movement within a broader definition of feminism and to reinterpret it in the light of current women's politics. This approach, which has been particularly apparent in West German scholarship, has also considered the logic of its vision of femininity in terms of the whole history of the interplay of class and gender consciousness within the German bourgeoisie. Elisabeth Meyer-Renschhausen has argued that the morality and abstinence campaigns of the turn of the century should be seen not as a distraction from or a substitute for political engagement, but as the manifestation of a genuinely feminist, woman-centered politics which challenged the social as well as the gender order. Looking back to the origins of the middle-class women's movement, she has also emphasized how the 'radically traditional' self-image of its members was rooted in the emancipatory aspects of bourgeois ideology in the eighteenth and early nineteenth centuries. The feminine character proposed by that ideology was not, in the first instance, subordinate or necessarily inferior to the masculine; the two were conceived of as fully complementary. The union of man and woman as moral equals created a family tied together by bonds of rational affection, and it was through this model of human and sexual relations that the articulate middle classes raised their challenge to the power and values of the aristocracy in pre-industrial Germany. Indeed, in deliberate contrast to the extravagance, brutality and licentiousness of the aristocracy, the image of the bourgeois man at this early period included many characteristics later associated with the feminine principle, including those of sentiment and attachment to domestic life.[33]

Herrad-Ulrike Bussemer argued in a similar vein when studying the model of 'intellectual motherliness' that was adopted by women in the 1860s and 1870s – a model that articulated the belief that women could contribute humane social concern in an increasingly cynical and power-oriented society. She proposes that this movement represented a reassertion of the values of a *Bildungsbürgertum* (educated middle class) in crisis, which explains why it drew upon the family- and child-centered educational theories of the late eighteenth and early nineteenth centuries.[34]

Thus, where work that focused on the relationship of the women's movement to mainstream political developments has interpreted its move to the right before the First World War as part of the general middle-class response to intensified class conflict, studies that situate the attitudes of the movement within a continuous feminist tradition have illuminated the way in which its apparent conservatism preserved the critical impulses inherent in bourgeois ideology at its birth. This literature is beginning to be echoed in the general literature relating to the social and political attitudes of the German middle classes that was inspired by the discussion, in the context of the *Sonderweg* debate, about the relative 'bourgeoisness' of nineteenth-century German society. The encounter between feminist historians and structural social history has so far succeeded in highlighting the ambivalences of bourgeois feminism. It has also revealed a gulf between the conviction of the structuralists that, over time, the rights attaching to bourgeois individuality can be extended to women as well as men, and the feminist proposition that the subordination of women is inherent in the terms of bourgeois individuality itself.[35]

WOMEN AND THE (WELFARE) STATE

The contradictions inherent in the aim of the women's movement to install 'motherliness' at the center of public life have been rehearsed in the growing literature on women's social work and their position in the welfare state. The commitment to the provision of social welfare services to families as of right, which emerged during the First World War and became one of the hallmarks of the Weimar Republic, was of epochal significance – a development in which Germany led the Western world and which in turn shaped the character of German public policy for much of the twentieth century. Women had a central role in this development.[36] Among the earliest activities of the bourgeois women's movement had been voluntary charity and social work, and this had developed by the end of the nineteenth century into a movement for social work education, where social work was understood both as a field of employment (mainly unpaid) for women and as a necessary service by women to women. This network was available for mobilization in wartime through the Nationaler Frauendienst, and in the process women's voluntary work was absorbed into the expanding machinery of state welfare provision. The end of the war, with the anticipated continuation of the welfare system and the establishment of welfare work as a paid public-sector occupation, witnessed the official accreditation of a large number of schools of social work, and the beginning of a process of professionalization. At the same time, members of the Social Democratic women's movement urged, and achieved, the creation of a socialist welfare organization, the Arbeiterwohlfahrt; motivated by the desire to protect working-class women from the patronage and indoctrination implicit in the middle-class character of professional social work, conceiving of social work in terms of the defence of rights rather than of direct assistance, the Arbeiterwohlfahrt developed an apparatus and an ethos that closely echoed those of the social work 'establishment'. The result has been characterized as the 'bureaucratization of motherliness' (*Sachße*), but this process did not imply significant empowerment of women. In spite of pretensions to professionalization, they continued to suffer the low pay levels characteristic of women's occupations. At the same time they found their ideals and their energies eroded in a system which, because it was chronically under review and underfunded, placed social workers and clients in an adversarial relationship. Mass unemployment after 1930 heightened these contradictions. The National Socialist takeover was rapidly followed by measures to streamline the welfare system and to adapt it for the purposes of social and eugenic screening and counselling. It was through the machinery of welfare that both material incentives were provided for healthy families and others were selected for sterilization and euthanasia. Those women who did not leave the welfare service or were not forced out on the grounds of racial or political disqualification thus stood at the cutting edge of Nazism's most inhumane policies.[37]

A particular feature of this problem is the role of women in the medicalization of social policy, and particularly in the trend towards solving social problems by eugenic means.[38] From the late nineteenth century the control of the reproductive capacity of women began to become a preoccupation of the German state, reflecting, in the first instance, concern about the size of the population.[39] The question of the right of women to abortion and contraception became one of the major issues in which organized (and unorganized) women engaged across a broad social and political spectrum during the Weimar Republic. At the same time there developed a consensus within the medical establishment and among policy makers that the quality of births was more important than the quantity; in this eugenic consensus, a wide range of forms of social deviance, and even poverty itself, were attributed to genetic inheritance. The consensus extended beyond the state's interest in exercising social control through women's bodies to include the attitudes of progressive and socially concerned physicians. These men and women helped to build up a system of public and private counselling centers offering advice on aspects of sexuality, marriage and childrearing. Intended as a service to the working class, these centers none the less dispensed help and advice on eugenic principles, as did many individual doctors active in the flouting of the laws on contraception and abortion. Because of their high degree of social engagement and the particular difficulties they faced in setting up private practices, women were very deeply involved in this advice movement. They thus appear in retrospect among the pioneers of a tendency that National Socialism would develop to its most dreadful consequences through the policies of compulsory sterilization, eugenic abortion and selective murder.

The question of how we read this evidence of women's 'complicity', of whether women are to be regarded as culprits or as victims in the tragic history and prehistory of National Socialism, represents the single most explosive point of controversy in recent West German scholarship on women's history.[40] Although leading historians such as Gisela Bock and Claudia Koonz (who may be said to represent as nearly opposite positions as possible) have engaged with the question, it is not one that can be answered through recourse to empirical research. It refers to an issue in feminist theory: whether it is possible for women to contribute to their own subordination. From that point of view, it need not detain us here; in the passion it arouses, it reflects both the intense engagement of West German scholars with their own past and the fact that placing women in history is indeed a conceptual as well as an empirical task. The same might be said of the tendency, stronger again in West German literature than in British or American, to replace the image of National Socialist reaction with one that sees all the features of modern industrial society tending towards the negation of all humane values that Nazism represents – whether the feature in question be modern technology, bureaucracy, medicine, or social welfare.[41] Looking back from the last decade, it is apparent that National Socialism was *not* the end of German society. The study of women's role in Germany's path to modernity, while drawing attention to a continuity of injustice and subordination, has nevertheless contributed substantially to pointing up the range of destinations implicit at its beginning.

NOTES

1 On the Federal Republic, see most recently R. G. Moeller, 'Reconstructing the family in reconstruction Germany: women and social policy in the Federal Republic, 1949–1955', *Feminist Studies*, vol. 15 (1989), pp. 137–70; A.-E. Freier and A. Kuhn (eds), *Frauen in der Geschichte V* (Düsseldorf, 1984); E. Kolinsky, *Women in West Germany* (Oxford, 1989). The historical literature on the GDR is less rich; cf. H. Kuhrig and W. Speigner (eds), *Zur gesellschaftlichen Stellung der Frau in der DDR* (Leipzig, 1978), and on the most recent developments to the 1980s: B. Eichhorn, 'Socialist emancipation. The women's movement in the German Democratic Republic', in S. Kruks, R. Rapp and M. B. Young (eds), *Promissory Notes. Women in the Transition to Socialism* (New York, 1989), pp. 282–305. In the interests of space, and because historical interpretation of the postwar period is at a relatively early stage and is bound to be thrown further into flux in the wake of the events of 1989–90, I offer no specific discussion here of the situation of German women after 1945.

2   This view is represented in the standard studies by Jill Stephenson, *Women in Nazi Society* (London, 1975) and *The Nazi Organisation of Women* (London, 1981), as well as numerous general histories.

3   The following account draws on Stephenson, *Women* and *Nazi Organisation*; T. Mason, 'Women in Germany 1925–1940: family, work and welfare', *History Workshop*, 1 and 2 (summer and autumn 1976); C. Koonz, *Mothers in the Fatherland* (London, 1987). U. Frevert, *Frauen-Geschichte. Von der bürgerlichen Verbesserung zur neuen Weiblichkeit* (Frankfurt, 1986), pp. 209–32 gives a good overview of current knowledge.

4   A. Grossmann, 'Berliner Ärztinnen und Volksgesundheit in der Weimarer Republik: Zwischen Sexualreform und Eugenik', in C. Eifert and S. Rouette (eds), *Unter allen Umständen. Frauengeschichte(n) in Berlin* (Berlin, 1986), pp. 183–217.

5   D. Winkler, *Frauenarbeit im 'Dritten Reich'* (Hamburg, 1977), pp. 42 ff; D. Petzina, W. Abelshauser and A. Faust, *Sozialgeschichtliches Arbeitsbuch III* (Munich, 1978), p. 4; W. H. Hubbard, *Familiengeschichte. Materialien zur deutschen Familie seit dem Ende des 18. Jahrhunderts* (Munich, 1983), p. 156.

6   cf. M. Schmidt, 'Krieg der Männer – Chance der Frauen? Die Frauen ziehen in die Büros der Thyssen AG', in L. Niethammer (ed.), *'Die Jahre weiss Man nicht, wo man die heute hinsetzen soll'. Faschismuserfahrungen im Ruhrgebiet* (Berlin and Bonn, 1983), pp. 133–62.

7   D. Winkler, 'Frauenarbeit versus Frauenideologie. Probleme der weiblichen Erwerbstätigkeit in Deutschland 1930–1945', *Archiv für Sozialgeschichte*, vol. 17 (1977), pp. 99–126; S. Bajohr, 'Weiblicher Arbeitsdienst im 'Dritten Reich'. Ein Konflikt zwischen Ideologie und Ökonomie', *Vierteljahrshefte für Zeitgeschichte*, vol. 28 (1980), pp. 331–57; S. Salter, 'Class harmony or class conflict? The industrial working class and the National Socialist regime 1933–1945', in J. Noakes (ed.), *Government, Party and People in Nazi Germany* (Exeter, 1980), pp. 89–91; Stephenson, *Nazi Organisation*, pp. 180 ff; Frevert, *Frauen-Geschichte*, p. 220.

8   E.g. D. Schoenbaum, *Hitler's Social Revolution* (Garden City, NY, 1966).

9   Figures for labor-force participation vary. A relatively accurate figure for the proportion of women actually doing paid work in 1939 is 36.2 per cent: Petzina, Abelshauser, Faust, *Arbeitsbuch*, p. 54. cf. C. Sachse, 'Fabrik, Familie und kein Feierabend. Frauenarbeit im Nationalsozialismus', *Gewerkschaftliche Monatshefte*, vol. 35 (1984), pp. 571 ff; R. Overy, 'Mobilisation for total war in Germany 1939–1941', *English Historical Review*, vol. 103 (1988), pp. 627–9; Stephenson, *Women*, p. 101; L.J. Rupp, *Mobilising Women for War* (Princeton, NJ, 1978).

10 Petzina, Abelshauser, Faust, *Arbeitsbuch*, p. 54; R. Rytlewski and M. Opp de Hipt, *Die Bundesrepublik Deutschland in Zahlen 1945/49–1980* (Munich, 1987), p. 78.

11 Schmidt, 'Krieg der Männer'; M. Prinz, *Vom neuen Mittelstand zum Volksgenossen* (Munich, 1986).

12 A. Tröger, 'The creation of a female assembly-line proletariat', in R. Bridenthal, A. Grossmann and M. Kaplan (eds), *When Biology Became Destiny. Women in Weimar and Nazi Germany* (New York, 1984), pp. 237–70.

13 G. Bock, *Zwangssterilisation im Nationalsozialismus* (Opladen, 1986), p. 136.

14 K. Hausen, 'Die Polarisierung der "Geschlechtscharaktere" – Eine Dissozia-
    tion von Erwerbs- und Familienleben', in W. Conze (ed.), *Sozialgeschichte
    der Familie in der Neuzeit Europas* (Stuttgart, 1977), pp. 363–93.
15 R. J. Evans, *The Feminist Movement in Germany 1894–1933* (London and
    Beverly Hills, Calif., 1976), pp. 40 ff; U. Gerhard, '"Bis an die Wurzeln des
    Ubels". Rechtsgeschichte und Rechtskämpfe der Radikalen', *Feministische
    Studien*, vol. 3 (1984), pp. 80–2.
16 Hubbard, *Familiengeschichte*, p. 156; G. Hohorst, J. Kocka and G. Ritter,
    Sozialgeschichtliches Arbeitsbuch (Munich, 1975), p. 67.
17 Evans, *Feminist Movement*, chs 3 and 4.
18 E. Meyer-Renschhausen, 'Zur Geschichte der Gefühle. Das Reden von
    "Scham" und "Ehre" innerhalb der Frauenbewegung um die Jahrhun-
    dertwende', in Eifert and Rouette, *Unter allen Umständen*, pp. 99–122.
19 See Evans, *Feminist Movement*, ch. 6, for an account of the anti-feminist
    movement.
20 Frevert, *Frauen-Geschichte*, p. 151; C. Lorenz, 'Die gewerbliche Frauenarbeit
    während des Krieges', in P. Umbreit and C. Lorenz (eds), *Der Krieg und die
    Arbeitsverhältnisse* (Stuttgart, 1928), p. 347.
21 E.g. Lorenz, 'Frauenarbeit'; J. Kocka, *Facing Total War* (Leamington Spa,
    1984); S. Bajohr, *Die Hälfte der Fabrik. Geschichte der Frauenarbeit in
    Deutschland 1914–1945* (Marburg, 1979). On the postwar period: Schoen-
    baum, *Hitler's Social Revolution*, p. 178.
22 U. Daniel, 'Women's work in industry and family: Germany, 1914–18', in R.
    Wall and J. Winter (eds), *The Upheaval of War* (Cambridge, 1988), pp.
    267–96.
23 R. Bessel, '"Eine nicht allzu grosse Beunruhigung des Arbeitsmarkts":
    Frauenarbeit und Demobilmachung in Deutschland nach dem Ersten
    Weltkrieg', *Geschichte und Gesellschaft*, vol. 9 (1983), pp. 211–29.
24 R. Bridenthal, 'Beyond *Kinder, Küche, Kirche*: Weimar women at work',
    Central European History, vol. 6 (1973), pp. 148–66.
25 For the following, see especially C. Sachse, *Siemens, der Nationalsozialis-
    mus und die moderne Familie. Eine Untersuchung zur sozialen
    Rationalisierung in Deutschland im 20. Jahrhundert* (Frankfurt, 1990);
    idem, 'Industrial housewives: women's social work in the factories of Nazi
    Germany', *Women and History*, vols 11 and 12 (special issue), 1987.
26 H. Kramer, '"Rationelle Haushaltsführung" und die "Neue Frau" der
    zwanziger Jahre', *Feministische Studien*, vol. 1 (1982); pp. 117–26; A.
    Grossmann, 'The new woman and the rationalisation of sexuality in Weimar
    Germany', in A. Snitow, C. Stansell and S. Thompson, *Powers of Desire. The
    Politics of Sexuality* (New York, 1983), pp. 153–71.
27 A. Grossmann, 'Girlkultur or thoroughly rationalized female: a new woman
    in Weimar Germany?' in J. Friedlander *et al.* (eds), *Women in Culture and
    Politics* (Bloomington, Ind., 1986), pp. 62–80.
28 K. Hausen, 'Mother's Day in the Weimar Republic', in Bridenthal, Grossmann
    and Kaplan, *When Biology became Destiny*, pp. 131–52.
29 K. Theweleit, *Male Fantasies*, 2 vols (Cambridge, 1987 and 1989).
30 T. Childers, *The Nazi Voter* (Chapel Hill, NC, 1983), pp. 188 ff, 259 ff.
31 Evans, *Feminist Movement*; idem, 'Liberalism and society: the feminist
    movement and social change', in idem (ed.), *Society and Politics in
    Wilhelmine Germany* (London, 1978), pp. 186–214.
32 Koonz, *Mothers*; cf. her response to critics in *Radical History Review*, 43
    (winter 1989), pp. 81–5.

33 E. Meyer-Renschhausen, *Weibliche Kultur und soziale Arbeit* (Cologne and Vienna, 1989).

34 H.-U. Bussemer, *Frauenemanzipation und Bildungsbürgertum* (Weinheim and Basel, 1985).

35 cf. U. Frevert (ed.), *Bürgerinnen und Bürger* (Göttingen, 1988), especially the contrasting afterwords by Jürgen Kocka and Ute Gerhard.

36 For the following, see C. Sachße, *Mütterlichkeit als Beruf* (Frankfurt, 1986); I. Stoehr, "'Organisierte Mütterlichkeit". Zur Politik der deutschen Frauen-bewegung um 1900', in K. Hausen (ed.), *Frauen suchen ihre Geschichte* 2nd edn (Munich, 1987), pp. 225–53; S. Zeller, *Volksmütter. Frauen im Wohlfahrtswesen der zwanziger Jahre* (Düsseldorf, 1987).

37 H. Knüppel-Dahne and E. Mitrovic, 'Helfen und Dienen. Die Arbeit von Fürsorgerinnen im Hamburger öffentlichen Dienst während des National-sozialismus', in H.-U. Otto and H. Sünker (eds), *Soziale Arbeit und Faschismus* (2nd edn, Frankfurt, 1989), pp. 176–97.

38 For the link between eugenics and welfare in the 1920s, see P. Weindling, 'Eugenics and the welfare state during the Weimar Republic', in W. R. Lee and E. Rosenhaft (eds), *The State and Social Change in Germany 1880–1980* (Oxford, 1990); pp. 131–60.

39 For what follows, see especially C. Usborne, 'Fertility control and population policy in Germany 1910–1928', PhD thesis, Open University, 1989; A. Grossmann, 'Abortion and economic crisis: the 1931 campaign against paragraph 218', in Bridenthal, Grossmann and Kaplan, *Biology*, pp. 66–86; idem, 'Berliner Ärztinnen'. For a conspectus of recent German research in the history of medicine and gender, see J. Geyer-Kordesch and A. Kuhn (eds), *Frauenkörper. Medizin. Sexualität* (Düsseldorf, 1986).

40 See for example the title of a recent anthology, A. Ebbinghaus, *Opfer und Täterinnen. Frauenbiographien im Nationalsozialismus* (Nördlingen, 1987). cf. K. Windaus-Walser, 'Gnade der weiblichen Geburt? Zum Umgang der Frauenforschung mit Nationalsozialismus und Antisemitismus', *Feministische Studien*, vol. 6 (1988), pp. 102–15; D. Schmidt, 'Die peinlichen Ver-wandtschaften – Frauenforschung zum Nationalsozialismus', in H. Gersten-berger and D. Schmidt (eds), *Normalität oder Normalisierung?* (Münster, 1987), pp. 50–65; G. Bock, review of Koonz, *Mothers*, in *Bulletin of the German Historical Institute, London*, vol. 11 (1989), pp. 16–25.

41 See for e.g. H. Kaupen-Haas (ed.), *Der Griff nach der Bevölkerung. Aktualität und Kontinuitat nazistischer Bevölkerungspolitik* (Nördlingen, 1986).

8 *Nazism and Social Revolution*

THOMAS SAUNDERS

*There is only one possible kind of revolution and it is not economic
or political or social, but racial.... All revolutions – and I have
studied them all – have been racial.*[1]

Adolf Hitler

Since the collapse of the Third Reich German history has been a
narrative in search of meaning. Prominent among its interpretive
paradigms has been the theory of the 'missing revolution'.[2] The much-
debated German *Sonderweg* revolves around the unsynchronized
experience of the two upheavals which have shaped the modern age, the
French Revolution and the Industrial Revolution. Germany's path to
modernity was characterized by disjunction between rapid economic
change and sociopolitical authoritarianism. Between 1848 and 1871,
precisely as industrial take-off began in earnest, Germany was unified by
conservative monarchists. Two generations later Germany's transformation from monarchy to republic came once again from above, forestalling
the revolution from below which could have effected a fundamental
democratization of German society. Still unfulfilled, that task fell to
National Socialism in 1933. What Hitler's regime did with the opportunity
to effect a more thorough redistribution of social power has been
debated ever since.[3]

The terms of that debate were initially set by national socialism's
principal opponents. Marxists dubbed fascism the political instrument of
monopoly capitalism bidding to stave off the inevitable triumph of the
working class.[4] Until the 1960s non-Marxist historians opposed this
reading of the Third Reich within the conceptual framework of
totalitarianism, paralleling fascism and communism as forms of political
domination.

Social questions were minimized.[5] Over the last quarter century the
terms of the debate have shifted considerably. The thaw in the Cold War,
burgeoning interest in social history and greater historical distance have
generated new conceptual and methodological approaches to the social
history of the Third Reich.

In the mid-1960s, studies by a German sociologist and an American
historian opened the subject for reconsideration.

Ralf Dahrendorf's controversial but influential study, *Society and Democracy in Germany*, set itself a political question – why liberal democracy failed to take root in Germany – but chose to answer by reference to social structures and values. Dahrendorf adopted the *Sonderweg* thesis, arguing that liberal democratic principles did not thrive because Germany failed to undergo social modernization to match its economic transformation. Writing amid stability and prosperity in the wake of the West German economic miracle, he sought to discover when it was that Germany had made the decisive turn to modernity capable of supporting democratic political forms. His answer was the period 1933 to 1945. Imperial Germany had 'managed to miss the road to [social] modernity', despite its high rate of industrialization and urbanization. The Weimar Republic likewise failed to turn the corner. Rupture came in 1933 when Hitler's totalitarian ambitions, quite contrary to his intent, destroyed the social basis for authoritarian government by corroding the bonds of family, class, religion and region. National Socialism therefore provided, against its will, Germany's missing social revolution.[6]

David Schoenbaum's full-length investigation of Nazi society, *Hitler's Social Revolution*, developed parallel conclusions. More nuanced and, in places, more ambiguous, Schoenbaum's study likewise posited contradiction between what the regime intended and what it achieved. Distinguishing between the revolution Hitler wanted to effect (a transformation of social consciousness and behavior), and the socio-economic continuity he needed to restore Germany's dominance in Europe and the upward mobility provided by penetration of the traditional order by Nazi social values, Schoenbaum argued that the Third Reich managed to destroy the correspondence of class and status in German society. Although an ambiguous achievement, in terms both of Nazi intent and capabilities, it laid a foundation for postwar liberal democracy. In this respect Hitler instigated a social revolution.[7]

Both Dahrendorf and Schoenbaum measured the Nazi social revolution by its contribution to Germany's modernization and West Germany's success as a democratic society. Since publication of their paradigmatic studies interpretive models have shifted and historical knowledge of the Third Reich has widened substantially. Monographic treatment has extended to virtually the entire spectrum of Nazi society – youth, women, the *Mittelstand*, white-collar workers, students and the working class. As the fate of specific social groups has been charted, the dominant themes of policy development (including coordination and indoctrination of Nazi society) and correspondence between policy and social reality have acquired greater nuance.[8] Most recently, the practice of oral history and study of everyday life have focused attention on public opinion, forms of sociability and continuity in daily life. [9] The result is a portrait of Nazi society rich in compromises, contradictions and ambiguities. Tradition and modernity, normalcy and a persistent state of crisis, 'coordination' and the resistance to conformity coexisted in such multifaceted ways that generalizations have become hazardous.[10]

In this context it is not accidental that two recent synthetic assessments take the thesis of social revolution as their point of departure only to emasculate it thoroughly. The first, by John Hiden and John Farquharson, devoted mainly to National Socialism's social support before 1933 and policy thereafter, concludes that the Third Reich should be examined within the context of the 'continuing German social revolution of the twentieth century', rather than as a revolution in its own right. By implication, National Socialism neither created nor destroyed.[11] The second, by Ian Kershaw, more systematic in its historiographical formulations, reaches more categorical conclusions. Because Hitler had little interest in social structures and because his following was far too heterogeneous to advance coherent goals, National Socialism's social project was essentially negative. The Third Reich neither witnessed significant shifts in class structure nor transformed social consciousness. Hitler's movement could only destroy: the real push to modernity came in the destruction and defeat of 1945.[12]

In both these cases revolutionary achievement is tied to the process of modernization. In this regard Dahrendorf's agenda remains with us. Again, however, generalizations of this breadth face conflicting evidence. The recent collection of essays on everyday life in the Third Reich edited by Richard Bessel suggests widely variant conclusions. The opening paper by Bessel adroitly describes the grassroots terrorist activity of the Sturmabteilung (SA) in the Nazi seizure of power, but is clearly uncomfortable with calling this a revolution (this and the term socialism are placed in quotation marks) and so concludes that the activism of the SA constituted merely hooliganism on behalf of an inherently contradictory political movement. By sharp contrast, the subsequent article on rural life by Gerhard Wilke ascribes revolutionary impact to Nazism in spawning generational conflict and female emancipation from traditional structures of authority. Detlev Peukert's paper on youth behavior likewise grants Nazi organizations an emancipatory, modernizing function, although it denies that this was their intent or that youth were thereby fully coordinated. Ulrich Herbert's oral history of working-class experience from the mid-1930s until the early 1960s suggests stability and normalcy in day-to-day life by contrast to the upheavals of the Weimar and postwar reconstruction periods.[13] The overall picture is therefore one of sharp contrasts.

By themselves such contrasts are not a peculiarity of German history. The challenge that they pose in this case arises from a fear that the normalcy of everyday life might serve to neutralize the (moral) peculiarities of National Socialism. In the aftermath of the *Historikerstreit*, a methodology that emphasizes the substratum of continuity in everyday life and treats the Third Reich like any other historical epoch might appear to relativize its barbarity.[14] Yet the debate over relativization, simultaneously about social history and the 'Final Solution', points toward a fresh conceptual framework. Kershaw's new chapter on this debate in the latest edition of his book suggests a different approach than that taken in his original chapter on social revolution. His response to prospects of 'normalization' or 'historicization' of National Socialism reaffirms the historian's ability to preserve the characteristic features of National Socialism even while treating its everyday social reality. In other words, he concedes the relevance of Nazi ideology to social change, ending with a plea to reintegrate categories that the previous chapter concluded ought to be divorced. 'Normalization' is not historically or morally objectionable if social developments are kept within their political–ideological context.[15]

Using Kershaw's conclusion as a point of departure, I would argue that National Socialism should be seen as a revolutionary movement, and that the kind of revolution proposed by Nazism, the extent to which it was realized and the social dynamism it unleashed deserve reconsideration. Both premise and answers to the questions derived from it depend heavily, of course, on the paradigm chosen for revolution. Marxist historiography has, from the first, denied Hitler's regime revolutionary significance because it made political and economic war on the working class. The combination of cooperation with authoritarian politicians and industrialists, the destruction of the independent workers' organizations and the elimination of the socialist and communist parties, clearly marked National Socialism as a counter-revolutionary enterprise, even if it stole much of its rhetoric and style from the left. Western historiography has partly shared that perspective while also applying, just as Dahrendorf, the test of modernization, thus investigating the Third Reich's contribution to industrial concentration, the welfare state, female emancipation, or social mobility. Fruitful though these paradigms have been, both judge Nazism against abstract types – Marxist revolution and modernization – as much as by historical models, such as the Russian Revolution, or in the context of interwar social problems. That National Socialism represents an ambiguous achievement in either respect goes without saying. It deserves, none the less, to be understood by reference to historical models.

It need hardly be demonstrated that the national socialist and Bolshevik revolutions had fundamentally different points of departure and goals. Nazism, though instituting far-reaching changes in governmental and legal practice, did not see ownership of the means of production, the proletariat, or class struggle as historical driving forces and, therefore, did not propose to overturn social or economic structures. Its violently anti-Bolshevik and anti-Semitic impulse meant that national uprising and racial cleansing were the prerequisites of social revolution. Instead of classes being made or destroyed, a 'race' was progressively marginalized, dispossessed and exterminated. However comparable Hitler's elimination of Jews may be to Stalin's war on the kulaks, Germany did not witness radical shifts in occupational profiles, industrial organization, or the composition of the social elite. Set against the Bolshevik upheaval, the Nazi revolution therefore appears more mythical than substantial.

These fundamental differences notwithstanding, Bolshevism and Nazism shared several assumptions about revolution. Both held that revolutions were made, not observed. For Hitler, this voluntarist political ethic, rooted in the assumption that life, individual or national, was struggle, linked the heroic era before 30 January 1933, the initial intense phase of *Gleichschaltung* in 1933–4 and the subsequent long-term crusade to prepare the nation for war, materially and ideologically. Both movements also saw themselves engaged in a world-historical task. Hitler's struggle – *Mein Kampf* – was inflated to apocalyptic proportions. Politics consisted of a prodigious effort to transfer his ideological convictions to a nation incapable of rendering its own experience in meaningful terms.[16] Most significantly, Bolshevism and National Socialism saw political power as the starting point for a more fundamental transformation – a social order that was to be peopled by a new human type. Both also saw the creation of this new man as a long-term struggle demanding attention to education and indoctrination as much as to material conditions. For Hitler, the ultimate test of success was the willingness of the German people to endorse his solipsistic reading of human history.[17]

Moving from presupposition to practice, one encounters commonality as well as contrast. Shorn of its ideological fanfare, the Russian Revolution represents, in the recent formulation of Sheila Fitzpatrick, terror, progress and upward mobility. It stands, in short, for a revolution of modernization based on violent state intervention.[18] From this perspective, the outstanding distinction between the Bolshevik and national socialist revolutions is their respective socioeconomic starting points. Bolshevism seized power when Russia was still an overwhelmingly pre-industrial, rural society. Both the full-time factory proletariat and the middle class comprised a tiny fraction of the total population. Consolidation of political power went hand in hand with creation of the socioeconomic structure essential for proletarian revolution. The Bolshevik program, all personal and power rivalries apart, demanded economic and social modernization, ultimately effected via industrialization and collectivization of agriculture by brutal means under Stalin. Germany, by contrast, already exhibited social characteristics common to advanced industrial societies: high levels of urbanization, a large working class, relative decline of the old middle class (*Mittelstand*), growth of the white-collar class and an extension of female employment. National Socialism, which drew disproportionate support from the 'losers' in this process, is usually read as a reaction against modernization. But it would be more accurate to say that, in social terms, Nazism represented a distinct mode of dealing with and instrumentalizing modernity. It had no intention of pastoralizing the country, a socially counter-revolutionary project, which would have been the only upheaval which Germany could have experienced commensurate with the forced industrialization of Stalinist Russia.

The categories of terror, progress and upward mobility derive, of course, from a non-Marxist reading of an ostensibly Marxist event. Once granted the differences already noted, however, they are relevant to the Nazi revolution. The first, a holdover of totalitarian interpretations of fascism and communism, is the least controversial of the three. Terror, understood as the maintenance of a monopoly on political power and the enforcement of social conformity, played a role in every aspect of National Socialism, from psychological intimidation of the populace to elimination of the biologically or racially unfit. It was unleashed against elements within the movement, primarily the SA, which, however ideologically motivated, threatened that monopoly, just as it was directed against undiscipline on the shop floor. It comprised, in short, both a defining feature of the political–legal process and, in as much as fear of denunciation contributed to social atomization, a constitutive part of social reality in the Third Reich.[19] Progress and upward mobility present, by comparison, more elusive models for revolution. The question of whether Nazism stalled or accelerated modernization and social opportunity – which was central to Schoenbaum – provokes a variety of responses. It can be adequately addressed only by historicizing National Socialism.

Historicization neither means to deny National Socialism's uniqueness nor does it mean that we ought to surrender critical or moral distance in the service of historical empathy. Rather, it signifies that, although morally repellent, Nazism had its own revolutionary agenda – however twisted or confused – and established its own logical nexus between theory and practice. That nexus has, admittedly, been difficult for historians to grasp. From Hermann Rauschning's description of Nazism as a revolution of nihilism, through A. J. P. Taylor's characterization of Nazism as fraud, to Jeremy Noakes's recent conclusion that Nazi ideology and practice were contradictory and destructive, historians have, in Noakes's phrase, been 'baffled' by the Nazi phenomenon. Socially at once revolutionary and conservative, modern and anti-modern, ideological and pragmatic, the Third Reich has defied firm categorization in conventional terms.[20]

The quotation with which this chapter began defines Hitler's revolutionary project in a manner that aptly illustrates the problem. Hitler disposed of the three types of revolution most often discussed by historians – political, social and economic – as irrelevant or, at best, derivative. In their place he substituted the racial revolution, a construct both preposterous and perverse. One can easily debunk his affected erudition. In this case it formed part of a polemic against the section of the party around Otto Strasser that claimed to take the 'socialism' of the party's 25-point program rather more seriously than did its principal author.[21] Measured against Hitler's earlier and later behavior, the specific refusal to valorize political revolution is brazenly untruthful. Finally, in light of functionalist readings of the Nazi state, a pronouncement from 1930 need not be seen as normative for action after 1933.[22] But all this being said, there is abundant, gruesome evidence that Hitler and his associates took realization of a racial revolution very seriously, indeed more seriously than anything else they proposed. What then does the racial revolution have to do with social aims?

The centrality of racism to Hitler's world-view was first systematically enunciated by Eberhard Jäckel in 1969 and has since been widely accepted.[23] Its social ramifications, though obvious with respect to Jews, are only slowly receiving programmatic formulation. Recent writing which takes Hitler's 'pseudo-biological racism' as the key to National Socialism's domestic and international revolution points in the right direction. Milan Hauner, though nominating Hitler as the most consistent revolutionary of our time, denies that his third way between capitalism and communism offered a 'genuine social revolution'. He does, however, insist that the impetus for racial purification through expansionism had immediate social repercussions, unleashing a dynamic which created the conditions for social mobility. The racial base of Nazi ideology therefore supports the superstructure of foreign policy and social change.[24] MacGregor Knox likewise welds domestic and foreign policy through racism. Without elaborating on the social revolution inherent in Hitler's amalgam of racism and nationalism, he leaves no doubt that the ultimate goal was the overthrow of German society through the uprooting of 'inherited institutions and values', as much as it was of the European state system.[25] Jeremy Noakes, who is more wide-ranging in his treatment of social issues, nevertheless agrees with Kershaw in denying that Nazism offered a consistent or constructive social vision. Though revolutionary in political terms, it could develop no stable forms because it was intrinsically destructive and self-destructive.[26]

The hypothesis that extreme racist nationalism constituted a powerful, if purely destructive, force for social change qualifies National Socialism as a revolutionary creed but demonstrates neither that Hitler desired and had a blueprint for social revolution, nor that a social revolution actually occurred. It subordinates social concerns to the primacy of politics conceived as a world-historical mission to eliminate the biologically inferior. Marxists, committed to the concept of revolution as political and social emancipation, view this mission as a red herring. For liberal historians, Nazism's authoritarian political objectives, in tandem with the undeniably reactionary aspects of its social vision, mark it as counter-revolutionary and confused. The anti-urban, anti-industrial, anti-feminist, blood-and-soil values espoused in social theory, party propaganda and cultural production sit awkwardly with the notion that National Socialism possessed a forward-looking social vision. Both objections can be challenged: the supposition that evolution must be historically and morally progressive derives from nineteenth-century assumptions, while the charge of inconsistency is scarcely unique to the Nazis. But the task of establishing ideological credentials for a Nazi social revolution remains.

Rainer Zitelmann's recent study of Hitler's world view provides the most systematic attempt to establish these credentials. While confirming the familiar picture of Hitler's social prejudices, Zitelmann argues that Hitler exhibited much more than casual or self-serving interest in social questions.[27] Hitler's social project presented a consistent and truly revolutionary expression of his fundamental convictions about human development: the centrality of struggle, the necessity of equal opportunity and the primacy of personality. It aimed to shatter the social framework within which he had matured and substitute for it a modern, upwardly mobile, equal opportunity society. This signified not social egalitarianism but a hierarchy based on talent and loyalty. According to Zitelmann, Hitler, who had no intention of turning back the socio-economic clock to a romanticized agrarian world, sought to balance agricultural and industrial sectors in the interests of the national community. In sum, Hitler had a coherent and unmistakably modern social vision. The realization of this vision, in so far as war permitted, was neither accidental – as Dahrendorf and Schoenbaum suggest – nor merely the result of war and destruction.[28]

At the core of this social project, as historians have long recognized, was the *Volksgemeinschaft*, a national community uniting leaders and followers irrespective of social background. Its historical precedent was the national uprising that occurred in August 1914. Substituting national for international socialism, Hitler conceived the ideal society as one which had internalized and institutionalized the fortress truce (*Burgfrieden*) and the trench experience of the Great War. Burial of social and political conflict in the national interest represented, of course, an older conservative ideal. But in Nazi hands the *Volksgemeinschaft* became a revolutionary force. The primary test for membership was racial 'purity'.

Disqualification of Jews, which entailed progressive exclusion from the civil service, citizenship, property ownership and the human race, paralleled sterilization and extermination of the physically or mentally handicapped, who were likewise considered unfit for life. Persons expressing undesirable political convictions similarly forfeited a place in the community.

But the requirements of membership were not necessarily met by proof of racial, physical, mental and ideological soundness. Social performance or achievement (*Leistung*) had also to be demonstrated. The progressive side of that demand, in theory at least, was the career open to talent and the freedom to realize personal ambition. Its ominous side was refusal of membership in the *Volksgemeinschaft* to a widening range of persons, from criminals, vagrants and gypsies to asocials, unproductive workers, and wayward or rebellious youth. The price of belonging was unquestioning conformity to prescribed social and political norms.[29]

Against this backcloth, the national community must be seen as a privilege reserved ultimately only for those whose social behavior corresponded to the national interest as defined by Hitler. Its principal admission requirement was service to the nation, whether of youth engaged in the Labor Service, women bearing children for the fatherland, or farmers fighting the battle for production when income and labor conditions undermined their economic position. One of its more revealing institutional forms was the plant or factory community (*Betriebsgemeinschaft*) which, under the guidance of a mini-Führer, ostensibly harmonized labor and management, henceforth known as retinue and leader. Its quintessence, what Hitler identified as the model socialist institution, was the military. Indeed, according to the terms of the *Volksgemeinschaft*, socialism signified sacrifice for the national cause. Its apotheosis was willingness to die for Führer and fatherland.[30]

The degree to which the *Volksgemeinschaft* constituted a vehicle for social modernization remains disputed. Historians who make anti-Semitism the pivot of Hitler's world view have abundant corroboration in the initially fitful but inexorable momentum of the Nazi racial revolution. By contrast, even to agree with Zitelmann's description of Hitler as a consistent social revolutionary in a modernizing tradition, prevented from implementing his more radical social designs by the exigencies of war, leaves unresolved the question of whether a social revolution occurred. That question can be answered only by examination of social ambitions, opportunity and mobility, and by measurement of subjective experience, namely, the ability of the regime to reshape social consciousness within the *Volksgemeinschaft*.

It is not, in the first instance, clear that Hitler's aims can be equated with the social impulse behind the Nazi revolution. Every attempt to evaluate the revolutionary purpose of National Socialism quickly confronts the heterogeneous, indeed syncretic character of its make-up and ambitions. The movement represented, both before and after 1933, such a cross-section of German society that no clear measure of its revolutionary potential can be gained from its class composition. For whatever circumstantial reasons – depression, socioeconomic depriva-tion, political crisis – National Socialism overcame boundaries of class, religion and region. Anti-Marxism provided much of the cement for this unusual alliance, but it does not automatically qualify the movement as reactionary or counter-revolutionary.[31] Attractive as the promises of preservation or restoration were for some sections of the movement – craftsmen, farmers and small businessmen – for activists, particularly for those in the SA, the idea of a return to a bygone era was anathema. Hostile to socialism, they planned a reckoning with the entire Weimar system. If left unchecked, their revolution would have been self-perpetuating as well as violent.[32]

Revolutionary impetus need not then be credited solely to the national socialist leadership. What we know of the initial stage of *Gleichschaltung* indicates that in many instances Reich policy lagged behind, indeed responded to, the activism of local units of the party and SA, which took 'coordination' into their own hands. Hitler's appointment as Chancellor and the March election unleashed a revolution from below in which old scores were settled, Jews and political opponents were ousted from city councils and Nazis assumed prominent positions in local affairs. Orchestration of the boycott of Jewish shops and businesses on 1 April, or the Law for the Restoration of the Civil Service later that month, provided Hitler's regime, which was still a coalition, with the means to channel and control this grassroots uprising.[33] It has been suggested that over a much longer term the same social dynamism provided a crucial ingredient of Nazi foreign policy. Expectations of national restoration and social opportunity, thwarted by accommodation with traditional elites, generated expansionist tendencies that would eventually destroy the domestic social structure. Moreover, while an independent factor in the equation that resulted in social revolution, the activist or radical Nazis espoused social ambitions that were shared by Hitler.[34]

The objectives of the activist core of the party can only partly be described as violent and destructive. Among its ambitions must also be included social climbing. Although historians still differ over the extent of social mobility in the Third Reich, the combination of political or racial discrimination and the growth of the bureaucracy created opportunities for social advancement.[35] In this respect Schoenbaum's claims have been developed into a case for a revolution driven by frustrated place-seekers. According to William Jannen, National Socialism represented a short cut to position for out-groups, which were defined by their relative lack of education. The process of *Gleichschaltung* at the local level was as much social as political, a chance for younger, less well-educated and comparatively inexperienced persons to attain administrative and political posts. Moreover, even when Nazis did not oust the old elite, the proliferation of party organizations (witness the massive bureaucracy of the Labor Front) and the creation of new state ministries headed by Nazi leaders (propaganda and the air force) opened positions for functionaries of all levels.[36] Finally, Jannen cites Nazi plans to restructure the educational system and the curricular emphases of the select Nazi schools to argue that the Third Reich aimed to substitute political and character qualifications for academic achievement in the training of a new elite.[37]

The failure of the Third Reich to conduct a wholesale administrative purge has generally been considered a consequence of its ambiguous social purpose, the need to compromise for pragmatic reasons and the willing adaptation of traditional elites to coordination.[38] Social harmony, national rejuvenation and rapid rearmament could not be squared with drastic upheaval in the civil service or the purge of industrial and intellectual elites. What applies to personnel policy can be extended to society and the economy as a whole. It has frequently been remarked that the anti-urban, anti-big finance, anti-department store rhetoric of the party could not be reconciled with the drive to maximize industrial potential and establish continental hegemony. Nor could rapid rearmament be squared with the wholesale purges of the civil service or industrial and intellectual elites that some activists desired. Nor could ambitions to return women to hearth and children be realized under the conditions of growing labor shortages after 1938.[39] Henry Turner, who claims that a consistent, Utopian anti-modernism informed National Socialism, suggests that the only viable means at hand to achieve this Utopia were modern ones.[40] Paradoxically, a parallel argument can be employed even if one posits an opposite, modernizing aim for Nazism. Revolutionary impulses were tamed less by opportunistic adjustment to governmental responsibility – Hitler and company conducted government in an exceedingly unorthodox manner – than by the fact that Hitler's multiple aims defied simultaneous realization. Whether one follows Turner or Zitelmann, Hitler's willingness to compromise with traditional bureaucrats, industrialists and officers to permit economic recovery and the pursuit of grandiose foreign policy objectives represents a temporary accommodation, even though it meant 'betrayal' of the revolution.[41]

Nazi social policy must be evaluated in light of these tensions and compromises. Early, by no means negligible, legislative action on behalf of social groups who formed the backbone of the movement – the *Mittelstand* of small businessmen, farmers and craftsmen – increasingly confronted limitations imposed by the efforts that were made to conciliate industry and win the allegiance of the largest social group which had resisted National Socialism: the working class. As the price of agricultural produce found its limits in the demands of industry and labor, so in turn was the conciliation of labor circumscribed by the imperatives of rearmament. Eventually, all the ambitions of Nazism were to find their limit in the context of total war.

Initially, farmers, shopkeepers and self-employed artisans had many of their central demands met. The agricultural community received guaranteed prices for their produce as well as protection against debt foreclosure on the medium-sized farms that Nazi ideologues claimed would anchor the master race in German soil. Shopkeepers won a ban on new department stores and restrictions on entry into the retail trade, which they considered essential for their survival. Artisans gained compulsory association, in effect a national guild that regulated the qualifications for entry into the trades. Most benefited, moreover, from economic recovery and the state-driven campaign for autarky.[42] But none of these groups proved the principal economic beneficiary of Nazi policy. Migration from the land continued, and even accelerated, as agricultural prices and wages fell behind those of industry, despite the Nazi apotheosis of the farmer as the progenitor of healthy racial stock. Small retail and manufacturing interests likewise received an ever-decreasing share of the national income. National Socialism provided the appearance of restoration, in organizational terms, without actually arresting the economic trends that had emerged in the late nineteenth century.[43]

For the German working class, National Socialism likewise posed anything but an unambiguous bane or blessing. Although. workers comprised a significant portion of the party's following before January 1933, the majority had remained loyal to their socialist or communist heritage. Hitler saw the winning of their allegiance as a *sine qua non* of domestic stability and international strength. With a combination of carrot and stick (what Hitler preferred to call bread and circuses), the new government moved quickly to defuse any revolutionary threat and to reconcile workers to national socialist rule. Destroying the political and organizational base of the working class, the regime sought to create new allegiances and organizational forms. The German Labor Front (DAF) was the institutional mechanism that was used to conciliate, indoctrinate and integrate the worker. With its programs of *Strength Through Joy* and *Beauty of Labor* the DAF oversaw everything from cleaner washrooms in factories to affordable holiday packages. Its success, however, depended upon Germany's economic recovery and the creation of new jobs. Victories on both these fronts did not alter the reality of a labor force whose real wages and standard of living improved only marginally over depression levels, whose share of national income declined steadily and whose hours of work increased under the pressure of rearmament.[44] Wage controls in the midst of soaring business profits, concentration on military production to the disadvantage of consumer goods, militarization of the labor market through restrictions on mobility and of the factory through introduction of the leadership principle: these were the objective realities of life for the working class in the Third Reich. Acquiescence continued only because the regime presided over a general economic recovery and thus provided, if less expeditiously than it liked to boast, full employment.[45]

In all these cases Nazi policy is less suggestive of the implementation of a revolutionary design that foresaw the creation of a harmonious national community than it is of a piecemeal, haphazard process by which popular support for the regime was maintained. Hitler's government thus appears, like that of any other modern state, a broker between multiple interests. However, the regime neither sacrificed the principle of national above sectional interests nor abandonded the criterion of social achievement (*Leistung*). In supporting the *Mittelstand* the Nazi regime never committed itself to rescue the poor and inefficient. Social legislation was intended, rather, to release the productive energies of the strong while allowing the weak to go to the wall.[46] Furthermore, the national community was conceived primarily as a matter of coordinating consciousness rather than as an instrument of social egalitarianism. At stake was not the relative economic wellbeing of different social groups, but what Schoenbaum termed 'interpreted social reality'.[47] To test the *Volksgemeinschaft* means to shift attention from class structures to subjective reality. It thus involves recognizing, if not dignifying, National Socialism's attention to social consciousness and behavior. The emotive appeal of the *Volksgemeinschaft* in a nation riven with political and class antagonisms has long been admitted. The question is, to what degree did that emotive appeal override traditional social distinctions.

Since compulsion and/or terror were behind the whole program of national service – from Hitler Youth to the armed forces – outward participation fails to measure the success of the *Volksgemeinschaft*. Since, however, the regime's preoccupation with coordinating national opinion through an extensive propaganda apparatus found a logical counterpart in soundings of the popular mood by the local authorities, security police, informers and, of course, prosecution of deviant attitudes or behavior, some measurement of public opinion is possible. This documentary record, considered along with reports filed with the Social Democratic Party in exile and the findings of recent oral history projects, offers insight into how thoroughly the values of the *Volksgemeinschaft* permeated German society. Generalizations are unlikely ever to be tidy, but enough has been done to demonstrate that, while the Third Reich did not achieve the kind of homogeneity of consciousness it sought, the *Volksgemeinschaft* cannot be dismissed as pure propaganda. It did not manage to obliterate awareness of socioeconomic distinctions: the working class, though provided with employment and distracted by the programs of *Strength Through Joy* and *Beauty of Labor*, reacted adversely to longer working hours and expectations of increased productivity. Slowdowns and absenteeism became expressions of socioeconomic grievance. The *Mittelstand* likewise lent the regime more passive than active support.[48] It cannot, furthermore, be maintained that the government succeeded in making German citizens selfless crusaders for a Utopian social vision, any more than it transformed them into fanatical anti-Semites.[49] And, as the study of everyday life suggests, conformity enforced in public encouraged withdrawal into privacy; policies that were supposed to stimulate political enthusiasm resulted in passivity.[50]

Nonetheless, grievances rooted in material conditions did not preclude changes in social consciousness, nor can it be argued that the regime was upheld only by the practice or threat of terror. Michael Prinz suggests that Nazi attempts to break the status barrier between blue-collar and white-collar workers both ended the isolation of the former and compelled the latter to devise a social identity no longer based on opposition to the proletariat.[51] Although economic upturn provided the basis for political stability, National Socialism also represented social values which had deep roots in German society. Detlev Peukert cites appreciation for the imposition of order and discipline – bicycles could be left outside unlocked and loafers were refused a free ride.[52] Ian Kershaw's studies of popular opinion document, amidst complaints about a host of other issues, widespread and remarkably durable admiration for the Führer. The cult of Hitler propagated by Goebbels provided a powerful integrative myth, upheld by economic revival and a chain of foreign policy successes. That the regime never suffered a serious threat of internal collapse even as Germany was being buried under Allied bombs gives a fair measure of social cohesion.[53]

Against this backdrop, Nazism's immense faith in human malleability and colossal appetite for socio-psychological engineering have more than curiosity value. Public language and spectacle became instruments of a totalizing vision to overcome class distinctions and social conflict. Everything from schools to women's organizations, the cinema and callisthenics were pressed into service of the *Volksgemeinschaft*. Schoenbaum is certainly right that conflict continued, transferred in part from society to the state, despite efforts to legislate and propagandize it out of existence.[54] Yet Detlev Peukert's discussion of the *Volksgemeinschaft*, by no means flattering, makes abundantly clear that it cannot be dismissed as a propaganda phrase. Commitment to racial purification was by itself revolutionary. The fact that social behavior supplanted racial origins as the criterion for membership in – or exclusion from – the national community made the racial revolution, with its quasi-scientific rationale, a potent force for revolutionizing society.[55] The result was a far cry from the image projected by Goebbels' propaganda, and anything but emancipatory, but still had its own revolutionary dynamic. In Peukert's words: 'The fellow-traveller and the non-participant, then, were equally threatened by the atomization of everyday life, the dissolution of social bonds, the isolation of modes of perception, the shrinking of prospects and hence the loss of the capacity for social action.'[56] This conclusion, paradigmatic in relating Nazism's totalizing social ambitions and its destructive impact, substantiates, however unwittingly, the view that Nazism contributed to the break down of traditional social norms.[57] By the same token, it offers an ironic commentary on the ambiguity of modernization.

In a recent study of Robert Ley, head of the German Labor Front, Ronald Smelser suggests that had the Third Reich outlasted the war Germany would have become a thoroughly modernized society, boasting equal opportunity, upward mobility and a cradle-to-grave welfare scheme.[58] Paralleling the Labor Front with contemporary information and service institutions, and describing the *Volksgemeinschaft* as a fictional but effective basis for social consensus, Smelser intimates that the postwar generation owes more to the Third Reich than it prefers to acknowledge. He then damns the entire enterprise, rightly, as fundamentally perverted because of its devotion to racism and war. These, the dynamos of social change, represented the first monstrous steps en route to a very peculiar type of modernity.[59]

There is, in sum, abundant evidence of divergence between Nazi ambitions, themselves diverse, and social reality in the Third Reich. There are also good grounds for questioning the sincerity and feasibility of those ambitions, not to mention their assimilation by the population. There is, finally, every reason to condemn the Nazi social vision as perverse and sadistic. It is less easy to dismiss it as empty window-dressing. National Socialism did not, thankfully, have the opportunity to complete its social revolution, conditional as it was on the racial reorganization of Europe. A glance at eastern Europe under Nazi occupation gives an approximate picture of the social consequences of racial revolution.[60]

NOTES

1 Quoted in Milan Hauner, *Hitler: A Chronology of his Life and Times* (London, 1983), p. 64.

2   For a critical survey see Richard Evans, 'The myth of Germany's missing revolution', *New Left Review*, no. 149 (January/February 1985), pp. 67–94.

3   Among a voluminous literature see David Blackbourn and Geoff Eley, *The Peculiarities of German History* (Oxford, 1984), and the recent critical summary by Jürgen Kocka, 'German history before Hitler: the debate about the German *Sonderweg*', *Journal of Contemporary History*, vol. 23 (1988), pp. 3–16.

4   See Horst Matzerath and Heinrich Volkmann, 'Modernisierungstheorie und Nationalsozialismus', in Jürgen Kocka (ed.), *Theorien in der Praxis des Historikers* (Göttingen, 1977), pp. 89–90.

5   Pierre Ayçoberry, *The Nazi Question* (New York, 1981), ch. 8; Ian Kershaw, *The Nazi Dictatorship* (2nd edn, London, 1989), ch. 2.

6   Ralf Dahrendorf, *Society and Democracy in Germany* (New York, 1967), pp. 64, 402–38.

7   David Schoenbaum, *Hitler's Social Revolution* (New York, 1966).

8   Apart from the general overviews by Frederic Grunfeld, *The Hitler File: A Social History of Germany and the Nazis 1918–1945* (London, 1974), and Richard Grunberger, *The 12-Year Reich* (New York, 1971), see, for instance, Tim Mason, *Sozialpolitik im Dritten Reich* (Opladen, 1977); John Farquharson, *The Plough and the Swastika* (London, 1976); Jill Stephenson, *The Nazi Organization of Women* (London, 1981). The more recent literature is cited below.

9   See the review article by Richard Bessel, 'Living with the Nazis: some recent writing on the social history of the Third Reich', *European History Quarterly*, vol. 14 (1984), pp. 211–20; the essays reprinted in R. Bessel (ed.), *Life in the Third Reich* (Oxford, 1987). Representative among the German material is Detlev Peukert and Jürgen Reulecke (eds), *Die Reihen fast geschlossen* (Wuppertal, 1981).

10   As, for example, in the strained formulations of Matzerath and Volkmann, 'Modernisierungstheorie und Nationalsozialismus', p. 100.

11   John Hiden and John Farquharson, *Explaining Hitler's Germany* (2nd edn, London, 1989), ch. 4.

12   Kershaw, *The Nazi Dictatorship*, ch. 7.

13   Bessel, *Life in the Third Reich*.

14   See the controversial article by Martin Broszat, 'Plädoyer für eine Historisierung des Nationalsozialismus', in his *Nach Hitler* (Munich, 1987), pp. 159–73; Saul Friedländer, 'Some reflections on the historicization of national socialism', *Tel Aviver Jahrbuch für deutsche Geschichte*, vol. 16 (1987), pp. 310–24; Otto Kulka, 'Singularity and its relativization', *Yad Vashem Studies*, vol. 19 (1988), pp. 151–86; Broszat's clarification 'Was heisst Historisierung des Nationalsozialismus?' *Historische Zeitschrift*, no. 247 (1988), pp. 1–14, and the exchange of letters with Saul Friedländer in *Vierteljahreshefte für Zeitgeschichte*, vol. 36 (1988), pp. 339–72.

15   Kershaw, *The Nazi Dictatorship*, ch. 8.

16   cf. MacGregor Knox, 'Conquest, domestic and foreign in fascist Italy and Nazi Germany', *Journal of Modern History*, vol. 56 (1984), pp. 1–57; J. P. Stern, *Hitler: The Führer and the People* (London, 1975).

17   See Hitler's May Day speech of 1934 cited in J. Noakes and G. Pridham (eds), *Nazism 1919–1945*, Vol. 2 (Exeter, 1984), p. 354; cf. Rainer Zitelmann, *Hitler. Selbstverständnis eines Revolutionärs* (Hamburg, 1987), pp. 187–94; Jeremy Noakes, 'Nazism and revolution', in Noel O'Sullivan (ed.), *Revolutionary Theory and Political Reality* (Brighton, 1983), p. 76; Gilmer Blackburn,

Education in the Third Reich (Albany, NY, 1985), pp. 93–115. Robert Tucker, 'Lenin's Bolshevism as a culture in the making', in Abbott Gleason, Peter Kenez and Richard Stites (eds), *Bolshevik Culture* (Bloomington, Ind., 1985), pp. 25–38.

18 Sheila Fitzpatrick, *The Russian Revolution 1917–1932* (Oxford, 1982), p. 8. Also see her 'The Russian Revolution and social mobility: a re-examination of the question of social support for the soviet regime in the 1920s and 1930s', *Politics and Society*, vol. 13 (1984), pp. 119–41, and the recent discussion between herself, Ronald Suny and Daniel Orlovsky in *Slavic Review*, vol. 49 (1988), pp. 599–626.

19 Jeremy Noakes, 'The origins, structure and functions of Nazi terror', in Noel O'Sullivan (ed.), *Terrorism, Ideology, and Revolution* (Brighton, 1985), pp. 67–87.

20 Hermann Rauschning, *The Revolution of Nihilism* (New York, 1939); A. J. P. Taylor, 'Hitler's seizure of power', in his *Europe: Grandeur and Decline* (New York, 1967), pp. 204–19; Noakes, 'Nazism and revolution', p. 86.

21 See Schoenbaum, *Hitler's Social Revolution*, p. 29.

22 See the debate between Tim Mason, Hans Mommsen and Klaus Hildebrand in Gerhard Hirschfeld and Lothar Kettenacker (eds), *The Führer State: Myth and Reality* (Stuttgart, 1981), pp. 23–132; Kershaw, *The Nazi Dictatorship*, ch. 4; Hiden and Farquharson, *Explaining Hitler's Germany*, ch. 3.

23 In English as *Hitler's World View* (Cambridge, Mass., 1972). The historiographical background is surveyed in Kulka, 'Singularity and its relativization', pp. 154–6.

24 Milan Hauner, 'A German racial revolution?', *Journal of Contemporary History*, vol. 19 (1984), pp. 669–87.

25 Knox, 'Conquest, domestic and foreign'.

26 Noakes, 'Nazism and revolution'; cf. Peukert, *Inside Nazi Germany*, p. 174.

27 cf. Michael Kater, 'Hitler in a social context', *Central European History*, vol. 14 (1981), pp. 243–72.

28 Zitelmann, *Hitler*, pp. 15–18, 93–5, 458.

29 Peukert, *Inside Nazi Germany*, pp. 208–9, gives a convenient summary.

30 See J. Noakes and G. Pridham (eds), *Nazism 1919–1945*, Vol. 3 (Exeter, 1988), p. 629.

31 Amidst a large literature see Thomas Childers, *The Nazi Voter* (Chapel Hill, NC, 1983); Michael Kater, *The Nazi Party* (Cambridge, Mass., 1983); and the recent historiographical survey by Peter Baldwin, 'Social interpretations of Nazism: renewing a tradition', *Journal of Contemporary History*, vol. 25 (1990), pp. 5–37.

32 See Bessel, 'Political violence and the Nazi seizure of power', and his *Political Violence and the Rise of Nazism* (New Haven, Conn., 1984), ch. 7; Conan Fischer, *Stormtroopers* (London, 1983), ch. 6; Peter Merkl, *The Making of a Stormtrooper* (Princeton, NJ, 1980). An illuminating case study is Ulrich Klein, 'SA-Terror und Bevölkerung in Wuppertal 1933/34', in Peukert and Reulecke, *Die Reihen fast geschlossen*, pp. 45–61.

33 Martin Broszat, *The Hitler State* (New York, 1981), pp. 77–84; Bessel, 'Political violence and the Nazi seizure of power'.

34 Ronald Smelser, 'Nazi dynamics, German foreign policy and appeasement', in Lothar Kettenacker and Wolfgang Mommsen (eds), *The Fascist Challenge and the Policy of Appeasement*, (Boston, Mass., 1983), pp. 31–47.

35 Noakes, 'Nazism and Revolution', p. 85, and Kershaw, *The Nazi Dictatorship*, pp. 143–4, minimize social opportunity.

36 Noakes and Pridham, *Nazism 1919–1945*, Vol. 2, p. 379; cf. Kater, *Nazi Party*, pp. 238–9.

37 William Jannen Jr, 'National socialists and social mobility', *Journal of Social History*, vol. 9 (1975/6), pp. 339–68; cf. Broszat, 'Plädoyer', pp. 167–9; Noakes and Pridham, *Nazism 1919–1945*, Vol. 2, p. 379. Fischer, *Stormtroopers*, pp. 59–61, indicates that rank rose consistently with educational/class background.

38 See, for instance, Kater, *Nazi Party*, pp. 237–8.

39 Matzerath and Volkmann, 'Modernisierungstheorie und Nationalsozialismus', p. 99, blame this on the absence of practical policy. For an illuminating example of the way in which the shortage of male professionals resulted in unprecedented numbers of women attending university see Jacques Pawels, *Women, Nazis, and Universities* (Westport, Conn., 1984).

40 Henry Turner, 'Fascism and Modernization', in his *Resappraisals of Fascism* (New York, 1975), pp. 117–39. For a recent statement of Nazism's ideological confusion see Peukert, *Inside Nazi Germany*, pp. 39–41.

41 See Kater, 'Hitler in a social context'.

42 Details are in Adelheid von Saldern, *Mittelstand im 'Dritten Reich'*, 2nd edn (Frankfurt/New York, 1985), ch. I; cf. Peukert, *Inside Nazi Germany*, pp. 87–93.

43 On agriculture see Farquharson, *The Plough and the Swastika*, pp. 187–8, 253, and the conclusion in Anna Bramwell, *Blood and Soil* (Abbotsbrook, 1985).

44 See Richard Overy, *The Nazi Economic Recovery 1932–1938* (London, 1982), pp. 44–5.

45 Tim Mason, *Sozialpolitik im dritten Reich* (Opladen, 1977), and 'Labour in the Third Reich, 1933–1939', *Past and Present*, no. 33 (1966), pp. 112–41; cf. Stephen Salter, 'Class harmony or class conflict? The Industrial working class and the national socialist regime 1933–1945', in Jeremy Noakes (ed.), *Government, Party and People in Nazi Germany* (Exeter, 1980), pp. 76–97; Schoenbaum, *Hitler's Social Revolution*, ch. 3.

46 von Saldern, *Mittelstand im 'Dritten Reich'*, p. 91.

47 In the words of Robert Ley, leader of the DAF: 'The social question is not a matter of wage agreements but a matter of training and education.' Quoted in Ronald Smelser, *Robert Ley* (Oxford, 1988), p. 146.

48 Ian Kershaw, *Popular Opinion and Political Dissent in the Third Reich* (New York, 1983) emphasizes the chimerical character of the *Volksgemeinschaft*; cf. von Saldern, *Mittelstand im 'Dritten Reich'*, ch. 3.

49 Lawrence Stokes, 'The German people and the destruction of the European Jews', *Central European History*, vol. 6 (1972), pp. 167–91; Ian Kershaw, 'The persecution of the Jews and German popular opinion in the Third Reich', *Leo Baeck Institute Yearbook*, vol. 26 (1981), pp. 261–89; Otto Kulka, 'Public opinion in Nazi Germany and the Jewish question', *Jerusalem Quarterly*, vol. 25 (1982), pp. 121–44; vol. 26 (1983), pp. 34–45; Sarah Gordon, *Hitler, Germans and the 'Jewish Question'* (Princeton, NJ, 1984), ch. 6.

50 Peukert, *Inside Nazi Germany*, pp. 50, 65.

51 Michael Prinz, *Vom neuen Mittelstand zum Volksgenossen* (Munich, 1986), pp. 334–5; cf. Zitelmann, *Hitler*, pp. 164–7.

52 Peukert, *Inside Nazi Germany*, p. 198; cf. Lothar Kettenacker, 'Social and psychological aspects of the Führer's rule', in H. W. Koch (ed.), *Aspects of the Third Reich* (London, 1985), pp. 96–132.

53 Kershaw, *Popular Opinion and Political Dissent*, and *The Hitler Myth* (Oxford, 1987).

54 Schoenbaum, *Hitler's Social Revolution*, p. 275.

55 Peukert, *Inside Nazi Germany*, pp. 215, 248.

56 ibid., p. 239. The two-edged character of policy is spelled out in Gisela Bock, 'Racism and sexism in Nazi Germany: motherhood, compulsory sterilization, and the state', in Renate Bridenthal, Anita Grossmann and Marion Kaplan (eds), *When Biology Became Destiny* (New York, 1984), pp. 271–96.

57 On the destructive force of National Socialism cf. Noakes, 'Nazism and revolution', p. 95.; Kershaw, *Nazi Dictatorship*, p. 149; also the conclusion in the recent survey by Jackson Spielvogel, *Hitler and Nazi Germany* (Englewood Cliffs, NJ, 1988), pp. 300–2.

58 cf. Marie-Louise Recker, *Nationalsozialistische Sozialpolitik im Zweiten Weltkrieg* (Munich, 1985); Broszat, 'Plädoyer', pp. 171–2.

59 Smelser, *Robert Ley*, pp. 303–7.

60 For an overview see Norman Rich, *Hitler's War Aims*, Vol. 2 (New York, 1974).

9 Hitler and the Coming of the War

DAVID E. KAISER

Thirty years after the publication of A.J.P. Taylor's controversial work, *The Origins of the Second World War*, the essential goals of Hitler's foreign policy are not a source of much dispute. Taylor's most contentious statements – that Hitler did not intend war to break out in September 1939, that he lacked a real plan for the conquest of Europe or the world, and that other governments had played a critical role in unleashing German expansion – have not held up. Recent treatments agree that Hitler *did* have a comprehensive plan for German expansion dating from before his accession to power and did intend a war in September 1939.[1]

Establishing Hitler's fundamental goals, however, does not clear up two other questions that have become the source of considerable debate: the extent of the roots of these goals in earlier eras of German foreign policy, and the role of tactical, domestic–political and economic considerations in the years leading up to the outbreak of the war. The question of continuity of German policy throughout the era of the two world wars was raised most emphatically by another seminal work, Fritz Fischer's *Griff nach der Weltmacht*,[2] which appeared nearly simultaneously with Taylor's and immediately became equally controversial, especially within its country of origin. By establishing quite clearly the extent of Germany's aims in the First World War – including territorial expansion in the west and the east, a large new colonial empire and, by 1918, a network of vassal states comprising much of the now-collapsed Russian empire including the Ukraine – Fischer inevitably invited comparisons with Hitler's goals as well. In so doing, of course, he threatened several myths dear to the West German historical establishment, including both the failure to accept primary German responsibility for the outbreak of the war of 1914, and its view of the Nazis as a definite break in the history of Germany as a whole. The attempt to refute his thesis – led by Gerhard Ritter – focused mainly upon Germany's war aims during the war.[3]

On the whole, the researches of the last 30 years have tended to confirm not only some basic similarities between German war aims in the two world wars, but also some longer-term continuities in German imperialist theory and practice. Perhaps the single most informative work on German imperialism in the years 1871–1945 is now Woodruff Smith's *The Ideological Origins of Nazi Imperialism* (1986), which traced two distinct currents of German expansionism through the imperial and Weimar periods and argued that Hitler attempted to combine them. In *Reshaping the German Right* (1980), Geoff Eley identified a very vocal party of German radical nationalists before the First World War, suggesting that even before 1914 large numbers of politically active Germans found their government's foreign policy too timid. Lastly, Fischer's student Imanuel Geiss, in his work on German war aims in Poland during the First World War, showed that German military and academic circles had planned not only the annexation of large parts of Russian Poland, but also the resettlement of much of the existing population and its replacement with Germans, thereby foreshadowing some – but not all – of the Nazis' most drastic plans for eastern Europe.[4]

All this tends to confirm that the main planks of Hitler's program – which have been well established for several decades – were anything but original. Hitler wanted to create a new Greater Germany by adding Austria, Bohemia and Moravia to the Reich, and to regain the territories lost to Poland and Lithuania as well. Then, having created this new Reich, he intended to move further eastward, destroying the Soviet Union and establishing a German agricultural empire in the Ukraine, while securing German influence over the whole of eastern and southeastern Europe. Well before the seizure of power, he had suggested that some peoples, such as the Balts, might be fully Germanized, while others must submit unconditionally to German will, accepting either resettlement or the status of fully colonized peoples. Hitler, during the 1920s, had decided against attempting to recover an overseas colonial empire in order to make an alliance with Great Britain possible, but after coming to power he was eventually persuaded to revive dreams of a central African empire as well.[5]

These goals combined the *Grossdeutschland* vision of the Austrian sections of the prewar Pan-German League, which had advocated the dissolution of the Hapsburg Empire and the inclusion of its German-speaking citizens in a Greater Germany, with the expansionist plans in eastern Europe developed by the German government and High Command during the First World War. While much of what Hitler planned to do had been foreshadowed by the policy of the imperial government in 1914–18, his plans for the east differed both qualitatively and quantitatively. Thus, while the Wilhelmine government had intended to remove the Polish and Jewish population from the 'frontier strip' which they planned to annex from Poland during the First World War, and to resettle it with Germans from Russia, these plans did not compare in scale with the Nazi plans to move or exterminate tens of millions of Jews, Poles, Ukrainians and Russians, whose implementation began immediately after the outbreak of war in September 1939.

In addition, most German politicians, diplomats and generals – in sharp contrast to Hitler – had drawn some lessons from the experience of 1914–18, and modified their aims accordingly. Hitler's revival of Germany's 1914–18 war aims did mark a sharp break from the foreign policy of the Weimar Republic. While no Weimar government had ever really accepted the terms of the Treaty of Versailles – including the new German-Polish frontier – no evidence that we have tends to show that the politicians, diplomats and generals of the Weimar Republic ever seriously intended to provoke a new war. Successive Weimar governments had fought the provisions of the Versailles treaty and had successfully removed a few of the restraints upon German national sovereignty.[6] In the years 1930–2, after the evacuation of the Rhineland, the Brüning government was already planning to use the Disarmament Conference to achieve a significant degree of German rearmament, while attempting to use German economic power to increase its influence in southeastern Europe, and perhaps to bring about some territorial changes.[7] But while ample evidence suggests that the political and military leadership wanted to regain roughly the position of 1914, subsequent evidence indicates that the traditional elites understood the danger of renewing the attempt to go beyond it. We shall see that Hitler's first steps towards a new European war in 1938 met with considerable opposition from diplomats and generals who had drawn appropriate lessons from the outcome of the First World War.

Hitler could not, of course, proceed at once to the realization of his ambitious goals after reaching power in January 1933, although he did encourage national socialist attempts to overthrow the government of Austria – attempts which failed dramatically in June 1934. During the first three years of his rule, he cast off many of the restrictions upon German national sovereignty imposed by the Treaty of Versailles. Thus he left the League of Nations and the Disarmament Conference in October 1933, proclaimed his intention to triple the size of the German army in 1934, denounced the disarmament clauses of the Versailles treaty altogether in early 1935 and remilitarized the Rhineland in March 1936. These steps had become possible as a result of the failure of the French government to compel the observance of the Versailles treaty in 1922–4, when they had to end the occupation of the Ruhr and undertake not to resume it, and by further allied concessions to the Weimar government in subsequent years, including the evacuation of the Rhineland in 1930 and the end of reparations in 1932. The French government, in short, had abandoned the idea of holding Germany to the Treaty of Versailles by force – a fact confirmed in 1936, when the government found that the French army had no plan to react promptly to the remilitarization of the Rhineland.[8] Hitler also began rearming Germany, but the extent of rearmament remained quite limited in 1936.

The nature of Hitler's ultimate goals, and some of the key problems involved in pursuing them, first emerged in early 1936, when the government had to deal with a new economic crisis. From 1933 through 1935, a combination of public works, rearmament and the recovery of the world economy had almost eliminated unemployment within Germany, contributing massively to the popularity of the Nazi regime. In late 1935, however, new problems were emerging. In order to carry on foreign trade despite continuing exchange controls, Hjalmar Schacht, Minister of Economics and President of the Reichsbank, had instituted the New Plan in 1934. The plan effectively rationed available foreign exchange among importers and attempted to balance much of German trade on a bilateral basis. Because Schacht, who was following Hitler's wishes, gave priority to imports of raw materials for rearmament over imports of foodstuffs, German importers by late 1935 could no longer meet the growing demand for various foods, including butter. In addition, the emphasis upon rearmament was starving Germany's export industries, making it more difficult for exports to keep pace with imports.

For all these reasons, in early 1936 Schacht proposed several measures designed to return Germany to economic normalcy while taking advantage of rearmament to achieve some long-standing political goals. Specifically, he wanted to lift exchange controls, slow down rearmament, encourage production for exports and, perhaps, devalue the Reichsmark to bring it in line with the pound and the dollar. Schacht also believed that the time was ripe to ask the Western powers for the return of Germany's lost colonies and for a revision of the German–Polish frontier. Germany, in short, would recover the position of 1914, while taking further advantage of the recovery of the world economy. Schacht, in essence, was arguing that the time had come to realize the major long-term goals of the foreign policy of the Weimar Republic.

Hitler's response definitely committed him to an entirely different course. After several months, he rejected Schacht's policies and appointed Göring head of the Four Year Plan, a new agency designed to assert greater control over the German economy. He specifically ordered Göring to press on with rearmament as rapidly as possible and to make the German economy self-sufficient in several important raw materials, including oil and rubber, by developing synthetic production. He added that foreign exchange must not be diverted to the purchase of foodstuffs at the expense of rearmament.[9] As Hitler made clear several times before and after the seizure of power, he did not believe in world trade as a solution to Germany's economic problems. The only solution, in his view, was the conquest of *Lebensraum* in the east, and this required accelerated rearmament, not production for export.[10]

Göring's measures under the Four Year Plan enabled rearmament to proceed for another 18 months. He tried to solve the food crisis by making massive grain purchases from the countries of southeastern Europe, whose governments lacked other markets and had to accept Reichsmarks for their goods. The government also began encouraging arms exports to improve the trade balance. Such policies were not altogether successful. Food shortages persisted, German consumers often had to eat bread adulterated with corn and potato flour, and a labor shortage became a serious problem by early 1938.[11] Goebbels, who in late 1935 had justified the butter shortage on the grounds that foreign exchange was needed for raw materials with which to make guns, now argued increasingly that an international Jewish conspiracy was responsible for Germany's economic hardship. Meanwhile, Hitler undertook no new dramatic diplomatic initiatives during late 1936 and 1937.

This brief review of the early years of the Nazi regime suggests that the question of continuity in German foreign policy cannot be resolved simply by comparing war aims during the two world wars, or by tracing Hitler's policies to their pre-1914 ideological roots. While ideas such as Hitler's had been current for decades, the possibilities for their realization had changed, and many important German figures who had endorsed expansionism on a massive scale during the First World War had moderated their views. In short, Hitler could not simply announce his intention to resume the struggle for world power and expect the rest of German society to come to his support. Moreover, he faced a diplomatic constellation which seemed, if anything, less favorable for Germany than that of 1914–18, and a much weaker economic situation. For these reasons, tactical considerations played a critical role in Hitler's approach to the Second World War. Both because of certain critical weaknesses in Germany's economic and diplomatic position, and because of the doubts entertained by the traditional elites concerning the wisdom of a new war, Hitler had to maneuver very carefully in undertaking the expansion of German power and territory from 1938 through the summer of 1941. Nazi foreign policy did not begin and end with the building and use of a new war machine, but reflected a very complex series of problems – problems which, as Hitler well knew, had eventually proved fatal to Germany during the First World War. To begin expansion anew, Hitler had to build up sufficient armed forces despite severe new economic constraints. He also wanted to avoid the diplomatic mistakes which, as he saw it, had helped to doom the German empire in 1914–18, and to avoid losing the support of the German people and provoking a collapse on the home front like that of November 1918. In an attempt to avoid these mistakes, he played upon key elements of the international climate of the 1930s and took advantage of changes in military technology and tactics. His clever mix of diplomacy, intrigue and strategy won him the mastery of central and western Europe, but failed in the end to create the great Eurasian empire with which he hoped to meet the British Empire and the United States on at least equal terms.

Hitler discussed the critical issues facing his policies with leading diplomats and generals during the so-called Hossbach Conference of 5 November, 1937. The conference dealt both with Hitler's aims and with the economic, diplomatic and internal political obstacles to their realization. The history of the next four years is largely the history of his attempts to overcome both those obstacles. To understand those four years, we must look first at Hitler's aims as reflected in the conference itself and then at the ways in which he managed to overcome the diplomatic, economic and domestic political obstacles to their achievement.

Speaking to Foreign Minister Constantin von Neurath, Göring and the leaders of the army and navy, Hitler reaffirmed the need for the conquest of living space in the east, which he foresaw sometime during the years 1943–5. He also noted the continuing economic difficulties occasioned by rearmament, Germany's increasing consumption of foodstuffs and the danger that a food and foreign exchange crisis might threaten the regime at any time. To begin solving these problems, he proposed the almost immediate conquest of Austria and Czechoslovakia, which in his view would provide a partial, short-term solution to the food crisis. He implicitly recognized that Germany was not ready to fight the British and French, but suggested that either civil war in France or war in the Mediterranean between Italy and Great Britain would make it possible for Germany to fall upon Austria and Czechoslovakia without their intervention during the coming year.[12] In reply, Neurath and Generals Blomberg and Fritsch questioned the likelihood of an Anglo-Italian war and argued that France and Britain were still much too strong for Germany and Italy. According to Neurath's testimony at Nuremberg, the foreign minister reiterated his views some weeks later, warning Hitler that his plans could lead to a world war.

In one way or another, all four of the major obstacles in the way of Hitler's plans emerged at the Hossbach Conference. First, the diplomats, the generals and, implicitly, Hitler himself, recognized the need to avoid an immediate conflict with the British and French while trying to annex Austria and destroy Czechoslovakia. All those present seemed to understand that a new world war, in which Germany and Italy would face Britain, France and perhaps the Soviet Union must be avoided, at least at present.

Second, as Hitler seemed to understand, continued rearmament was putting enormous strains on the German economy. Labor shortages, food shortages and the combination of an increased demand for imported foodstuffs and continuing diversion of production away from export industries threatened to produce a real crisis in the German economy. Hitler hoped that the immediate annexation of Austria and parts of Czechoslovakia would help solve this problem.

Third, the conference and its aftermath showed Hitler that the traditional military and diplomatic elites rejected his policies. This raised the danger that they would not give him their support and that they might possibly move against him if things went badly.

The fourth problem, which was only alluded to indirectly, was related to the second and third. The German people, who had initially welcomed the economic recovery under the Nazis and Hitler's reassertion of German national sovereignty, were still undergoing serious hardships. Hitler, who had never forgotten the events of November 1918, took their feelings very seriously.[13] As time went on, they needed proof that their sacrifices were necessary, and that they would be rewarded.

Hitler's diplomatic, military and political strategy from 1938 through 1940 was designed to overcome these obstacles. It succeeded brilliantly. During 1938, Hitler managed to annex Austria in March and to acquire the German-populated areas of Czechoslovakia, the Sudetenland, in the Munich agreement of 30 September. In March 1939 he destroyed the rest of Czechoslovakia, annexing Bohemia-Moravia and Memel from Lithuania. In September, shortly after signing the Nazi-Soviet Pact, he attacked and conquered Poland. In April 1940 he conquered Denmark and Norway and in May he successfully attacked and defeated France. In carrying out these moves he was not following a prescribed timetable, but rather taking advantage of various political, diplomatic and military aspects of the international situation to overcome the four major obstacles to the realization of his long-range goals.

The events of 1938, including the *Anschluss* and the annexation of the Sudetenland, did not reflect the scenario that Hitler had sketched at the Hossbach Conference. Neither civil war in France nor an Anglo-Italian war took place, confirming the skepticism of Neurath, Blomberg and Fritsch. Other elements of the European political situation, however, enabled Hitler to achieve most of his goals without firing a shot. He took advantage of both the re-emergence of German nationalism in central Europe and the attitudes of the Western powers towards another war.

Essentially, Hitler managed to exploit the principle of nationality to undermine the legitimacy of the governments of Austria and Czechoslovakia. While this principle had constituted the theoretical basis of the new European frontiers drawn at Paris in 1919, it had been applied in such a way that Germans in Austria and Danzig were denied the right of self-determination, while the claims of the Germans of Bohemia and

Moravia were rejected in favor of the Czechs. By late 1937, Hitler's success within Germany had strengthened National Socialism in Austria to a point where the Austrian Nazis could lay claim to a significant position in the government. Meanwhile, in Czechoslovakia, Konrad Henlein's Sudeten German Party had emerged as the clear representative of the German minority – and Henlein was in close touch with Hitler.[14]

Moreover, as Hitler came to understand, neither the French nor the British were willing to fight to maintain the provisions of the peace settlement of 1919 that violated the nationality principle to Germany's disadvantage. This British government in particular signalled as much to Hitler in November 1937 when Lord Halifax, visiting Hitler, referred to Danzig, Austria and Czechoslovakia as 'questions which fall into the category of possible alterations in the European order', and added that Britain's interest was 'to see that any alterations should come through the course of peaceful evolution'. And, indeed, the new British prime minister, Neville Chamberlain, had decided to accept the realization of Germany's goals through negotiation in an attempt to avoid war. The French government had also written off Austria and was weakening in its commitment to Czechoslovakia – partly, though not exclusively, because of Chamberlain's attitude.[15]

In February 1938, Hitler presented Schuschnigg, the Austrian chancellor, with a series of demands designed virtually to destroy the independence of his government. When Schuschnigg suddenly called for a plebiscite to reaffirm Austrian independence, Hitler dispatched an ultimatum and marched his troops into Austria following the collapse of Schuschnigg's government. The European powers, having already accepted the inevitability of *Anschluss*, stood by.

In Czechoslovakia, where the *Anschluss* further increased the appetite of the German minority, Hitler told Henlein to make demands for autonomy so sweeping that the Prague government would have to refuse them. In May, after a brief crisis, he ordered his generals to prepare for an attack upon Czechoslovakia, while insisting that the British and French would not intervene. While Henlein gradually increased his demands upon the Prague government, Hitler's statements became more and more ominous. The emerging crisis over Czechoslovakia brought to light the critical divergence in views between Hitler and such generals and diplomats as Ludwig Beck, who resigned as chief of staff of the army during the summer of 1938, and Ernst von Weizsäcker, state secretary of the foreign office, who tried to convince his chief, Joachim von Ribbentrop, that another general war would be disastrous. Should war break out between Germany, Italy and Japan on one side, and Britain, France and perhaps the Soviet Union on the other, 'the common loser with us', Weizsäcker argued prophetically, 'would be the whole of

Europe, the victors chiefly the non-European continents and the anti-social powers'.[16] When faced with such arguments, Hitler countered that Britain and France would stand aside. In the summer of 1938 Hitler had embarked upon an exercise that would, had it occurred in the 1950s, be regarded as brinkmanship.

In September, the threat of a German attack on Czechoslovakia and the prospect of a European war induced Chamberlain to fly to Germany to meet Hitler. There he promised to arrange the peaceful transfer of the German-populated Sudetenland to Germany. Since Hitler wanted both a local war and the annexation of all of Bohemia and Moravia, he prepared a further set of demands designed to split Prague from the Western powers, and presented them to Chamberlain at their second meeting in Godesberg. After some hesitation, the British and then the French governments refused to accede to these demands, threatening war should Hitler attack Czechoslovakia. At the last moment, Hitler canceled his plans for the attack and agreed to meet with Chamberlain, Daladier and Mussolini at Munich, where he accepted the peaceful transfer of the Sudetenland. Rather than risk war with the Western powers, he had taken advantage of their fear and their willingness to meet his nationalist claims to achieve a more limited victory. An impressive combination of threats and diplomatic compromise had resulted in a remarkable triumph for Hitler.

The lively and continuing debate over the wisdom of British appeasement, in my judgment, has largely missed the point of the crisis over Czechoslovakia by assuming that it was Chamberlain, rather than Hitler, who decided against war. Thus, Williamson Murray, in *The Change of the European Balance of Power, 1938–1939* (1984) argues that Britain and France would have defeated Hitler in a war over Czechoslovakia, while a number of authors, including D.C. Watt, have suggested that various strategic, diplomatic, economic and military factors rightly inclined Chamberlain away from war and toward peace in 1938. Yet the evidence we have suggests that Hitler, like his generals, recognized in 1938 that he could not yet fight Britain and France and therefore took what he could get without war when London and Paris finally firmed up on 29 September. Had Paris and London recognized this, the crisis might have produced a different result.

The debate so far has focused on the outcome of a war that no one intended to fight. Considerable evidence suggests that the crisis was an exercise in brinkmanship, one in which Hitler demonstrated superior skill.

Meanwhile, the *Anschluss* and the Munich agreement also won Hitler a decisive victory in the continuing struggle with his diplomats and generals. The German-Austrian crisis of February 1938, which led to the *Anschluss*, occurred just at the moment at which Hitler had dismissed

Neurath, Blomberg and Fritsch, who had opposed his policies at the Hossbach Conference, and the successful outcome of the international crisis enabled him to escape unscathed from the domestic crisis.[17] During the summer of 1938 a number of generals and diplomats planned to arrest Hitler if a general war broke out, but their conspiracy collapsed when Chamberlain agreed to fly to Berchtesgaden.[18] The Munich agreement secured Hitler's control.

During the next six months, Hitler used intrigues among the Slovaks and Hungary's designs upon Ruthenia to destroy the remainder of the Czechoslovak state. He succeeded and occupied Prague in March 1939 and also secured another peaceful, quasi-legal victory in Memel, which Lithuania was compelled to return to Germany. Meanwhile, Ribbentrop was attempting to negotiate with the Polish government the return of Danzig and the granting of extra-territorial transportation rights across the Polish corridor. Hitler, in short, was using the momentum of the Munich agreement to complete the creation of Greater Germany. His subsequent plans were not yet clear.

The situation changed in late March when the British and French governments promised to protect Poland against a German attack. Hitler immediately decided to attack Poland, and repudiated his previous offers of a deal. The decision, which clearly carried with it a much greater risk of war than his designs upon Czechoslovakia, required new diplomatic moves. While Hitler, in the summer of 1939, was somewhat stronger militarily than in the previous summer, the Western Allies were becoming stronger as well.

German rearmament was continuing and the occupation of Bohemia and Moravia had allowed the confiscation of enough Czech military equipment to equip several new German divisions. At the same time, Germany's economic crisis was becoming more severe. Any plans for an attack on Poland and a war against Britain and France required further diplomatic preparation, as well as a strategy for meeting the vastly increased economic needs of a new war.

While historians continue to debate the influence of the economic situation upon German policy, growing evidence suggests that the economic picture was inclining Hitler towards war in 1939.[19] As Hans-Erich Volkmann has shown, the German economy in 1939 was coming up against the limits of its resources and productive capacity. German heavy industrial production had reached its maximum capacity in 1937 and increased in 1938 and 1939 only because of the annexations of Austria, the Sudetenland and Bohemia–Moravia. Efforts to become self-sufficient in food and raw materials, or to import them only from eastern European states that traded with Germany in Reichsmarks, had not succeeded and demands for foreign exchange to pay for overseas imports remained high. German exports, moreover, were *falling* during

1939 – despite a general upturn in the world economy – because so much productive capacity had been diverted to rearmament and public construction projects. Germany would clearly have run out of foreign exchange and goods with which to pay for exports within a few more months had the war not begun in September 1939. Labor shortages had reached 1 million workers, and Göring had already made some attempts to control the use of labor throughout the German economy, with a view to restricting labor in non-essential areas.[20]

Hitler was determined to push rearmament ahead at an even faster pace and war may have been the only way in which to do so. Some evidence suggests that Hitler and other German authorities decided upon further expansion as a solution to some of these problems during 1939. The late Tim Mason recently suggested that new rearmament targets adopted by Hitler early in 1939 were so grandiose as to have required a major enlargement of the German economic base.[21] Elements within German industry, especially the chemical giant IG Farben and heavy industrial concerns, were already planning the organization of German-dominated markets in eastern Europe before the war began, and moved immediately to implement some of their plans, such as the integration of the heavy industry of Polish Silesia into the German war economy, as soon as the war made this possible.[22] Hitler also told his generals on 22 August 1939 that, 'because of our restrictions [*Einschränkungen*, or bottlenecks] our economic situation is such that we can only hold out for a few more years. Göring can confirm this.'[23] In attacking Poland, Hitler was choosing a strategy which Nazi economic theorists had put forward for years: a strategy of small, predatory wars to increase self-sufficiency.[24]

Before unleashing a war of expansion, however, Hitler had to prepare the war diplomatically and to ensure that secure supplies of necessary foodstuffs and raw materials would be available as soon as the war began. For a real war he needed allies. He initially sought a tripartite alliance with Italy and Japan that would commit all three powers to fight in a war against France, Britain and the Soviet Union. But the Japanese government refused to commit itself and Hitler decided to come to terms with the Soviet Union instead.[25] Negotiations between Ribbentrop and Molotov in Moscow in late August agreed upon German and Russian spheres of influence in Poland and the rest of eastern Europe. The Nazi–Soviet Pact guaranteed Soviet neutrality in a war between Germany and Britain and France.

The pact also solved some critical short-term economic problems. In the months before the outbreak of war, a study prepared by IG Farben had concluded that Germany needed the resources of the Soviet Union, as well as those of northern and eastern Europe, to withstand a blockade.[26] The economic clauses of the pact also promised Germany large immediate deliveries of food and raw materials in exchange for future deliveries of industrial goods. Having secured his eastern military flank and opened up a way around an allied blockade, on 1 September 1939, Hitler attacked Poland despite the risk of a European war.

The blitzkrieg tactics of armored war and close air support that defeated the Poles within a few weeks were another key element in Hitler's overall strategy. Germany was spared a protracted conflict and the rapidity of Poland's defeat encouraged the Western powers not to undertake an immediate offensive. While Hitler was apparently planning for a full-scale, protracted war in the 1943–5 period – as R.J. Overy has stressed – all his projected campaigns between 1938 and 1941, from the planned attack on Czechoslovakia to the attack on the Soviet Union, depended upon rapid success.[27] War helped solve some of Germany's immediate economic problems, especially the labor shortage. Planning for the use of prisoners of war in German agriculture began as early as January 1939 and the recruitment of Polish workers started days after the attack. The use of Polish and then French prisoners of war on a massive scale more than made up for losses of German men to the military at least until 1941.[28]

Other economic problems, however, became more serious and encouraged a broadening of the conflict. German imports and exports suffered a sharp fall, largely because of Germany's inability to pay for imports. The occupation of Denmark, Norway and the Benelux countries was largely designed to put the resources of these countries at Germany's disposal.[29] Hitler also ordered an immediate attack upon France partly because he believed that Germany's economic position must worsen in comparison to the Anglo-French allies and because he feared continued dependence upon Soviet supplies.[30] Generals and civilian officials opposed to the attack on France revived the conspiracy against Hitler in the winter of 1939/40,[31] but after Hitler's victories in western Europe it collapsed, not to revive until Germany was clearly losing the war. The Führer was well aware of the domestic political impact of these victories. As he declared in August 1939, every one of his dramatic foreign policy initiatives had been opposed by subordinates, but he had been proven right again and again.[32]

Hitler's victories in 1938–40 also seem to have helped reconcile the German people to their continuing hardship. By 1938, despite the end of unemployment, the effects of rearmament – including continual consumer-goods shortages, labor shortages in agriculture and upward pressure on wages – had seriously disturbed the population, resulting in police and other reports of increasing discontent.[33] Unless Hitler cut down on rearmament, all of these problems must get worse, not better and, far from cutting down on rearmament, Hitler was insisting that it be drastically increased once again, apparently to prepare for the great war that he anticipated was several years away. In this context, the political and economic significance of a series of crises and small wars becomes clear. Crisis and war provided some excuse for the hardships imposed upon the German people. A continuing stream of triumphs enormously enhanced Hitler's prestige, apparently encouraging the people to credit him with Germany's triumphs while blaming their hardships – and other unpopular aspects of the Nazi regime – upon his subordinates. Meanwhile, expansion provided at least some short-term solutions to Germany's economic problems. As preparations for war increasingly disrupted the German economy, it behoved Hitler to show that these preparations would lead not to a repetition of the catastrophe of 1914–18, but instead to the rapid expansion of German power and the eventual achievement of world-power status.

Two recent studies suggest that even before 1938 Hitler's foreign policy was extremely popular and probably made up among the population for considerable economic hardship and other unpopular domestic moves. His more dramatic foreign policy successes from 1938 through 1940 had a tremendous effect upon his popularity at a time when hardships were becoming even greater.[34] While the outbreak of war in 1939 seems initially to have depressed the population, the victories over Poland, Norway and France strengthened the emerging myth of Hitler's genius and raised his popularity to new heights. Still, he apparently believed that the German people simply would not tolerate a long war. And while intelligence reports in early 1941 showed a high level of approval of Hitler in the populace at large, the people also expected a decisive stroke which would bring about peace. A continuing string of foreign policy and military successes had become something of a necessity.

Hitler in mid-1940 had not achieved his long-term foreign policy goals. The victory over France placed much larger resources of food, raw materials, arms and labor at his disposal. The human and material resources of most of Europe enabled the Germans in 1939–41 to increase arms production more rapidly during these three years than at any other time under the Nazi regime.[35] But despite all this, Hitler in 1941 was still far from ready for the great war that he anticipated. In addition, he seemed to have run out of diplomatic options.

Although after the fall of France Hitler shifted armament priorities towards the army and navy – probably, as Andreas Hillgruber has argued, in preparation for an eventual worldwide struggle against the Anglo-Saxon powers and the Japanese – he lacked the means as yet to conquer the British Isles. He hoped during the summer of 1940 to compel the British to make a compromise peace by bombing, or perhaps to make an invasion possible by securing control of the air, but this plan failed and plans for the invasion of Britain had to be canceled. Meanwhile, feelers to enlist either Franco's Spain or Vichy France as allies against the British had failed, partly because of the irreconcilable goals of France, Spain and Mussolini's Italy. A brief attempt to enlist the Soviet Union in an anti-British coalition – an episode the seriousness of which is difficult to evaluate – also went nowhere. The long-term threat from the Anglo-Saxons became more serious as the United States government in the summer of 1940 extended more aid to Britain, and in January 1941 made clear its intention to put American industry at the disposal of the British in the lend-lease bill. By 1942, Hitler concluded, American rearmament would be in full swing and the Anglo-Saxon coalition would be a formidable foe whether the United States entered the war or not.

Hitler therefore decided to undertake the conquest of the Soviet Union at once in order to create his planned European empire before American rearmament had been completed. By this time he had convinced most of the old elites that they could safely pursue the goal of world power and that another blitzkrieg could vanquish the Soviet Union at relatively little cost. The attack which the generals planned for May 1941, however, and which was subsequently postponed until June, was not designed to unleash the great war for which Hitler was still planning. The plan anticipated that the Soviet Union, like France, would collapse politically after an initial series of German victories. This would clear the way for the realization of plans for the resettlement or extermination of much of the existing population of western Russia, and its colonization with Germans or other Aryans. With the grain of the Ukraine and the oil of the Caucasus at his disposal, Hitler would feel prepared to face the Western powers.[36] In anticipation of a quick victory over the Soviets, German arms production was already shifting to aircraft and ships, so as to defend the European empire against the Anglo-Americans and prepare for future conflict on a world scale.[37]

The failure of the blitzkrieg against the Soviets, whose authority held together despite crushing initial defeats, and the American entry into the war in December 1941 left Hitler in exactly the situation that he had hoped to avoid: a long-term struggle with industrially superior powers.[38] Helped by the occupation of most of Europe, the German economy performed remarkably well from 1942 through most of 1944. An impressive system of inflated 'occupation costs' and clearings which allowed the Germans an almost unlimited claim upon the resources of western Europe enabled them to use western European agriculture, heavy industrial resources and labor to raise production far above 1914–18 levels. Their brutal methods in eastern Europe were less successful economically, but one authority has found that the campaign in Russia was supported principally from Russian resources. With the help of more than 7 million foreign workers, Germany raised production of heavy industrial products and munitions to new heights.[39]

With all this, however, the Germans could not match the British and

Americans. The demands of the huge campaign on the eastern front, coupled with first an air and then a land war in western Europe, were too much. The Second World War confirmed the lesson of the First: that no European power had the economic resources to compete with the economic might of the United States, which furnished most of the supplies for the entire Allied war effort and simultaneously defeated Japan as well. While the Germans, British and Soviets each produced between 112,000 and 137,000 aircraft during the war, the United States built 300,000; while the Germans produced 45,000 tanks, the United States built 87,000 and the Soviets 103,000.[40] Although both the Soviet Union and the Western Allies eventually learned to use the techniques of blitzkrieg to defeat the German armies and reconquer Europe, they consistently relied upon material superiority to win their victories. German production collapsed when German armies had to retreat from Russia and France in 1944–5. In retrospect, Hitler's whole strategy was doomed from the moment that the Soviet regime failed to collapse in the summer of 1941.

This account of the early stages of the Second World War also illuminates another controversial issue, that of the role of Hitler within the Nazi government. The course of events from 1937 through 1941 shows that in foreign policy he frequently played a critical role. It is true, as Hans Mommsen in particular has suggested, that Hitler himself was lazy, that he himself principally played the role of a propagandist and that his chronic failure to define clear lines of authority helped create a situation in which various different Nazi potentates competed to achieve both ideological and personal goals.[41] Many aspects of Nazi policy – including the policy of extermination – may owe as much or more to low-level initiatives as to direction from Hitler himself. But in foreign policy in the years 1937–41 Hitler was not simply a weak mediator, but the prime mover who made the critical decisions. It was he who directed the campaign of brinkmanship against the Czechs, who decided on the alliance with the Soviets and who ordered the attacks upon Poland and France. He did so often in the teeth of opposition from his diplomats and generals; and his successes increased his authority over them. His role is more apparent in foreign policy than in any other realm of Nazi government action.

In order to resolve the continuity question, we must take a somewhat broader view of the sources of historical events and in particular of the relationship between particular individuals and long-term historical trends. On the one hand, many elements of an expansionist, imperialist policy were present within Germany well before Hitler, including a sense of the inadequacy of Germany's frontiers, a widespread (though hardly universal) belief in the need for *Lebensraum*, persistent nationalist claims to German-inhabited territory and, of course, the skill of the General

Staff. But the evidence suggests that these elements would not have led to another war of conquest had not Hitler skillfully taken advantage of the very rickety structure of European international politics in the late 1930s to overcome the obstacles to such a war.

Indeed, as Karl-Dietrich Bracher pointed out in the early 1960s, Hitler's tactics in foreign policy closely resembled his domestic political strategy before and after his seizure of power. Both relied upon dramatic measures and announcements, decisive displays of force and a knack for seizing and keeping the initiative. Both also took advantage of the structural weaknesses within contemporary domestic and international politics and of the confusion, disunity and paralysis that characterized the opposition to him.[42] Hitler, in short, succeeded largely because he knew how to take advantage of the opportunities offered by the existing situation. And to a large extent, both his domestic and foreign opportunities resulted from the cataclysm of the First World War.[43] At home, the collapse of imperial Germany, the Treaty of Versailles, the reparations question and the depression prevented the Weimar Republic from establishing itself upon a secure footing. Abroad – as A.J.P. Taylor argued in one of his more brilliant insights – the simultaneous defeat of Germany and Russia, combined with the collapse of Austria-Hungary, left behind a new territorial structure in central and eastern Europe that was likely to unravel as soon as the first few threads were pulled away.

The collapse of traditional authority and the weaknesses of the interwar settlement enabled Hitler temporarily to make himself the master of almost all of Europe, but he never succeeded in making Germany into a self-sufficient world power capable of taking on the British Empire and the United States. Instead, his attempt to do so led to the utter defeat of Germany and to the occupation of Germany and Europe by American and Soviet forces for the next 45 years. All this, in turn, has now come to an end as this work goes to press, and Germany has regained sovereignty as well as unity. With this comes an opportunity to prove that the two world wars and the experience of totalitarianism represented a discontinuity in German history which destroyed Germany's potential role as the leading nation in a peaceful Europe. History is never free of the influence of current events and views of Hitler and the origins of the Second World War will undoubtedly be affected by the consequences of German reunification and the building of a new Europe.

NOTES

1   See Gerhard L. Weinberg, *The Foreign Policy of Hitler's Germany. Starting World War II 1937–39* (Chicago, 1980), and Donald Cameron Watt, *How*

War Came. The Immediate Origins of the Second World War, 1938–39 (New York, 1989); and Norman Rich, 'Hitler's foreign policy', in Gordon Martel (ed.), *The Origins of the Second World War Reconsidered. The A.J.P. Taylor Debate after Twenty-five Years* (Boston, 1986), pp. 119–39.

2 (Düsseldorf, 1961).

3 As embodied in Gerhard Ritter, *The Sword and the Sceptre*, vols 3–4 (Coral Gables, Fl., 1972).

4 Imanuel Geiss, *Die Polnischen Grenzstreifen 1914–1918* (Lübeck, 1960).

5 Analyses of Hitler's program and its historical antecedents include Axel Kuhn, *Hitlers aussenpolitisches Programm. Entstehung und Entwicklung 1919–1939* (Stuttgart, 1970); Eberhard Jäckel, *Hitler's Weltanschauung: A Blueprint for World Power* (Middletown, Conn., 1972); Norman Rich, *Hitler's War Aims. Ideology, the Nazi State and the Course of Expansion* (New York, 1973). On colonial aims see Klaus Hildebrand, *Vom Reich zum Weltreich: Hitler, HSDAP und koloniale Frage 1919–1945* (Munich, 1969). For a succinct statement of Hitler's eventual aims in 1932 see Hermann Rauschning, *The Voice of Destruction* (New York, 1940), pp. 32–49.

6 Franz Knipping, *Deutschland, Frankreich und das Ende der Locarno-Ära 1928–1931* (Munich, 1987), covers the last phase of his process.

7 See Edward W. Bennett, *German Rearmament and the West, 1932–1933* (Princeton, 1979), pp. 11–77, and David E. Kaiser, *Economic Diplomacy and the Origins of the Second World War. Germany, Britain, France and Eastern Europe, 1930–39* (Princeton, NJ, 1980), pp. 17–56.

8 See Stephen A. Schuker, 'France and the remilitarization of the Rhineland, 1936', *French Historical Studies*, vol. 14 (1986), pp. 309–38.

9 On this crisis and its conclusion see Kaiser, *Economic Diplomacy*, pp. 151–4.

10 On Hitler's views of world trade see Adolf Hitler, *Hitlers Zweites Buch. Ein Dokument aus dem Jahr 1928*, ed. Gerhard L. Weinberg (Stuttgart, 1961), pp. 53–4, 59–60, 123–4, and *Hitler's Secret Conversations 1941–44* (New York, 1953), pp. 35–6.

11 Kaiser, *Economic Diplomacy*, pp. 155–64.

12 See Jonathan Wright and Paul Stafford, 'Hitler, Britain and the Hossbach memorandum', *Militärgeschichtliche Mitteilungen*, vol. 42 (1987), pp. 77–123. Wright and Stafford stress that Hitler by 1937 had generally abandoned hopes of an alliance with Great Britain, but had concluded, based upon British weakness during the Italo-Ethiopian War and the Spanish Civil War, that an alliance with Italy would actually be more valuable.

13 On this point see especially Albert Speer, *Inside the Third Reich* (New York, 1970), p. 281.

14 '...the status quo', writes Gerhard Weinberg, 'especially in Austria, was crumbling steadily and could quite easily dissolve without the kind of overt international crisis in which any foreign power might usefully intervene.' (Weinberg, *Starting World War II*, p. 284).

15 See Kaiser, *Economic Diplomacy*, pp. 191–6, 236–44.

16 Weizsäcker to Ribbentrop, 20 June 1938, quoted in Kaiser, *Economic Diplomacy*, p. 222.

17 This crisis is covered most thoroughly in Harold C. Deutsch, *Hitler and His Generals. The Hidden Crisis, January–June 1938* (Minneapolis, Minn., 1974).

18 See Peter Hoffmann, *The History of the German Resistance 1933–1945* (Cambridge, Mass., 1977), pp. 49–98.

19 See the comments by Tim Mason and myself, and the reply by R. J. Overy,

'Debate: Germany, 'domestic crisis' and war in 1939', *Past and Present*, no. 122 (1989), pp. 200–40.

20 Hans-Erich Volkmann, 'Die NS-Wirtschaft in Vorbereitung des Krieges', Militärgeschichtliche Forschungsamt (ed.) *Ursachen und Voraussetzungen der deutschen Kriegspolitik. Das deutsche Reich und der zweite Weltkrieg*, Vol. 1 (Stuttgart, 1979), pp. 177–370; see especially pp. 190–8, 310–70. It has been argued convincingly that the economic crisis grew partly out of the political anarchy characteristic of the Nazi regime, which in this case had allowed Hitler to approve separate, enormous expenditures for the navy, the Siegfried Line of fortifications against France, and numerous public construction projects without any governmental mechanism for assessing or resolving competing claims upon resources (see Jost Dülffer), 'Der Beginn des Krieges 1939: Hitler, die innere Krise und das Mächtesystem', *Geschichte und Gesellschaft*, vol. 2 (1976), pp. 443–57.

21 'There is no possible way in which the armaments plans of 1939 could be even approximately fulfilled within Germany's boundaries of March 1939 and under the prevailing social and constitutional order' (*Past and Present*, no. 122 (1989), p. 217).

22 Waclaw Dlugoborski and Czeslaw Madjaczyk, 'Ausbeutungssysteme in den besetzten Gebieten Polens und der UdSSR', Friedrich Forstmeier and Hans-Erich Volkmann (eds), *Kriegswirtschaft und Rüstung 1939–1945* (Düsseldorf, 1971), pp. 384–400.

23 *Documents on German Foreign Policy*, series D, vol. 7, no. 172. Another account of this talk gives a different version of this remark, however, and refers to 10–15 years, see Jeremy Noakes and Geoffrey Pridham, *Documents on Nazism, 1919–45* (New York, 1975), p. 563.

24 Volkmann, 'Die NS-Wirtschaft', pp. 190–8.

25 Weinberg, *Starting World War II*, pp. 600–11.

26 Kaiser, *Economic Diplomacy*, p. 278.

27 See R. J. Overy, 'Hitler's war and the German economy: a reinterpretation', *Economic History Review*, 2nd series, vol. 35 (1982), pp. 272–91, and Weinberg, *Starting World War II*, pp. 18–24.

28 Ian Kershaw, *Popular Opinion and Political Dissent in the Third Reich* (Oxford, 1983), pp. 281–8, discusses the impact of Polish workers upon the desperate Bavarian peasantry. See also Ulrich Herbert, *Fremdarbeiter. Politik und Praxis des 'Ausländer-Einstatzes' in der Kriegswirtschaft des dritten Reiches* (Berlin and Bonn, 1985), pp. 66–7.

29 Hans-Erich Volkmann, 'NS-Aufenhandel im "geschlossenen" Kriegswirtschaftraum (1939–1941)', Forstmeier and Volkmann, *Kriegwirtschaft und Rüstung 1939–1945*, pp. 92–101.

30 Hans-Adolf Jacobsen, *Fall Gelb. Der Kampf um den deutschen Operationsplan zur Westoffensive 1940* (Wiesbaden, 1957), pp. 143–53; Jehuda L. Wallach, *The Dogma of the Battle of Annihilation. The Theories of Clausewitz and Schlieffen and their Impact on the German Conduct of Two World Wars* (Westport, Conn., 1986), pp. 252–62.

31 Harold C. Deutsch, *The Conspiracy against Hitler in the Twilight War* (Minneapolis, Minn., 1968).

32 Remarks of 22 August 1939, Noakes and Pridham, *Documents on Nazism*, pp. 564–5.

33 See Mason, *Arbeiterklasse und Volksgemeinschaft*, and two works by Ian Kershaw, *Popular Opinion* and *The 'Hitler Myth'. Image and Reality in the Third Reich* (Oxford, 1987).

34 See Marlis G. Steinert, *Hitler's War and the Germans. Public Mood and Attitude during the Second World War* (Athens, Ohio, 1977), pp. 1–132, and Kershaw, *'Hitler Myth'*, pp. 121–60.

35 The increase was accomplished largely at the expense of domestic consumption, which dropped significantly, suggesting that T.W. Mason's belief that the war enabled the government to demand more from the civilian population was correct. See Overy, 'Hitler's war and the German economy', p. 283.

36 All these points have been covered brilliantly by Andreas Hillgruber, *Hitlers Strategie. Politik und Kriegführung 1940–41* (Frankfurt, 1965), especially pp. 352–88, 511–12, 542–3, 553, 555.

37 ibid., pp. 377–88.

38 'Once the strategy of the aggressors had failed [in early 1942],' Alan Milward writes, 'the strategies of all the major combatants became aligned, and the most important element in each was production' (Milward, *War, Economy, and Society* (Berkeley, Calif., 1977), p. 56).

39 ibid., pp. 377–88. On the Russian campaign see Alexander Dallin, *German Rule in Russia, 1941–45. A Study in Occupation Politics* (London, 1957), pp. 365–75.

40 Milward, *War, Economy, and Society*, p. 74.

41 Hans Mommsen, 'Ausnahmezustand als Herschaftstechnik des NS-regimes', Manfred Funke (ed.), *Hitler, Deutschland und die Mächte* (Düsseldorf, 1976), pp. 30–45. *et passim*.

42 This analogy has been drawn very strikingly by Karl Dietrich Bracher. See Bracher, Wolfgang Sauer and Gerhard Schulz, *Die nationalsozialistische Machtergriefung. Studien zur Errichtung des totalitären Herrschaftssystems in Deutschland 1933/34* (Cologne, 1962), pp. 232–41.

43 I have developed this point at greater length in David Kaiser, *Politics and War. European Conflict from Philip II to Hitler* (Cambridge, Mass., 1990).

10   *The 'Final Solution'*

RICHARD BREITMAN

> *I hereby charge you with making all necessary organization, functional, and material preparations for a complete solution of the Jewish question in the German sphere of influence in Europe.... I charge you furthermore with submitting to me in the near future an overall plan of the organizational, functional, and material measures to be taken in preparing for the implementation of the aspired final solution of the Jewish question.*
>
> Göring to Heydrich, 31 July 1941, Reinhard Heydrich's SS File

The literature on what is generally called the Holocaust has grown to proportions where one could not cover all the recent important developments and controversies even in a book.[1] This subject is of prime concern not only for Jews or for Germans attempting to come to terms with the past, but for western civilization generally. Nazi policies of mass murder grew out of a complete rejection of western moral standards – even of civilized behavior. Any attempt to understand and to describe this barbarism toward Jews and a number of other groups has a moral dimension that charges the discussion and broadens the audience.

The mass murders in Nazi Germany were so far removed from what we think of as normal human behavior that those who did not live through the experience may have difficulty accepting it. The commandant of Auschwitz once said: 'Our system is so terrible that no one in the world will believe it to be possible ... if someone should succeed in escaping from Auschwitz and in telling the world, the world will brand him as a fantastic liar.'[2] Books, articles, films and television have transmitted enough information about Nazi mass murders to reduce the tendency to disbelieve, but they have not dispelled it. Neo-Nazis, Nazi apologists, and anti-Semites in various countries who deny that Nazi Germany ever carried out the systematic murder of Jews have unwittingly raised scholars' consciousness in one respect. They have impelled us to collect and preserve the raw materials of history: to record the experiences of those who lived through the catastrophe while there is still time, to preserve original documents and artifacts carefully and to demonstrate their provenance, and to heighten our normal concern for carefully footnoting our findings in our writings.

Even without the Holocaust revisionists, this subject sparks controversy aplenty. 'Holocaust' is derived from an ancient Greek translation of the

Old Testament term signifying a burnt offering or sacrifice exclusively to God.[3] At best, the literal meaning may convey the sense that millions of Jews died because of their religion. At worst, the term may be taken as an indication that the victims were somehow sacrificed to God. In any case, the Nazis considered Jews a race, not a religious group. Nonbelievers and Jews who had converted to Christianity were not exempted from the transports to the death camps.

Jewish communities and spokesmen in Israel, the United States and elsewhere have seized upon the term Holocaust to summarize the fate of Jews under the Nazis, but there is also a debate over whether Nazi mass killings of civilians in other groups – Poles, Russians, gypsies, Jehovah's Witnesses, homosexuals, political prisoners and others – are part of the Holocaust.

Historians prefer to avoid moral or theological judgments and to find useful analytical concepts. In the journal *Holocaust and Genocide Studies* and elsewhere,[4] Yehuda Bauer of the Hebrew University of Jerusalem has distinguished the Jewish experience from the other victims on empirical grounds. The Nazis did try to wipe out virtually all Jews, whereas their murderous policies for other groups were more selective. In some cases, for example that of the gypsies, further research is needed to show what distinctions were made, why some were killed and others spared.

Bauer's 'holocaust' is, however, not exclusively Jewish. He uses holocaust for any case where the ruling power tries to kill off a designated enemy people entirely – men, women and children. He employs the word genocide not as a synonym for holocaust, but for attempts to wipe out the national identity and culture of a people by methods including (but not limited to) mass murder, but falling short of total annihilation. So the Nazis practised genocide against Poles and gypsies in this view, but holocaust may apply elsewhere. Bauer argues, for example, that Turkish policies toward the Armenians in 1915 resulted in a near holocaust; this was more than a case of genocide. His definition of genocide, however, runs counter to the more common meaning (and the literal meaning of the Greek and Latin roots) – killing of a people – and is unlikely to win complete acceptance.

The term holocaust was not used, of course, during the Third Reich. The phrase 'Final Solution of the Jewish question' allowed Nazi officials to avoid dirtying their lips with words like mass murder or extermination. Though it is not widely known, it seems that Hitler himself originated use of the phrase 'Final Solution of the Jewish question', the meaning of which initially was not clear.[5]

The program known as the Final Solution was an attempt to eliminate the Jewish 'race' from the Earth. It was to be accomplished largely through mass murder, though working people to death and allowing some small categories of Jews to die out peacefully were also significant parts of the process. Precisely when the Final Solution came to have this unambiguous meaning is but one of many issues still disputed. Historians who use 'Final Solution' at least implicitly emphasize the experience of the perpetrators, rather than the victims. Although Jewish historians still debate the degree of Jewish passivity and resistance in the course of the Final Solution, my focus here will be on interpretations of German policy and behavior.

Whatever the problems caused by use of a Nazi term that was designed partly to veil the reality, 'Final Solution' at least denotes a specific group defined by descent. The Nazis are not known to have spoken of the Final Solution of the Polish problem or of the gypsy problem. Those who write today about the Final Solution enjoy the grim irony of knowing that, in spite of the death of between 5 and 6 million Jews, the Final Solution was not final.

Although there were some significant findings in Gerald Reitlinger's work *The Final Solution*, Raul Hilberg originated systematic, careful and detailed study of the Final Solution with his mammoth 1961 volume, *The Destruction of the European Jews*, which appeared in expanded (three-volume) and updated form in 1985 and which remains the single most important work on the subject.[6] Although Hilberg is a political scientist, not a historian by training, the community of historians has taken to his work and his approach with great enthusiasm. Rarely has a single work defined the contours of such an important subject for so long.

Using primarily the vast array of German documents selected by Allied war crimes investigators and prosecutors for use at the Nuremberg trials, Hilberg portrayed an intricate system of cooperation among Nazi Party and SS officials, the civil service, major German corporations and the military that led to, and made it possible to implement, the Final Solution. Seeking ways to translate Nazi hostility to Jews into practice, this alliance of bureaucracies defined who was and who was not Jewish, expropriated Jewish assets, separated Jews from the non-Jewish population, deported them to suitable sites where they were either shut up in ghettos or worked to death, arranged for killing on the spot (primarily in the Soviet territories), or shipped them to newly constructed extermination camps where poison gas and crematoria provided assembly-line efficiency in mass murder. Although this pattern emerged again and again in territories under German control or influence, Hilberg denied that it resulted from an original long-range plan.[7] These operations were simply logical steps in a sequence, with the administrators seldom able to see more than one step ahead. Still, since they all shared or understood the climate of hostility toward Jews, they easily reached agreement.

Hilberg was concerned more with the overall pattern of events than with the historical sequence of events, which is reflected in the book's frequent deviations from chronology. Definition, expropriation, concentration and deportation might represent four chronological stages in a gradual sequence, but in some countries stages occurred almost simultaneously. Hilberg also showed greater interest in the unfolding of the basically similar elements in each location than with the differences in timing or substance from country to country. The entire process in Poland, for example, was virtually completed before it began to gather momentum in Denmark or Hungary.

Hilberg's emphasis on bureaucratic methods and on the complicity of a wide range of people and organizations overshadowed his references to Nazi ideology or to particular Nazi leaders such as Hitler or Himmler, without entirely eclipsing them. In this sense, the original Hilberg study provided carefully documented and detailed coverage of the scope of the Final Solution, which helps to explain why it is the only successful synthesis.

In spite of its length and excellent documentation, Hilberg's work left room for other scholars to follow him with more detailed studies of the involvement of particular organizations, offices and individuals in the early stages of Nazi persecution of the Jews or in the Final Solution. Hilberg's successors could and did draw upon plenty of captured German records not prepared for Nuremberg, newly discovered wartime documents inside and outside the two German states compiled both by perpetrators and victims and, increasingly, documents and witness testimony accumulated in the course of war crimes investigations and trials in various countries. Israel's trial of Adolf Eichmann was but the most famous of literally hundreds of proceedings that accumulated significant amounts of information about the Final Solution. Enough Nazi documents survived to make the Final Solution the best documented case of genocide in history.

These records, however, were quite unequally distributed in a number of respects. Some agencies kept excellent records and preserved them; others kept less on paper, managed to destroy records toward the end of the Third Reich, or simply lost them to the vicissitudes of war. We know, therefore, a great deal about the German Foreign Office in the Third Reich, but relatively little about the Führer Chancellery. Although most records of Auschwitz-Birkenau were destroyed, Commandant Rudolf Höss was captured and tried after the war, and he wrote relatively honest memoirs before he was executed in Poland. In contrast, Christian Wirth, a key figure in the development of poison gas facilities for the so-called euthanasia program, inspector for Belzec, Sobibor, and Treblinka and also commandant of Belzec, died before the end of the war and remains a blurry figure.

Another inequality in the surviving records is vertical. Generally speaking, record-keeping on policies related to Jews (and certain other especially sensitive matters) was far better at the middle and lower levels of bureaucracies than at the top. High officials can choose to omit sensitive episodes or not record decisions at all – particularly if they sense that written evidence may come back to haunt them. Of course, where records are kept more or less automatically and accurately, they can still be destroyed after the fact. Nixon's White House tapes had a now famous eighteen-minute gap. Hilberg followed the main line of the surviving Nazi documents, partly because he was eager to demonstrate the scope of bureaucratic involvement in the Final Solution. But the weight of records did not necessarily correspond to the weight of influence in Nazi Germany or degree of control over the Final Solution.

Hitler epitomized this problem, for he was notorious for avoiding paperwork. The traditional view, which dated back to the 1930s, was that Hitler dominated the Third Reich. Since Hitler's virulent anti-Semitism was well known, it was only logical to conclude that Hitler was responsible for the Final Solution. This deduction did not really depend upon documentation of Hitler's precise role during the course of the Final Solution, since there were at least some generally relevant records. In public speeches and private gatherings with his cronies, Hitler had fulminated against Jews and threatened to destroy them. It seemed to matter little that historians had found no order signed by Hitler for the annihilation of the Jewish race or that he apparently had never visited an extermination camp.

Reitlinger believed that Hitler had planned the destruction of the Jewish race well before he gave the order during the summer of 1941, and Hilberg retained a mid-1941 order from Hitler, even if the thrust of his argument was directed elsewhere.[8] The first major scholarly study of Hitler's early political ideology supported the notion that Hitler arrived at an early decision to physically eliminate the Jews. Although Eberhard Jäckel's *Hitler's Weltanschauung* did not examine the anti-Semitic policies of the Third Reich, it presented a clear and convincing portrait of a virulent anti-Semite whose views of history and German foreign policy objectives in the 1920s were connected with his desire to destroy what he saw as an international Jewish conspiracy. There were also early foreshadowings of future events. In *Mein Kampf*, for example, Hitler had claimed that the killing of 12,000 to 15,000 Jews in Germany during the First World War by means of poison gas (!) might have saved the lives of hundreds of thousands of German soldiers.[9]

A number of years later, and in partial agreement with Jäckel, Lucy S. Dawidowicz sketched a pattern that differed from Hilberg's. In her *The War Against the Jews* there were direct links between nineteenth-century German anti-Semites and Hitler, and between the Hitler of the 1920s and the chancellor who told the German Reichstag on 30 January 1939 that, if world Jewry forced Germany into another world war, the result would be the destruction of the Jewish race. In Dawidowicz's view, it was hard to view escalating Nazi persecution of German Jews after 1933 and the Final Solution as anything but the gradual implementation of his preconceived notions. Hitler did not react to outside events so much as try to impose his will upon reality. Hitler intended to bring about the Final Solution.[10]

In 1970 Karl Schleunes of the University of North Carolina, Greensboro, argued that the road to Auschwitz was not straight, but twisted. During the years 1933–9, Schleunes demonstrated, the Nazi regime had employed a number of different methods to persecute Jews, at times permitting private or party violence against Jews, but more often restraining it, while introducing one piece of legislation after another against Jews. Schleunes pointed out that there were a number of party and government agencies which took initiatives to 'resolve' the Jewish question, but, in contrast with Hilberg, he emphasized the clashes and contradictions among them. For whatever reasons, Hitler sometimes reined in the radical anti-Semites who wanted to escalate persecution. Meanwhile, the regime encouraged, even forced, Jewish emigration from Germany during the entire period. These zig-zag policies reflected Nazi hostility toward Jews and even a desire to be 'rid' of Jews, but they did not lead inevitably to the conclusion that Hitler had a preconceived plan to wipe out all the Jews of Europe. In fact, they suggested that if he did have a Final Solution in mind, no one else knew about it. Schleunes, however, ended his study in early 1939, suggesting that Hitler turned Jewish matters over to the SS at that point.[11]

Other historians who expressly rejected the 'great-man approach' to history and emphasized the influence of structural conditions then took a longer journey on Schleunes's 'twisted road' to Auschwitz. West German scholars such as Uwe Dietrich Adam, Martin Broszat and Hans Mommsen extended into the Second World War the pattern of stops and starts, trial and error, bureaucratic competition as well as cooperation to resolve the fate of the Jews.[12] In spite of differences of opinion among them, each of the scholars in this school, unfortunately given the awkward label of 'functionalist', concluded from the sequence of events that the Nazi regime had no preordained plan for the mass murder of the Jews. The Nazis were determined to rid Germany of Jews, but thought initially of allowing them – or forcing them – to emigrate. After emigration became impossible for all but a limited number of Jews, the Nazis supposedly turned to the idea of a Jewish 'reservation in Poland'. In 1940 there was a Nazi plan to ship millions of Jews to Madagascar, which, however, the continuation of the war against Britain precluded. After the German invasion of the Soviet Union, some saw a further possibility of expelling Jews farther to the east. Meanwhile, wartime shortages of food and housing intensified the pressures to get rid of the Jews. Then the unexpected continuation of the war in the east precluded the idea of deporting Jews deep into the USSR.[13] In short, according to this school, the Final Solution was improvised after other Nazi efforts to resolve the Jewish question failed. It was a last resort – the only option remaining consistent with the Nazi belief that Jews represented a mortal danger to the Third Reich.

In another recent hybrid interpretation, Princeton University historian Arno Mayer accepted the notion that the initial methods to resolve the 'Jewish problem' were emigration and resettlement. Mayer claimed that in December 1941 Hitler and his military commanders turned toward mass murder of the Jews out of frustration over the failure of the blitzkrieg against the Soviet Union, and out of a desire for revenge against the most accessible component of a perceived Judeo-Bolshevist partnership. Genocide became, in this view, an unplanned byproduct of the deteriorating war in the east.[14]

In contrast with functionalist studies, Mayer avoided detailed study of conflicts among party, government, and military officials. He apparently did no archival research, and there are no footnotes throughout the book – even for direct quotations. There are also serious problems with his argument itself. In the first place, there is no reliable contemporary evidence explicitly drawing this link between the military situation and the Final Solution; even if we accept Mayer's selection of relevant events, his argument is *post hoc, propter hoc*. Second, respected military historians do not see Hitler perceiving a turning point in December 1941,[15] and, third, we are given no reason why Hitler, who believed in the inferiority of the Slavs, should have been so pessimistic about the military situation so early. At another point Mayer related that even in early 1945, 'Hitler continued to underestimate the Red Army, as he always had. He dismissed reports about its capability to launch yet another winter drive.'[16] Why then would Hitler have been 'despondent' in December 1941?

Mayer's work nonetheless reflects a more general tendency by the functionalists to adopt a 'late' date for the formulation of the Final Solution. If the Final Solution was improvised during the midst of the war, there is reason for scholars studying it to stress the conditions and atmosphere engendered by the war itself, the role of bureaucrats, the reasons for the failure of other attempted 'solutions of the Jewish question', and the killing initiatives in the field as essential causes of genocide. The earlier the existence of high-level plans for mass murder, or actions that could only stem from such plans, on the other hand, the greater the importance of Nazi ideology as a fundamental cause and the less the importance of mid-war imperatives and of improvization from below. Determining the chronology of planning helps to identify the basic causes and primary agents of the Final Solution.

Along with changes in the critical date of decision, there were functionalist reassessments of Hitler's role. Broszat believed that Hitler shaped the climate and context of decision making, but did not personally plan genocide and did not approve it until the end of 1941 or early 1942, after the killing was well underway.[17] Mommsen revised the received picture of Hitler even more radically. His Hitler could not cope with the measures implied by his own anti-Semitic rhetoric; he was a charismatic figurehead – Mommsen regarded him as a weak dictator – who left the hard decisions for others. Mommsen pointed out the absence of evidence that anyone in Hitler's headquarters even discussed the extermination of the Jews – and took this to mean that it was not discussed. The most important force behind the escalating persecution of the Jews, Mommsen stated, was Heinrich Himmler, whose ambition made him determined to outbid the other officials seeking a role in Jewish policy and whose organization gave him the means to carry out mass murder.[18] The non-academic writer David Irving took the depreciation of Hitler's involvement in the Final Solution beyond its logical extreme, claiming that Hitler had no knowledge of the Final Solution until 1943.[19]

Alarmed at both the tendency to read the Final Solution as an improvisation and the depreciation of Hitler, the 'intentionalists' counterattacked. A British scholar, Gerald Fleming, wrote a short, provocative study entitled *Hitler and the Final Solution*, designed to rebut Irving's foolish argument. Fleming gave no quarter to the improvisers, arguing that Hitler's mind became set on mass murder of the Jews from the early 1920s. From 1933 on, Fleming implied, the Führer was simply waiting for the proper moment to strike.[20] It is doubtful whether any human being is as rigid as Fleming's Hitler. In any case, Fleming's interpretation can neither be proved nor disproved; it will never convince those who do not share his view of Hitler.

In spite of these weaknesses, Fleming's book made progress in two areas. First, he demonstrated that Hitler frequently kept his cards close to his vest and even boasted of his refusal to confide in others, of his willingness to lie to them and surprise them later.[21] Fleming constructed a psychological profile of the man, partly based on new and independent evidence, and then used it to explain Hitler's *modus operandi* for the Final Solution. Other Nazi officials pursued different policies for years simply because Hitler kept them in the dark. There was no signed Hitler order for the mass extermination of the Jews because this kind of man would never have written one. He instead expressed his 'wish' to Himmler, who set in motion the machinery of death, according to Fleming. Hitler kept himself insulated from the worst crimes, as a skillful, deceptive politician would.

In a short cogent article, Stuttgart University historian Eberhard Jäckel pointed out that only Hitler had advocated systematic murder by the state as a means of resolving the 'Jewish problem', that those who testified at Nuremberg and elsewhere uniformly cited Hitler as giving authorization for the Final Solution, and that the structure of the Third Reich precluded subordinate agencies or officials from taking such an initiative. Jäckel suggested that there was not a single decision by Hitler on one key date, but a series of related decisions over a considerable period of time.[22]

Hermann Graml of the Institute for Contemporary History in Munich traced a number of indications from the autumn of 1938 onwards that Hitler and certain other Nazi officials already had the extermination of Jews in mind. Graml also questioned the functionalist assumption that in the spring of 1941 the Nazi elite could have simultaneously planned both the invasion of the Soviet Union, which was to be accompanied by massive killings of Jews, communists and other perceived enemies, and an actual resettlement of European Jewry into the far reaches of the USSR. It was far more likely that any references to 'resettlement' were simply euphemisms for mass extermination.[23]

Although identifying himself with the functionalists and focusing on bureaucratic conflict and initiatives, Christopher Browning, professor at Pacific Lutheran University, defined a middle ground. His careful reconstructions of events and initiatives at the middle and lower level of government and party agencies, based on an impressive array of primary sources, added substantially to Hilberg's contribution. At higher levels, Browning retained the notion that Hitler had no original plan for genocide; there was, rather, a Nazi policy of resettling Jews, which led to bureaucratic trial and error, and eventually to the Final Solution. Nor did he think the Jewish question was high on Hitler's and Himmler's agendas early in the war.[24] Yet he dissented from others' efforts to devalue Hitler's influence and, in conjunction with Hilberg's view, he still saw the key decision for extermination coming out of the Führer's headquarters in the late summer of 1941, during the euphoria of expected victory over the Soviet Union.

Despite the merits of Browning's compromise, he may have a problem of consistency. If Hitler was indeed powerful and violently anti-Semitic (and I think he was both), then one has to ask why the Jewish question did not rank high in Hitler's priorities at the outset of the war and why Hitler's subordinates did not then seek to gain the Führer's favor by escalating persecution of Jews into wholesale mass murder.

Since Hitler, Himmler and other leading Nazis believed in the dominating power of international Jewry not only in the Soviet Union but also in the west, the most likely explanation for delaying mass murders of Jews is that Hitler was concerned about potential foreign policy and military repercussions. Indeed, Heydrich hinted at this fact during the autumn 1939 campaign against Poland.[25] If the Final Solution was conceived early but implemented later, then one cannot use the timing of implementation to gauge the timing of the original conception.

It is clear in retrospect that both intentionalists and functionalists have exhibited characteristic flaws. Some of those who believe that Hitler planned and ordered the Final Solution found it sufficient to analyze his political ideology in the 1920s and to quote his later speeches in which he prophesied the destruction of the Jews; then they shift to the Nazi preparations for mass murder. They overlooked the significance of Nazi pro-emigration policies during the 1930s and dismissed out of hand Hitler's occasional comments about relocating Jews in Madagascar or in the Soviet Union. They also assumed that everyone would accept their selection of Hitler's rhetoric as evidence – not only of consistent and serious intent, but also of Hitler's direct role in events. But the functionalists either discounted Hitler's rhetoric or chose to believe his occasional comments about resettling Jews. In any case, the intentionalists did not provide enough connecting links between Hitler's views and the preparations for, or decisions on, the Final Solution. They also did not allow for the possibility that Hitler had decided early to kill Jews, but that the scope and geographical limits of killing remained open for quite some time.

Discounting Hitler's rhetoric and in some cases his influence as well, some functionalists burrowed in archives that contained records of mid-level officials, field operations and ghettos. They uncovered evidence that Nazi officials at these levels had no inkling of an early master plan for the Jews: bureaucrats, party and SS authorities and the police fought among themselves regarding the best way to handle the Jews. They found that some officials proposed mass murder and that others opposed it. These discoveries demonstrated that mid-level or lower-level bureaucrats could often influence the course of events and the fate of many thousands of Jews for a considerable length of time. Not content with the importance of this finding, the improvisers argued either that there was no Nazi master plan, or that it was approved quite late, after the critical initiatives had come from below.

Even where documents are basically accurate, they may reflect only a limited portion of the decision making. The functionalists overlooked the possibility that Hitler and Himmler may have concealed their intentions for the Jews, withholding them from subordinates in the ministries and in the field, until the opportune moment, and avoided direct documentation of their own plans and decisions. It is, after all, possible to have planning from above and improvization from below simultaneously. Lack of communication inside government and political parties is not uncommon, all the more so in the Third Reich. So it is not really possible to determine Hitler's policies or role by drawing inferences from the policies or the records of ghetto administrators.

In short, surviving documents may not reflect the full reality and Nazi documents are no different in this regard. If anything, we must suspect that the records of the decisions to proceed with the Final Solution are less complete than records of non-criminal policies. Other cases of genocide in history have not left much evidence of advance plans. If the Final Solution was planned in advance, then Hitler's secretive nature and Himmler's tactics of deception have misled a prominent school of historians.

In spite of the often emotional debate, a number of intentionalists and functionalists agree that there is a need to focus more closely on Himmler's SS empire to gain further information regarding these gaps and problems. The intentionalist–functionalist controversy has uncovered substantial gaps in our knowledge of the Final Solution, which is itself a positive contribution. It may be difficult to get answers to certain questions because of incomplete or imperfect records, but we can try harder.

In a way, this controversy is a model for the field of history. It is not only concerned with uncovering and interpreting evidence, but in setting particular events in order and understanding the logic or illogic of that order. A political scientist or a sociologist might concentrate more on the overall patterns of genocide during the entire war; a lawyer or a philosopher might look at the crimes committed and the legal or moral implications. But for them, it might well not matter whether the Nazis planned and carried out killings in 1940 or 1943. No one would be as sensitive as the historian to the implications of the chronology itself.

Another less productive dispute, which the West Germans called the historians' controversy (*Historikerstreit*), exploded onto the pages of the West German press in the 1980s. This battle erupted after a number of prominent West German scholars and writers complained of too much weight being placed on the Nazi era, as compared with prior German history and with postwar West German success. If the Nazi era became a standard for absolute evil overshadowing all else, how would it be possible for Germans to recognize political, social and economic continuities without simultaneously poisoning all German history? And if all German traditions and achievements were tainted, how could West German citizens develop a healthy sense of national consciousness and political allegiance?[26]

The most outspoken advocates of a new approach, the West Berlin historian-philosopher Ernst Nolte and Joachim Fest, biographer of Hitler and publisher of the *Frankfurter Allgemeine Zeitung*, specifically questioned whether the Nazi effort at genocide was unique in the context of the twentieth century. In this view, the Turkish massacre of Armenians during First World War, the bloodshed of the Russian civil war, the Bolshevik rhetoric about extermination of the bourgeoisie and the

Stalinist purges and violence against the peasantry and suspected political opponents helped to pave the way for the Holocaust – and were more original. The Khmer Rouge massacres in Cambodia were also cited as evidence that genocide did not end with the Second World War. In the context of this debate, these comparisons were meant to demonstrate that other nations had committed horrible crimes without losing faith in their entire history, without being forced to surrender their national consciousness. Nolte and Fest raised further controversy by speculating that reports of communist mass killings in the Soviet Union might have provoked Hitler to act against what he saw as a Jewish-communist conspiracy: the Final Solution might have been, at least in Hitler's mind, they suggested, an act of preventive warfare.[27] This hypothesis is also, quite obviously, an attempt to shift some moral opprobrium from Nazi Germany to the Soviet Union.

Opponents, such as the German philosopher-sociologist Jürgen Habermas, denounced such genocide analogies as an effort to diminish the magnitude of German crimes (and as an attempt to clear the way for a more assertive and nationalistic German role in world affairs). Other scholars strongly asserted the originality and uniqueness of the Holocaust. In the words of Eberhard Jäckel: never before had a state with the authority of its responsible leader decided and announced that a specific human group, including its aged, its women, its children and infants, would be killed as quickly as possible, and then carried through this resolution using every possible means of state power.[28]

It is possible to draw comparisons between the Holocaust and other instances of genocide, but in many ways the Final Solution remains *sui generis*. The question of Nazi motivation for the Final Solution, however, requires a more careful, scholarly analysis than is possible in the pages of the popular press. With such an important and sensitive subject, it is dangerous to toss out 'possible' Nazi motives unsupported by detailed research. It is also contradictory to defend an argument containing a political agenda by rejecting criticism as politically motivated.

Like Schleunes's twisted road to Auschwitz, historical scholarship often follows a zig-zag pattern of provocative hypothesis and criticism, detailed studies and contradictory studies, cacophony rather than harmony. Eventually, someone may provide a synthesis that does justice to all the evidence and satisfies many, if not all, of the combatants or their successors. In the meantime, however, all the disagreements can be confusing or even alarming to an outsider who looks to the experts for 'the truth'.

In this case, perhaps more than most, there is good reason for concern. The Holocaust was probably the worst chapter in the history of the modern world, possibly the worst in all human history. It is hard to see how, some 45 years after the end of the Second World War, we can have absorbed all the lessons of the past if we still are not confident of the answers to basic questions such as how, when and why the Final Solution came about, or who was primarily responsible.

NOTES

1 See nonetheless the cogent discussion in Michael R. Marrus, *The Holocaust in History* (Hanover, NH, 1987). Marrus has now also compiled nine volumes of recent articles on the Holocaust: *The Nazi Holocaust: Historical Articles on the Destruction of European Jews*, ed. Michael R. Marrus (Westport, Conn., 1989). Readers in search of further articles and synthesis of this literature may wish to consult: Konrad Kwiet, 'Judenverfolgung und Judenvernichtung im Dritten Reich: ein historiographischer Überblick', in Dan Diner (ed.), *Ist der Nationalsozialismus Geschichte?* (Frankfurt, 1988), pp. 237–64; Otto Dov Kulka, 'Major trends and tendencies of German historiography on national socialism and the "Jewish question" (1924–1984)', *Yearbook of the Leo Baeck Institute*, vol. 21 (1985), pp. 215–42; and Ian Kershaw, *The Nazi Dictatorship: Problems and Perspectives of Interpretation* (London, 1985), pp. 61–105.

2 Affidavit of Isaak Egon Ochshorn, 14 September 1945, United States National Archives (hereafter NA), Record Group (hereafter RG) 238, NO-1934.

3 Marrus, *Holocaust in History*, p. 3.

4 Yehuda Bauer, *The Holocaust in Historical Perspective* (London, 1978); *A History of the Holocaust* (New York, 1982).

5 Interrogation of Hermann von Stutterheim, 11 March 1947, NA RG 238, microfilm series M-1019/roll 72/frame 774.

6 Gerald Reitlinger, *The Final Solution: The Attempt to Exterminate the Jews of Europe* (London, 1953). Raul Hilberg, *The Destruction of the European Jews* (Chicago, 1961); revised, expanded edition in 3 volumes (New York, 1985).

7 Hilberg, *Destruction* (original edition), p. 31.

8 Reitlinger, *Final Solution*, esp. pp. 80–4. Hilberg, *Destruction*, expanded edition, pp. 402 and 402 n. 30.

9 Eberhard Jäckel, *Hitler's Weltanschauung. A Blueprint for Power*, tr. Herbert Arnold (Middletown, Conn., 1972), gassing reference on p. 60.

10 Lucy S. Dawidowicz, *The War Against the Jews 1933–1945* (New York, 1975), esp. pp. 201–23.

11 Karl A. Schleunes, *The Twisted Road to Auschwitz: Nazi Policy Toward German Jews 1933–1939* (Urbana, Ill., 1970). See also his 'Retracing the twisted road: Nazi policies toward German Jews 1933–1939', in François Furet (ed.), *Unanswered Questions: Nazi Germany and the Genocide of the Jews* (New York, 1989), pp. 54–70.

12 The most important functionalist book is still Uwe Dietrich Adam, *Judenpolitik im Dritten Reich* (Düsseldorf, 1972). See also his 'An overall plan for anti-Jewish legislation in the Third Reich?', *Yad Vashem Studies* 11 (1976), pp. 33–55; and 'Nazi actions concerning the Jews between the beginning of World War II and the German attack on the USSR', in Furet, *Unanswered Questions*, pp. 84–95. Mommsen has contributed quite a number of related articles of which the best known is 'The realization of the unthinkable: "The Final Solution of the Jewish question" in the Third Reich', tr. and repr. in Gerhard Hirschfeld (ed.), *The Politics of Genocide: Jews and*

Soviet Prisoners of War in Nazi Germany (London, 1986), pp. 93–144. Martin Broszat's best known and most detailed article is 'Hitler und die Genesis der 'Endlösung': Aus Anlass der Thesen von David Irving', *Vierteljahrshefte für Zeitgeschichte*, vol. 25 (1977), pp. 737–75.

13   Adam, *Judenpolitik*, pp. 310–16; Broszat, 'Hitler und die Genesis', p. 759.

14   Arno Mayer, *Why Did the Heavens not Darken?: The 'Final Solution' in History* (New York, 1988), esp. pp. 279, 289, 299.

15   Earl F. Ziemke and Magna E. Bauer, *Moscow to Stalingrad: Decision in the East* (Washington, DC, 1987), p. 119, for example, mention that on 1 January 1942 Hitler wrote to the army commanders that if they held firm against the Russian counteroffensive that was using the last Soviet resources, this would assure the final victory in the summer of 1942.

16   Mayer, *Why Did the Heavens not Darken?*, pp. 240–1, 267–8, 298, 416.

17   Broszat, 'Hitler und die Genesis', pp. 756–8.

18   Mommsen, 'The realization', esp. pp. 110–14.

19   David Irving, *Hitler's War* (New York, 1977), esp. pp. xiv, 392, 504.

20   Gerald Fleming, *Hitler and the Final Solution* (Berkeley, Calif., 1984).

21   Fleming, *Hitler and the Final Solution*, p. 18.

22   Eberhard Jäckel, 'Hitler orders the Holocaust', in Jäckel, *Hitler in History* (Hanover, NH, 1984), pp. 44–65.

23   Hermann Graml, 'Zur Genesis der "Endlösung"', in Walter H. Pehle (ed.), *Der Judenpogrom 1938: Von der 'Reichskristallnacht' zum Völkermord* (Frankfurt, 1988), pp. 160–75.

24   Christopher R. Browning, *The Final Solution and the German Foreign Office* (New York, 1978); his *Fateful Months: Essays on the Emergence of the Final Solution* (New York, 1985), esp. pp. 8–38; his 'Zur Genesis der "Endlösung": Eine Antwort an Martin Broszat', *Vierteljahrshefte für Zeitgeschichte*, vol. 29 (1981), esp. pp. 98, 103–9; and his 'Nazi resettlement policy and the search for a solution to the Jewish question', *German Studies Review*, vol. 9 (1986), pp. 516–19.

25   Heydrich reported on 14 September that Himmler was presenting all suggestions on the Jewish question directly to the Führer, for only Hitler could make decisions with potentially far-reaching foreign-policy repercussions (Amtschefbesprechung, 14 September 1939, NA RG 242, T-175/R 279/2728514).

26   This argument is particularly associated with Michael Stürmer. See his 'Geschichte im geschichtlosem Land', in *'Historikerstreit': Die Dokumentation der Kontroverse um die Einzigartigkeit der nationalsozialistischen Judenvernichtung* (Munich, 1987), pp. 36–9.

27   Here especially Ernst Nolte, 'Die Sache auf dem Kopf gestellt', in *Historikerstreit*, pp. 223–31, and *Der europäische Bürgerkrieg. Nationalsozialismus und Bolschewismus* (Frankfurt, 1987). For a more thorough review of the literature and a more detailed analysis, see Charles S. Maier, *The Unmasterable Past: History, Holocaust, and German National Identity* (Cambridge, Mass., 1988), esp. pp. 66–99, and Richard J. Evans, *In Hitler's Shadow: West German Historians and the Attempt to Escape from the Nazi Past* (New York, 1989).

28   Jürgen Habermas, 'Eine Art Schadensabwicklung', and 'Leserbrief an die Frankfurter Allgemeine Zeitung', in *Historikerstreit*, pp. 62–76, 95–7. Quote from Eberhard Jäckel, 12 September 1986 article, originally in *Die Zeit*, reprinted in *Historikerstreit*, pp. 115–22; quoted in Maier, *Unmasterable Past*.

11 *The Economic Dimension in German History*

FRANK B. TIPTON

Eine Industrie läßt sich nicht von heute auf morgen schaffen.
Ernst Engel.[1]

INTRODUCTION

As both an economic and a political great power Germany has been at the center of the forces shaping the modern world, though in an oddly contradictory way. Economically, despite the wrenching interruptions of depression and war, Germany stands out as an obvious success when measured against any of the economist's standard yardsticks. Equally obviously, in the political realm Germany became the home of the most gruesome failure in world history. The nature of the connection between economic success and political failure has compelled the attention of many historians. However, none of those who attempt to link the development of German capitalism to the rise of Nazism has won general acceptance for their arguments, regardless of whether they believe that Germany was excessively capitalistic, or that Germany was not capitalist enough. Consideration of more limited questions has not fared much better. Numbers of scholars have argued that specific changes in Germany's political constitution exercised decisive influence on the economy, for instance with the foundation of the Bismarckian empire in 1871, the Nazi seizure of power in 1933 and the 'Nazi economic recovery', or the 'zero hour' of 1945 and the 'Wirtschaftswunder' in the West German Federal Republic. On the other hand, on other occasions economic development is held to have led to a political transformation. The Great Depression of 1873–95, the inflation of 1923 and the economic collapse of 1929 have all been cited in this way. However, unification, the Nazi economic recovery and 'zero hour' all tend to fade away when subjected to closer analysis, and the asserted impact of economic crises on political life also appear less certain when examined in detail.

The inconclusive nature of the debates over the relation between economics and politics has resulted in part from an implicit desire to

211

identify decisive turning points in economic development which correspond to dramatic political changes. Modern economies grow, change and fluctuate, but they do not experience the sort of sudden qualitative change implied in many historians' accounts. Failure to appreciate this has led to much of the confusion in the interpretation of the economic dimension in German history. The interaction of economic and political development cannot be analyzed without an examination of the long-term development of the economy to provide a framework for analysis. In particular historians need to distinguish between fundamental factors at play over relatively long periods of time, and cyclical factors of a more short-term nature. Such an approach allows us to see more clearly what linkages may connect political and economic developments. In addition, the comparative dimension embedded in such a general framework allows us to see whether specific economic factors were unique to Germany and therefore whether they can in fact have had unique repercussions in German history.

On balance, it seems that over the course of the past century and a half of modern economic development in Germany, the underlying thrust of economic development has resulted from factors over which politicians had little or no control. However, cyclical change, both in its timing and severity, has been more closely linked to political decisions. Moreover, the association has been a two-way relationship. Policies adopted by governments have affected cyclical fluctuations and, conversely, cyclical up- and downswings have influenced both large and small political changes. The relationship has not been a constant, for both political and economic structures have undergone profound changes; and it is the nature of those changes which makes up the substance of historical debate.

LONG-TERM TRENDS IN GERMAN DEVELOPMENT

The fundamental factors responsible for economic development are the growth of population, the development of the labor force, the supply of capital and especially changes in the available technology. Germany shares the major identifying characteristics of economic growth in the modern industrial period. Germany's long-term trends in total national product, industrial output, capital investment and labor force distribution match those of all the other advanced industrial economies, a group which remains limited in membership.[2] In the favored nations, high rates of growth in population, total income and income per capita have been accompanied by a decline in the share of agriculture in the economy, an initial rise in manufacturing industry and a later increase in the share of services. As population has shifted from rural districts to the cities, more women have sought employment outside the home, family firms in all sectors have declined in favor of more impersonal organizations and the birth rate has declined. In the background, technology has transformed modes of production and distribution beyond recognition.

How did these developments affect Germany? Volker Berghahn speaks for a large number of historians when he links modern economic growth to 'the extraordinarily violent course of Germany's development . . . . There would appear to be little doubt that this record of violence was connected with the experience of very rapid industrialisation.'[3] However, although the rates of growth and transformation which have characterized German economic and social development have indeed been high, they have not been exceptional among industrializing nations. In the mid-nineteenth century Germany was already far from being a poor or backward region. German per capita income in 1860 was slightly higher than that of France, but slightly lower than Italian income. All three were about half of British, but all were some two and a half times higher than Russian per capita income.[4] Over the next century, population, income and the shift away from agriculture and toward industry and the city all moved at rates which place Germany in the middle of the elite group of wealthy industrializing nations.[5] If Germany's social and political problems have economic foundations, they cannot lie simply in relatively high rates of growth.

As shown in Table 11.1, the German population nearly doubled from 35.3 million to 64.6 million between 1850 and 1910, but the rates of increase slowed in the twentieth century and the populations of both West and East Germany were declining in the 1980s. Germany lay in the middle of the 'demographic transition' which moved across Europe from northwest to southeast during the nineteenth and twentieth centuries. European birth rates and death rates fell, but following the Second World War birth rates continued to drop, to the point where in the 1980s the population of western Europe was not reproducing itself. In Germany the fall in the aggregate birth rate set in the 1880s and accelerated shortly after 1900. Over the next generation, the tendency to have fewer and fewer children, which began among affluent urban professional families, gradually spread to industrial workers, smaller towns and eventually to the agricultural countryside.[6]

Combined with increasing population have been even higher rates of growth of total income and corresponding increases in income per capita. German rates have been high but not exceptional. Walther Hoffmann's estimates show German national product in 1913 prices to have been 9.4 billion marks in 1850 and 48.5 billion marks in 1913, and the national product of West Germany alone to have been 71.0 billion

Table 11.1 Population in Germany.

	Total (thousands)	Birth rate (per 1000)	Death rate (per 1000)
Boundaries of 1913:			
1850	35,312	37.2	25.6
1860	37,611	36.4	23.2
1870	40,805	38.5	27.4
1880	45,095	37.6	26.0
1890	49,241	35.7	24.4
1900	56,046	35.6	22.1
1910	64,568	29.8	16.2
Boundaries of 1935:			
1922	61,900	23.0	14.4
1930	65,084	17.6	11.4
1938	68,558	19.7	11.7
West Germany:			
1950	49,989	16.2	10.5
1960	55,433	17.4	11.6
1970	60,651	13.4	12.1
1980	61,359	10.1	11.6
1987	61,170	10.5	11.2
East Germany:			
1950	18,388	16.5	11.9
1960	17,188	17.0	13.6
1970	17,068	13.9	14.1
1980	16,740	14.6	14.2
1987	16,661	13.3	12.9

Sources: Walther G. Hoffman, *Das Wachstum der deutschen Wirtschaft seit der Mitte des 19. Jahrhunderts* (Berlin, 1965), pp. 172–4; West Germany, Statistisches Bundesamt, *Statistisches Jahrbuch 1988 für die Bundesrepublik Deutschland* (Stuttgart, 1988), pp. 52, 70; East Germany, Staatliche Zentralverwaltung für Statistik, *Statistisches Jahrbuch der deutschen demokratischen Republik 1988* (Berlin, 1988), p. 356.

marks in 1959.[7] However, in the century from 1860 to 1960, substantially higher rates of growth of total and per capita product were recorded by Europe's overseas competitors, the United States, Canada, Australia and especially Japan. In Europe, Denmark, Norway and Sweden all grew more rapidly than Germany. These are small countries, but Russian total and per capita product also grew at rates well above the German figures and, on a per capita basis, both France and Italy matched or exceeded the German performance.[8]

A steady shift in the distribution of employment accompanied the growth of population and product. As shown in Table 11.2, agriculture employed well over half of the German labor force in the middle of the

Table 11.2 Labor force in Germany.

Labor force (thousands): Total		Agriculture	Industry	Services
Boundaries of 1913:				
1852	15,028	8,293	3,491	3,244
1875	18,643	9,230	5,439	3,974
1895	23,405	9,788	7,956	5,661
1911	30,034	10,627	11,377	8,030
Boundaries of 1935:				
1927	31,963	9,590	13,033	9,340
1936	35,352	9,020	16,227	10,105
West Germany:				
1950	20,459	4,973	8,613	6,873
1959	25,189	3,798	11,934	9,457
1971	26,817	2,134	12,988	11,695
1980	26,328	1,437	11,622	13,269
1987	25,971	1,327	10,523	14,121
East Germany:				
1960	7,686	1,304	3,238	3,144
1970	7,769	997	3,393	3,379
1980	8,225	879	3,711	3,635
1987	8,571	929	4,059	3,583

Labor force (% distribution): Female		Agriculture	Industry	Services
Boundaries of 1913:				
1852		55.2	23.2	21.6
1875	35.9 (1882)	49.5	29.2	21.3
1895	34.9	41.8	34.0	24.2
1911	34.9 (1907)	35.4	37.9	26.7
Boundaries of 1935:				
1927	37.4 (1925)	30.0	36.9	29.2
1936	37.7 (1939)	25.0	45.9	28.6
West Germany:				
1950	35.2	24.3	42.1	33.6
1959	37.2 (1958)	15.1	47.4	37.5
1971		8.0	48.4	43.6
1980		5.5	44.1	50.4
1987	38.5 (1986)	5.1	40.5	54.4
East Germany:				
1960	45.0	17.0	42.1	40.9
1970	48.3	12.8	43.7	43.5
1980	49.9	10.7	45.1	44.2
1987	49.0	10.8	47.4	41.8

Sources: Hoffmann, *Wachstum*, pp. 204–6; West Germany, *Jahrbuch 1988*, pp. 100–1; East Germany, *Jahrbuch 1988*, pp. 112, 117.

nineteenth century. Census results understated the total before 1907, but the numbers of agricultural workers may have been increasing until the turn of the century. They certainly began to drop after 1910, however, and by 1936 agriculture employed only a quarter of all German workers. The decline continued in both East and West Germany after the Second World War, and in the 1980s agriculture employed less than a tenth of the labor force. The obverse of the decline in agriculture was the increase in the share of industrial employment in the total and a general movement of workers into larger establishments. The numbers of self-employed persons declined, from 5.6 million in 1882 to 3.5 million in West Germany in 1959. Establishments with over 1,000 workers employed fewer than 2 per cent of all industrial workers in 1875, but 13.5 per cent in 1950.[9] However, following the Second World War the largest increase in employment came not in industry but in services. Services in turn were transformed by the decline in the category of mainly female household servants, from 1.6 million or 6 per cent of the entire labor force (equal to the numbers of workers in construction and twice those in mining, for instance) in 1907, to 580,000 or 2 per cent of the total in West Germany in 1959.[10]

Once again, the pattern and the timing place Germany in the middle of the development when viewed internationally. Neither did German agriculture decline especially rapidly, nor did the share of industry and later services rise at rates much above those common to other European nations. In Britain and the Low Countries the decline of agriculture began some decades before that in Germany, while in northern, southern and eastern Europe the decline began some decades afterwards.[11] Germany also resembled other developing nations in the response of government to changing labor-force distribution. The imperial, Weimar, Nazi and West German governments all attempted to protect and preserve their farmers with tariffs and subsidies and all failed to arrest the decline of the agricultural sector. In addition, attempts to restructure the sector achieved only the most limited success. Programs of peasant settlement under the imperial, Weimar and Nazi regimes affected only a few thousand individuals. The program of amalgamation of holdings in West Germany and even the collectivization of agriculture in East Germany did little to alter the distribution of holdings in the west or to improve productivity in the east. Agriculture changes, but it changes slowly, and attempts to alter the direction or rate of change seem in retrospect to have been largely futile.[12]

As in all other countries where it has occurred, the decline of agriculture created alarm and occasional panic in Germany. In the 1890s the question of whether Germany was becoming, or should become, an industrial state as opposed to an agrarian state erupted into a full-scale academic and political debate, and opposition to the relentless advance of industry constituted an important element in the more general conservative and anti-modernist movement.[13] One of the questions for German historians is whether this response was more passionate and more serious than elsewhere. The fact that the agricultural districts of eastern Prussia suffered both from the general decline of agriculture and from extremely heavy losses of population as workers moved to more favored urban and industrial centers did strike directly at the interests of the dominant Junker aristocracy, and this regional focus to the pattern of change may have contributed to the political response to economic development in Germany.[14]

Modern economic growth has also seen increasing ratios of saving and investment to total product. Rather than a sudden take-off following an increase in the investment ratio, the investment ratio appears to rise as development proceeds.[15] The pattern of German development matches that of other European nations.[16] From a possibly understated 7.3 per cent in the 1850s, the share of investment in German national product rose to an average of over 11 per cent during the next 30 years, and to over 14 per cent from 1890 to 1913. Investment declined during the interwar years, but then rose strongly following the Second World War. West German capital formation increased to more than 25 per cent of total product during the 1950s and touched 28 per cent during the 1960s; though dropping in the 1970s and 1980s, the ratio remained over 23 per cent, substantially above the levels recorded before the First World War. In East Germany capital formation accelerated from 17 per cent of total product during the 1950s to 24 per cent during the 1960s and over 30 per cent during the 1970s before falling back to 27 per cent during the 1980s.[17]

Massive and increasing investment in new capital has embodied the new technologies of the first, second and third industrial revolutions. As in other industrializing countries, in Germany increases in total output far outstripped increases in the labor force. For example, from 1850 to 1913 the German labor force increased by 1.18 per cent per year, but total output rose by 2.65 per cent per year, suggesting that new technologies contributed well over half of the total rise in output.[18] A more sophisticated total factor productivity approach, comparing actual output in 1913 to a hypothetical total assuming that technology had remained constant and the only change since 1850 had been increasing supplies of capital and labor, still produces the 'astounding' result that a 'residual' of fully 42 per cent of the total increase in output resulted from technological progress.[19] Technological change as measured by the residual method remained the major source of growth in the 1950s and 1960s, though interestingly less so in both Germany and Japan, where the very rapid growth of the capital stock played a large role, than in the United States.[20]

Table 11.3 Percentage distribution of population by size of community in Germany.

	Under 2,000	2,000–10,000	10,000–100,000	100,000+
Boundaries of 1913:				
1852	67.3	19.3	10.8	2.6
1871	63.9	18.7	12.6	4.8
1880	59.2	18.5	13.5	8.8
1890	53.0	19.1	15.8	12.1
1900	46.2	18.6	18.1	17.1
1910	40.0	18.9	19.8	21.3
Boundaries of 1935:				
1925	35.6	17.7	19.9	26.8
1939	30.1	18.2	20.1	31.6
West Germany:				
1950	29.0	23.0	21.0	27.0
1960	23.0	22.0	24.0	31.0
1970	19.0	21.0	28.0	32.0
1986	6.1	20.1	41.1	32.7
East Germany:				
1950	29.0	23.0	27.0	21.0
1960	28.0	22.0	29.0	21.0
1970	26.0	20.0	32.0	22.0
1980	23.7	19.3	31.1	25.9
1987	23.2	18.0	31.7	27.1

Sources: Hoffmann, *Wachstum*, p. 178; West Germany, *Jahrbuch 1988*, p. 60; East Germany, *Jahrbuch 1988*, p. 8.

A dramatic social transformation has accompanied the modern economic transformation. As people worked less and less in agriculture, so they also came to live less and less in the countryside. Over two-thirds of the German population lived in places of fewer than 2,000 inhabitants in 1852. As shown in Table 11.3, the proportion declined steadily, to less than half by 1900, less than a third in 1939, and under a fifth by the 1980s. At the other end of the scale, the share of the population living in cities of over 100,000 rose from only 2.6 per cent in 1852 to 17.1 per cent in 1900 and 31.6 per cent in 1939. The trend toward the largest cities continued after the Second World War, though at a lower rate. By the 1980s more than six of every ten persons in both East and West Germany lived in cities of more than 10,000 inhabitants. Because the territories lost in 1918 and 1945 contained relatively few large cities, these figures overstate the rate of change. Nevertheless, the spread of urbanization roughly matched the pattern of industrialization in its eastward movement across Europe, and again Germany lay in the middle.

The social and political consequences of the fundamental change in the position of women in the labor force are examined in the contribution by Eve Rosenhaft (ch. 7 above). The general growth of female employment and the concentration of women in certain occupations and industries in Germany once more parallel developments in other advanced economies. Women had always worked, as unpaid family members in agriculture, artisan manufacturing and shopkeeping, and most of the recorded increase in female agricultural employment merely reflects the increased willingness of official statisticians to include family members in their totals. However, in response to technological change and increasing bureaucratization, women increasingly took paid employment outside the home. By the 1880s women made up over one third of the recorded labor force. In industry the subsequent rise in the share of female employment followed a wave-like pattern depending on the relative rates of growth in those industrial branches in which women were concentrated: stable to 1900, rising to 1925, stable again until 1950. Following the Second World War, in West German industry the share of women rose again to 1962 and then stabilized once more, but women came to occupy over half of the positions remaining in agriculture and nearly half of the places in the expanding service sector. In East Germany a chronic shortage of labor accelerated the increase in the number of female workers. In the 1980s, 88 per cent of East German women of working age were either employed or in training, the highest female participation rate in the world.[21]

CYCLICAL FLUCTUATIONS IN GERMAN DEVELOPMENT

Despite the continuity of the underlying trends, however, modern economies do not grow at simple constant rates. The rates change and the historian must therefore also look at cyclical fluctuations in income, output, investment and employment. Through most of the modern period industrial economies have experienced three main types of cyclical behavior: three- to four-year trade or inventory cycles, seven- to eleven-year investment cycles, and long cycles of some 50 years. The long cycles remain particularly contentious. In the early 1920s Nikolai Kondratieff argued that 'long waves' in production and prices extending back into the late eighteenth century belonged 'to the same complex dynamic process' as the shorter cycles and were connected to major sectoral shifts in investment. During the long downswing, Kondratieff contended, prices decline and agriculture suffers a severe depression, but large numbers of technological discoveries are made. At the beginning of the long upswing, the new discoveries are applied. Gold production and prices rise and new markets are opened, but 'the period of high tension in the expansion of economic forces' is also marked by wars and revolutions.[22] Kondratieff's methods and conclusions have attracted much criticism, but the notion that there are underlying long cycles in economic development has continued to find adherents. Joseph Schumpeter argued in the 1930s that the introduction of crucial new technologies stimulated the upswings of the long cycles, Simon Kuznets in the 1950s that 'long swings' in economic activity were connected with investment required by expanding populations, and Walt Rostow in the 1970s that the 'lumpiness' of large-scale investment in natural resources lay behind the long cycle.[23] More recently Joshua Goldstein has linked the peaks of long economic cycles with periodic outbursts of warfare and the subsequent depressions with the destruction and exhaustion following in the wars' aftermath.[24]

The German statistics do show long 'growth' cycles of alternating periods of higher and lower average rates of expansion in total output, output per worker, total investment, and foreign trade. Tables 11.4, 11.5, 11.6 and 11.7 present the aggregate figures and break them down into some of their components to show the internal dynamics of the economy in each period. The upswing from 1850 to 1873 was marred by only three years of declining output, 1858, 1861 and 1870. In all three years the decline was marginal and resulted primarily from a drop in agricultural production. Net investment turned down sharply in 1856 and the effects of the 1857 commercial crisis could be seen in static output of clothing and food and a decline in metal and machinery production in 1859. Investment declined again in the mid-1860s and the impact of the American Civil War and the resulting 'cotton famine' showed in reduced textile output in 1862–4. Mining declined very slightly in 1860 and again in 1870; otherwise cyclical fluctuations had no impact on the long upswing.

The 1850–73 upswing saw especially large increases in output per worker in the industrial sector, but not as a result of large increases in industrial capital. Rather the improvement in the economy's efficiency appears to have resulted from the rapid expansion of the railway network. Investment in railways rose at nearly 8 per cent per year. The new transportation network created 'backward linkages' by providing markets for a broad range of industries, and permitted a large reduction in the amount of capital required for inventories.[26] Politically, an agreement to spend increases in government revenue on the railway system provided a new *modus vivendi* for the Prussian government and its former liberal opponents of 1848.[27] The supply of banknotes increased much more rapidly than previously, at over 12.5 per cent per year, making capital more readily available.[28] Zollverein exports rose at 4.9 per cent per year over the entire upswing and benefitted from the extension of an international network of liberal trade treaties during the 1860s.[29]

Table 11.4 Growth of output in Germany.

	Total	Agriculture	Industry	Services
Boundaries of 1913, five-year averages (million 1913 marks):				
1850–5	9,555	4,327	2,019	3,209
1871–5	16,376	6,130	5,336	4,910
1893–7	27,563	8,708	8,535	10,320
1909–13	44,761	10,619	19,758	14,384
Boundaries of 1935, five-year averages (million 1913 marks):				
1925–9	49,514	7,909	23,800	17,805
1934–8	58,765	9,826	28,965	19,974
West Germany (million 1913 marks):				
1950	40,052	4,521	20,821	14,710
1959	71,008	5,416	43,379	22,213
West Germany – net value added (million 1980 West German marks):				
1960	673,415	44,142	229,329	399,944
1970	1,020,250	37,037	383,845	599,368
1980	1,142,340	21,980	419,090	701,270
1986	1,388,925	22,453	460,116	906,356
East Germany – net material product (million 1985 East German marks):				
1950	30,352			
1960	79,379			
1970	121,563	22,596	83,639	
1980	193,644	25,112	138,903	
1987	261,200	29,966	194,050	
Percentage rate of increase:				
Boundaries of 1913:				
1853–73	2.73	1.76	4.98	2.15
1873–95	2.39	1.61	2.16	3.43
1895–1911	3.08	1.25	5.39	2.10
Boundaries of 1935:				
1927–36	1.92	2.44	2.21	1.29
West Germany:				
1950–9	5.89	1.82	7.62	4.21
1960–70	4.24	−1.74	5.29	4.13
1970–86	1.95	−3.08	1.14	2.62
East Germany:				
1950–70	7.18	1.98	8.00	
1979–87	4.60	1.67	5.08	

Sources: Hoffman, *Wachstum*, pp. 454–5; West Germany, *Jahrbuch 1988*, pp. 539–41; East Germany, *Jahrbuch 1988*, pp. 13, 15. Sectoral distribution of value added for West Germany for 1960, 1970 and 1980 calculated by applying an implicit deflator derived from the given constant price totals to current price sectoral figures. Note the inconsistency in the relative size of the service sector in Hoffmann's 1959 and the Statistisches Bundesamt's 1960 figures. Also note that East German net material product excludes most of the service sector's output.

Table 11.5 Growth of output per worker in Germany.

	Total	Agriculture	Industry	Services
Boundaries of 1913, five-year averages (1913 marks):				
1850–5	636	522	578	989
1871–5	878	664	981	1,235
1893–7	1,178	890	1,072	1,823
1909–13	1,490	999	1,737	1,791
Boundaries of 1935, five-year averages (1913 marks):				
1925–9	1,549	825	1,826	1,906
1934–8	1,662	1,089	1,785	1,977
West Germany (1913 marks):				
1950	1,958	909	2,417	2,140
1959	2,819	1,426	3,635	2,349
West Germany (1980 West German marks):				
1960	26,734	11,622	19,216	42,291
1970	38,045	17,356	29,554	51,250
1980	43,389	15,296	36,060	52,850
1986	53,480	16,920	43,725	64,185
East Germany (1985 East German marks):				
1970		22,664	24,650	
1980		28,569	37,430	
1987		32,256	47,807	
Percentage rate of increase:				
Boundaries of 1913:				
1853–73	1.63	1.15	2.98	1.12
1873–95	1.35	1.34	0.40	1.79
1895–1911	1.48	0.73	3.06	–0.11
Boundaries of 1935:				
1927–36	0.79	3.13	–0.25	0.41
West Germany:				
1950–9	3.71	4.61	4.17	0.94
1960–70	3.59	4.09	4.40	1.94
1970–86	2.15	–0.16	2.48	1.42
East Germany:				
1970–87		2.10	3.97	

Sources: Table 11.4 totals divided by Table 11.2 totals. Absolute levels are not comparable among the three series and a total figure for East Germany would be meaningless as the output of most service workers is excluded from the official definition of net material product. Also note that hours worked by each worker per year have declined over time, while wages have risen, both of which would have to be accounted for in a true measure of productivity.

Table 11.6 Growth of capital stock in Germany.

	Total	Agriculture	Industry	Railways	Non-agricultural housing	Government construction
Totals (billion 1913 marks):						
Boundaries of 1913:						
1850	46.77	24.99	7.16	1.15	6.98	6.99
1873	77.31	32.47	13.70	6.74	14.58	9.82
1895	141.18	40.36	34.60	14.25	35.69	16.28
1913	255.94	53.21	85.20	22.90	66.86	27.77
Boundaries of 1935:						
1924	226.80	44.46	73.55	21.00	62.00	25.79
1938	296.56	53.54	103.22	23.40	77.04	39.36
West Germany:						
1950	173.8	30.4	69.5	9.28	39.7	14.4
1959	267.5	35.3	126.7	12.4	59.8	19.5
Percentage rate of increase:						
Boundaries of 1913:						
1850–73	2.21	1.23	2.86	7.99	3.25	1.49
1873–95	2.78	0.99	4.30	3.46	4.15	2.32
1895–1913	3.36	1.55	5.13	2.67	3.55	3.01
Boundaries of 1935:						
1924–38	1.93	1.34	2.45	0.78	1.56	3.07
West Germany:						
1950–9	4.41	1.51	6.19	2.94	4.18	3.08

Source: Hoffmann, *Wachstum*, p. 253–5.

Table 11.7 Investment in West and East Germany.

West Germany (million 1980 West German marks):

	Total	Agriculture (%)	Industry (%)	
1960	189,870	9,640 (5.1)	54,770 (18.8)	
1970	291,910	9,760 (3.3)	86,410 (29.6)	
1980	335,880	9,280 (2.8)	84,920 (25.3)	
1986	324,890	8,210 (2.5)	82,660 (25.4)	

East Germany (million 1985 East German marks):

	Total	Agriculture (%)	Industry (%)	Housing (%)
1950	4,786	570 (11.9)	2,111 (44.1)	
1960	21,949	2,723 (12.4)	10,775 (49.1)	3,236 (14.7)
1970	43,707	6,038 (13.8)	22,823 (52.2)	3,248 (7.4)
1980	65,702	6,789 (10.3)	36,038 (54.9)	7,584 (11.5)
1987	71,205	5,646 (7.9)	41,595 (58.4)	8,706 (12.2)

Sources: West Germany, *Jahrbuch 1988*, p. 532; East Germany, *Jahrbuch 1988*, p. 105.

The Prussian army made efficient use of the railway system in the Danish, Austrian and French wars which punctuated the end of the upswing. Many historians have agreed with W.O. Henderson that the new imperial institution which resulted 'fostered future economic progress in Germany.... Many of the factors that had for so long hampered the expansion of industrial progress had now disappeared'.[30] However, this view gives insufficient weight to the preceding upswing. Knut Borchardt concludes that 'unification was not, contrary to the tenor of much German historical writing, a necessary condition of economic success.... The foundation of the empire may rather be seen as a result of Prussian growth than as a condition of growth in Germany.'[31] Certainly, the onset of the long cycle's downswing is an embarrassment to those who see unification as a decisive economic event.[32]

During the years from 1873 to 1895 the rate of growth in total output slowed. Investment in railways grew more slowly than in the upswing, reflecting the maturing of this key leading sector. Industrial investment quickened, but the rate of increase in output per industrial worker dropped, as the easier gains of the preceding period had now been largely exploited. Cyclical declines were more numerous and more sustained than in the upswing. Net investment fell in 1871, stagnated through the late 1870s, declined in 1879–80 and rose in the late 1880s only to slump again in 1891. Although the financial collapse of 1873 did not usher in a sudden decline, there was a two-year drop in total output in 1876 and 1877 and another in 1879 and 1880. The construction industry declined from 1875 to 1883 and did not regain its 1875 peak until 1892. The textile, metal and machinery industries all suffered during the mid-1870s as well. Agricultural output slowed substantially over the whole period and declined in 1874–7, 1879–80, 1889 and 1891. The protective tariffs passed in 1879 reflected these difficult circumstances, as well as the more generally competitive situation in international markets. The rate of growth of German exports dropped to 3.2 per cent per year over the downswing.[33] Credit was scarce. The new Reichsbank used its monopoly of note issue very restrictively, increasing the supply of currency by a mere 0.77 per cent per year. The total of currency and bank deposits rose only 5.2 per cent per year, less than half the 11.3 per cent of the preceding long upswing.[34]

In a widely influential article and subsequent book, Hans Rosenberg argued that the 1873 crash and the ensuing Great Depression led to the rise of 'neo-mercantilism', 'collective protectionism', interest group organization, the rise of mass parties, chauvinistic nationalism, increased militarism and 'modern anti-Semitism and pre-fascist currents'.[35] Rosenberg's work opens a promising approach linking economic trends to *mentalités*, but the line of causation is less straight than he pictures it.

None of the political developments which Rosenberg cites as consequences of the 1873–95 depression is as closely connected with the depression years as his argument seems to require. State intervention in the economy, for instance, had a history in the German states extending back to the eighteenth century at least. The anti-Semitism which Rosenberg identifies with the Great Depression clearly antedated 1873 and, significantly, the anti-Semitic political parties which might be seen as a response to the depression had all but disappeared by the 1890s.[36] Their re-emergence in the interwar years was linked with the trauma of a new and even more severe downswing.

The long cycle turned up again in the 1890s and Germany enjoyed very rapid growth from 1895 to 1913. The growth in total output was small consolation to agriculture, which continued to suffer from foreign competition, grew on average even more slowly than during the Great Depression and declined in 1898, 1901, 1905–7, 1909 and 1911–12. The upward thrust of the aggregate figures reflected the boom in industry. Industrial output dropped slightly in 1901 but was largely unaffected by the commercial crisis of 1907. Net investment sagged from 1899 to 1902, but recovered strongly and moved to new highs with only slight interruptions in 1908 and 1910. Investment in railways continued to slow, but the industries of the second industrial revolution emerged as the new leading sectors. Two generations of heavy investment in education at all levels had provided Germany with the human capital needed to seize the opportunities presented by industries based on chemistry, engineering and electricity.[37] The production of chemicals increased 6.6 per cent per year, the output of the metals and machinery industries 8.3 per cent each and electrical power output nearly 18 per cent per year. Much of the increased output found foreign buyers; total exports rose 5.9 per cent per year, exports of chemical products 8.9 per cent per year and exports of machinery 13.9 per cent per year.[38] A series of trade treaties sponsored by Bismarck's successor Caprivi in 1892–4 had lowered tariffs, but agrarian interests secured higher tariffs once again when the treaties expired in 1902.

Money for expansion was more readily available during the upswing. The Reichsbank increased its note issue 3.3 per cent per year, while the total of currency plus bank deposits also rose more rapidly than during the downswing, at 6.5 per cent per year.[39] The very highly developed system of 'mixed banks', which combined lending of their deposits with direct investment of their own capital, traditionally received credit for mobilizing these funds for industry. More recently it has been suggested that the banks may have misallocated their investments. Hugh Neuberger and Houston Stokes argue that German industry could have grown even more rapidly had more capital flowed to light industry and less to heavy industry.[40] The further suggestion that the banks responded to government pressure in favor of 'industries thought to have been making important contributions to national defense' reminds us that again the long upswing ended in war, a connection explored in the contribution by Holger Herwig (ch. 3 above).[41]

The First World War quickened several of the basic structural tendencies of development, but ushered in a period of very slow growth during the 1920s and 1930s, a long downswing of particular severity. The wartime withdrawal of mobilized workers, absence of new investment and shortage of manufactured inputs such as chemical fertilizer increased the pressure on agriculture. Heavy industry expanded during the war, and in all branches the government forced small firms to close or combine with their larger competitors.[42] Cartelization and 'rationalization' continued during the 1920s, but did not lead to notable improvements in efficiency. Output per worker actually declined. The industries of the second industrial revolution matured and began to slow. Exports fluctuated, but on balance dropped over the course of the downswing, as the disastrous slide of the 1930s wiped out the gains of the 1920s.[43] German producers faced increased international competition due to the rapid expansion of capacity in other countries during the war and the general spread of the new technologies. For example, Germany produced 80 per cent of the world output of dyes in 1913, but only 46 per cent in 1924.[44]

Slow growth reflected low investment, which rose at less than half the rate maintained during the preceding upswing. Much public and private debt disappeared in the 1923 inflation, but net investment rose above pre-1914 levels only in 1927, after which it declined steadily, becoming negative in 1931 and 1932 before turning upwards again.[45] Investment in railways and in housing[46] dropped to very low levels and, although the rate of agricultural investment rose, agriculture was no longer large enough to affect the entire economy. One factor unique to investment in the interwar period was reparations. Keynes and other observers considered the Allies' demand for 132 billion gold marks wildly excessive; in fact the manner of payment reduced the actual debt to 50 billion at most, but payments did reach 3 per cent of German national product in the late 1920s.[47] In addition, Knut Borchardt has argued that the relatively powerful position of labor unions in the Weimar period allowed workers to gain wage increases substantially in excess of productivity growth, which restricted investment by raising the share of wages in national income.[48] The banks imposed a very conservative pattern on the distribution of those funds which were available, withdrawing from dynamic sectors and concentrating in 'grandmotherly' areas such as brewing and textiles.[49] These institutional rigidities may be linked to recurrent cycles in the dominant type of investment. In the tradition of Schumpeter, Gerhard Mensch contends that periods of demand-creating 'expansionary' innovations alternate with times of cost-reducing 'rationalizing' innovations. In Mensch's view the stagnation of the 1920s and 1930s reflected the declining marginal returns to a preponderance of rationalizing innovations in established industries.[50]

Especially severe cyclical downturns marked the long downswing. Dietmar Petzina considers these declines fundamentally different from 'the pattern of classical economic cycles' because they did not lead to subsequent increases in output.[51] However, where yearly figures are available, they seem rather to suggest that not only did the underlying trends continue, but the patterns of the previous long downswing tended to repeat themselves. The German economy advanced from peak to peak, but compared to the preceding upswing the overall rates of increase were low and, as during the Great Depression, the interruptions were severe and prolonged. Despite the loss of Alsace-Lorraine and the Polish Corridor, in 1921 and 1922 output in the mining, metals and cotton industries recovered strongly, and output in most branches unaffected by the territorial losses equalled or exceeded 1913 levels.[52] The Franco-Belgian occupation of the Ruhr and the hyperinflation resulting from the Cuno government's policy of passive resistance together resulted in the collapse of the currency and worsened the downturn of 1923.[53] Output dropped sharply in 1923, but recovered after another setback in 1926 to reach new highs in most branches in 1929, 21 per cent above 1913 in the case of manufacturing output. A drop in both inventories and new investment caused a new cyclical downturn beginning in 1927–8. This was before the New York stock market crash and withdrawal of American short-term credits, which many historians have blamed for the depression in Germany.[54] The American crash, the banking crisis and the Brüning government's deflationary policies, however, transformed an already severe downturn into the deepest depression ever seen. Nevertheless, the decline of 1930–2 was in turn followed by another recovery lasting to the outbreak of war in 1939, and the new highs again exceeded the previous 1929 peaks.

The fluctuations in the interwar economy were bound up with equally violent political upheavals. The contributions by Larry Jones, Jane Caplan and Thomas Saunders (chs 4, 6 and 8, respectively) analyze these interrelationships, especially the way the Nazi Party exploited the crisis of 1930–2. Economic historians have explored the origins of the crisis and the role played by government policy. Borchardt insists that the weakness of the Weimar economy resulting from excessively high wages left no alternative to Brüning's program of deflation, which worsened the depression in the short run, but would in turn have hastened the recovery. This aspect of the 'Borchardt Thesis' has sparked a technical but very interesting debate.[55] East German Marxist historians see the depression as the product of a crisis in the capitalist system, and the Nazi seizure of power as the establishment of a regime of state monopoly capitalism. Business groups made large contributions to the Nazi Party, but the 'Stamokap' (state-monopoly capitalism) argument breaks down in the face of the well-documented divisions among industrial leaders and the general lack of enthusiasm for the Nazis among leaders of big business in particular.[56] David Abraham has attempted a more nuanced structural analysis, emphasizing the economic origins of divisions within the capitalist elite and their final turn to an 'extrasystemic solution' in 1931–2. Unfortunately, the debate over Abraham's use of statistical and archival evidence continues to divert attention from the substance of his argument.[57]

One positive aspect of the Nazi regime has appeared to be the rapid recovery from the depression. However, the output of producer goods and of consumer durables had already begun to rise from their troughs in mid-1932, and though unemployment continued to increase for another quarter, by early 1933 the inventory and investment cycles had turned upward, well before any possible impact of Nazi policy. The Nazi regime achieved full employment and high rates of growth during the late 1930s through heavy investments in military industries and to a lesser extent in housing, but 'paid the price of a slower and more uneven growth in productivity'.[58] In extending the highway system and proclaiming that the 'peoples' car', the Volkswagen, would be available to all,[59] the Nazi regime began to foster the largest leading sector of the next upswing, but then launched the world into the Second World War.

The outbreak of the Second World War at the end of a long downswing poses problems for Kondratieff's interpretation. Goldstein places the Second World War in the context of long swings in world economic development and cycles of major power conflict. From this perspective the war appears less the outcome of Nazi policy or Hitler's personal ambition than the final round in a cycle of hegemonic conflict resulting from the emergence of new major powers, similar to the Thirty Years' War and the French revolutionary and Napoleonic Wars. The fit is not a good one, however; although 'hegemonic war tends to occur on the war upswing of the long wave .... the synchrony is imperfect, as World War II shows'.[60]

In 1945 strategic bombing and invasion had left much of Germany in smoking ruins. Nevertheless, West Germany did not begin from 'zero hour'. Business and financial institutions remained essentially unchanged and the existing stock of human capital and a further inflow of skilled workers from eastern Europe provided ample resources.[61] Recovery in East Germany had also been essentially completed by the early 1950s. The German economy did more than merely recover, however; the long cycle had turned upwards once again and both East and West Germany grew very rapidly during the 1950s and 1960s. West German output rose more than 5 per cent per year in real terms from 1950 to 1970, the only slight downturn coming in 1967. Technical advances which had lain fallow during the interwar years now blossomed, employing workers drawn from agriculture and from foreign countries. Encouraged by favorable government policies, savings and investment rose to historically high levels. As Henry Wallich concluded in an early study, 'German business pulled itself up by its tax-exempt bootstraps.'[62] Banks continued to dominate the economy through direct holdings and proxies and persevered in their preference for large firms and mergers which provided them with business, but as in the 1895–1913 upswing this conservative bias did not hamper growth.[63]

A revolution in consumer spending patterns also marked the upswing in the west. West Germans spent a rapidly increasing percentage of their rising incomes on durables, especially the automobile. The share of food and drink in total consumption had declined from 60 per cent in 1850 to 52 per cent in 1910; now it dropped from 46 per cent in 1950 to 29 per cent in 1967.[64] The number of automobiles in West Germany increased by 18 per cent per year from 1950 to 1970.[65] As in previous upswings, exports rose dramatically, at 14.2 per cent per year during the 1950s and 7.5 per cent per year during the 1960s.[66] A general lowering of trade barriers and the foundation of the European Economic Community (EEC) in 1957 recalled the liberalization of the 1860s. On the other hand, although there were no major wars, in the late 1960s an outburst of strikes, student unrest and political terrorism provided evidence once again of the social strains created by rapid growth.

East Germany grew even more rapidly than West Germany during the upswing. Output rose over 7 per cent per year, despite the heavy loss of population before the closure of the border in 1961 and reparations and occupation costs imposed by the Soviet Union. Official statistics show foreign trade rising 6.6 per cent per year in 1985 prices. East Germany benefitted as a major supplier of industrial products to eastern Europe and from privileged access to the EEC as a result of the West German 'one Germany' policy.[67] Domestically, government policy favored heavy industry, but the consumer durables revolution seems to have fed the upswing as well. Though their incomes were only half those of their West German cousins, East Germans came to enjoy substantially higher living standards than other eastern Europeans. By 1970, 92 per cent of East German families owned a radio and 69 per cent owned a television.[68]

The long upswing slowed in the late 1960s, and the two Germanies endured slower growth once more during the 1970s and 1980s. German manufacturers faced higher prices for raw materials, especially oil, and the relatively easy gains from exploiting the backlog of technical innovations and shifting workers from agriculture to industry had been exhausted. Growth in West Germany averaged under 2 per cent per year

1971 to 1986 and total output declined in 1975, 1981 and 1982.[69] In East Germany increases in output slowed to 4.6 per cent per year. In both Germanies investment slackened relative to the upswing. Government reports, similar to those which appeared during the interwar downswing, criticized the large West German banks' influence over industry and accused them of increasing financial instability.[70] The initial boom in consumer durables had passed. The number of automobiles in West Germany rose 5.5 per cent per year during the 1970s, less than a third of the rate during the upswing. Across the border nearly half of East German households possessed a private automobile in 1987, compared to 3 per cent in 1960 and 16 per cent in 1970, but output remained small at some 200,000 per year.[71] The growth of West German exports dropped to 4.8 per cent per year and East Germany's official statistics showed a decline in the growth of foreign trade to 2.4 per cent per year.[72] These figures reflected both slower growth in foreign markets and increased competition, especially from Japan.

It is not the historian's business to predict the future, but should a new upswing arrive in the 1990s, in the context of the European Communities' new 'single market', extensive liberalization in eastern Europe and German reunification, West and East Germany appear well-positioned to seize the opportunity. Both have suffered relatively little during the downswing. West German industries have not been at the forefront of the third industrial revolution in electronics, and medium-sized firms might suffer in a general round of rationalization, but the West German economy remains by common consent the strongest in western Europe. Similarly, East Germany lags badly in the more modern areas of technology compared to West Germany, but in turn remains well in advance of the Soviet Union and most other eastern European countries, and would benefit from any flow of western capital eastwards.[73]

CONCLUSION

Not everyone agrees with the periodization adopted here. Reinhard Spree and Solomos Solomou, for instance, both doubt the existence of Kondratieff cycles and argue that even when long up- and downswings can be observed, the variations in growth rates have often not been statistically significant. They believe that those long swings which pass tests of statistical significance have been 'Kuznets swings' – discrete responses to specific population changes. Solomou contends that although these may resemble each other in their effect on investment and other economic variables, they do not form a regular recurring pattern.[74] The Great Depression of 1873–96 appears particularly vulnerable on statistical grounds. Hoffmann's figures may understate German output in the 1850s and overstate the downturn of the 1870s, which together would exaggerate the 1873 turning point. The transition from up- to downswing in 1970 also appears less dramatic if different dates are selected.

Yet the long cycles do appear across a wide range of variables and in the shift from one leading sector to another they appear connected in a manner analogous to the recurrent investment and inventory cycles. Further, Kondratieff's observation that the long swings add an upward or downward bias to other cyclical fluctuations seems to be confirmed; downturns resulting from inventory and investment cycles appear shorter and less severe during long upswings than during long downswings. The upswings are clearly associated with relatively expansive credit conditions, with the application of major new technologies and with very rapid growth of foreign trade. The importance of exports in the upswings highlights the connection of German growth to world economic development. As a privileged member of the industrial core, Germany reaped the benefits of the upswings but avoided some of the impact of the downswings, particularly during the 1970s and 1980s.

However, the connection of the long cycles to war and domestic unrest, and to politics in general, appears much less direct than Kondratieff thought. The most striking feature of German history remains the indeterminate nature of the relationship between politics and economics. Political actions obviously affect economic cycles, both in the long and short run. Investment in education and basic research, the provision of credit and securing access to foreign markets aid the economy over the long cycle, and monetary and fiscal management can smooth the fluctuations in investment and inventory cycles. And conversely; poorly chosen policies have negative consequences, as demonstrated disastrously during the interwar years. Similarly, economic cycles have political effects. Investment and inventory cycles can make and break governments. Long upswings create new interest groups, and downswings threaten the position of existing groups. Both sorts of movements affect the tone of public life along the lines suggested by Rosenberg. But all of these impulses are mediated through changing institutional structures, shifting psychological attitudes and individual ambition. 'Men make their own history, but they do not make it just as they please.'[75]

NOTES

I would like to thank Ayling Rubin, Department of Economic History, University of Sydney, and Matthias Spring, Economic Section, Consulate General of the

Federal Republic of Germany, Sydney, for assistance in locating some of the statistical material in this chapter. Thanks too to Robert Aldrich and Carole Adams for reading an earlier draft.

1 'An industry is not built in a day', Ernst Engel, *Die industrielle Enquête und die Gewerbezählung im deutschen Reiche und im preussischen Staate am Ende des Jahres 1875* (Berlin, 1878). Director of the Saxon Statistical Office in the 1850s, Engel became head of the Prussian Statistical Office in the 1860s and of the Imperial Statistical Office in the 1870s. His observation that the proportion of income spent on food declines as income rises is known to economists as 'Engel's Law'.
2 Immanuel Wallerstein, *The Modern World System III: The Second Era of Great Expansion of the Capitalist World-Economy, 1730–1840s* (San Diego, Calif., 1989); Simon Kuznets, *Modern Economic Growth: Rate, Structure and Spread* (New Haven, Conn., 1966).
3 Volker R. Berghahn, *Modern Germany: State, Economy and Politics in the Twentieth Century*, 2nd edn. (Cambridge, 1987), p. 267.
4 P. R. Gregory, *Russian National Income, 1885–1913* (Cambridge, 1982), pp. 155–7.
5 Hartmut Kaelble, 'Der Mythos von der rapiden Industrialisierung in Deutschland', *Geschichte und Gesellschaft*, vol. 9 (1983), pp. 108–18, using similar data, argues that German development before the First World War was 'unspectacular' in comparative perspective, and Angus Maddison, *The World Economy in the Twentieth Century* (Paris, 1989), places Germany somewhat below average in growth of total income in the twentieth century.
6 John E. Knodel, *The Decline of Fertility in Germany 1871–1939* (Princeton, NJ, 1974).
7 Walther G. Hoffmann, *Das Wachstum der deutschen Wirtschaft seit der Mitte des 19. Jahrhunderts* (Berlin, 1965), pp. 454–5.
8 Kuznets, *Modern Economic Growth*, pp. 64–5.
9 Hoffmann, *Wachstum*, pp. 209, 212.
10 ibid., pp. 205–6.
11 Kuznets, *Modern Economic Growth*, pp. 106–7; B.R. Mitchell, *European Historical Statistics, 1750–1970* (New York, 1976), pp. 153–63.
12 Hans-Jürgen Puhle, 'Lords and peasants in the Kaiserreich', in Robert G. Moeller (ed.), *Peasants and Lords in Modern Germany* (Boston, Mass., 1986), pp. 81–109; Dieter Gessner, 'The dilemma of German agriculture during the Weimar Republic', in Richard Bessel and E.J. Feuchtwanger (eds), *Social Change and Political Development in Weimar Germany* (London, 1981), pp. 134–54; David Schoenbaum, *Hitler's Social Revolution: Class and Status in Nazi Germany, 1933–1939* (New York, 1966), ch. 5; J. E. Farquharson, 'The agrarian policy of national socialist Germany', in Moeller, *Peasants*, pp. 233–59.
13 Kenneth D. Barkin, *The Controversy over German Industrialization, 1890–1902* (Chicago, 1970).
14 Frank B. Tipton, *Regional Variations in the Economic Development of Germany during the Nineteenth Century* (Middletown, Conn., 1976), ch. 6; James N. Retallack, *Notables of the Right: The Conservative Party and Political Mobilization in Germany, 1876–1918* (Boston, Mass., 1988).
15 W. W. Rostow, *The Stages of Economic Growth* (Cambridge, 1960); Kuznets, *Modern Economic Growth*, p. 247.
16 ibid., pp. 248–50; Mitchell, *European Historical Statistics*, pp. 781–95.
17 Calculated from data in Hoffmann, *Wachstum*, pp. 825–6; Mitchell, *European*

Historical Statistics, pp. 781, 785, 792; West Germany, Statistisches Bundesamt, *Statistisches Jahrbuch 1988 für die Bundesrepublik Deutschland* (Stuttgart, 1988), p. 532; East Germany, Staatliche Zentralverwaltung für Statistik, *Statistisches Jahrbuch der deutschen demokratischen Republik 1988* (Berlin, 1988), p. 105.

18 Calculated from data in Hoffmann, *Wachstum*.

19 Eckart Schremmer, 'Wie gross war der technische Fortschritt während der Industriellen Revolution in Deutschland, 1850–1913', *Vierteljahrschrift für Sozial- und Wirtschaftsgeschichte*, vol. 60 (1973), pp. 433–58.

20 E. D. Domar *et al.*, 'Economic growth and productivity in the U.S., Canada, U.K., Germany and Japan in the post-war period', *Review of Economics and Statistics*, vol. 46 (1964), pp. 33–40.

21 Reinhard Stockmann, 'Gewerbliche Frauenarbeit in Deutschland 1875–1980', *Geschichte und Gesellschaft*, vol. 11 (1985), pp. 447–75; Carole E. Adams, *Women Clerks in Wilhelmine Germany: Issues of Class and Gender* (Cambridge, 1988), ch. 2; Renate Bridenthal, 'Beyond Kinder, Küche, Kirche: Weimar women at work', *Central European History*, vol. 6 (1973), pp. 148–66; Ian Jeffries, 'The GDR in historical and international perspective', in Ian Jeffries and Manfred Melzer (eds), *The East German Economy* (London, 1987), p. 7.

22 Nikolai D. Kondratieff, 'The long waves in economic life' [1926], in Gottfried Haberler (ed.), *Readings in Business Cycle Theory* (Philadelphia, Pa, 1951), pp. 31–2.

23 Joseph A. Schumpeter, 'The analysis of economic change' [1935], in Haberler, *Readings*, pp. 1–19; Simon Kuznets, 'Long swings in population Growth and related economic variables' [1958], in *Economic Growth and Structure: Selected Essays* (New York, 1965), pp. 328–78; W. W. Rostow, *Why the Poor Get Richer and the Rich Slow Down: Essays in the Marshallian Long Period* (Austin, Tex., 1980).

24 Joshua S. Goldstein, *Long Cycles: Prosperity and War in the Modern Age* (New Haven, Conn., 1988).

25 Hoffmann, *Wachstum*, pp. 257, 338–43, 390–5, 454–5.

26 Rainer Fremdling, 'Railroads and German economic growth: a leading sector analysis with a comparison to the United States and Great Britain', *Journal of Economic History*, vol. 37 (1977), pp. 583–604; Kuznets, *Modern Economic Growth*, pp. 252, 257.

27 Richard H. Tilly, 'The political economy of public finance and the industrialization of Prussia, 1815–1866', *Journal of Economic History*, vol. 26 (1966), pp. 484–97.

28 Mitchell, *European Historical Statistics*, pp. 672–6.

29 Hoffmann, *Wachstum*, pp. 530–2.

30 W.O. Henderson, *The Rise of German Industrial Power, 1834–1914* (London, 1975), pp. 159–60.

31 Knut Borchardt, 'Germany, 1700–1914', in Carlo M. Cipolla (ed.), *The Fontana Economic History of Europe*, Vol. 4, pt 1 (Glasgow, 1973), pp. 115–16.

32 Frank B. Tipton, 'The national consensus in German economic history', *Central European History*, vol. 7 (1974), pp. 195–224.

33 Hoffmann, *Wachstum*, pp. 257, 390–5, 454–5, 530–2. Hoffman's figures for industrial output before 1895 have been criticized, particularly by W. Arthur Lewis, *Growth and Fluctuations, 1870–1913* (London, 1978), pp. 268–71.

However, even Lewis's recalculations show stagnation in the 1870s and slower growth in the 1870s and 1880s than from the early 1890s to 1913.

34 Mitchell, *European Historical Statistics*, pp. 672–96.

35 Hans Rosenberg, 'Political and social consequences of the Great Depression of 1873–1896 in central Europe', *Economic History Review* (1943), reprinted in James J. Sheehan (ed.), *Imperial Germany* (New York, 1976); idem, *Grosse Depression und Bismarckzeit* (Berlin, 1967), pp. 88–117.

36 W. O. Henderson, *The State and the Industrial Revolution in Prussia* (Liverpool, 1958); Richard S. Levy, *The Downfall of the Anti-Semitic Political Parties in Imperial Germany* (New Haven, Conn., 1975).

37 David S. Landes, *The Unbound Prometheus: Technological Change and Industrial Development in Western Europe from 1750 to the Present* (Cambridge, 1969), pp. 339–48.

38 Hoffmann, *Wachstum*, pp. 257–8, 388, 390–5, 454–5, 530–2.

39 Mitchell, *European Historical Statistics*, pp. 672–96.

40 Hugh Neuberger and Houston H. Stokes, 'German banks and German growth, 1883–1913: an empirical view', *Journal of Economic History*, vol. 34 (1974), pp. 710–31; Rainer Fremdling and Richard H. Tilly, 'German banks, German growth, and econometric history', ibid., vol. 36 (1976), pp. 416–24, and reply by Neuberger and Stokes, ibid., pp. 425–7.

41 Neuberger and Stokes, 'German banks', p.729.

42 Jürgen Kocka, *Klassengesellschaft im Krieg: Deutsche Sozialgeschichte, 1914–1918*, 2nd edn (Göttingen, 1978); Gerd Hardach, *The First World War, 1914–1918* (1973; Harmondsworth, 1987).

43 Hoffmann, *Wachstum*, pp. 530–2.

44 Derek H. Aldcroft, *From Versailles to Wall Street, 1919–1929* (1977; Harmondsworth, 1987), p. 49, citing V. Trivanovitch, *Rationalization of German Industry* (1931), p. 14.

45 Hoffmann, *Wachstum*, p. 258.

46 Dan P. Silverman, 'A pledge unredeemed: the housing crisis in Weimar Germany', *Central European History*, vol. 3 (1970), pp. 112–39.

47 Sally Marks, 'The myths of reparations', *Central European History*, vol. 11 (1978), pp. 231–55; Aldcroft, *Versailles to Wall Street*, pp. 81–92; Harold James, *The German Slump: Politics and Economics, 1924–1936* (Oxford, 1986), pp. 21–3.

48 Knut Borchardt, *Wachstum, Krisen, Handlungspielräume der Wirtschaftspolitik* (Göttingen, 1982), pp. 165–82; James, *German Slump*, ch. 6.

49 ibid., pp. 139–46.

50 Gerhard Mensch and Reinhard Schnopp, 'Stalemate in technology, 1925–1935: the interplay of stagnation and innovation', in Wilhelm H. Schröder and Reinhard Spree (eds), *Historische Konjunkturforschung* (Stuttgart, 1980), pp. 60–74; Mensch, *Stalemate in Technology* (Cambridge, 1979).

51 Dietmar Petzina, 'Problems in the social and economic development of the Weimar Republic', in Michael N. Dobkowski and Isidor Wallimann (eds), *Towards the Holocaust: The Social and Economic Collapse of the Weimar Republic* (Westport, Conn., 1983), pp. 37–59; idem, *Die deutsche Wirtschaft in der Zwischenkriegszeit* (Wiesbaden, 1977).

52 Hoffmann, *Wachstum*, pp. 343 (mining), 354 (metals), 358 (shipbuilding), 362 (rubber), 370 (textiles), 384–5 (foods).

53 Karl Erich Born, 'The German inflation after the First World War', *Journal of European Economic History*, vol. 6 (1977), pp. 109–16; Carl-Ludwig Holtferich, *The German Inflation, 1914–1923* (1980; Berlin, 1986); Gerald

D. Feldman (ed.), *Die deutsche Inflation: eine Zwischenbilanz* (Berlin, 1982), the first of four volumes by a group of predominantly West German and American scholars.

54 For instance, Berghahn, *Modern Germany*, p. 100, and Aldcroft, *Versailles to Wall Street*, p. 85. See Peter Temin, 'The beginning of the depression in Germany', *Economic History Review*, vol. 24 (1971), pp. 240–8; M. E. Falkus, 'The German business cycle in the 1920s', ibid., vol. 28 (1975), pp. 451–65.

55 Heinrich A. Winkler (ed.), 'Kontroversen über die Wirtschaftspolitik in der Weimar Republik', *Geschichte und Gesellschaft*, vol. 11 (1985).

56 Andreas Dorpalen, *German History in Marxist Perspective* (London, 1985), chs 7–8; Henry A. Turner, Jr, *German Big Business and the Rise of Hitler* (New York, 1985).

57 David Abraham, *The Collapse of the Weimar Republic: Political Economy and Crisis*, 2nd edn (New York, 1986). See Peter Hayes, 'History in an off key: David Abraham's second *Collapse*', *Business History Review*, vol. 61 (1987), pp. 452–72.

58 R. J. Overy, *The Nazi Economic Recovery, 1932–1938* (Basingstoke, 1982), p. 9; James, *German Slump*, ch. 10.

59 Schoenbaum, *Hitler's Social Revolution*, p. 105.

60 Goldstein, *Long Cycles*, pp. 283–8, 336–42; Alan S. Milward, *War, Economy and Society, 1939–1945* (Berkeley, Calif., 1977).

61 Berghahn, *Modern Germany*, pp. 197–207; Karl Hardach, 'Germany, 1914–1970', in Carlo M. Cipolla (ed.), *The Fontana Economic History of Europe*, Vol. 6 (Glasgow, 1976), pp. 212, 217–21; Werner Abelshauser and Dietmar Petzina, 'Krise und Rekonstruktion: Zur Interpretation der gesamtwirtschaflichen Entwicklung Deutschlands im 20. Jahrhundert', in Schröder and Spree, *Historische Konjunkturforschung*, pp. 75–115.

62 Henry C. Wallich, *Mainsprings of the German Revival* (New Haven, Conn., 1955), p. 166.

63 Martin Schnitzer, *East and West Germany: A Comparative Economic Analysis* (New York, 1972), pp. 155–8.

64 Hoffmann, *Wachstum*, pp. 698–9; Berghahn, *Modern Germany*, p. 292.

65 Mitchell, *European Historical Statistics*, p. 643.

66 Hoffmann, *Wachstum*, p. 153 (1950–9 exports in constant 1913 prices); West Germany, *Jahrbuch 1988*, p. 88 (1960–70 exports in constant 1980 prices).

67 East Germany, *Jahrbuch 1988*, p. 239. East Germany publishes trade figures only in 'valuta marks' whose relation to domestic prices is unknown. See Hanns-Dieter Jacobsen, 'The foreign trade and payments of the GDR', in Jeffries and Melzer, *East German Economy*, pp. 235–60.

68 East Germany, *Jahrbuch 1988*, p. 291.

69 Frank B. Tipton and Robert Aldrich, *An Economic and Social History of Europe from 1939 to the Present* (London, 1987), chs 4 and 8; Organization for Economic Cooperation and Development, *OECD Economic Surveys – Germany 1975* (Paris), pp. 5–18; idem, *Germany 1982–83*, pp. 7–23; idem, *Germany 1987–1988*, pp. 33–4.

70 Owen E. Smith, *The West German Economy* (London, 1983), pp. 230–4, 267–9.

71 United Nations, *Statistical Yearbook 1981*; East Germany, *Jahrbuch 1988*, p.291; Vienna Institute for Comparative Economic Studies, *Comecon Data 1985* (London, 1986), p. 236.

72 West Germany, *Jahrbuch 1988*, p. 88; East Germany, *Jahrbuch 1988*, p. 239.

73   OECD, *Germany 1987–1988*; Raymond Bentley, *Technological Change in the German Democratic Republic* (Boulder, Colo., 1984).

74   Reinhard Spree, *Wachstumstrends und Konjunkturzyklen in der deutschen Wirtschaft von 1820 bis 1913: Quantitativer Rahmen für eine Konjunkturgeschichte des 19. Jahrhunderts* (Göttingen, 1978); idem, 'Was kommt nach der langen Wellen der Konjunktur?' in Schröder and Spree, *Historische Konjunkturforschung*, pp. 304–15; Solomos Solomou, *Phases of Economic Growth, 1850–1973: Kondratieff Waves and Kuznets Swings* (Cambridge, 1987).

75   Karl Marx, *The 18th Brumaire of Louis Bonaparte* (1852; New York, 1969), p. 15.

12 German History – Past, Present and Future

RICHARD J. EVANS

THE PAST

German history did not end in 1945. But for a long time historians tended to behave as if it did. As the contributions to this book show in their various different ways, the Third Reich stood at the center of most historians' concerns and at the end of most historians' narratives. This could in practice be implicit rather than explicit. But even in works devoted exclusively to earlier periods, as far back as the middle of the nineteenth century, the shadow of Nazism loomed unseen beyond the intervening decades. 1848 was refracted through the prism of 1933; 1866–71 through that of 1939; 1918 through that of 1945. Explaining how Hitler came to power, how the Nazi dictatorship could take a grip on German society and culture, and how the Third Reich could descend to such unparalleled depths of destruction and barbarity, has been an essential part of the intellectual enterprise of studying modern German history even for those historians who did not put these tasks explicitly at the top of their agenda.

There were good reasons why this was the case. The Third Reich may only have lasted a mere 12 years, but those 12 years saw Germany have a more profound effect on the rest of the world than in all the previous centuries put together. Argument may rage about the uniqueness or otherwise of the Nazis' genocidal policies towards the Jews, but within the history of Germany itself, the question of what caused those policies to be devised and implemented, what made Nazism in its wider sense acceptable to a majority of Germans for much of the time despite all its manifest horrors and injustices, is one that has steadfastly refused to go away. It is precisely the moral and historical abnormality of Nazism and its crimes that has impelled historians to identify what they see as abnormalities in the longer run of German history. Other countries, other societies have had their myths of progress and improvement, but in the case of Germany, the idea of history as a steady progression – even if occasionally interrupted – towards a better future has always seemed rather out of place, at least since 1945.

Moreover, those who studied the phenomenon of Nazism itself could make use almost from the beginning of an unprecedented quantity of documentation. Rarely can the evidence for the inner workings of a modern regime have become so accessible in such large quantities so soon after the regime's collapse. By contrast, documentation for what followed – for the history of the postwar era – has been much slower to reach the light of day. In the case of West Germany and the Western Allies, it has been subjected to the usual 30-year embargo before it has been made available to researchers. Given the fact that a PhD dissertation or a scholarly monograph takes at least five years from the beginning of research to final publication, and given the need to base such work on more than a couple of years' documentation if it is not to be completely trivial in scope, this means in effect that there has been an inevitable delay of about 40 years before historical research on postwar Germany has begun to be published in any quantity. Up to the 1980s, German history after 1945 was largely the preserve of the political scientists, whose sources, methods and approaches are very different from those of the historian.

There were political as well as practical reasons why German history for so long seemed to have come to an end in 1945. The division of Germany into East and West, the loss of the eastern territories to Russia and Poland, the liquidation of so many German traditions, from Prussian militarism to the power of the landed Junker aristocracy, and above all the establishment of stable political systems that differed markedly from anything that had previously been experienced in Germany's past, seemed to establish 1945 as a discontinuity far greater than previous dates such as 1871, 1918, or 1933. 1945 was 'zero hour', the moment when German history began again with a slate cleaned partly by the occupying Allies, partly by the Nazis themselves. Indeed, as time went on, and the political divisions created by the founding of two German states in 1949 hardened into the physical barrier erected with the building of the Berlin Wall in 1961, German history itself, as a single story, seemed to be over. The idea of Germany as a nation–state was increasingly replaced by the admission that there was not one German history but several. The East Germans in particular, following on the constitutional changes introduced in 1974, began to back-project their own statehood onto the historical identity of the part of Germany they occupied, so that Luther or Frederick the Great, for example, appeared retrospectively East German by virtue of having lived within the boundaries of what was now the German Democratic Republic.

West German historians, too, began to wonder whether regional identities had not in the end proved stronger than national ones. Bismarck's creation of the empire of 1871 seemed increasingly to have been a *tour de force*, its artificial nature underlined by the fact that its existence was followed within a few decades by two world wars for which it was largely responsible. Its boundaries did not stand the test of time; they were revised in 1918 by the Treaty of Versailles, in 1938 by the Anschluss of Austria and the annexation of the Sudetenland – a return to the 'big German' concept of national unity that Bismarck had so forcefully rejected in 1866 – and again during the Second World War, before final defeat in 1945 destroyed the existence of a single state for the Germans altogether. As the fortieth anniversary of the end of the Second World War came and went, Germany increasingly seemed to have reverted to what was arguably its natural condition of division into a number of different independent states.[1]

The 'modern Germany' that this book originally set out to reconsider, when its editor began gathering his list of contributors in 1988, therefore, was implicitly the nation–state, flawed and partial though that creation might have been, made by Bismarck in 1871 and unmade by Hitler in 1945. Indeed, this is the perspective adopted by the overwhelming bulk of research discussed by this book. 'Germany' is understood, for example, to have been different from Austria throughout. The 'little German' model ruled, with a traditional Prussian or National Liberal historiography, narrating the story of German history as an inevitable, almost predestined progress towards the unification of 1871 under Prussian leadership, being increasingly overlaid during the twentieth century by a second, much more critical model, telling the same story, but in more negative terms, as an inevitable, almost predestined progress towards the Third Reich of 1933–45. The point was that both models shared many of the same assumptions about the centrality of Prussia to modern German history, and the concomitant marginality of Austria.

Already by the time this book was conceived, however, changes were taking place that were beginning to bring this long-established situation into question. The first and most obvious was the increasing distance in time between the end of the Second World War and the present. During the 1980s, as archival research on the postwar period began to appear in rapidly growing quantities, a new historiography emerged, written from an entirely different perspective: the historiography of the Federal Republic. Whether it was critical or not, this historiography was starting to make an important contribution to the legitimation of the Federal Republic by asking questions about where it came from, how it was established, why it was structured as it was, and so on, that had little to do with the older perspective on German history as a whole. Of course, serious archival research on the history of the German Democratic Republic was not possible because there was no free access to the archives. Historical research was centrally planned to serve the interests of the state and the ruling Socialist Unity Party. Western scholars – mainly political scientists – were dependent on information supplied by defectors or deported dissidents. But by 1989, there was already a substantial body of archivally based historical scholarship on the political history of the early postwar years in the three Western zones. Social and economic history by its very nature tends to cover longer periods, since the pace of change is slower than in politics, but here too the years from 1945 to the early 1950s were taking on real historical contours by the late 1980s.[2]

This was a field that not only attracted large numbers of younger scholars, for whom it was by the 1980s as remote in time as the Third Reich and the Weimar Republic had been for the 'critical' historians who had begun their dissertations 20 or 30 years earlier, but also many more senior researchers who were fired by the opportunities and challenges that this new area of study presented.[3] The Munich-based Institute for Contemporary History, for example, which had begun in the early postwar years as a center for the study of National Socialism, shifted its focus increasingly to the years after 1945, as can be seen from the growing proportion of its publications – particularly in its journal the *Vierteljahreshefte für Zeitgeschichte* – devoted to this period. Historians, in other words, were now moving in where economists, sociologists and political scientists had previously held sway. The consequences of this new development of the 1980s were far from negligible.

Not only were historians of Germany now thinking increasingly of problems other than that of the Third Reich and its origins, but the move into the postwar era also began to alter their perspective on earlier periods. Nazi Germany inevitably began to seem less immediate, more historical; a development that was taken up and posed as a question, indeed, by the Munich Institute's Director, the late Martin Broszat, when he began to argue in the mid-1980s for a 'historicization' of National Socialism. Broszat's argument was put at times in rather obscure terms and gave rise to a good deal of controversy, not least because it was widely misunderstood. Perhaps this was hardly surprising, given the fact that he based it on the rather dubious claim that the Third Reich had somehow blocked the way to the development of a wider German historical consciousness, whatever that might be. And of course the notion that the phenomenon of the Nazi dictatorship has prevented historians from studying the broader sweep of German history is far from convincing, given the fact that a generation of historians has attempted since the 1960s to locate its origins in the development of German history in the eighteenth and nineteenth centuries.[4] Nevertheless, Broszat had a point.

Treating the Third Reich as history meant, for Broszat, ceasing to create demons of its agents and heroes of its victims and opponents. It meant instead recognizing the complexities and ambiguities of people's behavior and motivation in such circumstances. It meant shifting the focus of attention from high politics, ideology, military strategy, organized resistance and outright opposition, which presented a two-dimensional picture of Germany between 1933 and 1945, onto the everyday life which Germans lived in the period, onto the myriad varieties of accommodation with the regime, dissent from it, obedience to its dictates. It meant recognizing that, for most people, life in the Third Reich, at least almost until the end, had a kind of normality that shaped their experience and perceptions in a very powerful way and formed a continuum with the normality of life before 1933 and after 1945. Only in this way, said Broszat, would we be able, if we wished, to reach an accurate moral judgment on what they had done. History, he seemed to be suggesting, knows no heroes or villains, at least not of an unalloyed variety. The story of Nazi Germany should not be portrayed as a Victorian melodrama. Or, to put it another way, it was time to stop painting it in terms of black and white, time instead to represent it in shades of grey.[5]

The same point was put by Ernst Nolte, a well-known authority on the international history of fascism, in a newspaper article, followed by a book, which was one of the major contributions to the so-called *Historikerstreit*, the 'historians' debate', which raged in Germany from the summer of 1986 to the autumn of 1988. Nolte, along with other conservative or neo-conservative historians, sought to strengthen Germany's national self-confidence, to make Germans feel happier, or at least more comfortable, with being German, by arguing that the crimes of Nazism, above all the extermination of the Jews and the war crimes of 1939–45, were not uniquely horrible in human history, as many German (and other) historians had previously portrayed them, but were instead similar in degree, kind and scale to other twentieth-century crimes, including Stalin's liquidation of the kulaks and Pol Pot's 'autogenocide' against the people of Cambodia. Nolte, indeed, went even further and suggested that Auschwitz was a copy of and a response to the Gulag, the Bolshevik mass murder of the Russian urban and rural bourgeoisie and their threat to extend it to the rest of Europe.[6]

This is not the place to go into these arguments, which have not found wide acceptance among German historians.[7] What is important to emphasize here is the fact that, however sharply they may have differed in their political intentions and their historiographical direction, the arguments of both Broszat and Nolte expressed, in their various ways, a feeling that the nature of historical research into the Third Reich was beginning to shift, and that this feeling both expressed the lengthening temporal distance that the 1980s placed between the German present and the Nazi past, and reflected the fact that, as a consequence, it seemed increasingly absurd to take the Third Reich out of a broader continuity which started before it and – the crucial point – went on afterwards. What was 'normalizing' or 'historicizing' Nazi Germany, in other words, was the history of the postwar period. 1945 was beginning to seem less like the end of German history and more like a turning point in it.[8]

For more and more historians, therefore, this meant examining features of German history that cut across the boundary of 1945. The Bismarckian and Wilhelmine empires, for example, could appear as the sources not only of developments, such as the rise of racial anti-Semitism or the growth of extreme, populist nationalism, that led to the Third Reich, but also of more long-term developments such as the rise of cultural modernism or the beginnings of women's emancipation, that came to greater prominence in the Weimar Republic, were submerged under the Nazis, then found a much fuller development in the postwar decades.[9] On a more detailed level, it became clear that many crucial institutions of German society experienced after 1945 not a complete renewal but a partial restoration. It was, for example, only in the 1980s that serious critical studies began to appear documenting the active participation of the legal profession, the medical profession, social work, the army and other key professional bodies in the racial and genocidal policies of the Third Reich. Just as important, they documented the restoration of these bodies in the postwar period, along with many of their leading members from the Nazi years, and the subsequent taboo imposed on the subject of their involvement in the Nazi regime until a new generation of lawyers, doctors, social workers and army officers reached positions of prominence, until those who still had something to hide had died or retired from the scene.[10]

That such investigations ran counter to the neo-conservative attempt to place Nazism in more relativizing kinds of continuity is clear. The kind of locally based 'history of everyday life' with which Broszat was associated, and which found its most generalized expression in Detlev Peukert's *Inside Nazi Germany*, was very different from the philosophical history of ideas represented by Nolte, or the kind of diplomatic and military history favored by other neo-conservative historians.[11] Nevertheless, both approaches shared a common intention to situate Nazism in a broader contextual continuity reaching up to the present, even if the contexts in question – for Nolte, the continuities of the Cold War from 1917 to the 1980s, for the historians of everyday life, or at least for many of them, the continuities spanning the years before and after 1945 – were utterly different from one another.

THE PRESENT

As the development of interest in the history of everyday life suggests, methodological innovations in historical scholarship were also playing their part in the change of perspective on modern German history that came about during the 1980s. Traditionally, German historians had concentrated very much on political and diplomatic history, the history of the state; economic history had established itself mainly in the medieval field, but even where it did intervene in the study of the nineteenth and twentieth centuries, it was predominantly under the primacy of politics, so that the Customs Union of the 1830s, the industrialization of the 1860s, or the inflation of the 1920s, were all viewed primarily in terms of their political significance. Attempts to introduce modern social history had made little impact, not least because of the centrality of explaining the Third Reich and its origins, for some decades after the Second World War. While British, French and American historians came increasingly under the influence of social sciences such as demography, sociology, statistics, geography and anthropology in the 1950s and early 1960s, this approach was overwhelmingly rejected by the majority of German historians, who continued to pay allegiance to traditional notions of understanding the past in its own terms, of so-called *Historismus*, a way of arriving at an objective truth through critical assessment of the documents, which had been the principal contribution of the Germans to historical methodology in the nineteenth century.[12]

The critical reinterpretation of modern German history that began in the late 1960s was based on a conscious rejection of this tradition and on the deliberate adoption of the theory and methodology of the social sciences. The task of history was not to understand the past in its own terms, but to tell us how we became what we were and thus help us find out what we were, or ought to be, in the process of becoming. Social science theory, quantitative methods and other innovations were mobilized in the service of a progressive and, on the whole, optimistic vision of history and its purposes. This vision often emphasized the negative aspects of the past, such as social inequality, structurally determined poverty, authoritarianism and injustice, and frequently tried to harness historical scholarship into the service of helping humanity escape from these evils. A critical understanding of the German past could thus help people to understand why Nazism had come to power, to eliminate its residues in the present, and to guard against its recurrence in the future.

History, in this view, was not just about politics, or society, or the economy, or culture, but had to take all these things into account and demonstrate how they related to one another. It needed social science theory to help it carry out this task. It was important to avoid giving absolute primacy to one particular aspect, whether the economy, as in 'vulgar Marxist' approaches, or high politics and diplomacy, as in traditional German historical scholarship. A theory that allowed historians to take account of the process of modernization without falling into anachronistic judgments of the past, a theory such as that of Max Weber, would facilitate a synthetic general account of the past that held all the disparate strands of political, social, economic and cultural history together and wove them into a common pattern leading to the present: a theory such as this was the only proper basis for understanding the German past.[13]

Thus, history became impossible without the social sciences; indeed, in the educational politics of West Germany in the 1970s, it came near to being replaced by the social sciences altogether, as it was pressed into the service of civic and political education. History, in this view, was an essential part of training for citizenship in a democratic society. And in carrying out this task, it had to make use of the latest sociological concepts, quantitative methods and conceptual innovations. History, indeed, was a social science; and the classic studies of modern Germany published during the 1970s and 1980s were characteristically filled with statistical tables and packed with terms borrowed from sociology, economics and political science. This was a modernist version of history, in which industrialization and economic growth were seen in positive terms as being linked with social mobility and civic freedom, and the task of German historians was seen as lying in the explanation of why this conjuncture did not happen in the German case until the 1950s and 1960s. Here again, as German exceptionalism came to an end, so too did German history; everything that happened since was a postscript.

But the 1980s have undermined many of the sociopolitical assumptions which underlay this modernist vision of history. It was, for example, a vision which saw the past mainly in class terms, and explained German history through the concept of changing relations between the nobility, the bourgeoisie, the urban and rural petty-bourgeoisie and the proletariat. Such a view was still by no means out of place in the 1950s. But by the 1980s it was becoming clear that the social antagonisms characteristic of classic industrial societies were yielding to more complex conflicts, as the industrial sector dwindled and post-industrial social structures came to the fore. Gender, ethnicity, generational identity, sexual orientation, all of which (even ethnicity) had been neglected by the modernist historians, began to attract historical research as they became more important in the present. Enthusiasm for modern industrial and scientific progress encountered widespread disillusion and criticism, as the environmental damage caused by unrestrained growth became ever more obvious. As the leading edge of research in the natural sciences shifted from chemistry and physics, space exploration and similar areas where the financial costs of technological gigantism were spiralling out of control, towards biology and medicine, where the practical returns were a good deal more obvious, criticism of unfettered scientific progress became increasingly vociferous, with protestors ranging from anti-vivisectionists and feminists at one extreme to religious fundamentalists and Catholic moralists at the other. Long-term mass unemployment added to these other factors to draw attention to the human costs of economic and scientific expansion and growth.

By the middle of the 1980s, it was clear that the present from whose perspective the modernist historians were writing itself now lay in the past. Moreover, the conceptual and methodological tools they had used were being rapidly superseded. Quantitative history – 'cliometrics' – which had promised such gains in historical accuracy and certainty when it arrived with the age of the computer, had proved a disappointment. Studies of voting patterns in modern German history, for example, had reached an undreamt-of pitch of methodological sophistication, but they left the central question of what voters thought they were doing when they cast their ballot, of what voting actually meant, and of why voters supported the parties they did, as mysterious as ever.[14] Social-scientific concepts, like the modernist architecture of the 1960s, neglected the human dimension and reduced the people of the past to anonymous categories. It seemed more important to reinstate subjective experience at the center of history than to continue the futile search for a conclusively scientific explanation of the objective factors thought to have determined people's behavior in the past.[15]

The new history in Germany – *Alltagsgeschichte* or the 'history of everyday life' – focused on values, beliefs, mentalities and lifestyles rather than structures, class antagonisms, or economic fluctuations. It directed attention away from attempts to describe and analyze the structures of whole societies and towards the experience of the individual, the community, the small group, to the forgotten victims of history instead of the big battalions.[16] German historians proved unable to satisfy the new demand of readers and publishers for studies of values and feeling, the history of the senses and the emotions, and the 1980s saw, therefore, a flood of translations of works on these subjects from French, Italian and English into German, until a French medievalist such as Georges Duby or Emmanuel Le Roy Ladurie became more widely read in German than most German medievalists were. A book such as Alain Corbin's history of smell in eighteenth- and nineteenth-century France became a best-seller; there was no German equivalent.[17]

In pursuit of these new objectives in history, new methods and concepts began to be developed. Most obvious was perhaps the emergence of oral history as a means of recapturing the subjective experience of people in the past. But the way that values and feelings are expressed, through language, has also moved increasingly to the center of historians' attention. The study of symbols, ceremonies and iconography has provided a new perspective on the meaning of political and social events and actions which the modernist historians took for granted as unproblematical. Literary analysis, poststructuralism, anthropology, semiotics, are taking the place of Weberian sociology and Marxist or Keynsian economics. Foucault has displaced Weber.[18]

Moreover, whereas it was commonplace in the 1960s and 1970s to speak of a decline in public historical consciousness, a 'crisis of history', expressed both in practical terms (old buildings were torn down, new shopping centers replaced old alleyways, and so on), and intellectually (social science was making the running and it often seemed difficult to justify the study of history at all, at least for its own sake), the 1980s have seen a dramatic revival of history. As we look around at the latest postmodern buildings or read the latest postmodern novels, it becomes clear that a central feature of postmodernism lies in the rediscovery of the past. Art, literature and architecture now make a point of abandoning the search for new forms so characteristic of modernism, and mix together pastiches of old styles and genres into a new synthesis instead. Conservative governments in Britain and the United States as well as West Germany preferred history to sociology, which itself entered a state of crisis in the 1980s. The notion of history as a foundation for a strengthened national consciousness in West Germany went well beyond the protagonists of the *Historikerstreit* and entered political discourse in events such as the ceremony at the Bitburg military cemetery in 1985, where Chancellor Kohl and US President Ronald Reagan honored Germany's soldiers of the Second World War. The postmodern emphasis on mentalities has had a political counterpart in the positive reassessment by conservative historians of the supposed virtues of the Prussian Junkers. And the heritage industry, the fashion for historical exhibitions and the conservation of historical remains, has taken its place in Germany as well as in other Western countries.[19]

Modernist history was dominated not only by social science theory and methodology but also by the demand for relevance, and in pursuit of this objective, German historians, especially those in the younger generation, shifted their attention increasingly to periods near to the present: first of all to the Weimar Republic and the Third Reich, then finally to the postwar years. But the demand for relevance had its own perils. The Third Reich and its origins may have been the most relevant part of German history to the progressive historians of the 1960s and 1970s, who had either experienced the Nazi years themselves as children or had to confront the involvement in it of their parents, but this could no longer be assumed in the case of history students and graduate researchers born in the 1960s. For this generation, indeed, the origins of the Federal

Republic were in many ways of more direct relevance, and this may help explain why so many of them turned to the postwar years for their research topics if they started work on a doctoral dissertation. It was precisely this worry – how to make the Nazi phenomenon relevant to a generation which had not experienced it even indirectly, through its parents – that underlay many of the attempts of proponents of *Alltagsgeschichte*, the 'history of everyday life', such as Martin Broszat and Detlev Peukert, to replace the tendency to create heroes and demons of so much historical writing on the Third Reich with an approach that recognized the people of the period as human beings, complex, divided, indecisive and often only dimly aware of the significance of their actions: as people, in other words, like us.[20]

By the 1980s, in other words, the relevance of the Third Reich could no longer be assumed, it had to be argued for. But in shifting the focus to problems such as the role of medicine and disease, sport and leisure, the media and entertainment, women and the family, homosexuality and deviance, religious belief, work, the treatment and experience of minorities, and so on, these historians were in fact accommodating the study of Nazi Germany to a much profounder shift in historical sensibility in which 'relevance' played no part at all. For the postmodern recovery of history, in addressing subjects such as identity, belief, experience and subjectivity, has been a recovery of history as a whole, in which, indeed, the people of remote periods may be of more interest than those of the recent past, precisely because the otherness of the physical and emotional world in which they lived illuminates the limits and possibilities of the human condition in a richer and more varied way. Hence the popularity of books such as *Montaillou* and the revival of interest in the history of the Middle Ages, pioneered at first by the translation into German of the work of French historians but now being followed up actively by the Germans themselves.[21] To put it more concretely: for someone whose interest in history is inspired by feminist convictions, and perhaps also feminist doubts, a study of the female body, and ideas about it, in the early eighteenth century, may be just as 'relevant' as a study of women's place in the Third Reich, because the alien quality of the subject will provide a larger and richer understanding of what it is to be a woman, and what the relationship is, or might be, between the physical condition of femaleness and the social construction of gender.[22]

These shifts of focus in historical scholarship and consciousness during the 1980s have dramatically increased the fragmentation of history that began with the modernist historians of a generation earlier. Social science history created a whole new series of specialisms, some of them, such as demographic or econometric history, highly technical and often impenetrable to the uninitiated, others, such as urban history or family history, apparently unrelated to the central problematic of German history as a whole. But the institutional structures of German academia and perhaps even more importantly the continuing centrality of the Third Reich as a problem to be tackled through a politically oriented history, ensured that this process did not go as far in Germany as it did in France or Britain. The history of religion continued to be the preserve of theology departments in German universities, the history of medicine of medical schools, legal history of law departments, and so on, while mainstream historical scholarship oriented itself towards the 'social history of politics', not of other things.[23]

It was only in the 1980s that these institutional barriers began to crumble, that social historians in Germany began to take an interest in subjects such as disease, popular religion, divorce, or superstition. The result has been the undermining of any consensus over what the history of modern Germany is actually about. Even in the contributions to the present book, for example, the beginnings of this process of fragmentation can be seen; for while the majority of contributions still focus on rival grand narratives of the Nazi period and its origins in the nineteenth century, some of them deal with quite different problems, such as the role of women in German history, the economic development of modern Germany, or the culture of the Weimar Republic. The enterprise of 'reconsidering' modern Germany is still possible on the basis of the sociopolitical historiography of the 1960s and 1970s, and even to some extent that of the 1980s, but in the 1990s it will only be achievable on the basis of ignoring an increasing quantity of historical scholarship on modern Germany and focusing on an area – political history – that is itself becoming a specialism, and only one among many.

THE FUTURE

The study of modern German history was already undergoing profound changes, then, in the second half of the 1980s. In 1989, however, it was given a further jolt by the dramatic events that took place in East Germany: the fall of the Honecker regime, the breaching of the Berlin Wall, and then, in 1990, the final collapse of communism and the advent of German reunification. In many ways it is too early to judge the effect of these events on the study of German history. Nevertheless, a few things are clear. First, the rapid end of the East German state took everyone by surprise. Despite the evident discontent that had been simmering in the German Democratic Republic for some time – especially since the rigged municipal elections of the previous spring – and the growing numbers of citizens clamoring to leave, nothing significant happened until Soviet President Gorbachev publicly withdrew his support for the Honecker regime in October 1989. It was only the assurance that they were now in charge of their own destinies, that whatever happened, Russian tanks would not come rolling out onto the streets as they had done during the uprising of 1953, that galvanized the people of East Germany into action.

Thus the German revolution was made principally in East Germany; the West merely reacted. Historians were as surprised as anyone else by these events. The *Historikerstreit* had died down by 1989. The political thrust behind the attempt of neo-conservative West German historians in the mid-1980s to relativize the Third Reich and its misdeeds was directed towards strengthening the political backbone of West Germans against the alleged threat from the East. In the atmosphere of renewed anti-communist militancy encouraged in the NATO countries in the early years of the Reagan presidency in the USA – the years when Reagan was describing the Soviet Union as an 'evil empire' and pushing hard for increased military expenditure on the Star Wars program and the stationing of a new generation of nuclear weapons, including Cruise and Pershing missiles, in West Germany and other European countries – conservatives in Europe and America found the strength of popular resistance to these developments in West Germany deeply worrying. Indeed, one of the neo-conservative protagonists of the *Historikerstreit*, Michael Stürmer, thought that West German public opinion was so lacking in self-confidence that it was already falling victim to a campaign of fear and hate waged by the East in the global civil war against democracy, while another, the late Andreas Hillgruber, compared East Germany to the nineteenth-century Italian state of Piedmont, under whose leadership Italian unification had taken place and under whose institutions united Italy was eventually governed.[24]

The debate in question was not without its implications for an eventual reunification of Germany, as indeed Hillgruber's anxieties implied. If, as the neo-conservatives wanted, German national pride was strengthened by a lessening of the burden of the German past, by the view that Germany had nothing more to be ashamed of in its past than any other nation had, then the objective of reunification would undoubtedly gain in legitimacy. Such considerations may well have been present in the support given by the conservative daily newspaper the *Frankfurter Allgemeine Zeitung* for 'new revisionism' of this kind in the mid-1980s, given the fact that the newspaper was also showing considerable enthusiasm for the idea of a reunified Germany.[25] But on the whole the theme of reunification was of only secondary importance, a distant implication rather than a present concern. The main thrust of the neo-conservative historians' arguments was to strengthen anti-com-munism inside West Germany itself.

These arguments had already died down by the time of the revolution in East Germany in November 1989. By this time, the entire international scene had been transformed beyond recognition. Disarmament rather than rearmament was now the order of the day. The Soviet Union no longer appeared to be a serious threat to peace, and the claim that it was sweeping all before it in a global civil war against democracy appeared simply absurd. German reunification confirmed and deepened these changes and consigned the *Historikerstreit* and the political thrust behind it even more decisively to the past. But many of the opponents of the neo-conservatives were overtaken by events too. Those who, such as Heinrich August Winkler, declared that Germany's past made German reunification and the creation of a nation–state unnecessary and undesirable, as well as those who proclaimed that Germany had become a 'post-national' society in which regional identities at one level, and a European consciousness at another, had effectively superseded identification with a German nation, were proved equally wrong.[26]

The way in which German reunification took place gave the lie to the argument that German national self-confidence needed strengthening for such an event to happen. For the majority of East Germans, indeed, the justification for the assertion of identity with the West Germans lay primarily in the possibility it opened up of sharing in the prosperity and affluence that had been the hallmark of life in the Federal Republic for so long. In addition, unification seemed the quickest and most painless way to secure the civil rights and freedoms that had been denied to them for decades. In the mid-1980s, debate had raged between those who, like Stürmer, said that a shared national and cultural identity was the only basis on which the West German political system could strengthen its popular legitimacy, and those who, like the sociologist and philosopher Jürgen Habermas, argued that the West German constitution, the 'Basic Law' of 1949, was a satisfactory, indeed a superior, substitute. The attitude of the East Germans seemed to prove them both right.[27]

What took place was, initially at least, less a true unification than an *Anschluss*, the wholesale incorporation of East Germany into the West. Despite fears of what the East Germans' lack of experience in democratic ways might lead to, they are after all only 16 million people in a nation of nearly 80 million. While it is in some respects regrettable that the Federal Republic has not taken the opportunity to embark on a critical self-examination of its own institutions, and while the atmosphere of witch-hunting for supposed communist police agents and of the arrogant assumption that West Germans should determine which of the former East Germans should have access to these institutions and which should not, is distasteful, the fact of *Anschluss* has at least one major benefit in the context of dealing with the past, that is the probable extension across the whole of the reunited country of the current historiographical culture of the West. German historians, in other words, are not going to stop confronting the Nazi past just because of reunification.

If anything, indeed, current trends are likely to be strengthened by recent events. The addition to the Federal Republic of areas such as Saxony, where the environmental and other costs of industrialism are even more obvious than they have been in the West, the discrediting of the most teleologically optimistic of modernist approaches to history – Marxism-Leninism – and similar developments, will probably further weaken the influence of modernism over our German views of the past. Reunification has not given rise to a celebratory cult of Germanness; rather, it has led to a worried questioning of what being German actually means. As the inhabitants of the two halves of Germany have got to know each other, the differences between them have become as obvious as the similarities. At the same time regional allegiances have undergone a strong renaissance in areas such as Mecklenburg or Saxony. As a result, the classically postmodern concern with identity – regional, national, gender, class, generational, and so on – has moved even more decisively to the forefront of German historiography.

Even more striking, though as yet hardly explored, is the effect that reunification has on concepts of continuity in German history. On one level, of course, it makes 1945 seem even less of a turning point than it was already being depicted as by the late 1980s. The postwar division of Germany turns out, with the exception of Austrian independence, not to have been permanent after all. German history did not come to an end in 1945. Rather, the events of 1989 suggest that changing boundaries and state forms have been a feature of German history all along. However long they last, the boundaries of 1989 are unlikely to be regarded as the natural boundaries of Germany in the way that those of 1871 were for so long. All this places the question of national identity even more firmly at the center of the agenda. But it also divorces it more than ever before from the question of the state and its boundaries, and reveals it to have been – and to be – a mutable, contingent, changing thing.

All the indications so far are that German unification will speed the process of European integration and thereby integrate Germany and its intellectual culture more firmly into a broader European context. For historians this will mean not only a further quickening of the pace of the international exchange of ideas, through conferences, journals, translations of books, and the like, but also a progressive reorientation of historical study away from the national paradigm. These and other processes seem likely to be accelerated, in other words, rather than interrupted or reversed by the events of 1989–90. In the course of these changes, the place of the Third Reich and its origins in historical writing and research will change too. But it will not disappear. Rather than form the dominating centerpiece of a grand narrative of German history, it will more probably come to permeate, inform, or insert itself into the many different narratives which historians construct, according to the way in which they approach the German past or use it to illuminate wider human problems.

The Third Reich is not going to go away, but it is likely to assert itself in the writing of German history in a more varied manner than before, if only because the writing of German history is itself becoming more varied. But this does not mean that the challenge it poses to historical understanding is becoming any easier, still less that it is going to be evaded. The indications are that German historians are fully aware of the fact that unification demands a continuing open and honest confrontation with the German past. That the perspectives from which this confrontation takes place are becoming more diverse is part of history's richness as a subject. It should not be a cause for alarm or despondency, rather the reverse.

NOTES

1   For some reflections on these issues, see Hagen Schulze, *Gibt es überhaupt eine deutsche Geschichte?* (Berlin, 1989); John Breuilly, 'Nation and nationalism in modern German history', *Historical Journal*, vol. 33 (1990), pp. 659–75; Harold James, *A German Identity 1790–1990* (London, 1989); and on the development of German historiography more generally, Richard J. Evans, *Rethinking German History* (London, 1987).

2   Martin Broszat *et al.* (eds), *Von Stalingrad zur Währungsreform* (Munich, 1988), gives a useful selection of this work.

3   See for example the changing research focus of V.R. Berghahn, from *Der Tirpitz-Plan* (Düsseldorf, 1971) to *The Americanization of German Industry 1945–1965* (London, 1987).

4   Martin Broszat, *Nach Hitler: Der schwierige Umgang mit unserer Geschichte*, ed. Hermann Graml and Klaus-Dietmar Henke (Munich, 1987). For a penetrating critique of Broszat's argument, see Dieter Langewiesche, 'Der "Historikerstreit" und die "Historisierung" des Nationalsozialismus', in Klaus Oesterle and Siegfried Schulze (eds), *Historikerstreit und politische Bildung* (Stuttgart, 1989), pp. 20–40. See also the exchange of views in Martin Broszat and Saul Friedländer, 'A controversy about the historicization of national socialism', *New German Critique*, vol. 44 (1988), pp. 85–126. For a cogent defence of Broszat's position, see Ian Kershaw, *The Nazi Dictatorship*, 2nd edn (London, 1989), pp. 150–67.

5   Broszat, *Nach Hitler*, pp. 68–91 and 159–73.

6   Ernst Nolte, 'Vergangenheit, die nicht vergehen will', in Nolte, *Das Vergehen der Vergangenheit* 2nd edn, (Berlin, 1988), pp. 171–8; also Nolte, *Der europäische Bürgerkrieg 1917–1945: Nationalsozialismus und Bolschewismus* (Frankfurt, 1987), esp. pp. 181–5, 190, 204–9, 240, 317–18, 393, 517.

7   The literature on this subject is too large to be thoroughly documented here. For introductory surveys in English, see Richard J. Evans, *In Hitler's Shadow. West German Historians and the Attempt to Escape from the Nazi Past* (New York, 1989); Charles S. Maier, *The Unmasterable Past. History, Holocaust, and German National Identity* (Cambridge, Mass., 1988); Kershaw, *The Nazi Dictatorship*, pp. 168–91; Geoff Eley, 'Nazism, politics and the image of the

past: thoughts on the West German Historikerstreit 1986–1987', *Past and Present*, no. 121 (1988), pp. 171–208.

8 Saul Friedländer, 'West Germany and the burden of the past: the ongoing debate', *Jerusalem Quarterly*, vol. 42 (1987), pp. 3–18; idem, 'Some reflections on the historicization of National Socialism', *Tel Aviv Jahrbuch für deutsche Geschichte* vol. 16 (1987), pp. 310–24; Kershaw, *The Nazi Dictatorship*, pp. 150–91; Langewiesche, 'Der "Historikerstreit"'.

9 Thomas Nipperdey, 'Wehlers "Kaiserreich". Eine kritische Auseinandersetzung', *Geschichte und Gesellschaft*, vol. 1 (1975), pp. 539–40; Hans-Günther Zmarzlik, 'Das Kaiserreich in neuer Sicht?,' *Historische Zeitschrift*, vol. 222 (1976), pp. 105–26; idem, 'Das Kaiserreich als Einbahnstrasse?', in Karl Holl and Günther List (eds), *Liberalismus und imperialistischer Staat* (Göttingen, 1976), pp. 62–71 are all early examples of this trend.

10 For examples of such work see Ingo Müller, *Furchtbare Juristen* (Frankfurt, 1988); Benno Müller-Hill, *Tödliche Wissenschaft* (Reinbek, 1984); Christian Streit, *Keine Kameraden* (Stuttgart, 1978).

11 Detlev Peukert, *Inside Nazi Germany. Conformity and Opposition in Everyday Life* (London, 1987). See also Jürgen Kocka, 'Klassen oder Kultur? Durchbrüche und Sackgassen in der Alltagsgeschichte', *Merkur*, vol. 36 (1982), pp. 955–65; Martin Broszat, 'Plädoyer für Alltagsgeschichte', *Merkur*, vol. 36 (1989), pp. 1244–8.

12 Georg Iggers (ed.), *The Social History of Politics: Critical Perspectives in West German Historical Writing since 1945* (Leamington Spa, 1985), has a useful introduction surveying this situation.

13 Hans-Ulrich Wehler, *Aus der Geschichte lernen?* (Munich, 1988), esp. pp. 115–30.

14 For a guide to this situation, see Elizabeth Harvey, 'Elections, mass politics and social change in Germany 1890–1945: new perspectives', conference report in *German History*, vol. 8 (1990), pp. 325–33, and the forthcoming conference volume of the same title, edited by James N. Retallack (New York, 1992).

15 See the debate in Franz-Josef Brüggemeier and Jürgen Kocka (eds), *'Geschichte von unten – Geschichte von innen.' Kontroversen um die Alltagsgeschichte* (Hagen, 1985).

16 Gert Zang, *Die unaufhaltsame Annäherung an das Einzelne* (Konstanz, 1985).

17 Alain Corbin, *Pesthauch und Blütenduft* (Berlin, 1984).

18 See in general Lynn Hunt (ed.), *The New Cultural History* (Berkeley, Calif., 1989).

19 For a useful general discussion in the British context, see Raphael Samuel, 'The Return of History', *London Review of Books*, 14 June 1990, pp. 9–12. See also the discussion of exhibitions in *German History*, vol. 1 (1984), and the account of Bitburg in Evans, *In Hitler's Shadow*, pp. 16–17.

20 Broszat, *Nach Hitler*, esp. pp. 68–91; Peukert, *Inside Nazi Germany*.

21 For a significant pointer in these directions, see Hans Medick and David Sabean (eds), *Emotion and Material Interest* (Cambridge, 1985).

22 Barbara Duden, *Geschichte unter der Haut* (Munich, 1987).

23 See for example Wolfgang Schieder, 'Religion in the social history of the modern world', *European Studies Review*, vol. 12 (1982), pp. 289–99.

24 Evans, *In Hitler's Shadow*, pp. 21–2.

25 Hermannus Pfeiffer (ed.), *Die FAZ: Nachforschungen über ein Zentralorgan* (Cologne, 1988).

26 Heinrich August Winkler, 'Auf ewig in Hitlers Schatten?', in R. Piper (ed.), *'Historikerstreit'. Die Dokumentation der Kontroverse um die Einzigartigkeit der nationalsozialistischen Judenvernichtung* (Munich, 1987), pp. 256–63; Jürgen Habermas, *Eine Art Schadensabwicklung* (Frankfurt, 1987), esp. pp. 159–79.

27 Michael Stürmer, *Dissonanzen des Fortschritts* (Munich, 1986); see also the record of Stürmer's views in Hilmar Hoffmann (ed.), *Gegen den Versuch, Vergangenheit zu verbiegen: Eine Diskussion um politische Kultur in der Bundesrepublik aus Anlass der Frankfurter Römerberggespräche 1986* (Frankfurt, 1986); and Habermas, *Eine Art*.

13 *Bibliographical Essay*

TRACEY J. KAY

GENERAL WORKS

The vast majority of general works on modern Germany necessarily take more or less the same approach: they are essentially narrative accounts that concentrate on political history. Such works usually focus on unification, the establishment and maintenance of the Bismarckian Reich, the fall of this structure under the bumbling efforts of Bismarck's successors and the slow downward slide to the catastrophe of Nazism. Under this approach one can list: William A. Carr, *A History of Germany 1815–1945*, 2nd edn (London: St. Martins Press, 1979); Gordon A. Craig, *Germany 1866–1945* (New York: Oxford University Press, 1978); Hajo Holborn, *A History of Modern Germany 1840–1945* (Princeton, NJ: Princeton University Press, 1969); Agatha Ramm, *Germany 1789–1919: A Political History* (London: Methuen, 1968); Koppel S. Pinson, *Modern Germany: Its History and Civilization*, 2nd edn (New York: Macmillan, 1966); and Golo Mann, *The History of Germany since 1789* (New York: Praeger, 1968).

With the shift in emphasis to social history in the 1970s a few general works attempted to incorporate this theme. One of the first to do so was Volker R. Berghahn in his *Modern Germany: Society, Economy and Politics in the Twentieth Century* (Cambridge: Cambridge University Press, 1982), which is, nevertheless, a political narrative interspersed with a few notes on various social and economic factors. On the other hand, Eda Sagarra, *A Social History of Germany 1648–1914* (London: Methuen, 1977) attempts to create a completely different type of general survey. Unfortunately, while providing an interesting look at the life of the elites in nineteenth-century Germany, she manages to give only a cursory overview of the period in general.

A very different type of survey is that which concentrates on the

German people and, in particular, on the 'German mind'; see Gordon A. Craig, *The Germans* (New York: Meridian, 1982), for a noteworthy example. And consider the thematic overview of Joan Campbell in *Joy in Work, German Work: The National Debate, 1800–1945* (Princeton, NJ: Princeton University Press, 1989).

On the interpretation of Germany and German history see: Ralf Dahrendorf, *Society and Democracy in Germany* (New York: Doubleday, 1968); David Calleo, *The German Problem Reconsidered: Germany and the World Order, 1870–1945* (Cambridge: Cambridge University Press, 1978); and David Blackbourn and Geoff Eley, *The Pecularities of German History: Bourgeois Society and Politics in Nineteenth Century Germany* (Oxford: Oxford University Press, 1984).

BISMARCKIAN GERMANY

Although no bibliography can pretend to offer a comprehensive listing of all the literature on Bismarckian Germany, it is possible to point out some of the main issues of interest to scholars in recent years and the literature related to them. A good starting point for anyone interested in the historiography of the period is Geoff Eley and David Blackbourn, *The Peculiarities of German History: Bourgeois Society and Politics in Nineteenth Century Germany* (Oxford: Oxford University Press, 1984).

While the historiography of the Bismarckian period clearly reflects the drift away from studies of elite politics and toward the history of everyday life, there is still considerable interest with the era's main actor: the standard biographies of Bismarck remain A.J.P. Taylor, *Bismarck: The Man and the Statesman* (New York: Knopf, 1955) and Otto Pflanze, *Bismarck and the Development of Germany, 1815–1871* (Princeton, NJ: Princeton University Press, 1963). For more interesting and challenging accounts see Lothar Gall, *Bismarck: The White Revolutionary*, 2 vols (London: Allen & Unwin, 1980) and Fritz Stern, *Gold and Iron: Bismarck, Bleichröder and the Building of the German Empire* (New York: Alfred A. Knopf, 1977). See also the essay by A. Mitchell, 'Bonapartism as a model for Bismarckian politics', *Journal of Modern History*, 49 (1977), pp. 181–99.

For a general survey of the early Bismarckian period, Theodore S. Hamerow, *The Social Foundations of German Unification, 1858–1871* (Princeton, NJ: Princeton University Press, 1968) remains a reliable account. See also the applicable sections of Martin Kitchen, *The Political Economy of Germany, 1815–1914* (Montreal: McGill University Press, 1978) and of Richard Evans, *Death in Hamburg: Society and Politics in the Cholera Years 1830–1910* (Oxford: Oxford University Press, 1987). For the period following unification see Hans-Ulrich Wehler, *The*

German Empire, 1871–1918 (Leamington Spa: Berg, 1980) and the older, yet still relevant, account by Arthur Rosenberg, *Imperial Germany: The Birth of the German Republic, 1871–1918* (English tr., Boston, Mass: Beacon Press, 1964).

A considerable amount of scholarship has been devoted to questions concerning the role and influence of the so-called 'silent majority' in politics. On this topic see: J.C. Hunt, 'Peasants, tariffs and meat quotas: imperial German protectionism reexamined', *Central European History*, 7 (1974), pp. 311–31; David Blackbourn, 'Peasants and politics in Germany, 1871–1914', *European History Quarterly*, 14 (1984), pp. 47–75; and Blackbourn, 'The Mittelstand in German society and politics, 1871–1914', *Social History*, 2 (1977), pp. 409–33.

The socioeconomic development of Bismarckian Germany remains a matter of considerable contention. On this topic see Hans Rosenberg, 'Political and social consequences of the Great Depression of 1873–1896 in central Europe', *Economic History Review*, 13 (1943), pp. 58–73 and the critique by Geoff Eley, 'Hans Rosenberg and the Great Depression of 1873–1896: politics and economics in recent German historiography, 1960–1980', in Eley, *From Unification to Nazism: Reinterpreting the German Past* (London: Unwin Hyman, 1986). See also Helmut Böhme, 'Big business pressure groups and Bismarck's turn to protectionism, 1873–1879', *Historical Journal*, 10 (1967), pp. 218–36 and Ivo N. Lambi, *Free Trade and Protection in Germany* (Wiesbaden: F. Steiner, 1963). See also David F. Crew, *Town in the Ruhr: A Social History of Bochum 1860–1914* (New York: Columbia University Press, 1979).

The middle class in Bismarckian Germany has attracted a great deal of attention in recent years. A good place to begin is the collection of essays edited by David Blackbourn and Richard Evans, *The German Bourgeoisie* (London: Oxford University Press, 1989). See also E.K. Bramsted, *Aristocracy and the Middle Classes in Germany* (Chicago: University of Chicago Press, 1964). This is, however, only an introduction to a topic upon which the literature is immense. On the working class see Michael J. Neufeld, *The Skilled Metalworkers of Nuremberg: Craft and Class in the Industrial Revolution* (New Brunswick, NJ: Rutgers University Press, 1989).

The political history of the Bismarckian period has not gone unstudied in recent years, with major works appearing on most major, and some minor, political parties. The social democrats have received perhaps the most attention: G. Roth, *The Social Democrats in Imperial Germany: A Study in Working Class Isolation and National Integration* (Totowa, N.J: Barnes & Noble, 1963); Vernon T. Lidtke, *The Outlawed Party, 1878–1890* (Princeton, NJ: Princeton University Press, 1966); and the related work by John A. Moses, *German Trade Unionism from Bismarck to Hitler*, 2 vols (Totowa, NJ: Barnes & Noble, 1981). The Centre Party has also received considerable attention, mainly from historians who argue that the political parties of Bismarckian Germany were not merely ineffective dupes of a neo-feudal state. See J.K. Zeender, *The German Center Party, 1880–1906* (Philadelphia, Pa: American Philosophical Society, 1976) and Jonathan Sperber, *Popular Catholicism in Nineteenth Century Germany* (Princeton, NJ: Princeton University Press, 1984). On the conservatives see James N. Retallack, *Notables of the Right: The Conservative Party and Political Mobilization in Germany, 1876–1918* (Boston, Mass: Unwin Hyman, 1988). On the liberals see Dan S. White, *The Splintered Party: National Liberalism in Hessen and the Reich, 1867–1918* (Cambridge, Mass.: Harvard University Press, 1976), and Gordon Mork, 'Bismarck and the "capitulation" of German liberalism', *Journal of Modern History*, 43 (1971), pp. 59–75.

There are also several excellent collections of essays on the Bismarckian period. Among the best are: David Blackbourn, *Populists and Patricians: Essays in Modern German History* (London: Allen & Unwin, 1987); James J. Sheehan (ed.), *Imperial Germany* (New York: New Viewpoints, 1976); and the relevent sections of Geoff Eley, *From Unification to Nazism: Reinterpreting the German Past* (London: Unwin Hyman, 1986).

WILHELMINE GERMANY

Since a good deal of the general material in the preceding section also dealt with the Wilhelmine period there is no need to repeat those titles here. Instead, this section will focus on works pertaining exclusively to the Wilhelmine period. One of the major themes of post-Bismarckian literature concerns the perceived lack of effective leadership under Wilhelm II. On this topic see J.C.G. Röhl, *Germany without Bismarck: The Crisis of Government in the Second Reich* (Berkeley, Calif.: University of California Press, 1967) and J. Alden Nichols, *Germany after Bismarck: The Caprivi Era, 1890–1894* (Cambridge, Mass: Harvard University Press, 1958). See also the essays in Röhl and Nicolaus Sombart (eds), *Kaiser Wilhelm II: New Interpretations* (Cambridge: Cambridge University Press, 1982) and the work of Isabel Hull, *The Entourage of Kaiser Wilhelm II, 1888–1918* (Cambridge: Cambridge University Press, 1982). On the Bethmann-Hollweg era see the invaluable work of Konrad H. Jarausch, *The Enigmatic Chancellor: Bethmann-Hollweg and the Hubris of Imperial Germany* (New Haven, Conn., and London: Yale University Press, 1973).

The historiography of the Wilhelmine period, like that of its predecessor, is intensely concerned with developments among the major political parties and organizations. For a general overview of this topic see Stanley Suval, *Electoral Politics in Wilhelmine Germany* (Chapel Hill, NC: University of North Carolina Press, 1985). There is also considerable material on individual parties: for the social democrats see Molly Nolan, *Social Democracy and Society: Working Class Radicalism in Düsseldorf, 1890–1920* (Cambridge: Cambridge University Press, 1981) and Carl E. Schorske, *German Social Democracy, 1905–1917: The Development of the Great Schism* (Cambridge, Mass.: Harvard University Press, 1975); for the Center Party see David Blackbourn, *Class, Religion and Local Politics in Wilhelmine Germany: The Centre Party in Württemberg before 1914* (New Haven, Conn., and London: Yale University Press, 1980), Ellen L. Evans, *The German Center Party, 1890–1933* (Urbana, Ill.: Southern Illinois University Press, 1981), and R.J. Ross, *The Beleaguered Tower: The Dilemma of Political Catholicism in Wilhelmine Germany* (Notre Dame, Indiana: Notre Dame University Press, 1976). On other political groupings, formal and informal, see: Geoff Eley, *Reshaping the Radical Right: Radical Nationalism and Political Change after Bismarck* (New Haven, Conn., and London: Yale University Press, 1980); John C. Hunt, *The People's Party in Württemberg and Southern Germany, 1890–1914* (Stuttgart: Klett, 1975); A.J. Peck, *Radicals and Reactionaries: The Crisis of Conservatism in Wilhelmine Germany* (Washington, DC: The University Press of America, 1978); and B. Heckart, *From Bassermann to Bebel: The Grand Bloc's Quest for Reform in the Kaiserreich 1900–1914* (New Haven, Conn.: Yale University Press, 1974).

Wilhelmine historiography is not, however, exclusively preoccupied with the political elites and the growing interest in everyday life is now very much in evidence. See especially the essays in Richard J. Evans (ed.), *The German Working Class 1888–1945: The Politics of Everyday Life* (London: Croom Helm, 1982) and in Evans (ed.), *The Feminist Movement in Germany 1894–1933* (London: Sage, 1976). For other aspects of Wilhelmine social history see: Robert Gellately, *The Politics of Economic Despair: Shopkeepers and German Politics 1890–1914* (London: Sage, 1974); Stephen Hickey, *Workers in Imperial Germany: Miners in the Ruhr* (Oxford: Oxford University Press, 1985); and the works of Roger Chickering: *We Men Who Feel Most German: A Cultural Study of the Pan-German League* (Boston: Allen & Unwin, 1984), *Imperial Germany and a World without War* (Princeton, NJ: Princeton University Press, 1975) and Marilyn Shevin Coetzee, *The German Army League: Popular Nationalism in Wilhelmine Germany* (Oxford: Oxford University Press, 1990).

The relationship between domestic and foreign policy, especially in light of the events of July 1914, has increasingly preoccupied historians of the Wilhelmine period. For two early interpretations of this problem see the work of Eckart Kehr: *Economic Interest, Militarism and Foreign Policy* (tr. Grete Heinz, Berkeley, Calif.: University of California Press,

1970) and Pauline R. Anderson and Eugene N. Anderson (eds), *Battleship-Building and Party Politics in Germany 1894–1901* (Chicago: University of Chicago Press, 1973); as well as that of Ludwig Dehio, *Germany and World Politics in the Twentieth Century* (New York, Norton: 1959). For more recent work see: Geoff Eley, 'Sammlungspolitik, social imperialism and the navy law of 1898', *Militärgeschichtliche Mitteilungen*, 15 (1974), pp. 29–63; Holger Herwig, *'Luxury Fleet': The Imperial German Navy 1888–1918* (London: Allen & Unwin, 1980); Paul Kennedy, *The Rise of the Anglo-German Antagonism, 1860–1914* (London: Allen & Unwin, 1980); and Wolfgang Mommsen, 'Domestic factors in German foreign policy before 1914', *Central European History*, 6 (March 1973), pp. 11–43.

INDUSTRY, EMPIRE AND THE FIRST WORLD WAR

Unfortunately, most of the debate specifically related to the Fischer controversy has taken place in German. The most useful introduction to the debate, in English, remains John Moses, *The Politics of Illusion* (London: Prior, 1975). Fischer's own work, especially *Germany's Aims in the First World War* (New York: Norton, 1961) and *War of Illusion* (New York: Norton, 1969), continues to be provocative and challenging. For the point of view that inspired Fischer to put forward his own interpretation, see Gerhard Ritter, *The German Problem* (Chicago: Ohio State University Press, 1965). A more sophisticated version of the Ritter thesis can be found in Konrad Jarausch, '"The Illusion of limited war" Chancellor Bethmann Hollweg's calculated risk, July 1914', *Central European History*, 2 (1969), pp. 48–76. One of the most ardent defences of Fischer can be found in Volker Berghahn, *Germany and the Approach of War in 1914* (New York: Macmillan, 1973). A recent report on the status of the controversy can be found in David Kaiser's article, 'Germany and the origins of the First World War', *Journal of Modern History*, 55 (September 1983), pp. 442–74. On the impact of and reaction to Fischer's work in Germany see Holger H. Herwig, 'Clio deceived: patriotic self-censorship in Germany after the Great War', *International Security*, 12 (1987), pp. 5–44. In German, see the work of one of Fischer's students, Helmut Böhme, *Deutschlands Weg zur Groß macht*, 2nd edn (Köln: Kiepenheuer & Witsch, 1972) and also Arnold Swyottek's essay, 'Die Fischer-Kontroverse', in I. Geiss and B.-J. Wendt (eds), *Deutschland in der Weltpolitik des 19. und 20. Jahrhunderts* (Düsseldorf: Bertelsmann, 1973).

A considerable amount of work has been devoted to demonstrating that German imperialism was essentially a way for pre-industrial elites to avoid the social reforms which usually accompanied industrialization. For a pre-Bielefeld exposition of this thesis see Ludwig Dehio, *Germany and World Politics in the Twentieth Century* (New York: Norton, 1959). The most thorough discourse on this subject is, Hans-Ulrich Wehler, *The German Empire, 1871–1918* (English tr., K. Trayner, Leamington Spa: Berg, 1985). Wehler's ideas are summarized clearly in his articles on 'Bismarck's imperialism 1862–1890', *Past and Present*, no. 48 (1970), pp. 119–55 and 'Industrial growth and early German imperialism', in R. Owen and B. Sutcliffe (eds), *Studies in the Theory of Imperialism* (London: Longman, 1972), pp. 71–92. See also Paul Kennedy, *The Rise of the Anglo-German Antagonism* (London: Allen & Unwin, 1980) and Imanuel Geiss, *The Outbreak of the First World War* (New York: St. Martins Press, 1974). Geiss also addresses the ideological and psychological influences on German foreign policy. For a concise summary of this argument see Wolfgang Mommsen, 'Domestic factors in German foreign policy before 1914', *Central European History*, 6 (March 1973), pp. 11–43.

Recent revisionist work has questioned the whole idea of foreign policy as a way to offset latent domestic tension. Younger scholars have particularly objected to the assertion that pre-industrial elites had the ability to manipulate nationalism so efficiently as to divert attention from pressing internal concerns; see Geoff Eley, *Reshaping the German Right: Radical Nationalism after Bismarck* (New Haven, Conn.: Yale University Press, 1980) and David Schoenbaum, *Zabern 1913: Consensus Politics in Imperial Germany* (Boston, Mass.: Allen & Unwin, 1982).

THE WEIMAR REPUBLIC

The historiographical debate concerning the culture of the Weimar years has been intensely political and no consensus has been reached. Weimar culture is variously characterized as the triumph of the sons over the fathers, or used as proof of the strength of the fathers and the weakness of the sons. That is, on the one hand historians have used Weimar culture as proof of the rise of cultural modernity in Germany, while others point to the persistence of traditional culture even in an era of political change. Weimar culture can be regarded as either the harbinger of the modern era in Germany or the co-conspirator in the rise of Hitler.

On the persistence of tradition, namely, the irrational and the anti-modern, the works of George L. Mosse, *The Crisis of German Ideology: The Intellectual Origins of the Third Reich* (New York: Fertig, 1964) and Fritz Stern, *The Politics of Cultural Despair: A Study in the Rise of the Germanic Ideology* (Berkeley, Calif.: University of California Press, 1961), remain useful. Likewise Konrad Jarausch's work on academic illiberalism, *Students, Society and Politics in Imperial Germany* (Princeton, NJ:

Princeton University Press, 1982), remains an invaluable study of the anti-modern currents in German society.

On the side of modernity, Peter Gay, *Weimar Culture: The Outsider as Insider* (Westport, Conn.: Greenwood Press, 1968), offers a look at the aspects of Weimar culture which were 'new', if not unprecedented. The recent work of Modris Eksteins, *Rites of Spring: The Great War and the Birth of the Modern Age* (Toronto: Lester & Orpen Dennys, 1989) offers a persuasive argument for the 'modernity' case.

On modernism and its most cultural counterpart, expressionism, see: Peter Paret, *The Berlin Secession: Modernism and its Enemies in Imperial Germany* (Cambridge, Mass.: Harvard University Press, 1980); P. Jelavich, *Munich and Theatrical Modernism: Politics, Playwriting and Performance 1896–1914* (Cambridge, Mass.: Harvard University Press, 1985); B. Myers, *The German Expressionists: A Generation in Revolt* (New York: Praeger, 1957); Lotte Eisner, *The Haunted Screen: Expressionism in the German Cinema and the Influence of Max Reinhardt* (Berkeley, Calif.: University of California Press, 1969); and the essays in S.E. Bronner and D. Kellner (eds), *Passion and Rebellion: The Expressionist Heritage* (New York: Bergin & Garvey, 1988). For a study which attempts to argue both sides of the modernist/conservative point of view see J. Herf, *Reactionary Modernism: Technology, Culture, and Politics in Weimar and the Third Reich* (Cambridge: Cambridge University Press, 1984).

On the more specific question of the relationship between politics and culture see the essays in Keith Bullivant (ed.), *Culture and Society in the Weimar Republic* (Manchester: Manchester University Press, 1982), and the essays in Anthony Phelan (ed.), *The Weimar Dilemma: Intellectuals and the Weimar Republic* (Manchester: Manchester University Press, 1985), especially Stephen Lamb, 'Intellectuals and the challenge of power: the case of the Munich "Räterepublik"', pp. 132–61. See also Robin Lenman, 'Politics and culture: the state and the avant-garde in Munich, 1886–1914', in Richard Evans, *Society and Politics in Wilhelmine Germany* (London: Croom Helm, 1978); John Willett, *Art and Politics in the Weimar Period: The New Sobriety, 1917–1933* (Chapel Hill, NC: University of North Carolina Press, 1988); Istvàn Deàk, *Weimar Germany's Left-Wing Intellectuals: A Political History of the Weltbühne and its Critics* (Berkeley and Los Angeles, Calif.: University of California Press, 1968); Barbara Miller Lane, *Architecture and Politics in Germany 1918–1945* (Cambridge, Mass.: Harvard University Press, 1985); Paul Pörtner, 'The writer's revolution: Munich 1918–19', *Journal of Contemporary History*, 3 (1968); George L. Mosse and S.G. Lampert, 'Weimar intellectuals and the rise of national socialism', in J.E. Dimsdales (ed.), *Survivors, Victims, and Perpetrators: Essays on the Nazi Holocaust* (New York: Hemisphere, 1980); and the study by Joan Weinstein, *The End of Expressionism: Art and the November Revolution in Germany, 1918–1919*

(Chicago: University of Chicago Press, 1990). On working-class culture, consider Peter D. Stachura, *The Weimar Republic and the Younger Proletariat: An Economic and Social Analysis* (London: Macmillan, 1990) and Peter Fritzsche, *Rehearsals for Fascism: Populism and Political Mobilization in Weimar Germany* (Oxford: Oxford University Press, 1990) and W.L. Guttsman, *Workers' Culture in Weimar Germany: Between Tradition and Commitment* (Oxford: Berg, 1990).

LIBERALISM

Historians of German liberalism are no longer content to chronicle the failures of liberals, and scholars are now taking a more dispassionate look at the problems faced by German liberals in the nineteenth and twentieth centuries. On the shift from the 'chronicle of failure' approach see Gordon Mork, 'Bismarck and the "capitulation" of German liberalism', *Journal of Modern History*, 43 (1971), pp. 59–75.

Unfortunately, much of the work on liberalism is taking place in Germany and is as yet unavailable in English. The work of James Sheehan has, however, ensured that at least part of the debate is available to English-speaking audiences; for a concise summary of his ideas see 'Liberalism and society in Germany 1815–1848', *Journal of Modern History*, 45 (1973), pp. 583–604 and 'Liberalism and the city in nineteenth century Germany' *Past and Present*, no.51 (1971), pp. 116–37. For those who wish to pursue Sheehan's ideas further, see his *German Liberalism in the Nineteenth Century* (Chicago and London: University of Chicago Press, 1978) and also Geoff Eley, 'James Sheehan and German liberals: a critical appreciation', *Central European History*, 14 (1981), pp. 273–88.

Of the general surveys on German liberalism, Sheehan's book is certainly one of the best. See also the recent essays in Konrad Jarausch and Larry Eugene Jones (eds), *In Search of Liberal Germany* (Oxford: Oxford University Press, 1990).

As deeper investigations are made into the nature of German liberalism, some historians have begun to question the validity of the term 'liberal' in the German context. For an early examination of this problem see Leonard Krieger, *The German Idea of Freedom. History of a Political Tradition* (Chicago: University of Chicago Press, 1957). See also Donald G. Rohr, *The Origins of Social Liberalism in Germany* (Chicago: University of Chicago Press, 1964).

Above all, the chief concern of German liberals in the nineteenth century related to the national question. On this subject see: A. Schwan, 'German liberalism and the national question in the nineteenth century', in H. Schulze (ed.), *Nation-Building in Central Europe* (Leamington Spa: Berg, 1987), pp. 65–80; Dan S. White, *The Splintered Party: National*

Liberalism in Hessen and the Reich (Cambridge, Mass.: Harvard University Press, 1976); and R. Hinton-Thomas, *Liberalism, Nationalism and the German Intellectuals 1822–1847* (Cambridge, Mass.: Harvard University Press, 1951). On German liberalism's most prominent spokesmen see Stephen Zucker, *Ludwig Bamberger: German Liberal Politician and Social Critic* (Pittsburgh, Penn.: University of Pittsburgh Press, 1975) and J.F. Harris, 'Eduard Lasker and compromise liberalism', *Journal of Modern History*, 42 (1970), pp. 342–60.

German liberalism in the Weimar period has been the subject of considerable work by Larry Eugene Jones. For the most succinct summary of his ideas see Larry Eugene Jones, 'The dissolution of the bourgeois party system in the Weimar Republic', in R. Bessel and E.J. Feuchtwanger (eds), *Social Change and Political Development in Weimar Germany* (London: Croom Helm, 1981), pp. 268–88. On more specific issues see his 'Gustav Stresemann and the crisis of German liberalism', *European Studies Review*, 4 (1974), pp. 141–63 and 'In the shadow of stabilization: German liberalism and the legitimacy crisis', in Gerald Feldman (ed.), *Die Nachwirkungen der Inflation auf die deutsche Geschichte 1924–1933* (New York: De Gruyter, 1985), pp. 21–41. His ideas are further developed in *German Liberalism and the Dissolution of the Weimar Party System, 1918–1933* (Chapel Hill, NC, and London: University of North Carolina Press, 1988). A somewhat different point of view can be found in Luigi Albertini, 'German liberalism and the foundation of the Weimar Republic: a missed opportunity', in Anthony Nicholls and Erich Matthias (eds), *German Democracy and the Triumph of Hitler* (London: Allen & Unwin, 1971), pp. 29–46.

WOMEN IN MODERN GERMANY

In terms of English language monographs, the history of women in modern Germany is somewhat underdeveloped. There are, however, several collections of articles, with five in particular that stand out: Ruth-Ellen B. Joeres and Mary Jo Maynes (eds), *German Women in the Eighteenth and Nineteenth Centuries* (Bloomington, Ind.: Indiana University Press, 1986); John C. Fout (ed.), *German Women in the Nineteenth Century: A Social History* (London: Holmes & Meier, 1984); Renate Bridenthal *et al.* (eds), *When Biology becomes Destiny: Women in Weimar and Nazi Germany* (New York: Monthly Review Press, 1984); Ingeborg Drewitz (ed.), *The German Women's Movement* (Bonn: Hochwacht, 1983); and Judith Friedländer *et al.* (eds), *Women in Culture and Politics: A Century of Change* (Bloomington, Ind.: Indiana University Press, 1986). In addition, Richard Evans and W.R. Lee (eds), *The German Family: Essays on the Social History of the Family in Nineteenth and*

Twentieth Century Germany (London: St Martins Press, 1981) contains several useful articles on women in general and their roles within the traditional German family in particular.

On the effect of industrialization on women see B. Franzoi, *At the Very Least She Pays the Rent: Women and German Industrialization* (Westport, Conn.: Greenwood, 1985) and Carole Adams, *Women Clerks in Wilhelmine Germany: Issues of Class and Gender* (Cambridge: Cambridge University Press, 1989). For a short but thorough summary of the place of women in political life see Roger Chickering, '"Casting their gaze more broadly": women's patriotic activism in imperial Germany', *Past and Present*, no. 118 (1988), pp. 156–85. On the impact of the First World War see L.J. Rupp, *Mobilizing Women for War* (Princeton, NJ: Princeton University Press, 1978) and Ute Daniel, 'Women's work in industry and family: Germany, 1914–1918', in R. Wall and R. Winter (eds), *The Upheaval of War* (Cambridge: Cambridge University Press, 1988), pp. 267–96.

For a concise summary of the late Weimar and early Nazi period see Tim Mason, 'Women in Germany, 1925–1940: family, welfare and work' *History Workshop*, I and II (summer and autumn 1976), pp. 74–113 and 5–32. On Weimar see also Renate Bridenthal, 'Beyond Kinder, Küche, Kirche: Weimar Women at Work', *Central European History*, 6 (1973), pp. 148–66 and Anita Großmann, 'Girlkultur or thoroughly rationalized female: a new woman in Weimar Germany?', in J. Friedländer *et al.* (eds), *Women in Culture and Politics* (Bloomington, Ind.: Indiana University Press, 1986), pp. 62–80.

For a good overview of the feminist movement in Germany see Richard Evans, *The Feminist Movement in Germany, 1894–1933* (London: Sage, 1976) and his *Comrades and Sisters: Feminism, Socialism, and Pacifism in Europe, 1890–1945* (London: St Martins Press, 1987). Marion Kaplan addresses similar themes while dealing with the added complexity of the Jewish question in *The Jewish Feminist Movement in Germany: The Campaigns of the Jüdischer Frauenbund* (Westport, Conn.: Greenwood, 1979). Jean H. Quataert's *Reluctant Feminists in German Social Democracy 1885–1917* (Princeton, NJ: Princeton University Press, 1979) is a useful though somewhat more specialized treatment of feminism. Quataert considers the problems faced by social democrats in attempting to integrate women and the reluctance of many feminists to submerge their own goals to the greater social democratic cause. For a short summary of the problems of German feminism see Amy Hackett, 'The German women's movement and suffrage, 1890–1914: a study in national feminism', in R.J. Bezucha (ed.), *Modern European Social History* (Lexington, Mass.: D.C. Heath, 1972), pp. 354–86.

On the Nazi period the paucity of monographs is not nearly so evident as in the earlier period. Claudia Koonz, *Mothers in the Fatherland: Women, the Family, and Nazi Politics* (New York: St Martins Press, 1987), is the most readable and thorough account of the issues, problems and opportunities facing women during the Nazi era. The work of Jill Stephenson, especially *Women in Nazi Society* (New York: Harper & Row, 1975) and *The Nazi Organization of Women* (London: Croom Helm, 1981), remains seminal to the topic. On the problems that faced women pursuing higher education see Jacques Pauwels, *Women, Nazis and Universities: Female University Students in the Third Reich, 1933–1945* (Westport, Conn.: Greenwood Press, 1984).

THE GERMAN ECONOMY

German economic development has been the subject of a tremendous volume of research. There are a considerable number of general works in the field. Among the best of these are: Martin Kitchen, *The Political Economy of Germany 1815–1914* (Montreal: McGill University Press, 1978); Knut Borchardt, *The Industrial Revolution in Germany, 1700–1914* (tr. George Hammersley, London: Collins, 1972); W.O. Henderson, *The Rise of German Industrial Power, 1834–1914* (London: Temple Smith, 1975); Frank B. Tipton, *Regional Variations in the Economic Development of Germany during the Nineteenth Century* (Middletown, Conn.: Wesleyan University Press, 1976), and the now somewhat outdated but still interesting work by Thorsten Veblen, *Imperial Germany and the Industrial Revolution* (New York: Macmillan, 1915).

For more specific works on the Bismarckian and Wilhelmine periods see: Ivo N. Lambi, *Free Trade and Protection in Germany, 1868–1879* (Wiesbaden: Steiner, 1963); Robert Gellately, *The Politics of Economic Despair: Shopkeepers and German Politics 1890–1914* (London: Sage, 1974); Kenneth Barkin, *The Controversy over German Industrialization, 1890–1902* (Chicago: University of Chicago Press, 1970) and W. E. Mosse, *The German-Jewish Economic Élite, 1820–1935: A Socio-Cultural Profile* (Oxford: Clarendon Press, 1989). There are also a number of excellent articles on the imperial period. Among these see: Hans-Jürgen Puhle, 'Lords and peasants in the Kaiserreich' in Robert G. Moeller (ed.), *Peasants and Lords in Modern Germany* (Boston, Mass.: Allen & Unwin, 1986); Robert G. Moeller, 'Peasants and tariffs in the Kaiserreich: how backward were the 'Bauern'?', *Agricultural History*, 55 (1981), pp. 370–84; Richard H. Tilly, 'The political economy of public finance and the industrialization of Prussia, 1815–1866', *Journal of Economic History*, 26 (1966), pp. 484–97; the classic article by Hans Rosenberg, 'Political and social consequences of the Great Depression of 1873–1896 in central Europe' *Economic History Review*, 13 (1943); Hugh

Neuberger and Houston H. Stokes, 'German banks and German growth, 1883–1913: an empirical view', *Journal of Economic History*, 34 (1974), pp. 710–31, and J.C. Hunt, 'Peasants, grain tariffs, and meat quotas: imperial German protectionism reexamined', *Central European History*, 7 (1974), pp. 311–31.

On the impact of the First World War on the German economy see Gerald D. Feldman, *Army, Industry and Labour in Germany 1914–1918* (Princeton, NJ: Princeton University Press, 1966), Sally Marks, 'The myths of reparations', *Central European History*, 11 (1978), pp. 231–55, and Karl Erich Born, 'The German inflation after the First World War', *Journal of European Economic History*, 6 (1977), pp. 109–16.

The literature on the economic history of the Weimar period has largely been dominated by the debate over David Abraham's, *The Collapse of the Weimar Republic: Political Economy and Crisis*, 2nd edn (New York: Holmes & Meier, 1986). Abraham's chief opponents are Gerald D. Feldman and Henry Ashby Turner. For their views see Feldman, *Iron and Steel in the German Inflation 1916–1923* (Princeton, NJ: Princeton University Press, 1977) and Turner, *German Big Business and the Rise of Hitler* (New York: Oxford University Press, 1985). On the debate in general see *Central European History*, 17 (1984), pp. 159–293 and also Peter Hayes, 'History in an off key: David Abraham's second collapse', *Business History Review*, 61 (1987), pp. 452–72.

For other views on the economic problems of Weimar see: Dietmar Petzina, 'Problems in the social and economic development of the Weimar Republic', in Michael N. Dobkowski and Isidor Wallimann (eds), *Towards the Holocaust* (Westport, Conn.: Greenwood Press, 1983), pp. 37–59; H. Homburg, *Iron and Steel in the German Inflation, 1916–1923* (Princeton, NJ: Princeton University Press, 1977); Dieter Gessner, 'The dilemma of German agriculture during the Weimar Republic', in Richard Bessel and E.J. Feuchtwanger (eds), *Social Change and Political Development in Weimar Germany* (London: Croom Helm, 1981); Harold James, *The German Slump: Politics and Economics, 1924–1936* (Oxford: Oxford University Press, 1986); and Peter Temin, 'The beginning of the depression in Germany', *Economic History Review*, 24 (1971), pp. 240–8.

On the Nazi period there is a wealth of material. A good starting point is Richard Overy, *The Nazi Economic Recovery 1932–1938* (London: Macmillan, 1982). See also: J.D. Heyl, 'Hitler's economic thought: a reappraisal', *Central European History*, 6 (1973), pp. 83–96; William Carr, *Arms, Autarky and Aggression: A Study in German Foreign Policy 1933–1939* (New York: Norton, 1973); and J.E. Farquharson, 'The agrarian policy of national socialist Germany', in Robert G. Moeller, *Peasants and Lords in Modern Germany* (Boston, Mass.: Allen & Unwin, 1986), pp. 233–59. On the impact of the Second World War see: Overy,

'Germany, "domestic crisis", and War in 1939', *Past & Present*, 116 (August 1987); B. Carroll, *Total War: Arms and Economics in the Third Reich* (The Hague: Mouton, 1978); Alan S. Milward, *The German Economy at War* (London: Athlone Press, 1964), and Milward, *War, Economy and Society, 1939–1945* (Berkeley, Calif.: University of California Press, 1977).

THE RISE OF THE NSDAP

The seminal work on the growth of national socialism and the dissolution of Weimar remains Karl-Dietrich Bracher, *The German Dictatorship: The Origins, Structure, and Effects of National Socialism* (English tr. Jean Steinberg, New York: Praeger, 1970). It should be noted at the outset, however, that Bracher is firmly on the side of the Bielefeld School of historiography. For Bracher, national socialism is rooted in Germany's fundamentally anti-democratic political structure, a structure that persists into the modern age. A similarly structuralist account can be found in Martin Broszat, *The Hitler State: The Foundation and Development of the Internal Structure of the Third Reich* (New York: Longman, 1981). It should be noted, however, that the English edition of Broszat has been criticized for its faulty and misleading translation of the original German. Moving to more recent scholarship, Martin Broszat, *Hitler and the Collapse of Weimar Germany* (Leamington Spa: Berg, 1987), Peter Stachura (ed.), *The Nazi Machtergreifung* (London: Allen & Unwin, 1983) contains invaluable essays on the rise of the NSDAP. In terms of older works both Konrad Heiden, *Der Führer: Hitler's Rise to Power* (Boston: Houghton Mifflin, 1944) and Franz Neumann, *Behemoth: The Structure and Practice of National Socialism 1933–1944* (New York: Octagon Books, 1944) remain fascinating, if not totally reliable, studies. For those who wish to delve into the multitude of documents available on the subject, a good starting point is Jeremy Noakes and Geoffrey Pridham, *Nazism: Selected Documents*, 3 vols (Exeter: University of Exeter Press, 1983).

Of the many recent attempts to understand the social composition of Nazi support, Thomas Childers, *The Nazi Voter: The Social Foundations of Fascism in Germany, 1919–1933* (Chapel Hill, NC: University of North Carolina Press, 1983) is probably the best. Equally valuable is the collection of essays edited by Childers, *The Formation of the Nazi Constituency 1918–1933* (London: Croom Helm, 1986). For specific facts and figures concerning Hitler's electoral support see Richard F. Hamilton, *Who Voted for Hitler?* (Princeton, NJ: Princeton University Press, 1982). Considerable attention has been devoted to the rise of national socialism in specific localities. Among these four in particular stand out: Jeremy

Noakes, *The Nazi Party in Lower Saxony: 1921–1933* (Oxford: Oxford University Press, 1971), William S. Allen, *The Nazi Seizure of Power: The Experience of a Single German Town 1922–1945* (Chicago: Quadrangle, 1965/84), Johnpeter H. Grill, *The Nazi Movement in Baden, 1920–1945* (Chapel Hill, NJ: University of North Carolina Press, 1983), Geoffrey Pridham, *Hitler's Rise to Power: The Nazi Movement in Bavaria, 1923–1933* (New York: Harper & Row, 1973). A more general yet equally useful work on Nazism and local politics is Rudi Koshar, *Social Life, Local Politics and Nazism* (Chapel Hill, NC: University of North Carolina Press, 1986).

More specialized yet equally valuable accounts can be found in Richard Bessel, *Political Violence and the Rise of Nazism* (New Haven, Conn., and London: Yale University Press, 1984), Henry Ashby Turner, *German Big Business and the Rise of Hitler* (New York: Oxford University Press, 1985), Erich Matthias and Anthony Nicholls (eds), *German Democracy and the Triumph of Hitler*, 2nd edn (London: Allen & Unwin, 1981), Dietrich Orlow, *The History of the Nazi Party*, Vol. 1: *1919–1933* (Pittsburgh, Pa: University of Pittsburgh Press, 1969), David Welch (ed.), *Nazi Propaganda: The Power and the Limitations* (Totowa, NJ: Barnes & Noble, 1983) and David Jablonsky, *Nazi Party in Dissolution: Hitler and the Verbotzeit, 1923–1925* (London: Cass, 1989).

On Hitler's role in the triumph of national socialism, two works provide a good entry into a wealth of material. The first, Joachim Fest, *Hitler* (New York: Harcourt, Brace, Jovanovich, 1974), takes a more or less chronological approach to the rise of the movement and Hitler's role therein, interspersed with Fest's thoughts on the socioeconomic and political context within which Hitler was operating. The second work, J.P. Stern's *Hitler: The Führer and the People* (London: Fontana, 1975), takes a very different approach, focusing on several key components of Hitler's personal appeal, including will, the representative nature of Hitler's personal experience and the longing for transcendence in German society. On the validity of works such as Stern's see Ian Kershaw, *The Hitler Myth: Image and Reality in the Third Reich* (Oxford: Oxford University Press, 1987). The standard work in this area is Alan Bullock, *Hitler: A Study in Tyranny* (New York: Harper & Row, 1952/64). Also useful is William Carr, *Hitler. A Study in Personality and Politics* (London: Edward Arnold, 1978) and Charles B. Flood, *Hitler: The Path to Power* (London: Hamish Hamilton, 1989).

The rise of national socialism naturally raises questions about the rise of fascism in general. On this topic there are several standard works: Ernst Nolte, *Three Faces of Fascism* (New York: Holt, Rinehart & Winston, 1965), Barrington Moore, Jr, *Social Origins of Dictatorship and Democracy* (Boston, Mass.: Beacon Press, 1966), Francis L. Carsten, *The Rise of Fascism* (Berkeley, Calif.: University of California Press, 1967).

NAZISM AND SOCIAL REVOLUTION

Nazism as social revolution rather than Nazism as neo-conservative reaction is a relatively new concept, owing much to the pioneering, if problematic, work of David Schoenbaum, *Hitler's Social Revolution: Class and Status in Nazi Germany 1933–1939* (New York: Doubleday, 1966). This theme was echoed a year later by Ralf Dahrendorf in *Society and Democracy in Germany* (New York: Doubleday, 1967). For the deeper origins of the concept Hermann Rauschning's *The Revolution of Nihilism* (New York: Longman, Green, 1939) remains provocative, despite its questionable evidence.

But if Nazism was revolutionary, what kind of revolution did it represent? It has been variously interpreted as a racial revolution, a revolution of nihilism, a social revolution, a political revolution and an economic revolution. On this topic see: Milan Hauner, 'A German racial revolution?', *Journal of Contemporary History*, 19 (1984), pp. 669–87; Jeremy Noakes, 'Nazism and revolution', in Noel O'Sullivan (ed.), *Revolutionary Theory and Political Reality* (Brighton: Wheatsheaf, 1983); William Jannen Jr, 'National socialists and social mobility', *Journal of Social History*, 9 (1975/6), pp. 339–68; Michael H. Kater, *The Nazi Party: A Social Profile of Members and Leaders 1919–1945* (Cambridge, Mass.: Harvard University Press, 1983); Stephen Salter, 'Class harmony or class conflict? The industrial working class and the national socialist regime', in Jeremy Noakes (ed.), *Government, Party and People in Nazi Germany* (Exeter: University of Exeter Press, 1984), pp. 76–97; Ronald Smelser, 'Nazi dynamics, German foreign policy and appeasement', in Lothar Kettenacker and Wolfgang Mommsen (eds), *The Fascist Challenge and the Policy of Appeasement* (Boston, Mass.: Allen & Unwin, 1983), pp. 31–47; Gisela Bock, 'Racism and sexism in Nazi Germany: motherhood, compulsory sterilization, and the state', in Renate Bridenthal *et al.* (eds), *When Biology Became Destiny* (New York: Monthly Review Press, 1984), and Tim Mason, 'The primacy of politics', in S.J. Woolf (ed.), *The Nature of Fascism* (New York: Wiedenfeld & Nicolson, 1969). On the working class, see Ronald Smelser, *Robert Ley: Hitler's Labor Front Leader* (Oxford: Berg, 1988).

On the related question of the nature of life in the Third Reich, the essays in Richard Bessel (ed.), *Life in the Third Reich* (Oxford: Oxford University Press, 1987) provide an excellent starting point. See also: Ian Kershaw, *Popular Opinion and Political Dissent in the Third Reich* (New York: Oxford University Press, 1983); Gilmer Blackburn, *Education in the Third Reich* (Albany, NY: State University of New York Press, 1985); Detlev Peukert, *Inside Nazi Germany: Conformity and Opposition in Everyday Life* (New Haven, Conn.: Yale University Press, 1987); Hans-Peter Bleuel, *Strength through Joy: Sex and Society in Nazi Germany* (Philadelphia, tr.,

J. Maxwell Brown, John Lippincott, 1973). For particular sectors of society see: John E. Farquharson, *The Plough and the Swastika: The NSDAP and Agriculture in Germany 1928–1945* (London: Sage, 1976); Alan Beyerchen, *Scientists under Hitler: Politics and the Physics Community* (New Haven, Conn.: Yale University Press, 1977); and Werner T. Angress, *Between Fear and Hope: Jewish Youth in the Third Reich* (New York: Columbia University Press, 1988). See also the essays in Gerhard Hirschfeld and Lothar Kettenacker (eds), *The Führer State: Myth and Reality* (Stuttgart: Klett-Cotta, 1981).

HITLER AND THE COMING OF THE WAR

Given that most of the literature on Hitler and the coming of war in 1939 arose, either directly or indirectly, out of the controversy surrounding A.J.P. Taylor's *The Origins of The Second World War* (London: Atheneum, 1961), this is perhaps the best starting point for those unfamiliar with the topic. Taylor's book can be read in conjunction with the excellent essays in Gordon Martel (ed.), *The Origins of the Second World War Reconsidered: The A.J.P. Taylor Debate after Twenty-Five Years* (Boston, Mass.: Unwin Hyman, 1986).

On the ideological origins of Hitler's foreign policy, G. Stoakes, *Hitler and the Quest for World Dominion: Nazi Ideology and Politics in the 1920s* (Leamington Spa: Berg, 1986) is a good starting point, as is Milan Hauner, 'Did Hitler want a world dominion?', *Journal of Contemporary History*, 13 (1978), pp. 15–32. On the more specific question of ideology and Hitler's war aims, see Norman Rich, *Hitler's War Aims. Ideology, the Nazi State and the Course of Expansion*, 2 vols (New York: Norton, 1973) and M. Van Creveld, 'War Lord Hitler: some points reconsidered', *European Studies Review*, 4 (1974), pp. 57–79.

With respect to domestic influences on Hitler's foreign policy and the coming of war see William Carr, *Arms, Autarky and Aggression: A Study in German Foreign Policy* (New York: Norton, 1973). Ronald Smelser, 'Nazi dynamics, German foreign policy and appeasement', in Lothar Kettenacker and Wolfgang Mommsen (eds), *The Fascist Challenge and the Policy of Appeasement* (Boston, Mass.: Unwin Hyman, 1983), pp. 31–47 offers an interesting perspective on this issue as does Richard Overy, 'Germany, 'Domestic Crisis', and War in 1939', *Past and Present*, 116 (August 1987). See also: R.J. O'Neill, *The German Army and the Nazi Party 1933–1939* (London: Cassell, 1966); Wolfgang Michalka, 'Conflicts within the German leadership on the objectives and tactics of German foreign policy', in Kettenacker and Mommsen (eds), *The Fascist Challenge and the Policy of Appeasement* (Boston, Mass.: Unwin Hyman, 1983), pp. 31–47; and Harold C. Deutsch, *Hitler and His Generals: The*

Hidden Crisis, January–June 1938 (Minneapolis, Minn.: University of Minnesota Press, 1974).

The international context within which Hitler was operating is well covered in David E. Kaiser, *Economic Diplomacy and the Origins of the Second World War: Germany, Britain, France and Eastern Europe, 1930–1939* (Princeton, NJ: Princeton University Press, 1980). On the same point see also: Edward W. Bennett, *German Rearmament and the West, 1932–1933* (Princeton, NJ: Princeton University Press, 1979); E.M. Robertson, 'Hitler's planning for war and the response of the great powers', in H.W. Koch (ed.), *Aspects of the Third Reich* (London: St Martins Press, 1985), pp. 196–234; and John Hiden, *Germany and Europe, 1919–1939* (London: Longman, 1977).

On the impact of the German military on political thinking see: Francis L. Carsten, *The Reichswehr and Politics 1918–1933* (Oxford: Oxford University Press, 1966); Wilhelm Deist, *The Wehrmacht and German Rearmament* (London: Macmillan, 1982); and Gerald Weinberg, 'The German generals and the outbreak of war 1938–1939', in A. Preston (ed.), *General Staffs and Diplomacy before the Second World War* (London: Croom Helm, 1978), pp. 24–40. See also several of the essays in Wilhelm Deist (ed.), *The German Military in the Age of Total War* (Princeton, NJ: Princeton University Press, 1963).

THE FINAL SOLUTION

Without some insight into the history of the 'Jewish Question' in Germany, it is almost impossible to come to terms with the tremendous volume of material relating specifically to the Holocaust. Jehuda Reinharz, *Fatherland or Promised Land: The Dilemma of the German Jew, 1893–1914* (Ann Arbor, Mich.: University of Michigan Press, 1975) and George L. Mosse, *Germans and Jews: The Right, the Left and the Search for a Third Force in Germany* (New York: Fertig, 1970), provide a good place to begin. However, the true complexity of the situation faced by Jews in Germany emerges in Steven Aschheim's *Brothers and Strangers: The East European Jew in German and German-Jewish Consciousness, 1800–1923* (Madison: University of Wisconsin Press, 1982). On the Jewish response to pre-Nazi anti-Semitism see the pioneering work of Ismar Schorsch, *Jewish Reactions to German Anti-Semitism, 1870–1914* (New York: University of Columbia Press, 1972).

Turning to the Holocaust itself, several standard works remain useful. Raul Hilberg, *The Destruction of the European Jews* (Chicago: Quadrangle, 1961), Lucy S. Dawidowicz, *The War against the Jews, 1933–1945* (New York: Holt, Rinehart & Winston, 1975), and Hannah Arendt, *The Origins of Totalitarianism* (London: Secker & Warburg, 1951), each contribute to a broad, if not entirely dispassionate analysis of the Final Solution. Hilberg's book is now available either in a revised one-volume edition (New York: Holmes & Meier, 1985) or a completely revised three-volume edition (New York: Holmes & Meier, 1985).

In terms of more recent scholarship, Sarah Gordon's *Hitler, Germans, and the Jewish Question* (Princeton, NJ: Princeton University Press, 1984) provides a useful overview of the Holocaust in historical context as does Yehuda Bauer, *A History of the Holocaust* (New York: F. Watts, 1982). Christopher Browning's more specialized work, *Fateful Months: Essays on the Emergence of the Final Solution* (New York: Holmes & Meier, 1985) is a useful contribution to the debate on the origins of the Final Solution. See also Berel Lang, *Act and Idea in the Nazi Genocide* (Chicago: Chicago University Press, 1990), Benno Müller-Hill, *Murderous Science: Elimination by Scientific Selection of Jews, Gypsies and Others* (New York: Oxford University Press, 1988) and Jonathan Steinberg, *All or Nothing: The Axis and the Holocaust, 1941-1943* (London: Routledge, 1990).

In terms of the Holocaust and German public opinion see Ian Kershaw, 'The persecution of the Jews and German popular opinion in the Third Reich', *Leo Baeck Institute Yearbook*, 26 (1985) and Otto Dov Kulka, 'Public opinion in Nazi Germany: the Final Solution', *Jerusalem Quarterly* (1983) and Anthony Read and David Fischer, *Kristallnacht: Unleashing the Holocaust* (London: Michael Joseph, 1989).

There are also several very useful collections of essays on the topic of the Final Solution. See especially Henry Friedländer and Sybel Milton (eds), *The Holocaust: Ideology, Bureaucracy and Genocide* (New York: Kraus, 1980) and Michael Marrus (ed.), *The Nazi Holocaust* (Westport, Conn.: Meckler, 1989). The latter is a fifteen-volume series which brings together most of the important English-language material on the origins, course and results of the Holocaust.

A good deal of work has been devoted to examining the historiography of the Final Solution. Three of the most important works in this regard are Michael Marrus, *The Holocaust in History* (Toronto: Lester & Orpen Dennys, 1987), Lucy S. Dawidowicz, *The Holocaust and the Historians* (Cambridge, Mass.: Harvard University Press, 1981), Arno J. Mayer, *Why Did the Heavens Not Darken?: The Final Solution in History* (New York: Pantheon, 1988), Jehuda Reinharz, *The Holocaust in Historical Perspective* (Seattle: University of Washington Press, 1978), Charles S. Maier, *The Unmasterable Past: History, Holocaust and German National Identity* (Cambridge, Mass.: Harvard University Press, 1989) and James Young, *Writing and Rewriting the Holocaust: Narrative and the Consequences of Interpretation* (Bloomington, Ind.: Indiana University Press). For a short overview of the topic see Otto Dov Kulka, 'Major trends and tendencies in German historiography on national socialism and the "Jewish Question" (1924–1984)', *Leo Baeck Institute Yearbook*, 30 (1985), pp. 215–42.

For those wishing additional reading in this area see Gitta Sereny, *Into That Darkness: An Examination of Conscience*, 2nd edn (New York: Random House, 1983), Elie Wiesel, *The Night Trilogy: Night, Dawn, the Accident* (New York: Robson, 1962), Claude Lanzmann, *Shoah: An Oral History of the Holocaust* (New York: Pantheon, 1985), and Yaffa Eliach, *Hasidic Tales of the Holocaust* (Oxford: Oxford University Press, 1982).

GERMANY DIVIDED

Though no work can now claim to be completely up to date on the issue of the Germanies since 1945, Henry Ashby Turner, Jr, *The Two Germanies since 1945* (New Haven, Conn.: Yale University Press, 1987) is an authoritative and relatively complete account of the Germanies up to the 1980s. On the history of the West since 1945, Michael Balfour, *West Germany: A Contemporary History* (London: Croom Helm, 1982), provides a relatively complete account despite its predominantly political approach, and also see Dennis L. Bark and David R. Gress, *A History of West Germany*, 2 vols (Oxford: Basil Blackwell, 1989). On the East before the 1980s see David Childs, *The GDR: Moscow's German Ally* (London: Unwin Hyman, 1983) and Martin McCauley, *The German Democratic Republic since 1945* (London: Macmillan, 1983). Mike Dennis, *German Democratic Republic: Politics, Economics, and Society* (New York: University of Columbia Press, 1988) is a useful recent addition to the literature on the subject.

The postwar settlement and the roots of the Cold War have been the subject of a number of excellent works. Students might begin with Michael Balfour and John Mair, *Four Power Control in Germany and Austria* (London: Oxford University Press, 1956). More specialized is Ian Turner, *Reconstruction in Post-War Germany: British Occupation Policy and the Western Zone* (Oxford: Berg, 1989). On the roots of the East–West split and its origins in wartime Europe see Tony Sharp, *The Wartime Alliance and the Zonal Division of Germany* (Oxford: Oxford University Press, 1975), Daniel J. Nelson, *Wartime Origins of the Berlin Dilemma* (Alabama: Westview, 1978), and the older, but still useful work by John N. Snell, *Wartime Origins of the East-West Dilemma over Germany* (New Orleans: Hauser Press, 1959). Peter H. Merkl, *The Origin of the West German Republic* (New York: Oxford University Press, 1963) also contains much valuable information.

The politics of the Germanies since the war have been the subject of a variety of analyses. Among the best of these are: David Conradt, *The German Polity* (New York: Longman, 1978); Kurt Sontheimer, *The*

Government and Politics of West Germany (London: Hutchinson, 1972); Sontheimer and Wilhelm Bleek, *The Government and Politics of East Germany* (New York: Hutchinson, 1975); Arnold J. Heidenheimer, *The Governments of Germany*, 4th edn (New York: St Martins Press, 1977); Kenneth H.F. Dyson, *Party, State and Bureaucracy in West Germany* (New York: St Martins Press, 1977) and Barbara Marshall, *The Origins of Post-War German Politics* (London: Croom Helm, 1988).

In terms of the economic development of East and West Germany, Wolfgang E. Stopler, *The Structure of the East German Economy* (Cambridge, Mass.: Harvard University Press, 1960) remains invaluable, especially with respect to East German development in the immediate postwar period and the impact of reparations. Stopler's work is unfortunately somewhat outdated. To fill in the missing information see Karl Hardach, *The Political Economy of Germany in the Twentieth Century* (Berkeley, Calif., and New York: University of California Press, 1980).

On the history of German foreign policy up to the 1980s, William Griffith, *The Ostpolitik of the Federal Republic of Germany* (Cambridge, Mass.: Harvard University Press, 1978) is an informative and useful work as is Peter H. Merkl, *German Foreign Policies East and West* (Santa Barbara, Calif.: ABC-Clio, 1974). Almost every account of the reunification question necessarily remains inconclusive at this time. On the history of the early years of the reunification question, especially the diplomatic conferences of those years, see Frederic H. Hartmann, *Germany between East and West: The Reunification Problem* (Englewood Cliffs, NJ: Prentice-Hall 1965). On the strategic and global implications of reunification see Philip Windsor, *German Reunification* (London: Martin Elek, 1969). In all likelihood the next few years will see the appearance of more up-to-date works on the reunification issue.

INTERPRETATIONS OF MODERN GERMANY

Since German history has been so often a source of controversy there exists a plethora of historiographical material. On the history of German historiography one of the best works remains Georg G. Iggers, *The German Conception of History: The National Tradition of Historical Thought, from Herder to the Present* (Middletown, Conn.: Wesleyan University Press, 1968). For a more up-to-date treatment of West German writing in particular see Iggers, *The Social History of Politics: Critical Perspectives in West German Historical Writing since 1945* (Leamington Spa: Berg, 1985) and Richard Evans, *In Hitler's Shadow: West German Historians and the Attempt to Escape from the Nazi Past* (New York: Pantheon, 1989). For a brief overview of the historiography of modern

Germany see the excellent introductory article in Richard J. Evans, *Rethinking German History: Nineteenth Century Germany and the Origins of the Third Reich* (London: Unwin Hyman, 1987).

On the Nazi period specifically see Ian Kershaw, *The Nazi Dictatorship: Problems and Perspectives of Interpretation*, 2nd edn (London: Edward Arnold, 1989) and also John Hiden and John Farquharson, *Explaining Hitler's Germany. Historians and the Third Reich* (London: Batsford, 1983).

Much of the recent historiographical debate has revolved around the issue of continuity in German history: was the Third Reich a momentary aberration or the logical conclusion of several hundred years of historical development? Though the literature on this debate is immense a good starting point is David Blackbourn and Geoff Eley, *The Peculiarities of German History: Bourgeois Society and Politics in Nineteenth-Century Germany* (Oxford: Oxford University Press, 1984). Eley's, *From Unification to Nazism: Reinterpreting the German Past* (London: Unwin Hyman, 1986) is also helpful for understanding the parameters of the field. For the other side of the debate see John C.G. Röhl (ed.), *From Bismarck to Hitler: The Problem of Continuity in German History* (London: Longman, 1971). For a concise summary of both sides see Jürgen Kocka (ed.), 'German history before Hitler: the debate about the German Sonderweg', *Journal of Contemporary History*, 23 (1988), pp. 3–16.

There are an enormous number of articles on various aspects of German historiography. Among the most useful of these are: Robert G. Moeller, 'The Kaiserreich recast? Continuity and change in modern German historiography', *Journal of Social History*, 17 (1984), pp. 655–83; James N. Retallack, 'Social history with a vengeance? Some reactions to Hans-Ulrich Wehler's, *Das Deutsche Kaiserreich*', *German Studies Review*, 7 (1984), pp. 422–50; R. Fletcher, 'Recent developments in West German historiography: the Bielefeld School and its critics', *German Studies Review*, 7 (1984), pp. 451–80; Kenneth D. Barkin, 'From uniformity to pluralism: German historical writing since World War One', *German Life and Letters*, 34 (1981), pp. 234–47; Geoff Eley, 'Memories of underdevelopment: social history in Germany', *Social History*, 2 (1977), pp. 985–91; Hans-Ulrich Wehler, 'Historiography in Germany today', in J. Habermas (ed.), *Observations on 'The Spiritual Situation of the Age'* (Cambridge, Mass.: MIT Press, 1984); Kenneth D. Barkin and Margaret L. Anderson, 'The myth of the Puttkamer Purge and the reality of the Kaiserreich: some reflections on the historiography of imperial Germany', *Journal of Modern History*, 54 (1982), pp. 268–84; and Jane Caplan, '"The imaginary universality of particular interests": the "tradition" of the civil service in German history', *Social History*, 4 (1979), pp. 299–37; and Peter Baldwin, 'Social interpretations of Nazism: renewing a tradition', *Journal of Contemporary History*, 25 (1990), 5–37. On the historiography of national socialism and the Jewish question see Otto Dov Kulka, 'Major trends and tendencies in German historiography on national socialism and the Jewish question', *Leo Baeck Institute Yearbook*, 30 (1985), pp. 215–42.

Notes on Contributors

Richard D. Breitman is Professor of History at the American University. He is the author of *German Socialism and Weimar Democracy* and *The Architect of Genocide: Himmler and the Plans for the 'Final Solution'*. He has co-authored *Breaking the Silence* with Walter Laqueur and *American Refugee Policy and European Jewry, 1933–1945*.

Jane Caplan is Professor of History at Bryn Mawr College and has previously taught at Cambridge and Columbia Universities. She is the author of *Government Without Administration. State and Civil Service in Weimar and Nazi Germany* and of other publications on national socialism, fascism and gender history. She is now working on a study of the state and identity documentation in nineteenth-century Europe.

Geoff Eley is Professor of History at the University of Michigan. He is the author of *From Unification to Nazism: Reinterpreting the German Past* and *Reshaping the Radical Right: Radical Nationalism and Political Change after Bismarck*, and the co-author of *The Peculiarities of German History: Bourgeois Society and Politics in Ninteenth Century Germany*.

Richard Evans is Professor of History at Birkbeck College, the University of London. He is the author of: *The Feminist Movement in Germany, 1894–1933; Death in Hamburg: Society and Politics in the Cholera Years 1830–1910; Rethinking German History: Nineteenth-Century Germany and the Origins of the Third Reich*; and *In Hitler's Shadow. West German Historians and the Attempt to Escape from the Nazi Past*.

Holger H. Herwig is Professor of History at the University of Calgary. He is the author of: *The German Naval Officer Corps: A Social and Political History; Politics of Frustration: The United States in German Strategic Planning, 1888–1941; 'Luxury' Fleet: The Imperial German Navy 1888–1918*; and *Germany's Vision of Empire in Venezuela 1871–1914*, in addition to other works.

Larry Eugene Jones is Professor of History at Canisius College in Buffalo, New York. He is the author of *German Liberalism and the Dissolution of the Weimar Party System, 1918–1933*, and is the co-editor (with Konrad Jarausch) of *In Search of Liberal Germany: Studies in the History of German Liberalism from 1870 to the Present*.

David E. Kaiser is Professor of History at the Naval War College,

Newport, Rhode Island. He is the author of *Economic Diplomacy and the Origins of the Second World War: Germany, Britain, France and Eastern Europe, 1930–1939*.

Tracey J. Kay is a PhD candidate at the University of British Columbia, specializing in nineteenth- and early twentieth-century German social and cultural history. Her current research is related to the development of popular literature in the early nineteenth century.

Dieter Langewiesche occupies the Chair of Modern History at the University of Tübingen. He is the author of *Liberalismus in Deutschland* and is the editor of *Liberalismus im 19. Jahrhundert. Deutschland im europäischen Vergleich*.

Gordon Martel is Professor of History at Royal Roads Military College. He is the author of *Imperial Diplomacy* and *The Origins of the First World War*, and has edited *The Origins of the Second World War Reconsidered* and *Studies in British Imperial History*.

James Retallack is Associate Professor of History at the University of Toronto. The author of *Notables of the Right: The Conservative Party and Political Mobilization in Imperial Germany, 1876–1918*, he is currently editing *Elections, Mass Politics, and Social Change in Germany, 1890–1945* while working on a study of journalism and propaganda in Germany.

Eve Rosenhaft is Senior Lecturer in German at the University of Liverpool and has been a Fellow of the Institut für Europäische Geschichte (Mainz) and a Humboldt Fellow. She is the author of *Beating the Fascists? The German Communists and Political Violence 1929–1933* and the co-author, with W.R. Lee, of *The State and Social Change in Germany 1880–1980*.

Thomas J. Saunders is Assistant Professor in the Department of History at the University of Victoria, Canada. His research is focused on cinema and society and problems of cultural identity in Weimar Germany.

Frank B. Tipton is Associate Professor and Head of the Department of Economic History at the University of Sydney. He is the author of: *Regional Variations in the Economic Development of Germany during the 19th Century; An Economic and Social History of Europe, 1890–1939*; and *An Economic and Social History of Europe from 1939 to the Present*.

Index